LEGENDS

HOW TO PLAY AND COMPOSE LIKE THE WORLD'S GREATEST GUITARISTS

Design: David Houghton

Music Engraving: Cambridge Notation

CD Production: Jan Cyrka

Programming: Toby Bricheno

Printed by: ColourBooks Limited, Dublin

Published by: Sanctuary Publishing Limited, 82 Bishops Bridge Road, London W2 6BB

ISBN: 1 86074 220 3

LEGENDS

HOW TO PLAY AND COMPOSE LIKE THE WORLD'S GREATEST GUITARISTS

adrian clark

INTRODUCTION

Hello, and congratulations on getting this far – despite what they said about computers replacing everything, the art of opening a book is not dead!

Yes, that's right – this is yet another of those "Greatest Guitarists Of All Time" books, but before you stifle a yawn and politely explain that you've got to go and watch some paint dry, let me explain why this one is a bit different...

Ever since the explosion of accurate transcriptions, celebrity video lessons and other high quality instructional materials in the late 1980s, it's been incredibly easy for budding guitarists to learn practically any song or solo, right down to the minutest details. Now, there's nothing wrong with that; all the great players started off by copying their heroes, and the sheer quantity of accurate transcriptions in books and magazines has to be a positive thing. The problem is: where do you go from there? Learning from other people's playing is a great way of launching yourself into the musical world, but it can become a bit of a crutch – if you're intending to really go somewhere with music, it's essential that you develop your own voice. Unfortunately, that's not always easy.

So... what we need is a sort of "halfway house" to wean you away from simply duplicating other people's material, and that's exactly what I've done with this book. Instead of plunging you into the wild, scary world of composition with nothing but a blank piece of manuscript paper and a head full of music theory, I'm going to show you how you can use the work of your heroes as a jumping-off point. For each player covered, I've written a short, entirely original piece of music in the style of that player, using as many of their melodic, harmonic, rhythmic and structural characteristics as I could fit in. The reasoning behind this is to help you to see beyond the actual notes, to the underlying structure. Once you understand that structure – the "musical template" – you can add your own favourite licks or chords and – hey presto! – you've got an original piece of music on your hands!

So these pieces are not copies of the artists' work. They're not supposed to sound *exactly* like the player in question, they're just my personal interpretations of the twenty-four guitarists featured, based on what I've learnt about their musical personalities.

There's nothing new to this method of learning – for years, music students have learnt to apply their musical knowledge by writing pieces of music in the style of older, established composers. It provides a kick-start to your imagination and helps you avoid those dreaded ruts.

You'll notice that all of the players here are primarily electric guitarists. Believe me, there are plenty of other players I would like to have included – electric and acoustic – but there's only a finite amount of space in any book, and I wanted to avoid the trap of including a couple of "token" acoustic players. There are so many great acoustic players, it would take another entire book to do justice to the subject.

This book is aimed primarily at players who have already put in some work on the basics, but I've tried to include material suitable for guitarists of all levels. If you get stuck, the Theory and Technique Primers at the back of the book are designed to explain most of the concepts covered in the main body of the book. They're not exhaustive though, so use them more for an indication of what's possible, and if you're interested in exploring further, you could always find a reputable teacher.

Finally, if you like the idea of *Legends*, but are disappointed not to find your favourite player here, don't despair. *Legends* appears in *Guitarist* magazine as a column every month, so there must be something among the back issues that tickles your fancy!

ABOUT THE AUTHOR

Adrian Clark is twenty-eight and hails from Lincoln. He started playing guitar at the age of thirteen, driven by the parent-annoying potential of Heavy Metal. In the intervening years, he has expanded his tastes to cover almost everything from Coltrane to The Chemical Brothers, Stravinsky to Steve Vai, and caused himself to age prematurely by about fifty years in an attempt to expand his guitar playing abilities in a similar fashion.

Since 1994, Adrian has worked for *Guitarist* magazine, rising to the position of Music Editor. Responsible for various transcriptions and product reviews/demos as well as his regular monthly features "Legends" and "Solo Analysis", Adrian's handywork can be seen and heard each month in the magazine and on the accompanying CD. As well as this, Adrian teaches guitar privately from his home in the South London suburbs.

His biggest musical inspiration is Frank Zappa, and his list of favourite guitarists is too huge and ever-changing to include here, but usually includes Steve Vai, Charlie Hunter, Mike Keneally and Martin Taylor. Research suggests that Adrian must be the world's only left-handed, guitar-playing Zappa fan who writes for a major guitar magazine and has a degree in Swedish.

CONTENTS

CHAPTER 1
Jeff Beck

BORN:
24 June 1944.

ORIGIN:
Surrey, England.

FIRST SPOTTED:
Jeff made his first recordings in 1963 with a band called The Tridents.

BIG BREAK:
Two years later, in 1965, he stepped into the spotlight by replacing Eric Clapton in The Yardbirds.

DISTINGUISHING FEATURES:
Expect the unexpected. A growling low-string bend might give way to a stutter of chicken-picking, graceful washes of harmonics can merge into manic flurries of trilled notes, vicious power chords suddenly mutate into a gravity-defying triple-note bend...

SEEN IN THE COMPANY OF:
Are you ready? For a while, one of Jeff's fellow Yardbirds was none other than Jimmy Page. Rock's most famous mullet-wearer Rod Stewart sang in the earliest incarnation of The Jeff Beck Group (which also featured Ron Wood, now of The Rolling Stones). He's been in bands with Tim Bogert, Carmine Appice and Jan Hammer. He's done sessions with Tina Turner, Mick Jagger, Stevie Wonder, Kate Bush, Roger Waters... blimey!

THE GOOD BITS:
All of the above and much more. Throughout his career, Jeff has always been one of the most inspiring players on the planet. He's constantly experimented with new types of music and shattered preconceptions of what the guitar is supposed to sound like.

THE BAD BITS:
He's never really felt the need to hurry with his music, when there are classic cars to be tinkered with. As a result, a new album is an occasional luxury and live performances... well, forget it.

SOUND ADVICE:
Bet you scanned quickly down to this bit didn't you? Well, you're out of luck. If I knew the secret of the Jeff Beck sound, do you think I'd tell you? Here's a hint, though – use your fingers instead of a pick and learn to really snap those strings.

NUTS AND BOLTS:
Having originally been a Telecaster fan, Jeff vacillated between Strats and Les Pauls from the late sixties until he eventually settled with the Strat. Fender now make the Jeff Beck Signature Stratocaster complete with a huge neck for those mechanic's hands.

VITAL VINYL:
Despite the fact that Jeff now hates them, his jazz-rock albums *Blow By Blow* and *Wired* are a great example of how that sort of music can be very listenable. Listen to the Yardbirds material, such as 'Over Under Sideways Down' for some of his earliest sonic experiments. From more recent times, *Jeff Beck's Guitar Shop* is an absolutely stunning album.

biography TRACK 23

Before you start playing anything, first throw away your pick! I've written this little Beck-alike tune in the style of Jeff's more recent work in order to introduce you to the fine old tradition of plucking the strings with your fingers. Although you lose a lot of the speed and fluency by switching to fingerstyle (especially if, like me, you use a pick most of the time) there are some advantages, such as the increased tonal and dynamic ranges and the simple fact that you're closer to your guitar, having cut out that bit of plastic.

Ask any Beck fan what their favourite tune is, and it's pretty likely that they'll mention 'Where Were You', that haunting track from the album *Jeff Beck's Guitar Shop*. For the first section of this piece, I've gone for a similar approach, using volume swells, natural harmonics and advanced whammy bar techniques (yes, I must apologise to all the users of Gibsons or Telecasters out there!). Here's the part I played; I've also provided an approximation of the synth chords in case you'd like to play those. This bit is in the key of G major (G A B C D E F# G) which is a good one for open string harmonics.

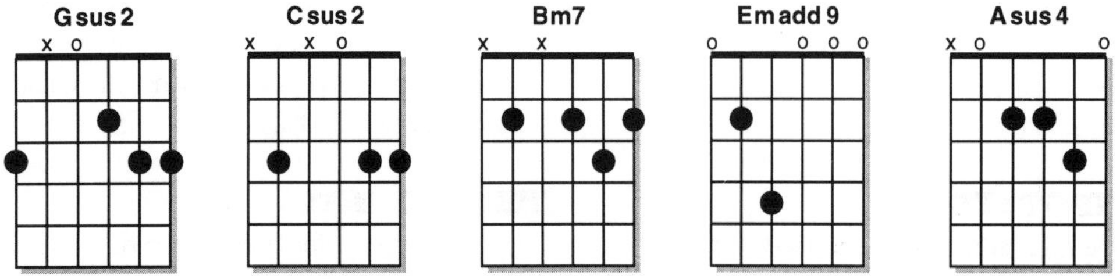

EX 1

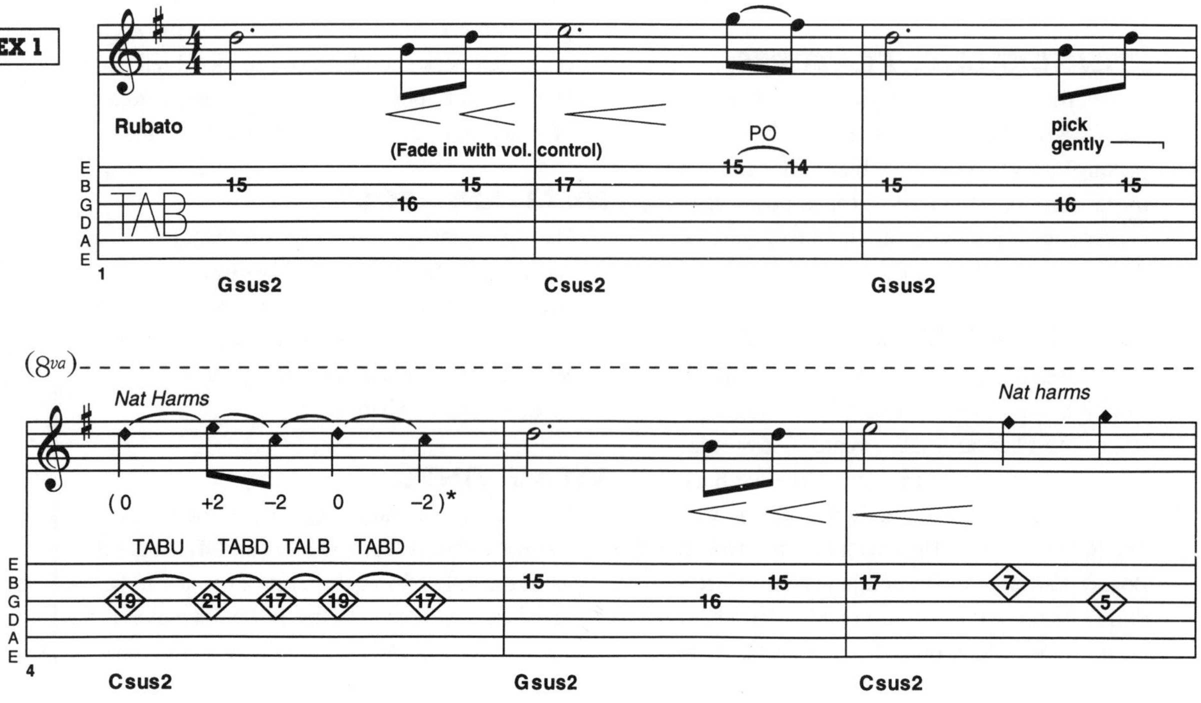

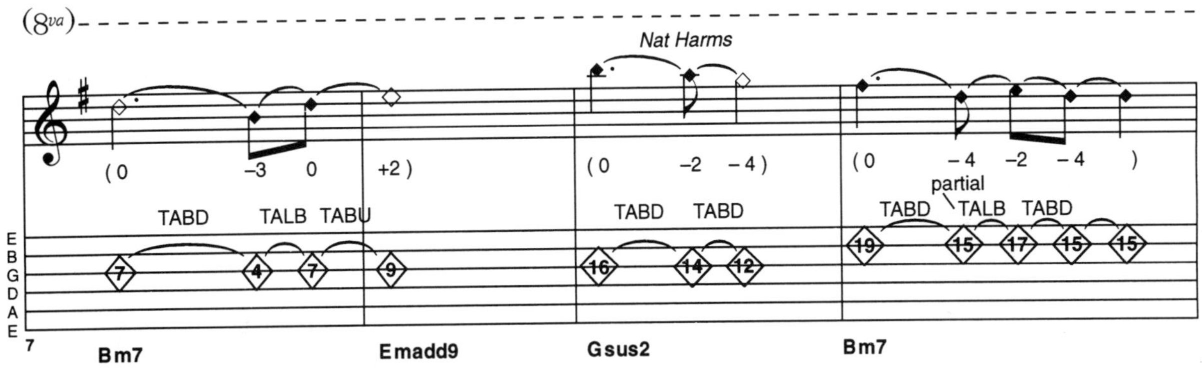

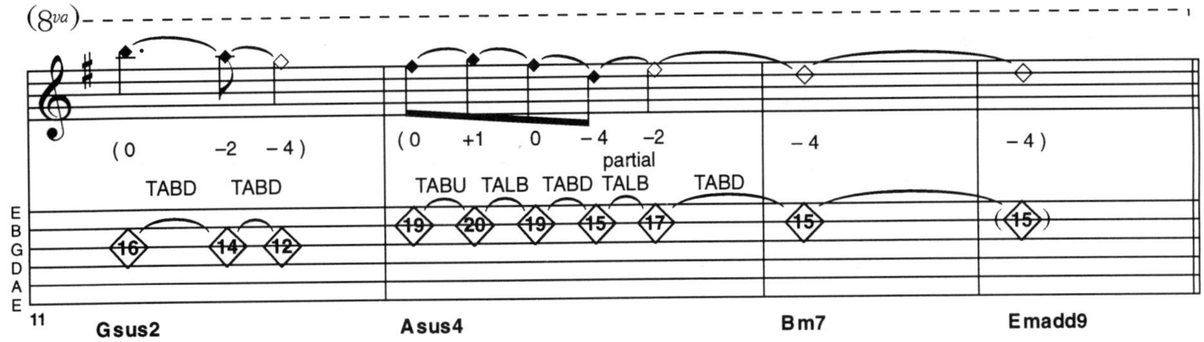

(* Numbers between staves show how many semitones the original note is raised or lowered with the tremolo bar.)

Now, if you've only ever used your tremolo bar (or wang bar, whammy or whatever else you like to call it) for the occasional subtle vibrato wiggle or eighties-metal divebomb, you'll need to put in a bit of practice before you can use it to play melody lines accurately. The best way to do this is to choose an open string harmonic and find its corresponding fretted note (Ex 2a). Next, make up a simple melodic phrase using the fretted note and other notes close to it (Ex 2b) and then try to match that melody exactly with just the harmonic and your tremolo bar (Ex 2c). Don't be disheartened if it sounds horrible; it really does take some practice to get this right. Also, resist the temptation to pile on the overdrive in an attempt to increase sustain – this will just deprive your sound of the important dynamic range.

EX 2A

EX 2B

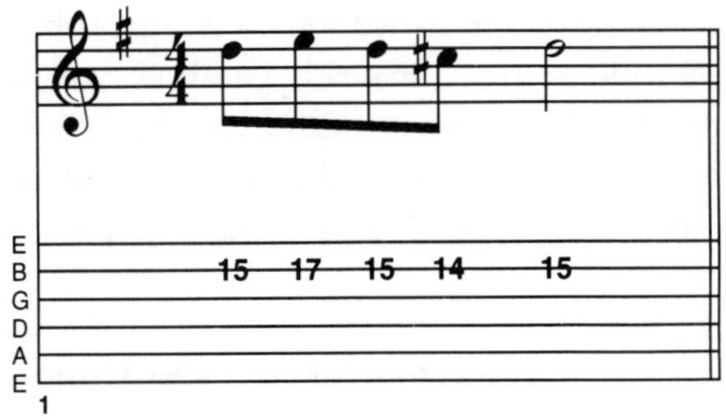

EX 2C

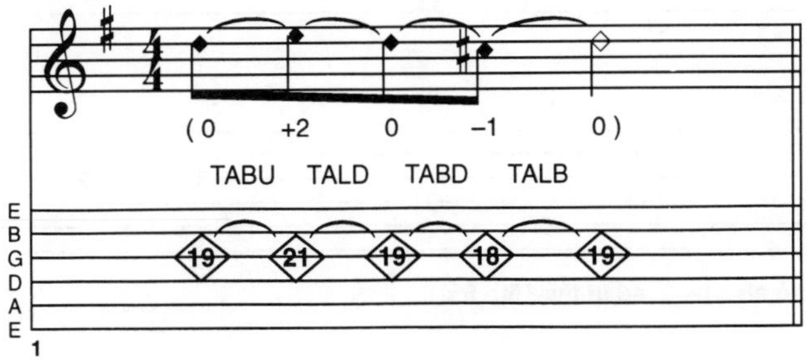

For the second section, I've upped the tempo, gone for more of a rock feel and taken the opportunity to use one of those swampy fingerpicked riffs that Jeff's so good at. Don't be afraid to get your fingers under the strings and give them a good yank – just be careful not to rip 'em clean off the guitar! By the way, I've switched to G minor for this bit, and all of the notes in the riff are from the G minor Pentatonic (G B♭ C D F G).

EX 3

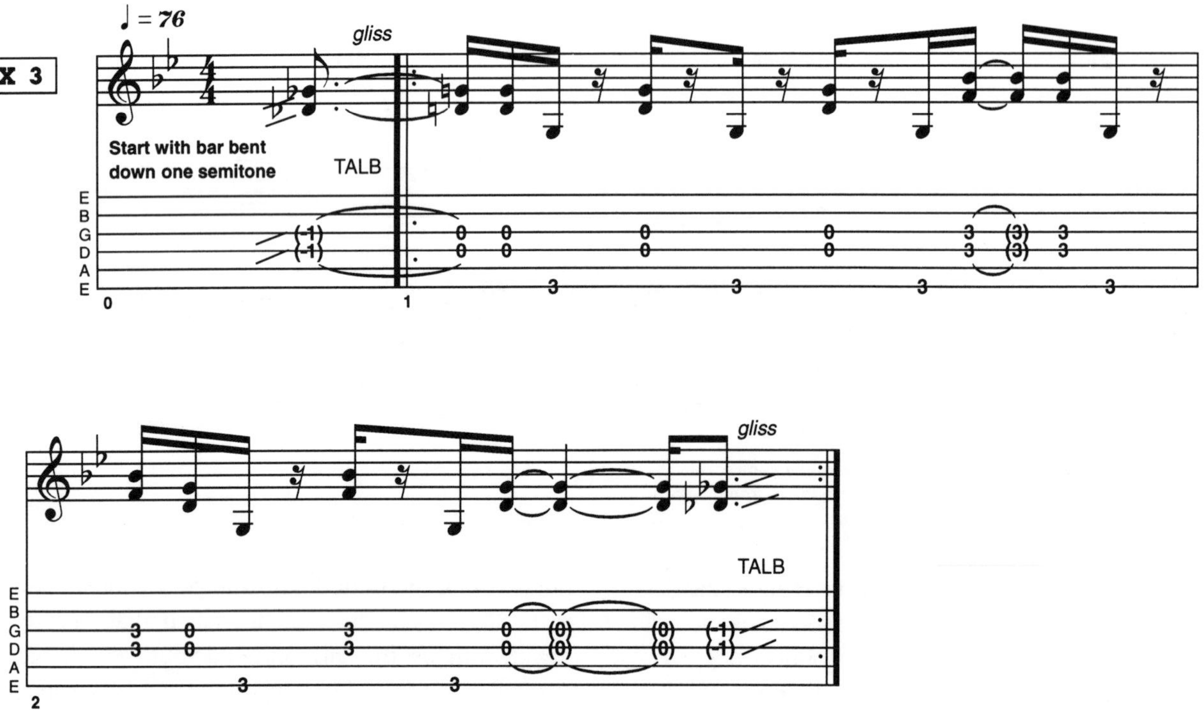

And over the top of that, I improvised a bit of a solo. Since my aim was to go for a typically free-form Beck-type excursion, I've decided not to do a note-for-note transcription, as it'd probably be too difficult to read. Instead, I'll show you the raw material I used, so you can have a go at coming up with your own ideas. Also, I didn't play anything particularly fast (I was using my bare fingers, dammit!) so if you're really curious, you should be able to work out roughly what I played.

First of all, the note choice. I stuck mainly to the G minor Pentatonic (some of my fingerings are shown in Ex 4a) with the only exception being the bluesy "flat 5" (D♭ in this key). Ex 4b shows how you can use this note for a menacing effect.

G MINOR PENTATONIC FINGERINGS

EX 4A

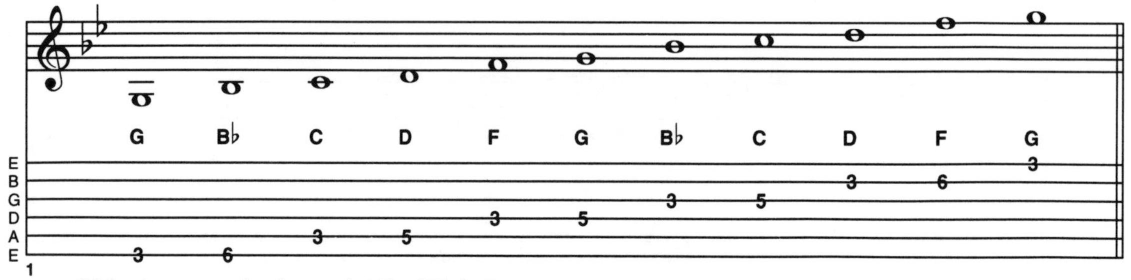

(This shape can also be used at the 15th fret)

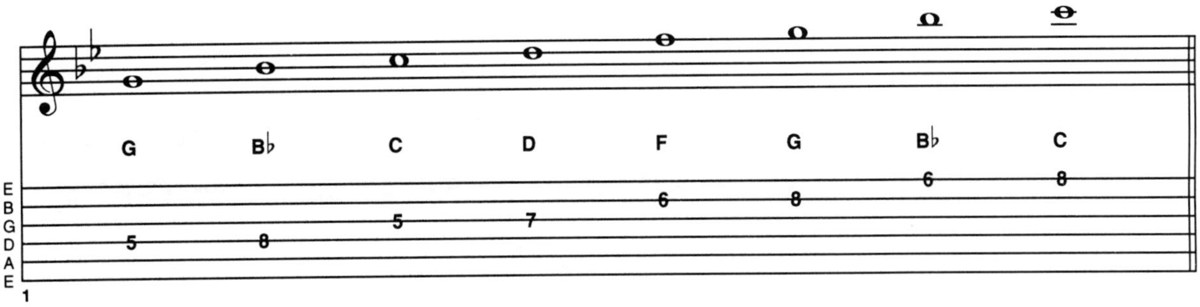

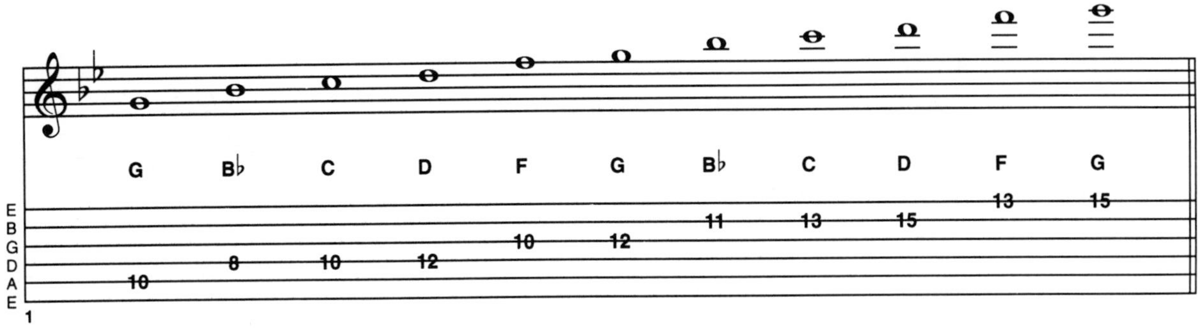

EX 4B

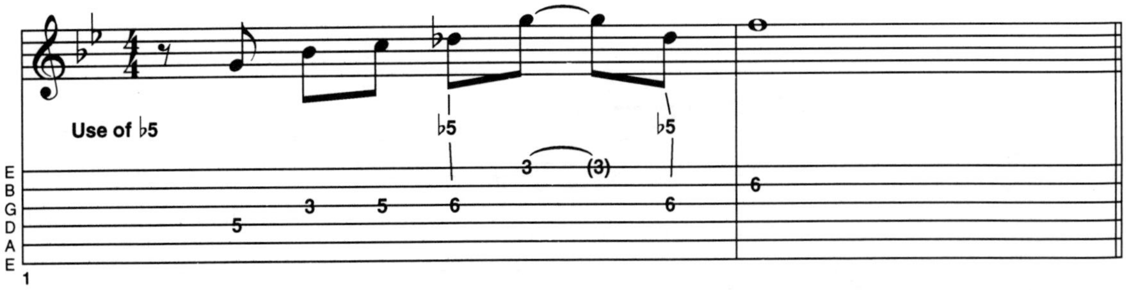

Finally, here are a few of the techniques I used in my attempt to get the Beck sound. Jeff's fifties influences are revealed in the Duane Eddy-esque low string bends (Ex 5a) while manic sliding taps bring us smartly up to date (Ex 5b). Try "scooping" into notes with the whammy bar (Ex 5c) or using the bar to highlight notes with a righteous shake (Ex 5d). Sudden, unexpected note blizzards can add drama to a solo (Ex 5e) – make sure you really snap that first note. And for the icing on the cake, why not add a bit of slide? I did this at the start of my solo so I could just drop the slide when I'd finished with it, and not have to pick it up in mid solo!

EX 5A

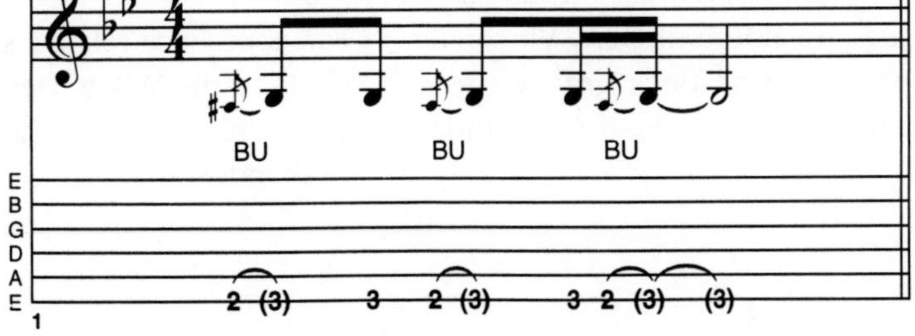

EX 5B

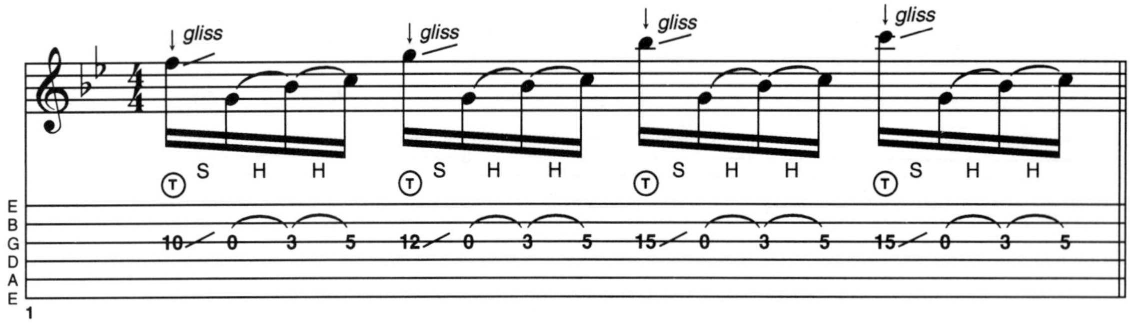

EX 5C

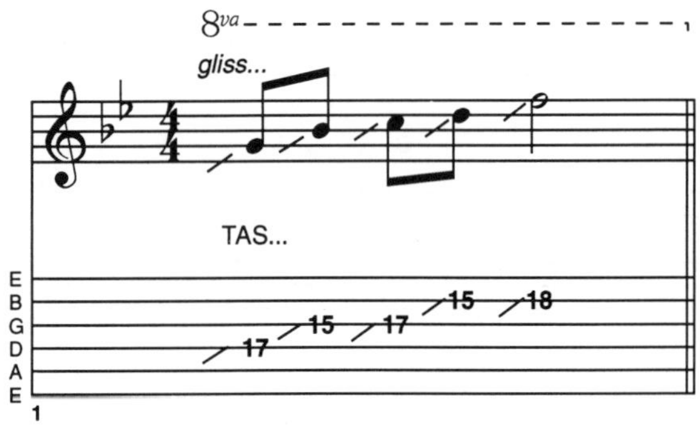

EX 5D

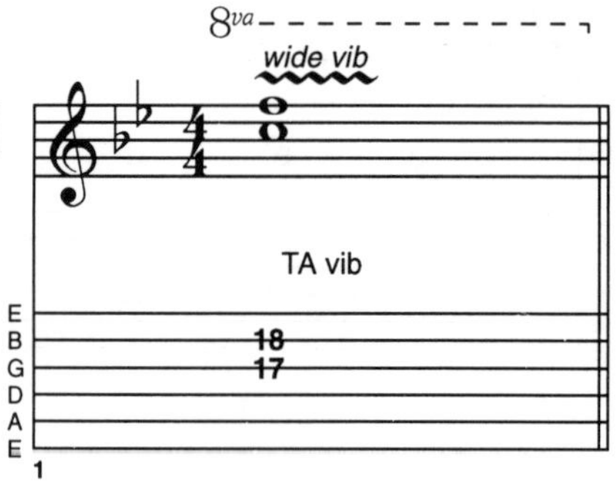

EX 5E

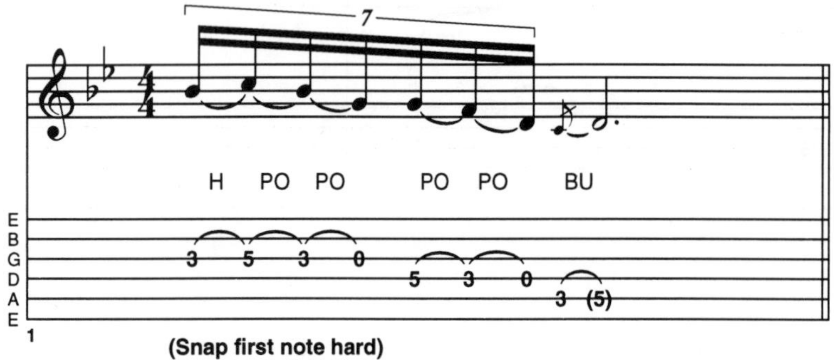

Time to go and bathe your bruised fingers, I think...

Further Exploration

Jeff's biggest influence of all time was probably the late Cliff Gallup, who played guitar with Gene Vincent; in fact, Jeff's admiration for the man's playing led to his recording *Crazy Legs*, an album of Gene Vincent covers. Otherwise, the young Beck grooved to the sounds of Hank Marvin, James Burton and Buddy Guy.

As one of the most influential players from one of the most fertile periods of musical development, it's not surprising that so many people mention Jeff Beck as a major influence. Steve Lukather, Joe Satriani, Eddie Van Halen and Slash are four of the most famous Beck-ophiles.

For your Beck-related surfing needs, get yourself along to the Yellow Deuce, a comprehensive Beck site which is at http://www.wsvn.com/~staff/beck/indexhtml

CHAPTER 2

Chuck Berry

BORN:

18 October 1926.

ORIGIN:

St Louis, Missouri, where the young Charles Edward Anderson Berry sang in his local church choir.

OCCUPATION:

The man entrusted with the important task of telling that pesky Beethoven to "roll over". He also found the time to write one of the most famous intros in the history of rock 'n' roll as well as practically defining the role of the electric guitar in rock music.

FIRST SPOTTED:

New Year's Eve, 1952. Chuck played a gig with pianist Johnnie Johnson's band. Johnson went on to play on many of Chuck's classic recordings.

BIG BREAK:

Having sent a demo tape to the famous Chess records, Chuck was invited to Chicago to record his first single, 'Maybellene', which was released in 1955. No doubt the ensuing fame and fortune allowed him to give up his job as a trainee hairdresser.

SEEN IN THE COMPANY OF:

Although Chuck has never recorded on anything but his own projects, he seems to have played with just about everyone, especially since artists such as Keith Richards, Eric Clapton and John Lennon revealed him as being such a major influence on their own styles.

THE GOOD BITS:

Countless classic songs and riffs, covered by just about every pub band ever to tread those hallowed lager-soaked carpets, he was a major influence on both The Beatles and the Rolling Stones... this man is a rock icon. Hell, he was even featured on the *Pulp Fiction* soundtrack.

THE BAD BITS:

I'm sorry, Mrs Berry, but your son just keeps getting into trouble: marijuana, tax irregularities, illicitly transporting a minor across a state line, that unfortunate business with the closed-circuit TV... Mind you, given the choice between a Chuck Berry record and a Cliff Richard record, which would you buy?

NUTS AND BOLTS:

That good old cherry red Gibson 335 (although he did very briefly use a black Les Paul Custom in the mid fifties).

VITAL VINYL:

As most of Chuck's best work comes from an age when albums were basically thirty-minute compilations of recent singles plus filler material, you might as well get yourself one of the stonking multi-CD compilations on the market. Just make sure it covers all the 1950s classics.

There are apparently people out there who are under the impression that it's not actually necessary to be able to do the duckwalk in order to play like Chuck Berry. In an effort to prevent this tide of scurrilous misinformation, I urge you to clear a space in your living room, put on a Chuck Berry record (or even better a video) and practise for at least a couple of hours before continuing with this chapter...

There. I'm sure you'll agree it's a most liberating sensation. So, you've learnt the steps... now it's time to work on the sounds. This intro uses a couple of Berry-isms, none more obvious than that augmented chord. The trick is – whatever key you're playing in, use the augmented chord built on the fifth note of that key; here we're in the key of B♭ (the B♭ major scale is B♭ C D E♭ F G A B♭) so we use an F augmented chord. The result is an expectant, very "intro-like" sound.

EX 1

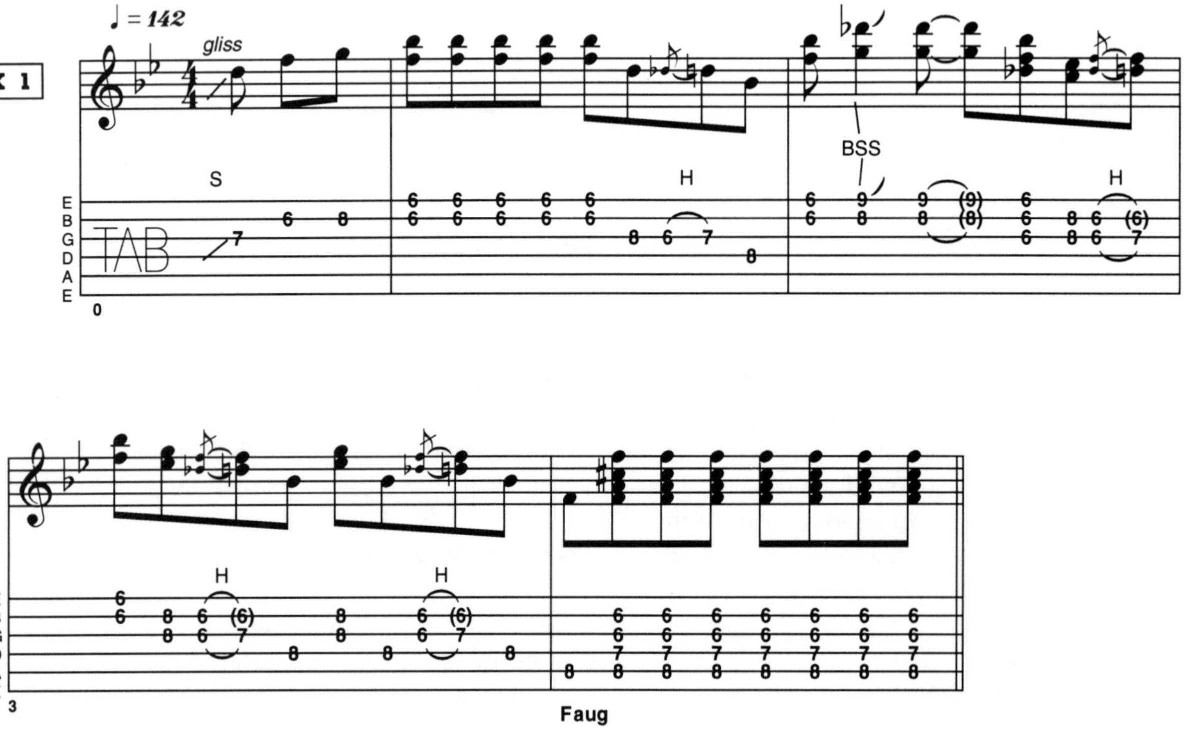

Now, rather than having a long intro solo like on 'Johnny B Goode', let's dive straight into the verse part. The basic structure for this little piece is based around the good old I-IV-V twelve-bar blues progression. Not all of Chuck's songs follow this sort of progression, but enough do for it to count as a kind of stylistic trait. Anyway, we're in the key of B♭, so the chords are...

EX 2

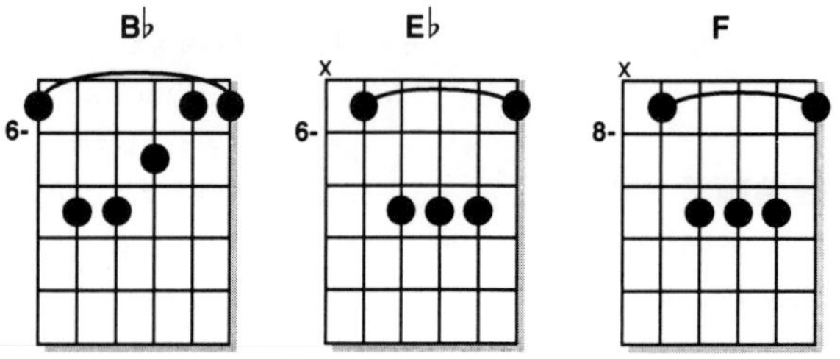

Incidentally, those of you who have had some experience of playing twelve-bar blues progressions may be wondering why I've put this tune in the key of B♭, rather than a more guitar-friendly key like A or E. The clue lies in Chuck's influences – he was particularly inspired by boogie-woogie pianists and big-band swing, where the "flat keys" are much more common. Given those influences, it's not surprising that Chuck used this bass-heavy pattern to play chords. Here are the three basic forms you'll need; all you have to do is fit them together as shown in Ex 2.

EX 3

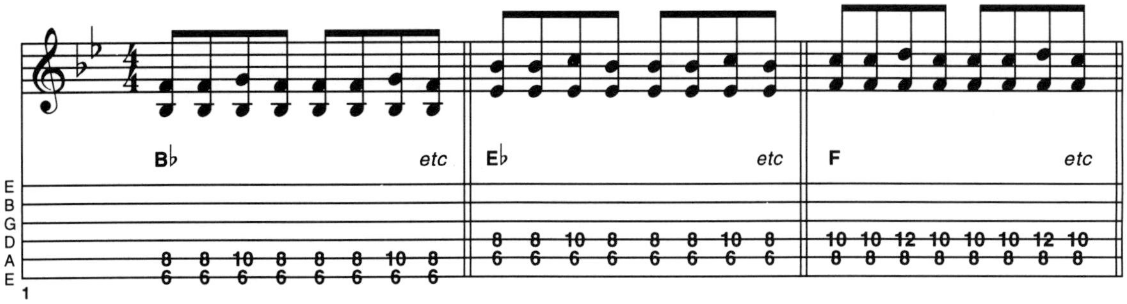

To make things more interesting, I've added a Chuck-type fill at the end of each line. If you're feeling adventurous, try switching quickly between rhythm and lead parts, otherwise get a friend (or an obedient tape recorder) to play the chords, while you add the fills over the top. Here are the fills for verse one...

EX 4

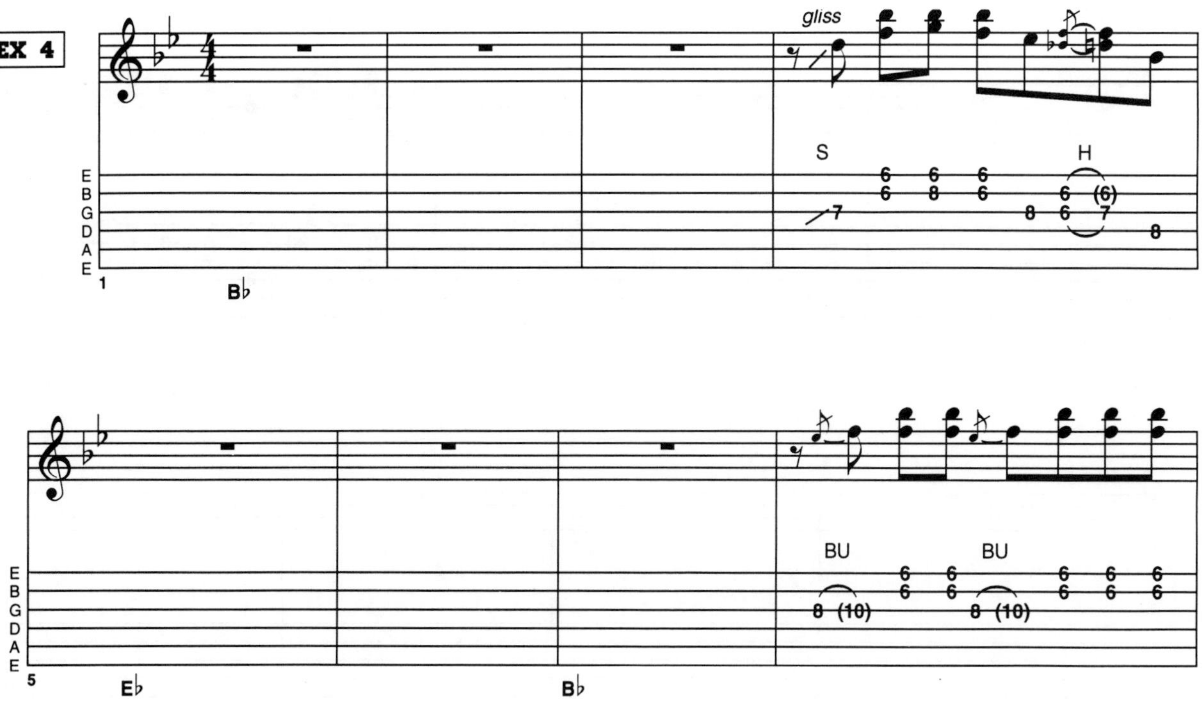

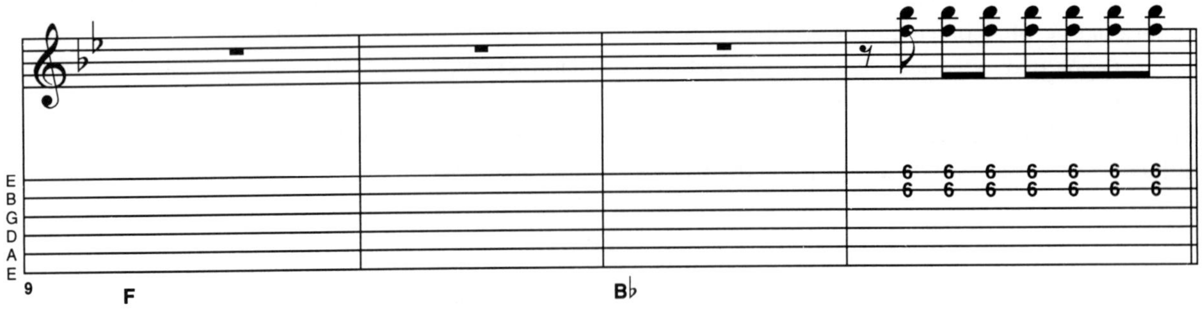

And the equivalent fills for verse two...

EX 5

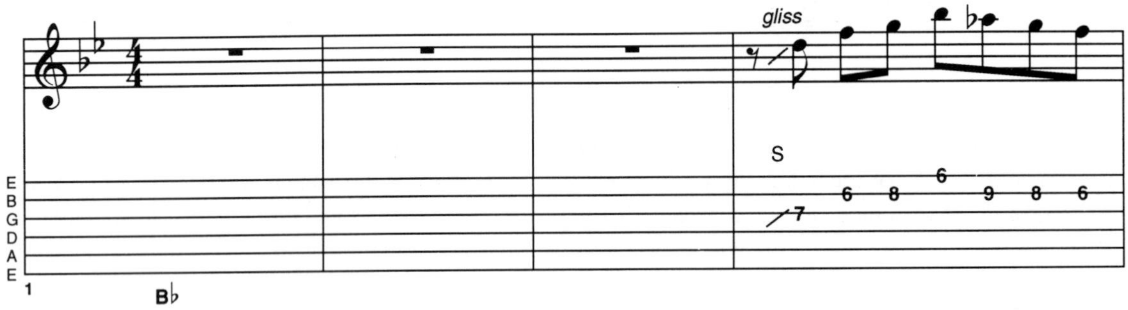

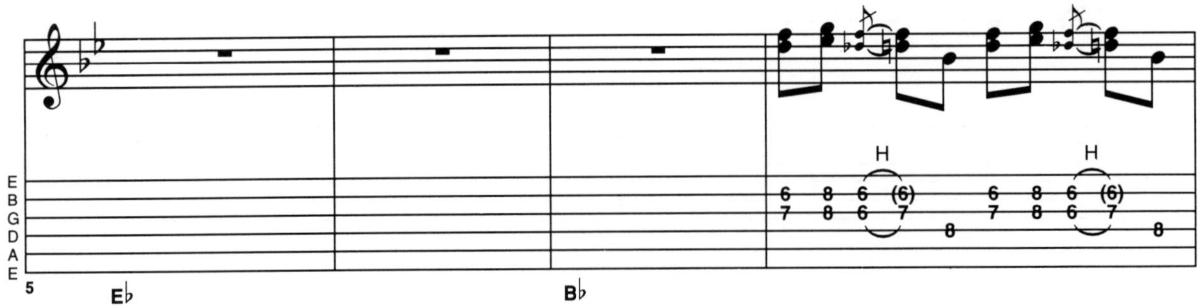

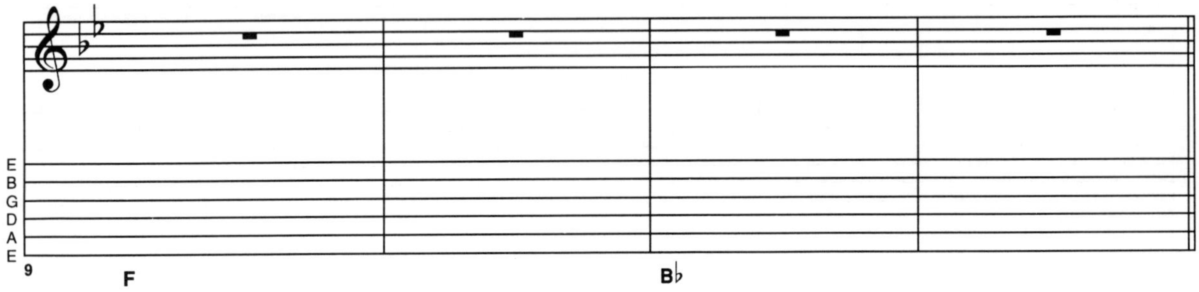

In the grand tradition of almost every great rock 'n' roll song, it's time to add a solo. In common with the intro and the verse fills, I've used a mixture of the B♭ major Pentatonic (B♭ C D F G B♭) and B♭ minor Pentatonic (B♭ D♭ E♭ F A♭ B♭) scales here; I could probably fill up the rest of this book with analysis of where you should use which scale, but as Chuck's playing is often built around box-position licks, it's probably better that you learn plenty of these and let your ears tell you where they work best. One bit of advice I will give you – when playing over the E♭7 (the IV chord) the minor Pentatonic works best as both the chord and the scale contain a D♭ note. The D (natural) in the major Pentatonic tends to clash a bit.

EX 6

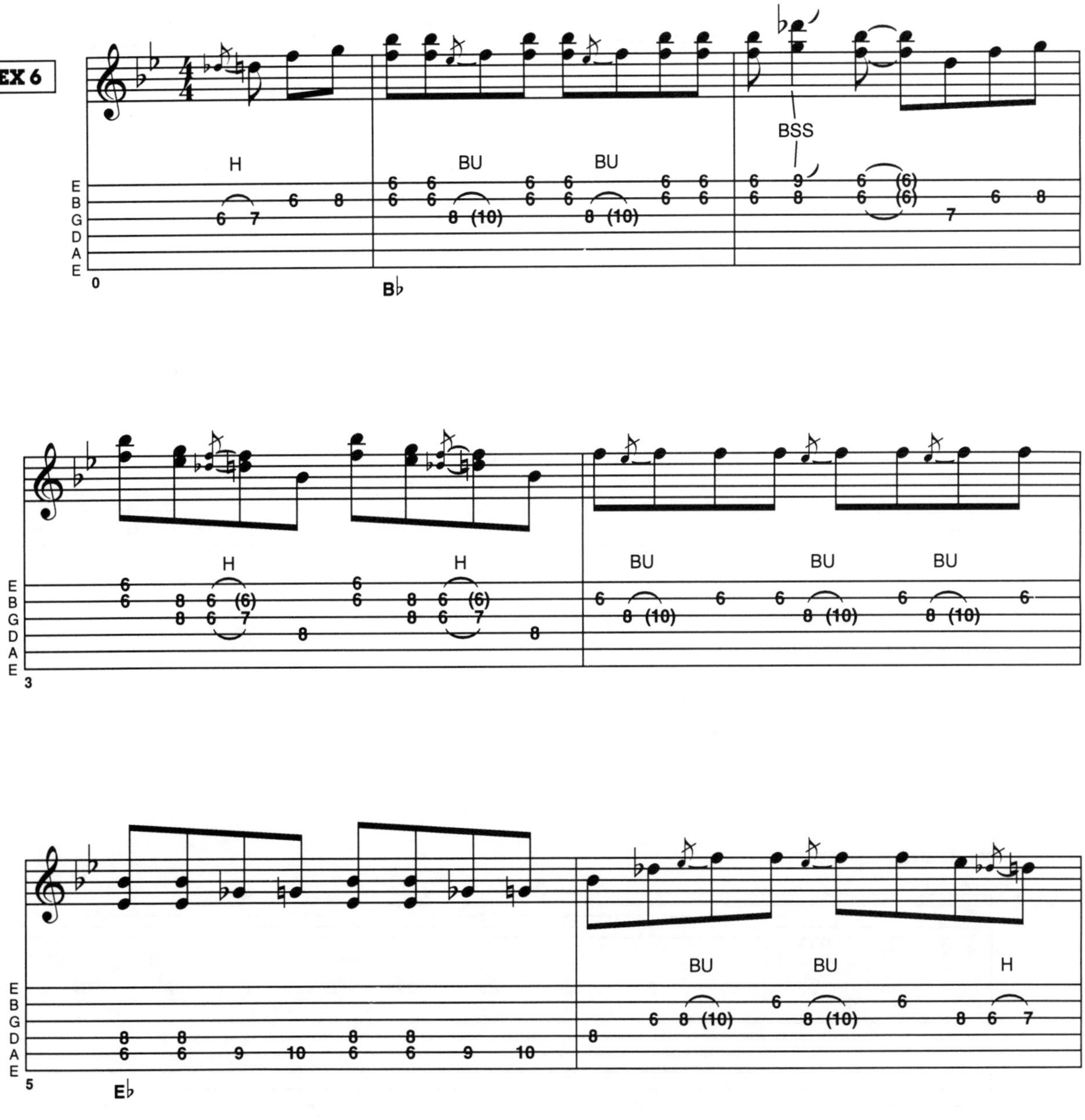

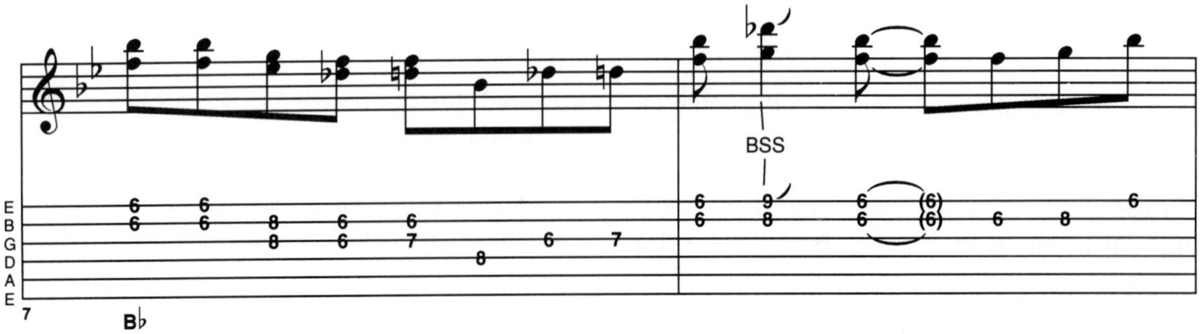

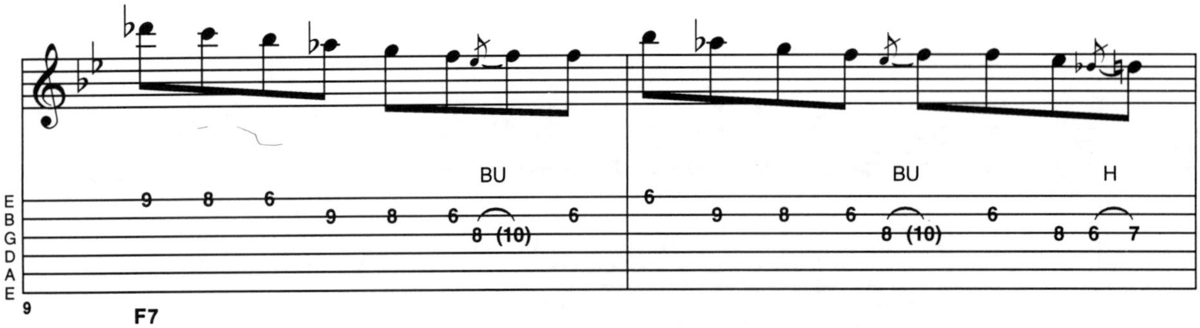

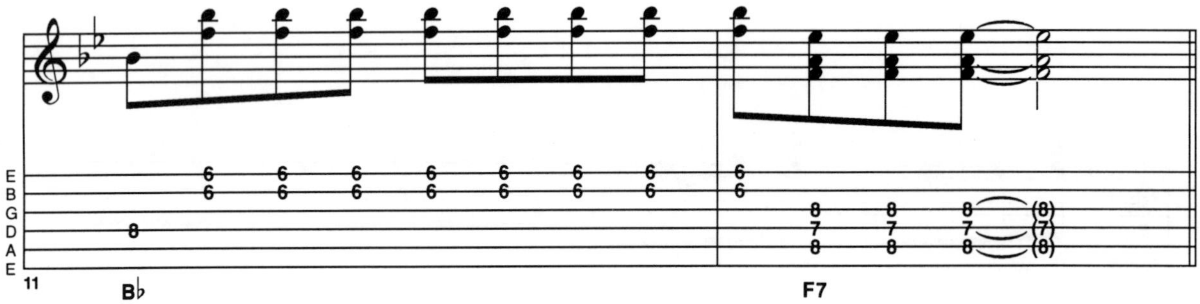

Just in case you're a bit baffled about those scales, here's your Free Bonus Special Offer Example...

B♭ MINOR PENTATONIC

EX 7A

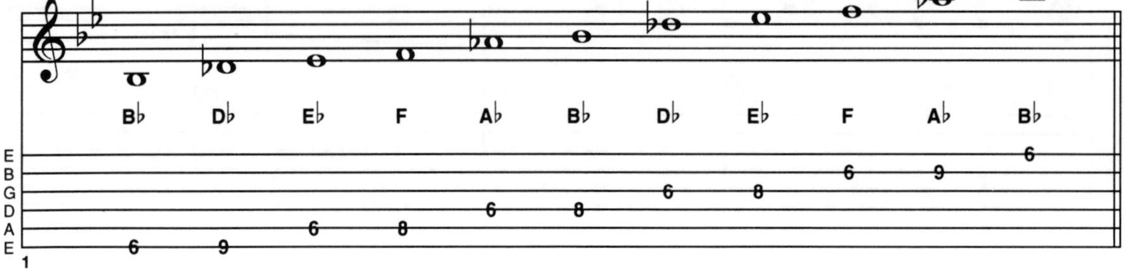

B♭ MAJOR PENTATONIC

EX 7B

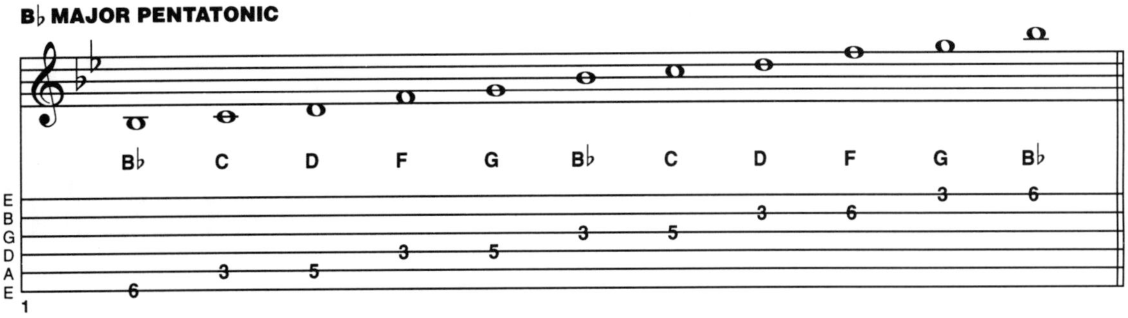

B♭ MAJOR PENTATONIC (ALTERNATIVE FINGERING)

EX 7C

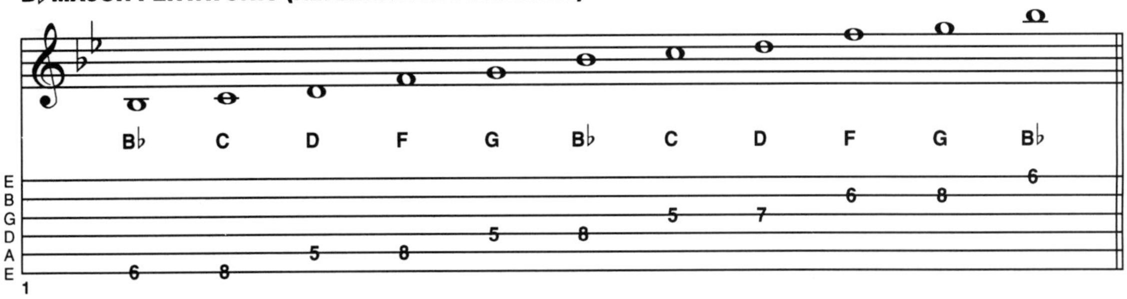

After that, I simply repeated the verse again, but I think by now you can probably try working out the fills I used for yourself. (Clue – they're pretty much the same as all the others, and all notes are from the two scales in Ex 7.)

Further Exploration

The revolutionary sound of Chuck's guitar style (at least to a 1950s audience) had a lot to do with his wide range of influences: as well as the obvious blues guitarists such as Muddy Waters, Elmore James and Lonnie Johnson, Chuck was a big fan of jazz guitarists Charlie Christian, T-Bone Walker and Django Reinhardt as well as saxophone and piano players. Country music also had an effect on Chuck, as can be heard from his use of a pedal steel on early recordings.

As you've probably already gathered, Chuck Berry had an enormous effect on rock music. Much of what is now accepted as "classic" rock guitar playing came from his huge hands, and without his influence, maybe much of the rawness and fire of rock music would never have existed.

As with many of the big, long-established guitar names, there's plenty of information on the Web regarding Chuck Berry and most of it is entirely unremarkable, being made up of brief "Hall of Fame" and encyclopedia entries. However, one site is well worth a visit – surf on down to http://www.shell.ihug.co.nz/~mauricef/frames9.html where you'll find biographical info, a discography and even some guitar chords.

CHAPTER 3
Ritchie Blackmore

biography

TRACK 3

BORN:
14 April 1945.

ORIGIN:
Weston-Super-Mare in South West England, a seaside town not usually known for its community of rock guitar heroes.

THE PRODUCT OF:
At the age of ten, Ritchie was given a guitar by his father, who threatened to bash him over the head with it unless he learned to play it "properly".

FIRST SPOTTED:
After spells with various unsuccessful groups, Ritchie got the guitar job with Screaming Lord Sutch And The Savages in 1962. For those of you not acquainted with the finer points of 1960s British popular culture, Screaming Lord Sutch was an eccentric pop singer. Nowadays, he's an equally eccentric wannabe politician, with his own Monster Raving Loony Party.

BIG BREAK:
In 1968, Ritchie put together the first line-up of Deep Purple (and probably started practising two-note power chord riffs in the key of G).

SEEN IN THE COMPANY OF:
Ritchie was one of the top London session players in the mid sixties, working extensively with the late Joe Meek, so he backed an enormous number of people. Mind you, this figure probably pales in comparison to the hordes featured in the numerous line-ups of Deep Purple and Rainbow.

THE GOOD BITS:
In a world full of Pentatonic box-position drudgery and talentless Clapton-style blues rip-offs, Ritchie Blackmore gave rock guitar the kiss of life by introducing classically-influenced sounds and exotic scales...

THE BAD BITS:
... thus leaving the field wide open for the creation of – oh no! – Neo-Classical Metal!

ECCENTRICITY RATING:
A good eighty per cent – this man has a well-known penchant for German castles.

NUTS AND BOLTS:
Ritchie's been using Fender Stratocasters for years and years. He uses a thicker tremolo bar, hollows out ("scallops") the wood between the frets, and never uses the middle pickup. His amps are generally souped-up Marshalls.

VITAL VINYL:
In Rock, *Machinehead* and *Fireball* are widely considered to be the Deep Purple classics – for a start, they feature the famous "Mark 2" line-up, with Ian Gillan and Roger Glover. The Rainbow output is a little bit patchy with lots of saccharine American Rawk, but the first couple of albums – *Ritchie Blackmore's Rainbow* and *Rainbow Rising* – are exceptional.

Sit still, relax and concentrate very carefully on what I am about to say. As you feel your arms and legs getting heavier and your eyelids beginning to droop, you will become receptive to my commands... you are NOT going to play 'Smoke On The Water'. In fact, once you've woken up, you may never play that riff ever again. You will realise the harm you have caused in music stores and jam sessions by playing "that riff" over and over again, and you will atone for your sins by learning about some of the other things that Ritchie Blackmore has done for guitar playing.

In fact, let's be really daring here... let's not use the key of G. Actually, I'm only joking; although many of Ritchie's best-known riffs are indeed in that saddest of all minor keys, he did use other ones. E minor is a particular favourite, so here's the intro part...

EX 1

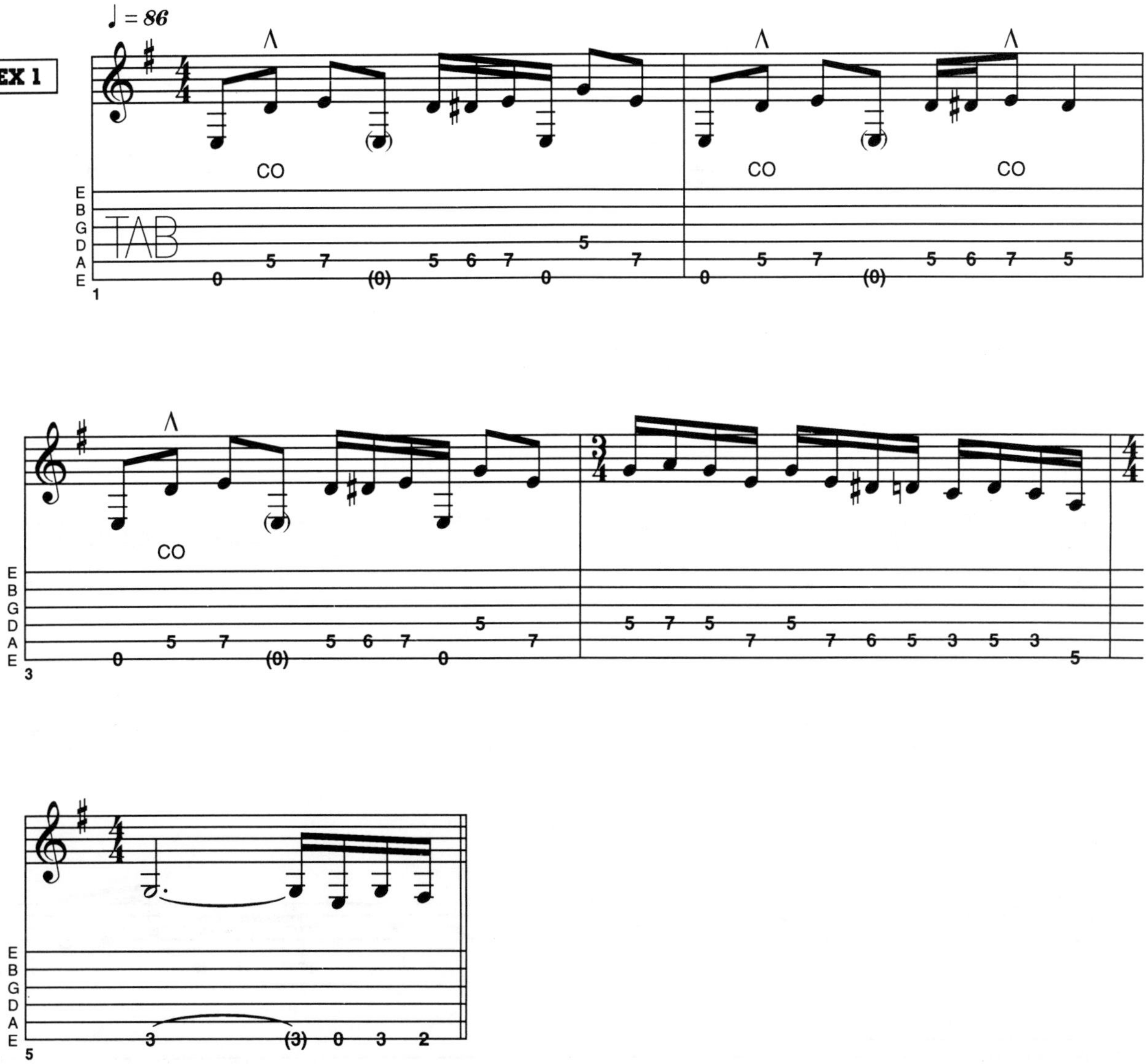

By recycling and mutating that riff a little bit, we have the makings of a verse part. For the first half, I've kept to E minor (and simplified things slightly, as this is where a vocal part would be superimposed) and for the second part, I've moved the pattern up to B minor and added some typically Blackmore-esque Phrygian Dominant bits.

EX 2

Yes, I know you're probably wondering what the hell the "Phrygian Dominant" is, and you'll probably regret it once I've told you, but here goes...

The Phrygian Dominant mode (sometimes known as the Spanish Gypsy Scale) is the fifth mode of the Harmonic Minor scale. So, if you take the E Harmonic Minor scale but root it around B (its fifth note) the result is the B Phrygian Dominant:

E HARMONIC MINOR

EX 3A

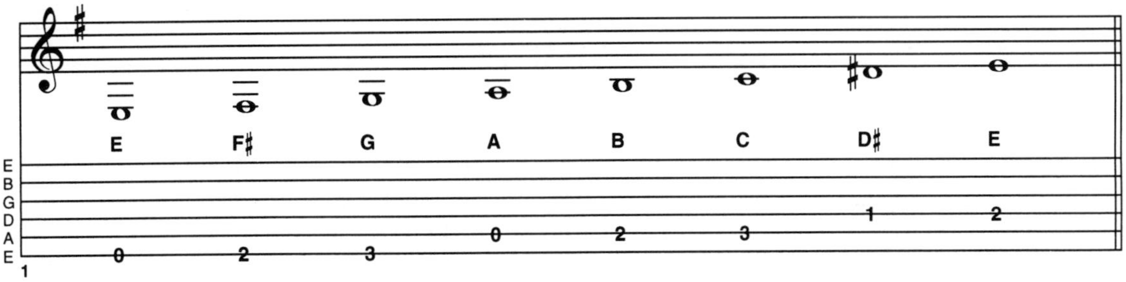

B PHRYGIAN DOMINANT

EX 3B

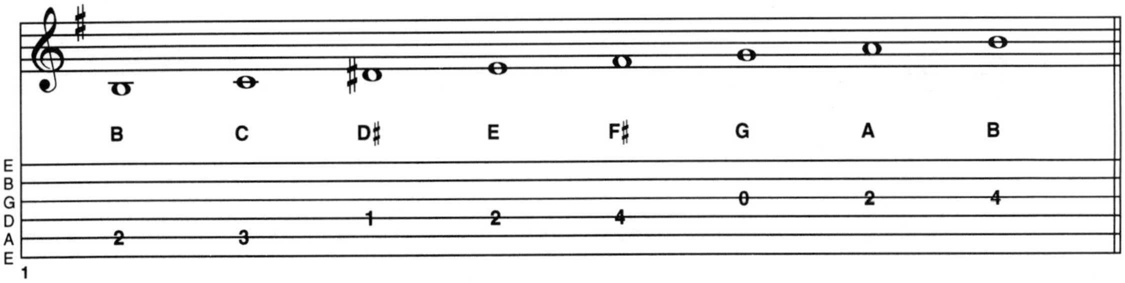

By the way, if you're completely confused by all this talk of modes and Harmonic Minor scales, you really ought to check out the Theory Primer at the back of the book.

Next we have the chorus. This is really just based around a simple Am-G-D-B7 chord progression, to which I've added the necessary Blackmore-isms. First of all, I created the main harmonic "body" of this section by playing a repeating arpeggio pattern which outlines the chords. To make this part flow, I used the fine old classical technique of "voice leading", whereby each note (or "voice") of a chord leads to the nearest possible note of the next chord, and so on. This means that you never get any huge leaps between notes, and the result is something like this...

EX 4

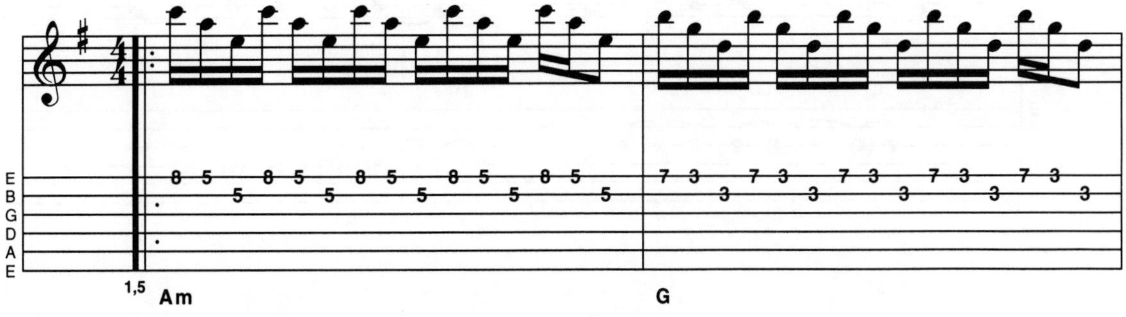

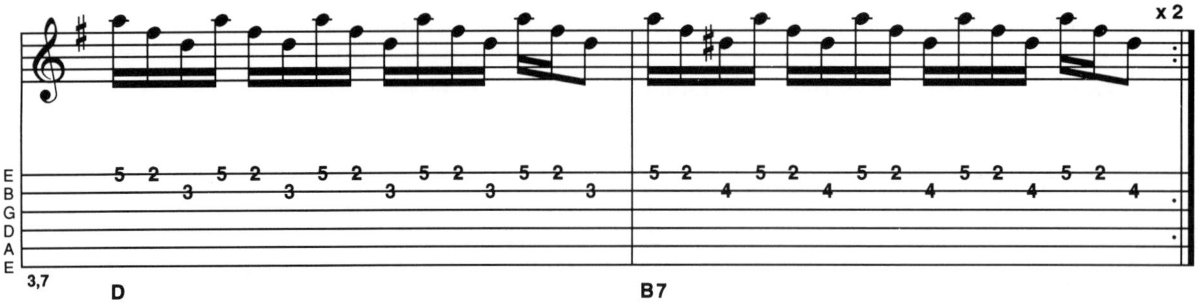

Since we haven't got a singer to fill the sonic space, I decided to go a step further and add a melody part (even with a singer, this could work) using long, sustaining notes. Unfortunately, it didn't sound full enough at first, so I added a harmony part. Harmonising a melody can be a matter of trial and error if you don't know what you're doing, but here I've kept things simple by building the original melody using only notes from the underlying chords. This means that I could do exactly the same with the harmony part, again using the "voice leading" concept to keep things smooth and logical.

EX 5

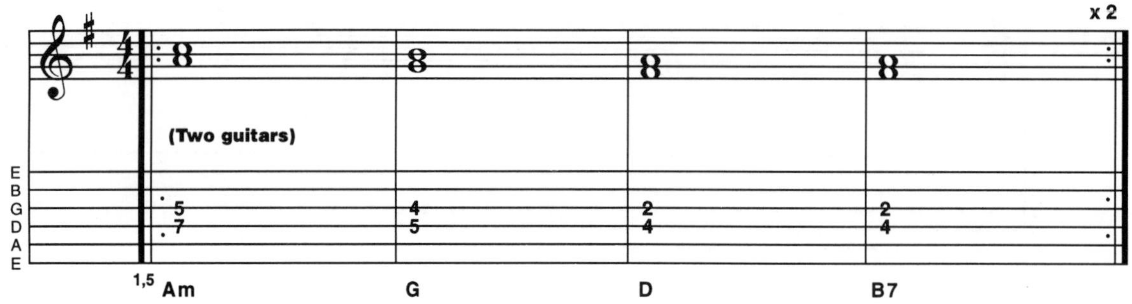

So that's the chorus, and you already know the next bit – it's just a straight repeat of the intro. See what I mean? This songwriting thing is just so easy! At least it is until you decide to play a solo in the style of Ritchie Blackmore... that's when things start to get a little more complicated again. Ah well, look on the bright side – this is an ideal opportunity to sharpen your knowledge of this chapter's new scale. That's right, it's the Phrygian Dominant once again, my friends. Here's the solo, anyway.

EX 6

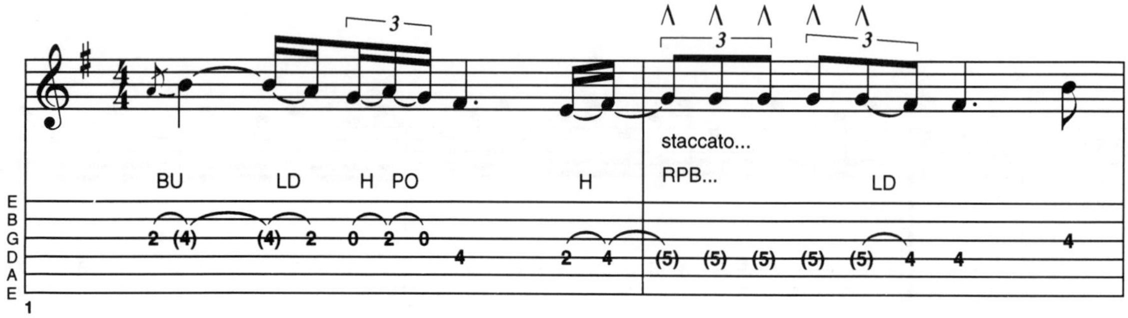

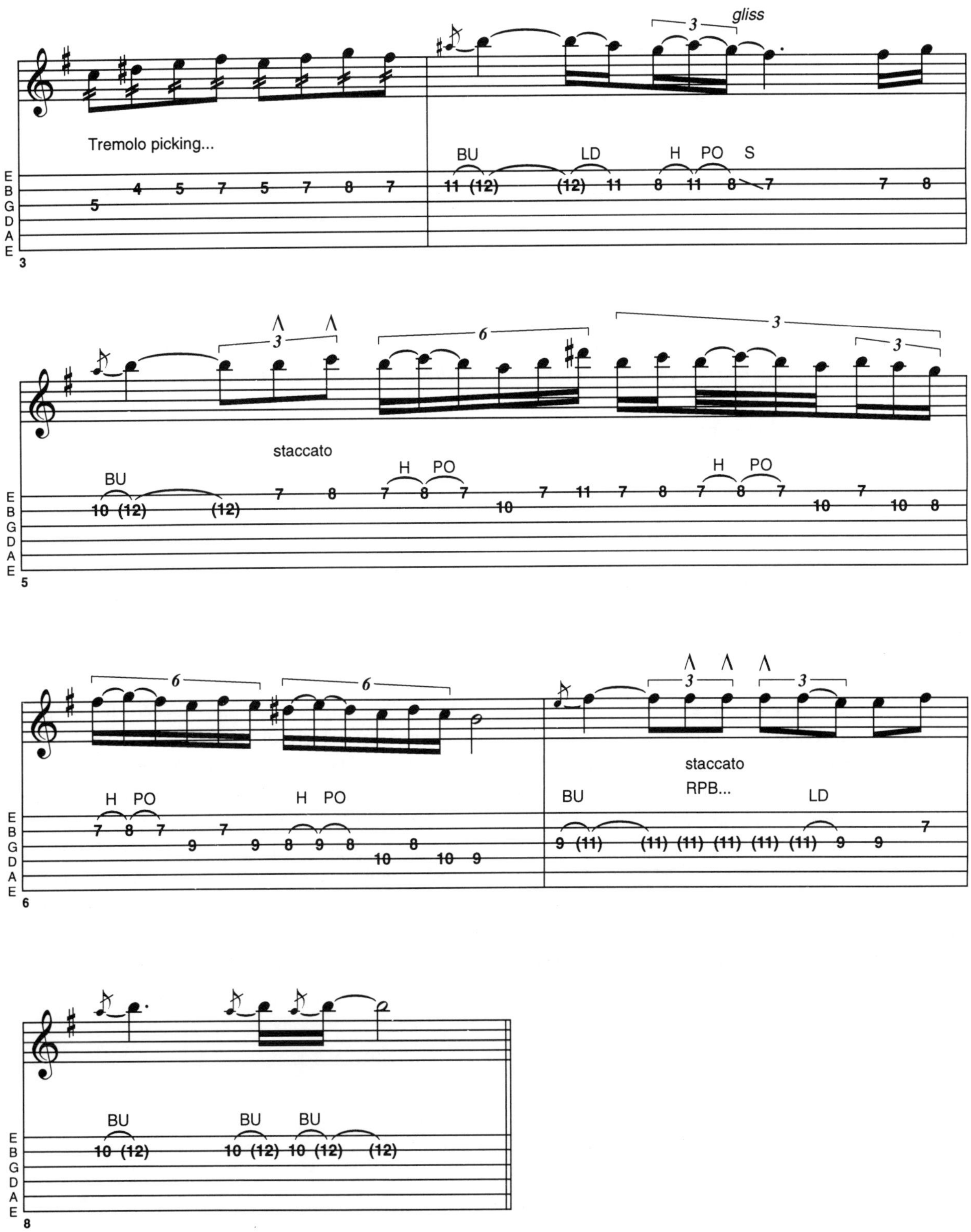

If you were to go through that solo in extreme detail, checking whether every single note is indeed taken from the B Phrygian Dominant... maybe you should get out more. Only joking, but if you did that, you'd see that there are in fact a few A# notes here and there. Looking back at Ex 3, it's clear that there's something amiss here – A# doesn't belong in this scale! Don't worry, because what we have here is a slice of prime Blackmore. Ritchie often replaces the standard ♭7 with the 7 when he uses the Phrygian Dominant, giving rise to what he calls his "snake-charmer scale"...

"SNAKE CHARMER" SCALE IN B

EX 7

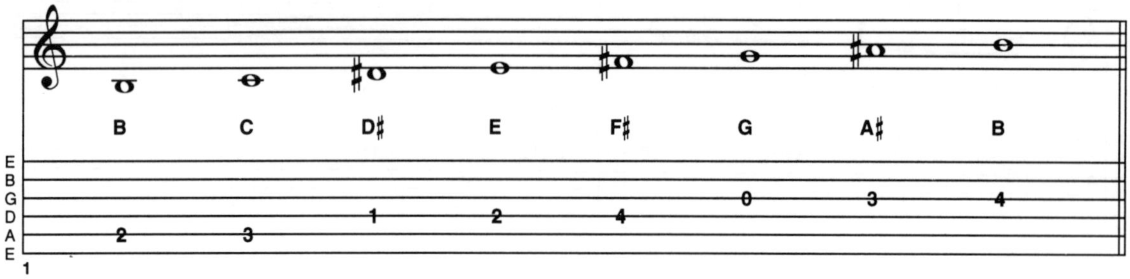

For a few final touches, remember that Ritchie often gets a very aggressive vibrato sound by using the tremolo bar. He also uses strict alternate picking where more recent guitarists (especially in the post-Malmsteen age!) would use sweep picking or economy picking. Try the alternate picking approach in Ex 4 above, and you'll probably find that although it slows you down at first, it actually enables you to get a more defined sound.

Further Exploration

Ritchie's main influences during his early years as a guitarist included Les Paul, Jimmy Bryant, James Burton, Scotty Moore and, of course, Hank Marvin – required listening for any young British player during the late fifties and early sixties. The way in which Ritchie's style developed must have had a lot to do with the lack of major blues influences and the fact that all of the players just mentioned are known for their technical precision.

With his unforgettable riffs, his flamboyant soloing style and his exploration into classically-influenced ideas, Ritchie paved the way for some of the most impressive players of our time: Randy Rhoads, Eddie Van Halen, Steve Morse and – ahem! – Yngwie Malmsteen all owe a major debt to the man in black.

Fans of Blackmore for whom his recorded output is just not enough should point their browsers in the direction of Purple Rainbows: A Tribute To Ritchie Blackmore In The 1970s. Ponderous title, but a great site... http://www.cri.com/~Lzrdking/purprain/index.shtml or if you prefer Ritchie's work with Rainbow, someone in Sweden has got just the thing for you; go to http://www.swepett.pp.se/rainbow/ and see how unofficial sites can be just as slick and professional as the official ones.

CHAPTER 4
Kenny Burrell

BORN:
31 July 1931.

ORIGIN:
Detroit, Michigan.

FIRST SPOTTED:
A bit of a prodigy, Kenny was playing with such jazz greats as Dizzy Gillespie by his late teens.

DISTINGUISHING FEATURES:
Like his old schoolfriend and fellow "house guitarist" at Blue Note Records, Grant Green, Kenny is known for his laid back, blues-meets-bebop style. The English jazz player Adrian Ingram once described Kenny's playing as "suave", which just about sums it up, really.

SEEN IN THE COMPANY OF:
It sounds like a Who's Who of jazz – Dizzy Gillespie, Oscar Peterson, John Coltrane, Quincy Jones, Jimmy Smith, Tommy Flanagan, Jack McDuff...

LAST SEEN:
In early 1997, Kenny became head of UCLA's Jazz Studies programme, having already attained full professorships in Music and Ethnomusicology. Kenny's no stranger to academia, having studied classical guitar with Joe Fava and gained a BMus degree from Wayne University.

THE GOOD BITS:
Kenny's music makes an ideal starting point for any newcomer to jazz guitar. The funky phrasing and blues-influenced lines are far more palatable than most fleet-fingered beboppers and his playing is always the epitome of class.

THE BAD BITS:
His forays into the poppier side of jazz have drawn a certain amount of criticism.

NUTS AND BOLTS:
Kenny's main guitar is a Gibson Super 400 CES, generally plugged into a Fender Twin Reverb or a Polytone amp.

VITAL VINYL:
His best work can be found on the famous Blue Note label, both as a leader (*Midnight Blue* and *Blue Lights*) and as a sideman (Jimmy Smith's *Back At The Chicken Shack*).

I mentioned earlier that much of Kenny Burrell's playing has a very bluesy feel. Taking the first step in jazz guitar can be a pretty daunting thing to do, so building your first solos around the good old familiar twelve-bar blues progression makes for a reasonably gentle introduction. In fact, that's exactly what I've done here – we're in the key of B♭, so here's the chord progression:

EX 1

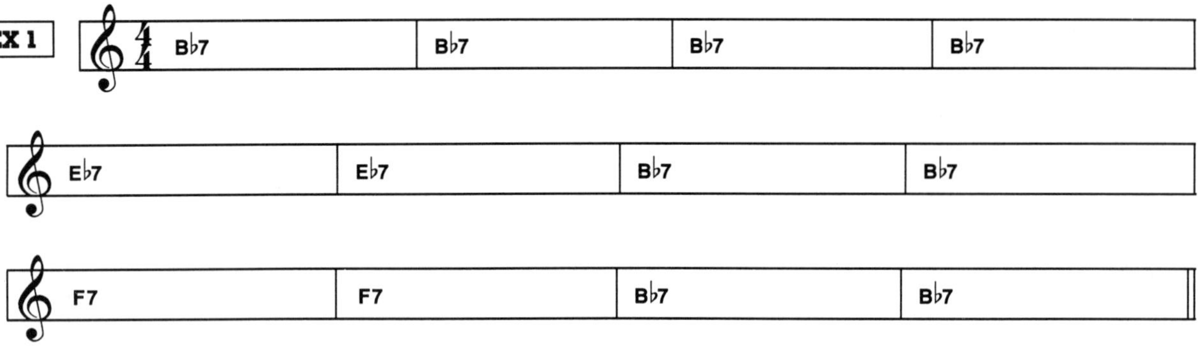

After a brief introduction played by the bass and drums, the guitar enters with the head section. This takes the form of a fairly simple melody using mainly the B♭ minor Pentatonic (B♭, D♭, E♭, F A♭, B♭), interspersed with partial chord "stabs". Take note of the double stop licks in bars 6 and 10 – these are Burrell trademarks, and you'll be using more of them later on.

EX 2

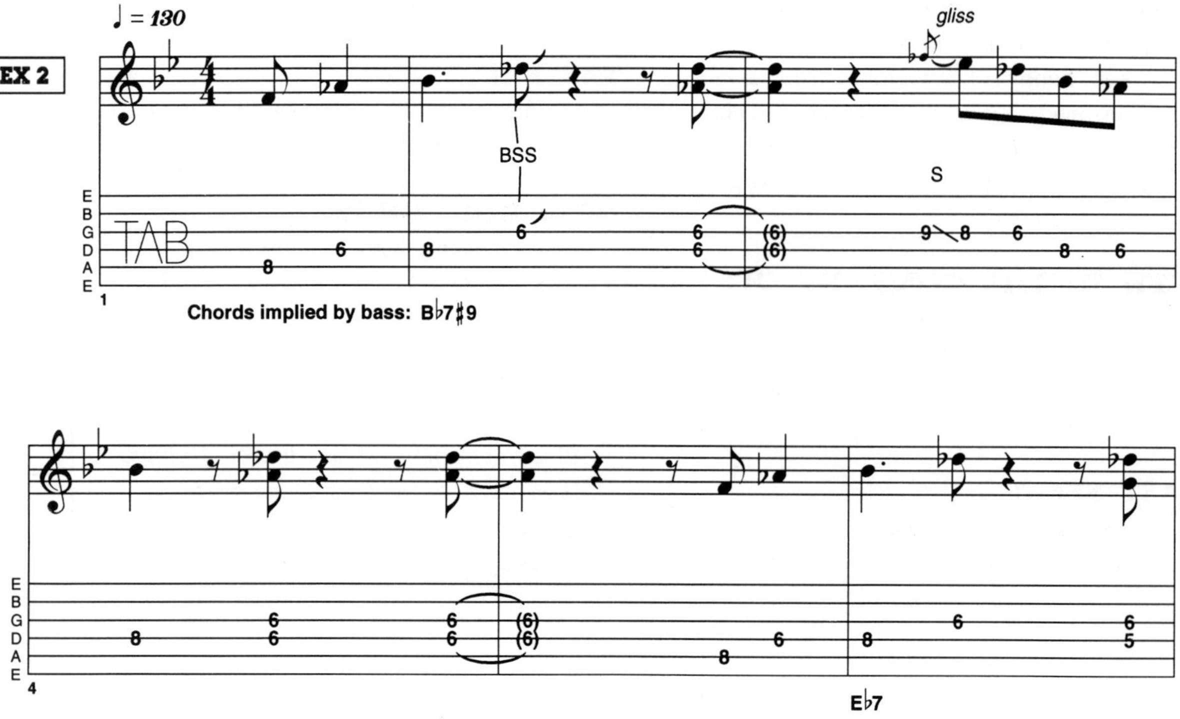

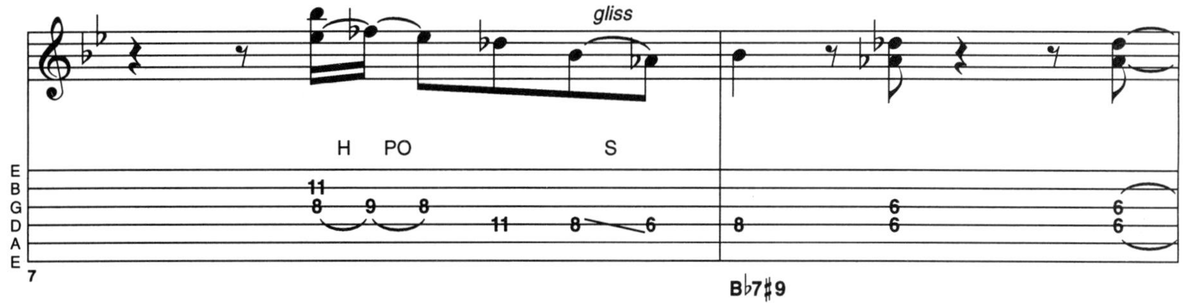

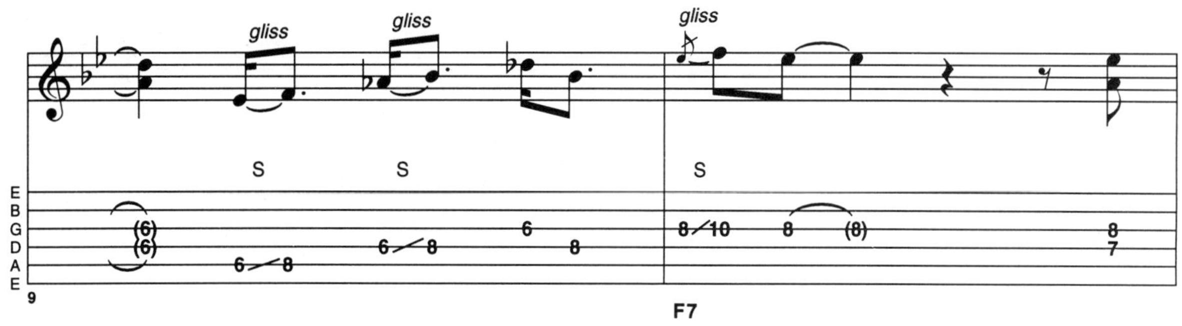

For the second twelve-bar cycle, I repeated the head, but with a few variations to keep it fresh...

EX 3

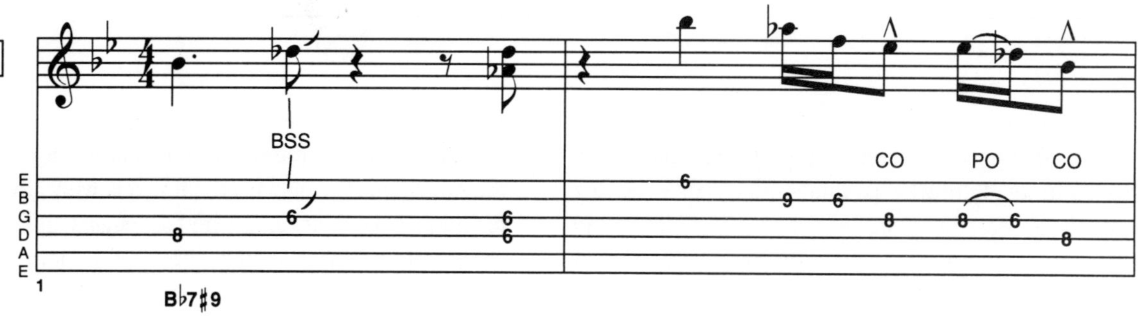

When soloing on this sort of tune (check out the album *Midnight Blue* for plenty of laid back blues-based tunes) Kenny keeps things quite sparse, leaving plenty of breathing space between the licks and resisting the temptation to drown everything in endless sixteenth notes. Also, he often provides occasional reminders of the underlying chords, by adding those little two-note stabs that we encountered in Ex 2 and 3; these give the listener a kind of aural point of reference. Here are two choruses of solo – again I've relied on the B♭ minor Pentatonic for most of the notes, but I've also used a few relatively advanced techniques, such as diminished arpeggios and altered chord tones. Unfortunately there's no room in this book to go into that sort of thing in the necessary detail, so just enjoy the sound of the non-Pentatonic phrases. You can always find a tutor if you're interested in delving deeper.

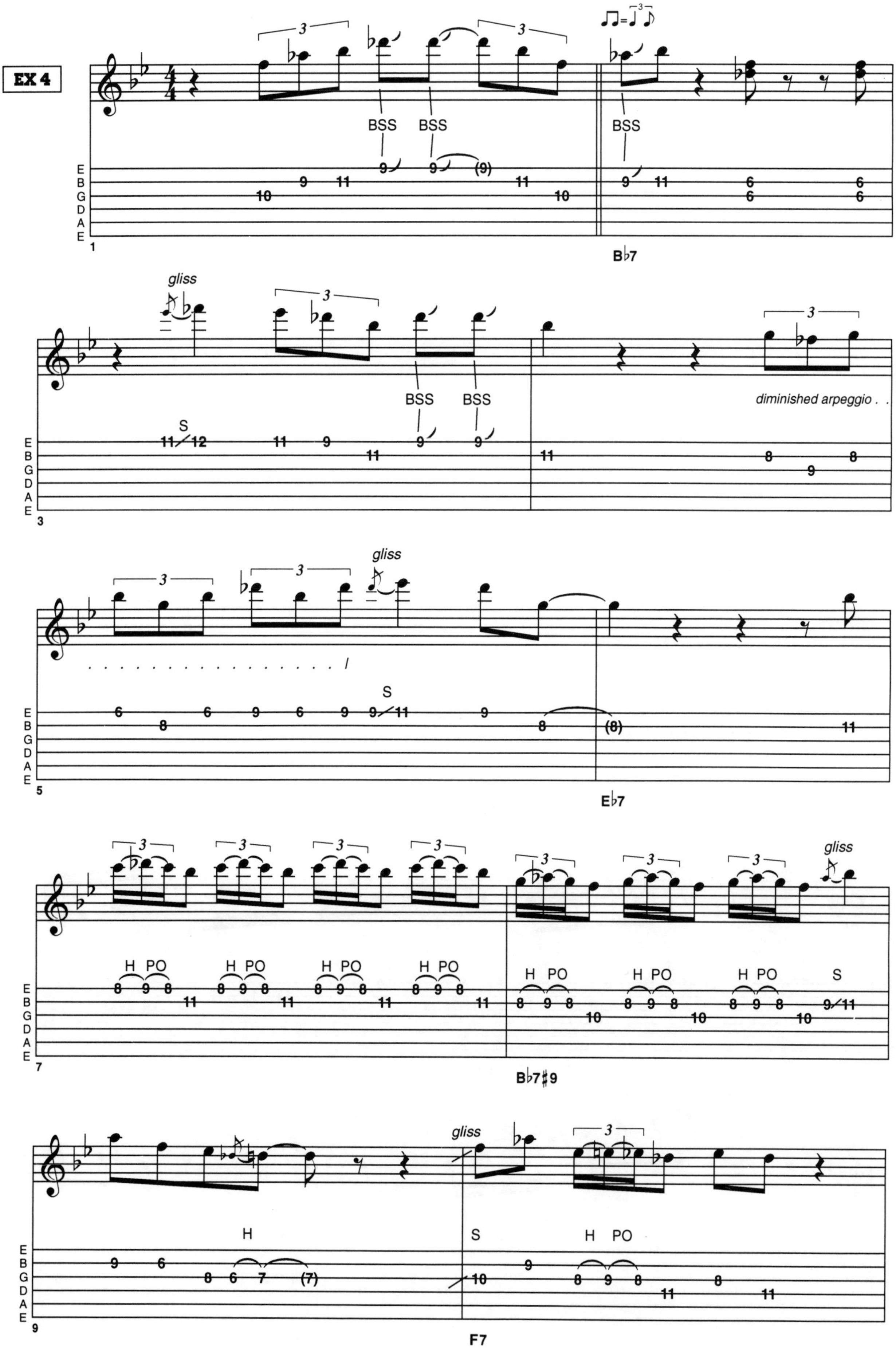
EX 4
BSS
BSS
BSS
B♭7
gliss
S
BSS
BSS
diminished arpeggio . . .
gliss
S
E♭7
H PO
S
gliss
B♭7♯9
gliss
H
S
H PO
F7

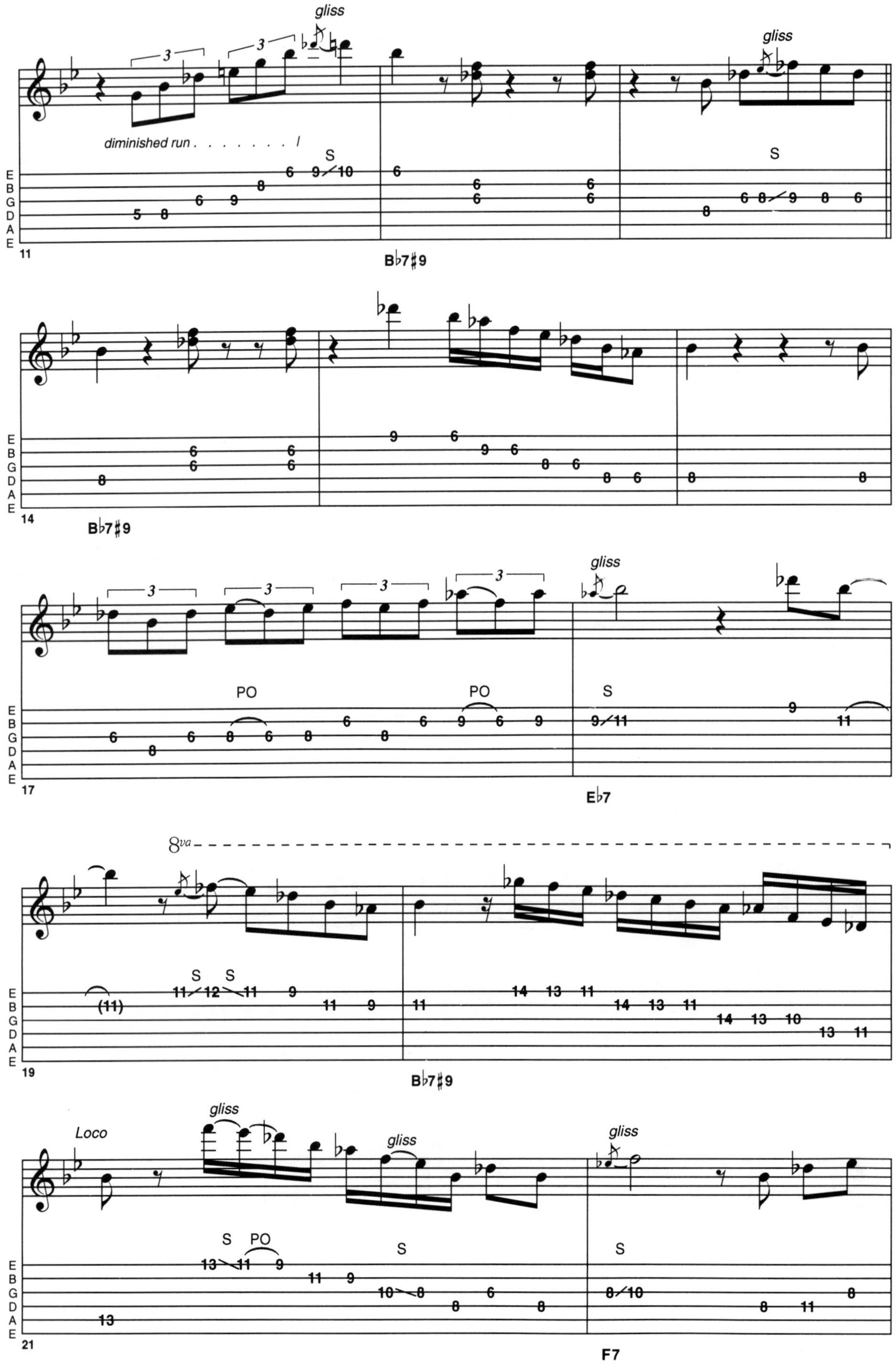
gliss
diminished run l
S
gliss
S
B♭7♯9
B♭7♯9
PO
PO
gliss
S
E♭7
8va
S S
B♭7♯9
Loco
gliss
gliss
S PO
S
gliss
S
F7

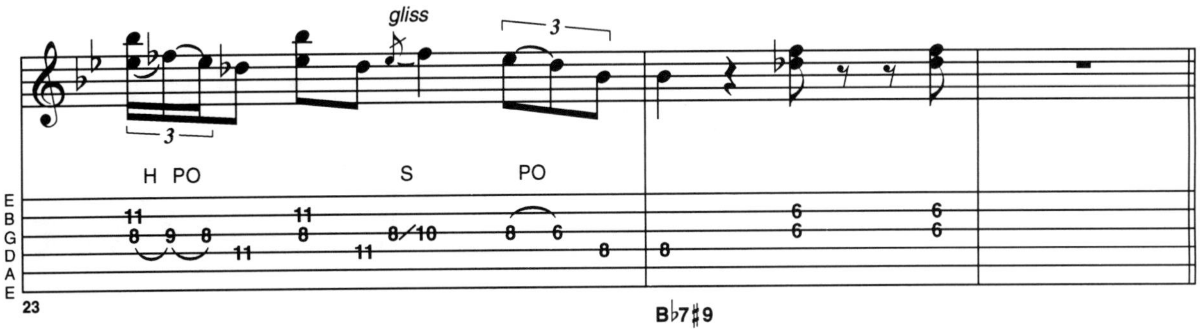

After the solo, I just went back to the head section one last time, but again added a few slight variations to preserve the loose, improvised feel of the whole thing. I haven't bothered transcribing this section, but by using the material we've covered so far, you ought to be able to figure out what I played. It'll be good for you, honest! The tune ends on this chord:

EX 5

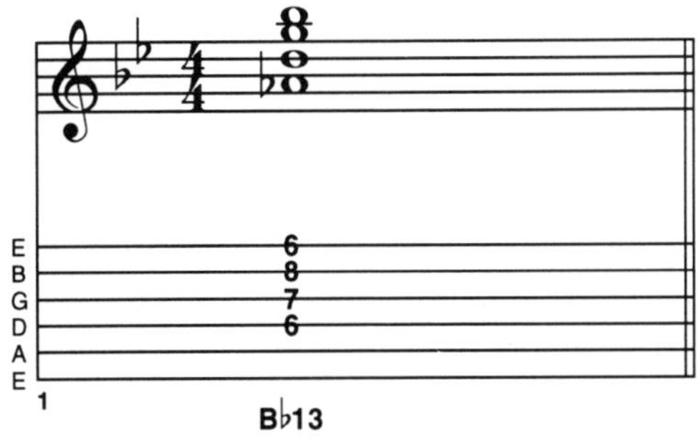

Further Exploration

As a teenager in Detroit, Kenny was first drawn to the guitar by the sounds of Charlie Christian (with Benny Goodman), Oscar Moore (with Nat King Cole) and T-Bone Walker.

Among the hordes of younger players to be inspired by Kenny's cool, bluesy jazz are Martin Taylor, Stevie Ray Vaughan, Andy Summers and Steve Howe.

On the Web... well, I hope you have better luck than I did! For a player of such stature and musical relevance, there's hardly any information regarding Kenny, save for the usual stock of record reviews and adverts. The nearest I could find was in a guide to the teaching staff in UCLA's department of music. Will someone please do something about this...

CHAPTER 5

Charlie Christian

biography TRACK 6

BORN:
29 July 1916.

DIED:
2 March 1942.

ORIGIN:
Born in Texas, grew up in a slum in Oklahoma City, built and played "cigar-box" guitars as a schoolboy. In other words, humble beginnings.

CLAIM TO FAME:
Possibly the first electric soloist. By the time Charlie appeared on the scene, Django Reinhardt was already amazing people in Europe with his acoustic solos, and Eddie Lang had done the same in the States, but electric lead guitar...?! Did this young man actually expect anyone to take this sort of thing seriously? Yup, and God bless his determination!

FIRST SPOTTED:
Charlie had already become a bit of a hometown hero by 1939, when the legendary talent-spotter and record producer John Hammond took him to New York...

BIG BREAK:
...where he met, and impressed the pants off bandleader Benny Goodman, who signed him up immediately.

SEEN IN THE COMPANY OF:
As well as being a regular member of Benny Goodman's Orchestra and Sextet, Charlie frequently took part (with Charlie Parker and Dizzy Gillespie) in the famous Harlem jam sessions which led to the birth of bebop.

THE GOOD BITS:
One of the best soloists of the time, he silenced the traditionalists with his virtuosity on the recently-invented electric guitar, carving out a future path for the instrument. His playing was flashy, confident and way ahead of its time, showing many aspects of what later came to be known as bebop.

THE BAD BITS:
His professional career only lasted eighteen months, as Charlie contracted tuberculosis. We always say this of players who die young, but with Charlie, it's particularly true: who knows what he might have achieved?

NUTS AND BOLTS:
Gibson ES250, complete with the "Charlie Christian" pickup.

VITAL VINYL:
It can be difficult, but try to track down as many Goodman/Christian recordings as you can – Charlie's playing is uniformly brilliant. The tune 'Seven Come Eleven' is a particular classic.

Now, as you'd probably expect, we couldn't afford to hire a full-size big band to do the backing for this track on the CD, so excuse the sparse qualities – think "MTV Unplugged is proud to present Charlie Christian – Back From The Grave".

One of the characteristics of jazz during the Swing Era was the use of riffs. Just in case you're one of those people who didn't spend their teenage years playing 'Smoke On The Water', 'Iron Man' or 'Black Dog', I'll get right down to basics and tell you what a riff actually is. I like to think of riffs as being a versatile midpoint between melody and harmony. They're often used in place of a standard chord part, and yet they're usually made up of single notes, like a melody. Of course, you can get chord-based riffs, but that's just getting a little too specialised...

If you'd prefer a more academic description, here's what Chambers' dictionary has to say: "a phrase or figure played repeatedly". Simple and to the point, eh? Well, here's a "head" section, based on a simple swing-style riff...

Chords used in this chapter

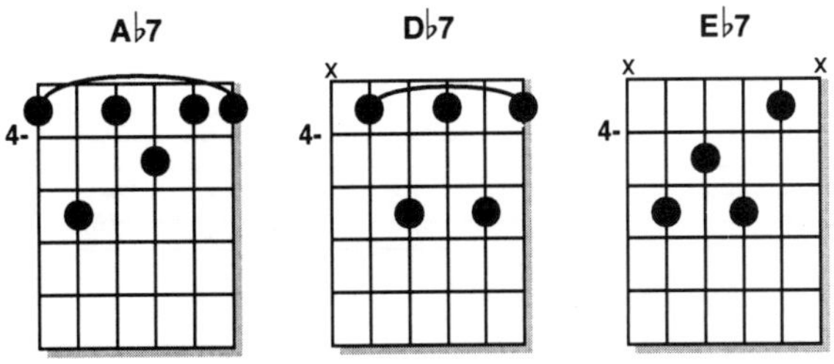

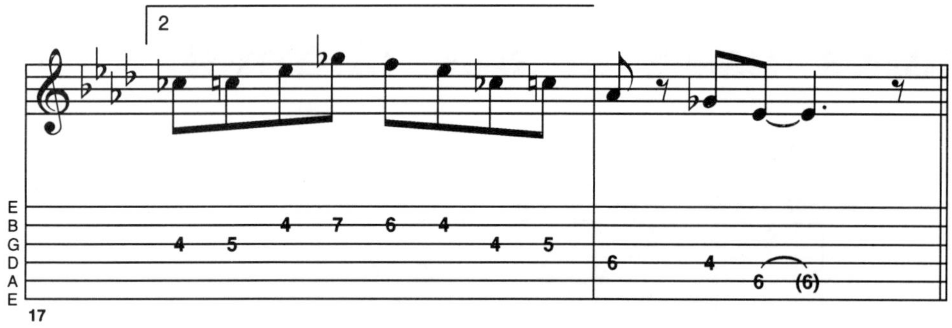

To provide a reasonably non-specific backdrop for the solo section, I've used the old favourite twelve-bar blues structure. Jazz tunes are often played in the "flat" keys (such as F, B♭, E♭ or A♭) as these keys are easier for the primary jazz instruments – tenor and alto saxophones, clarinet and trumpet. Unfortunately for us guitarists, these are often the worst keys to play in, as they don't involve many open string notes! However, if you are interested in jazz (of any era, not just swing) it's important to become familiar with these keys, which is why I've written this tune in the literally terrifying key of A♭. Here's the twelve-bar chord progression for the solo.

EX 2

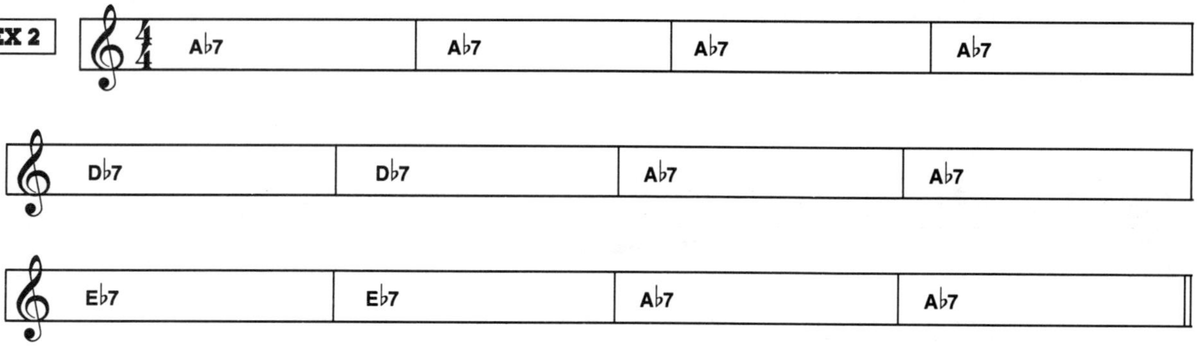

And now, the solo. On most of his recordings with Benny Goodman, Charlie tends to solo for two choruses (ie two complete twelve-bar cycles) as do the other soloists. However, since we don't have any other soloists here, I've written out three choruses of Christian-style lines for you to try. Don't just learn or sight-read the whole thing as one long piece of music – try to see how I've introduced a new lick, phrase or melodic idea for each chord change. After a while, you'll be able to mix the licks up, modify them and even start to build your own solos. I know that sounds simplistic, but that's how all of the great jazz musicians learned their trade. Here's chorus #1...

SOLO CHORUS I

EX 3

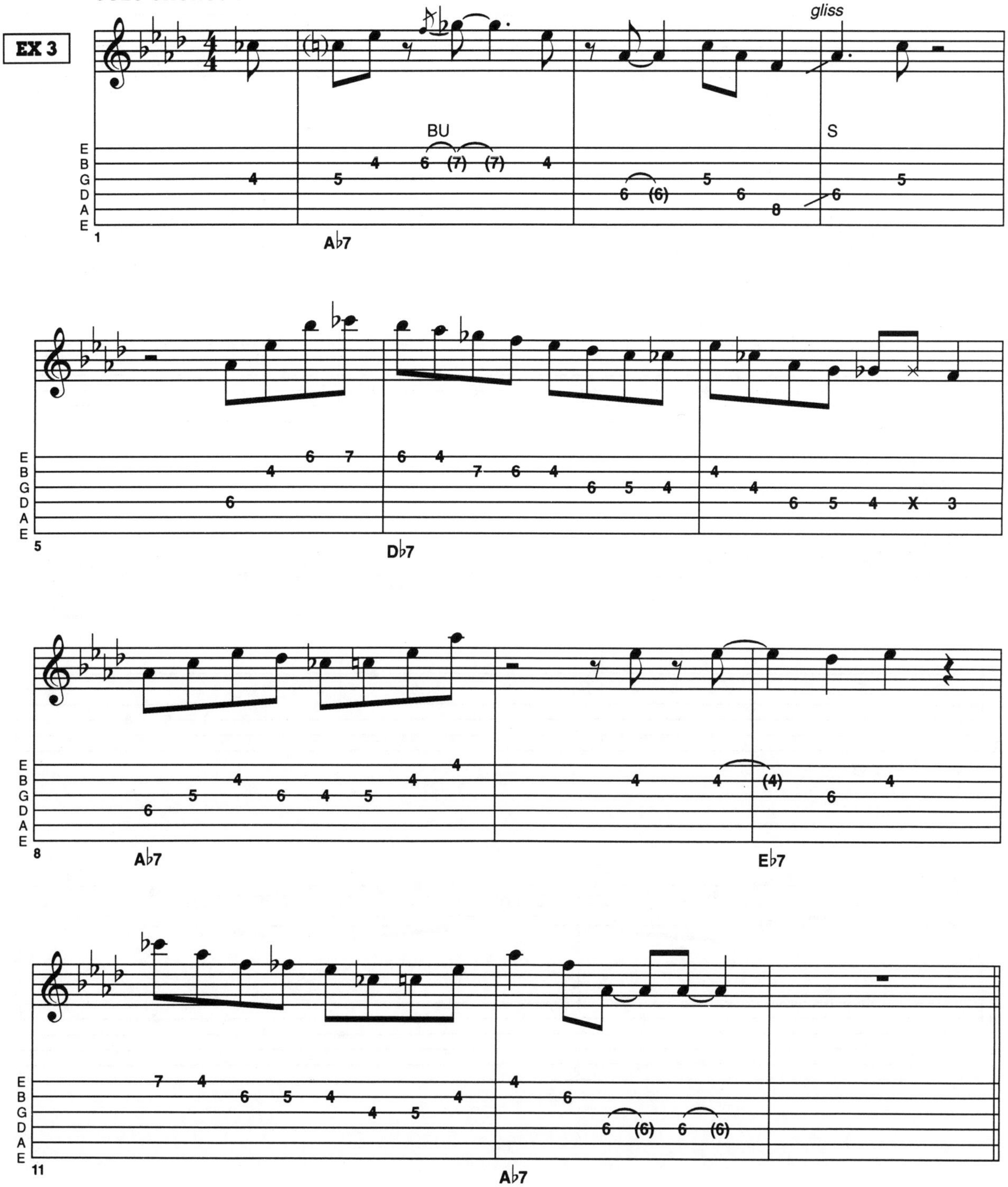

And chorus #2...

SOLO CHORUS II

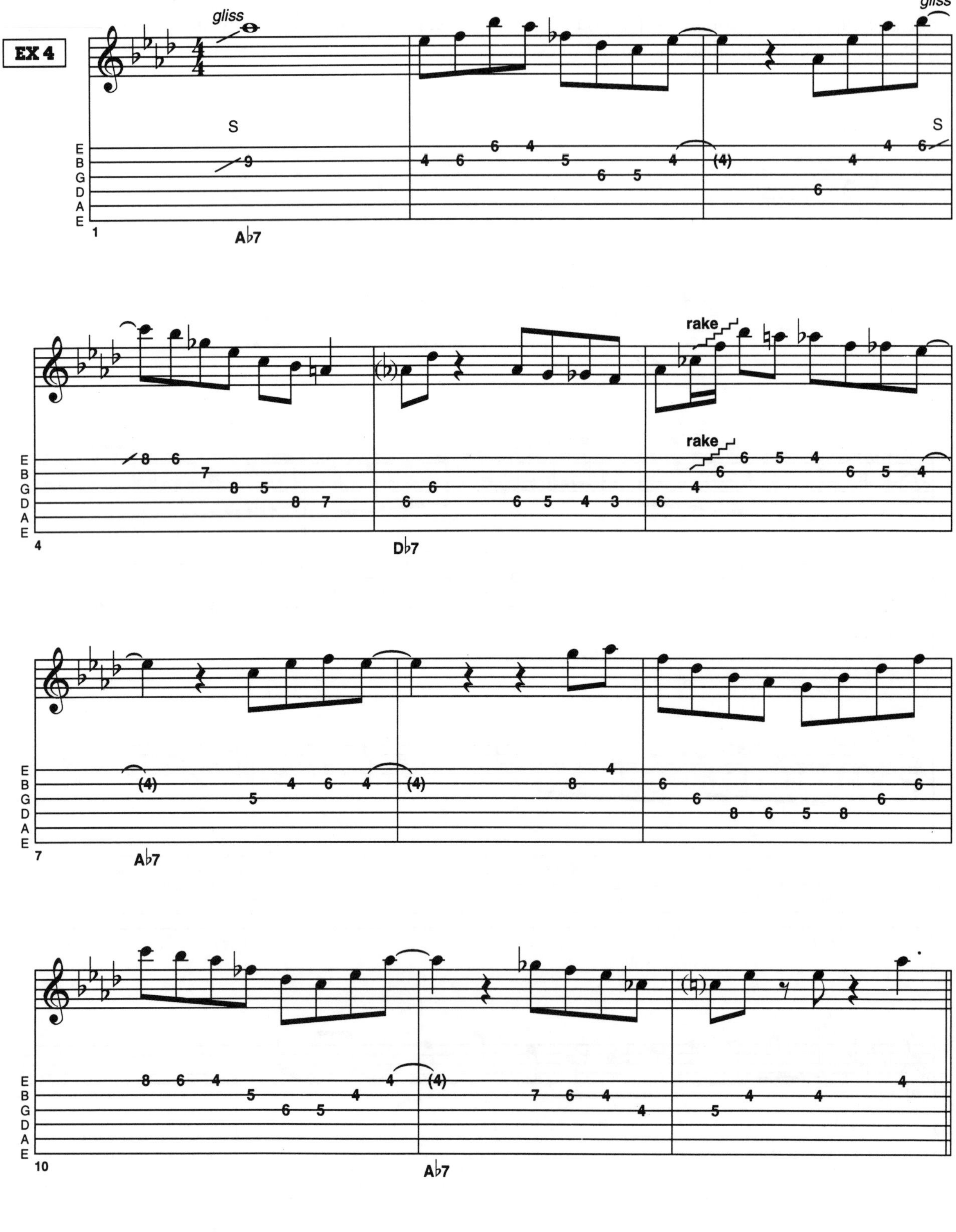

And finally, chorus #3...

SOLO CHORUS III

EX 5

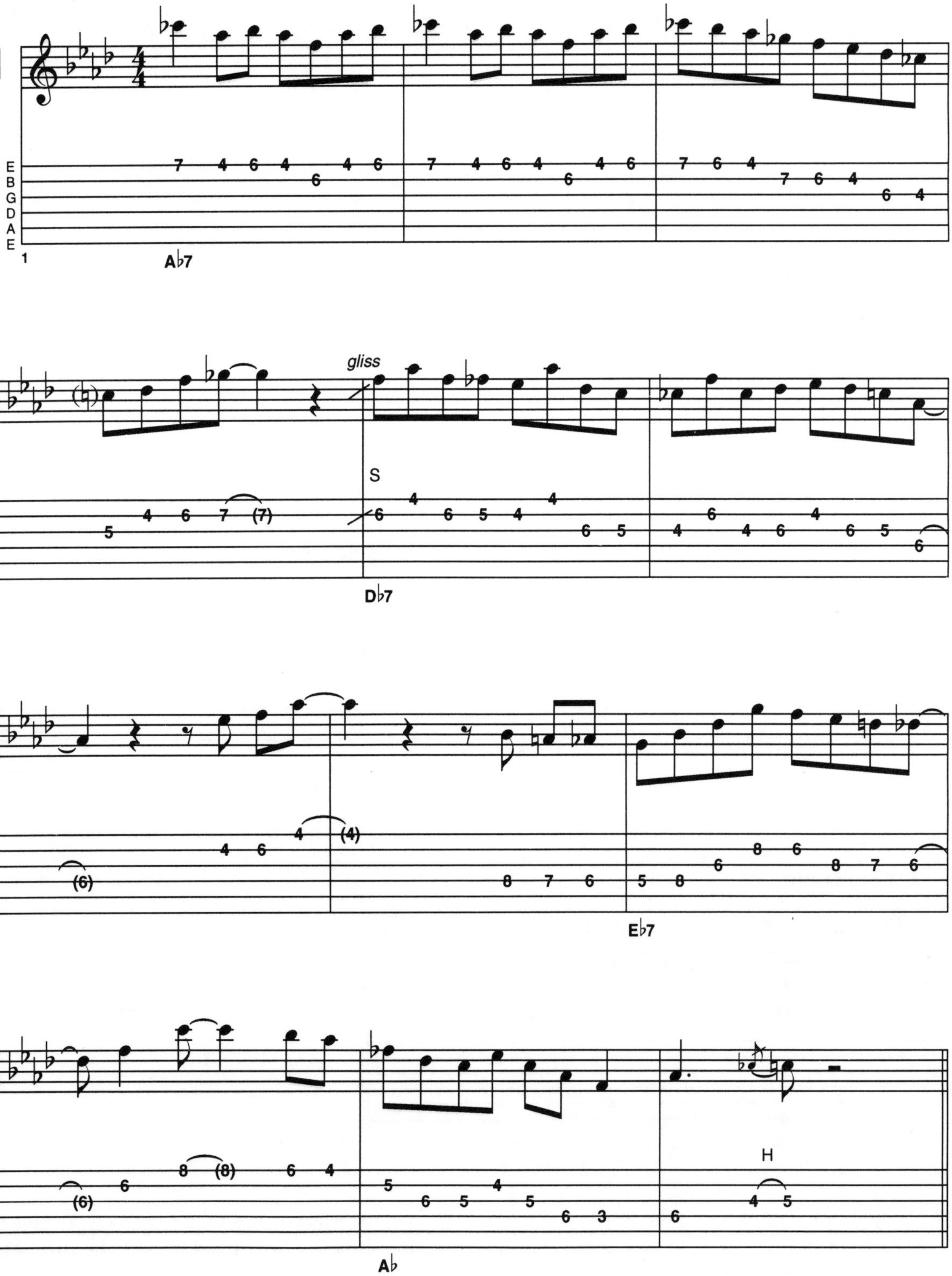

To round things off neatly, I then decided to repeat the head section, but with a slightly different ending. All you have to do is replace the "2" box in Ex 1 with the following.

EX 6

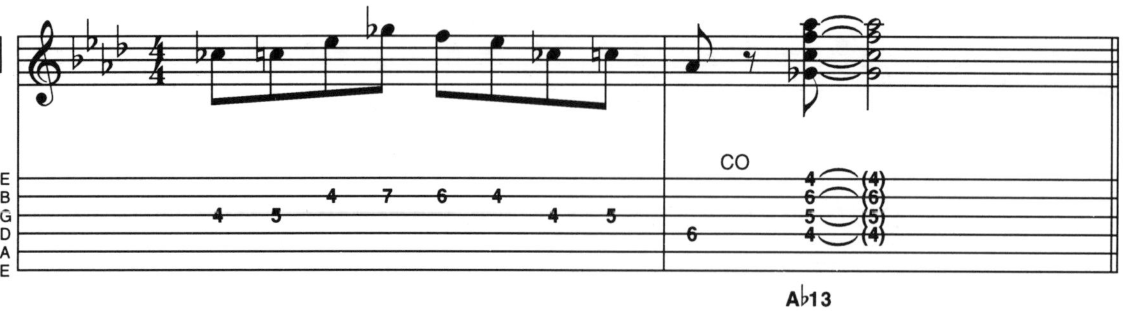

By learning all that, you'll have quite a few Charlie Christian-style licks and ideas to play with, but in jazz that's not really enough – you need to be able to expand on them and create something of your own. So... here's a rough guide to some of the scales used.

For the I chord (A♭ in this key), Charlie would generally use a composite scale made up of notes from the minor Pentatonic and the Mixolydian mode (and therefore containing notes from the A♭7 chord)...

EX 7A

A♭ MINOR PENTATONIC **A♭ MIXOLYDIAN**

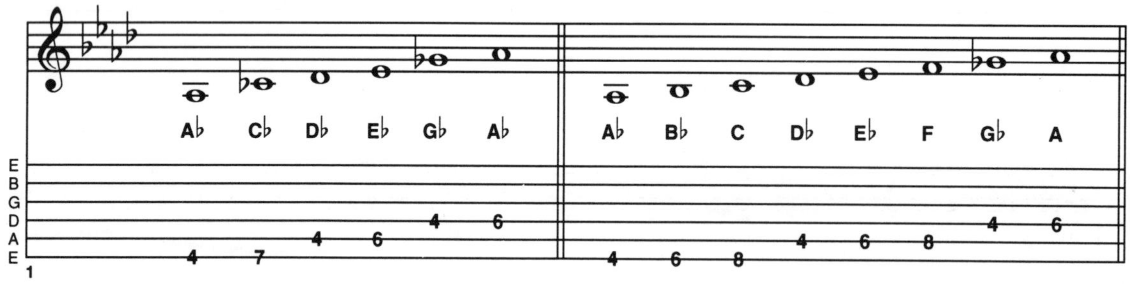

A♭7 ARPEGGIO

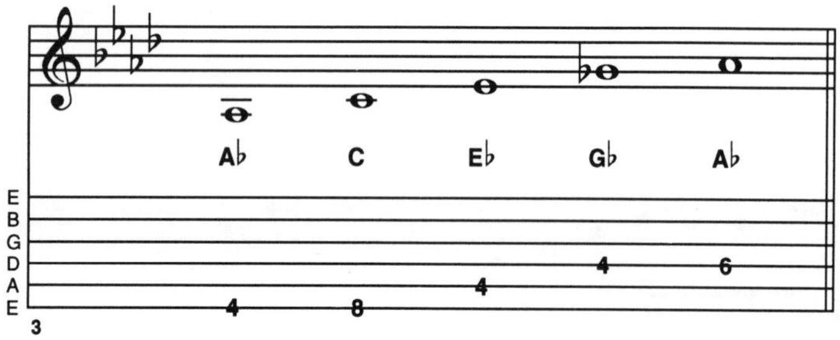

With that sort of scale, you must resist the temptation simply to run up and down through the notes, like a rock player would. The trick is to use the scale as a source of licks – consult Ex 3-5 above to see how I did it, and then try a few of your own.

Now, for the IV chord (D♭ in the key of A♭) you can either continue to play around the scale in Ex 7a, or build phrases around the notes of a D♭7 chord. For our solo, I stuck more or less to the scale for the first chorus and then built phrases around the standard D♭7 bar chord shape (with added chromatic passing notes) for the other two choruses. Another method used by Charlie is to build licks around a conveniently-situated D♭13 arpeggio...

EX 7B

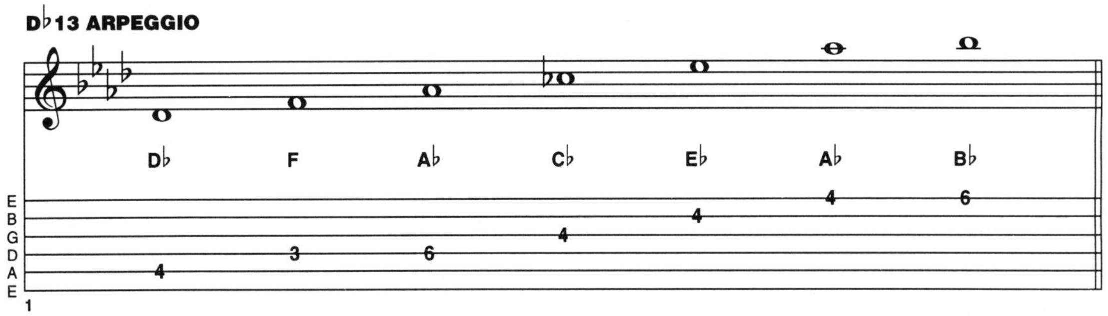

Finally, we need some material for the V chord (E♭ in this particular key). Again, with a bit of care you can weave some pretty impressive lines using just the composite scale from Ex 7a, but there are other alternatives. In the second solo chorus, I used an E♭13 arpeggio shape and in the third, I used the E♭7 bar chord shape as a starting point.

EX 7C

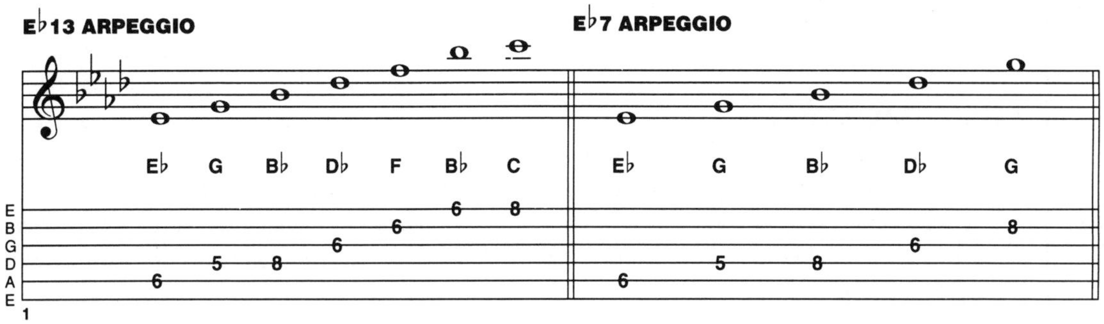

Further Exploration

Charlie Christian was born into a family of musicians, and was therefore exposed to a wide range of musical styles; in 1920s Oklahoma City, even the poorest black children had access to music appreciation classes. Among Charlie's influences were saxophonist Lester Young, guitarists Eddie Lang and Lonnie Johnson and early Western Swing bands, featuring guitarists such as Leon McAuliffe and Bob Dunn.

Charlie Christian's career, though short, could be described as one of the major milestones in the history of the guitar, so in a way, we all have reasons to be grateful for what he did. Players who were particularly influenced by his style include Barney Kessel, BB King, T-Bone Walker and Chuck Berry.

Exploding the myth that the Web only ever caters for the latest new trend, there's a fantastic site called Charlie Christian – Legend Of The Jazz Guitar. It features masses of biographical info, pictures, transcriptions and even MIDI files of some of the great man's solos. Direct your Web-browser to http://www3.nbnet.nb.ca/hansen/Charlie/

CHAPTER 6
Eric Clapton

biography TRACK 2

BORN:
30 March 1945.

ORIGIN:
Ripley, Surrey.

OCCUPATION:
God. No, I'm not trying to invoke the wrath of any Christians who may be reading – "Clapton is God" was a common toilet-wall daubing in 1960s London.

FIRST SPOTTED:
In the jazz and blues clubs of suburban London, a fertile breeding ground for many future legends. Eric started off as an enthusiastic fan, before eventually forming his first band, The Roosters, in 1963.

BIG BREAK:
Although Eric had already begun to make a name for himself with The Yardbirds, their pop-orientated material placed too many restrictions on his blossoming guitar talents. The real break came in 1965, when EC joined John Mayall's Bluesbreakers and recorded *that* album.

SEEN IN THE COMPANY OF:
Like his namesake, Eric seems to have been everywhere and played with everyone. He has recorded with The Beatles, Buddy Guy, Freddie King and George Harrison, to name a few, jammed with numerous others and was even part of Live Aid in those guitar-free mid eighties.

THE GOOD BITS:
Despite being a middle-class white boy from comfortable south-eastern England, Eric has become one of the all-time greats of blues guitar, demonstrating its universal nature.

THE BAD BITS:
Eric's recent career has tended to focus more on pop and songwriting than pure blues. Nothing wrong with that, of course, but if you've just been blown away by his work with John Mayall and Cream, you may be disappointed by some of the later stuff.

NUTS AND BOLTS:
Blackie, the famous mongrel Strat, has now retired after nearly twenty years of service, so Eric is usually seen nowadays with a Fender Clapton Strat. Before the Strat phase started, though, Eric was a loyal Gibson man, using a Les Paul with The Bluesbreakers and an SG or a 335 with Cream. Although Eric tends to use Soldano amps these days, his most famous amp was the forty-five-watt Marshall "1962" combo he used in the 1960s, now reissued as the "Bluesbreaker" model.

VITAL VINYL:
Start with the "Beano" album (*John Mayall's Bluesbreakers Featuring Eric Clapton*) taking care to secure any loose objects. The Cream albums are also classics, demonstrating a less traditional application of Eric's blues playing. Then there's *Layla And Other Assorted Love Songs* and, more recently, *Unplugged* and *From The Cradle*.

Faced with a variety of blues-related styles from Eric's long career, I've decided to base this particular "in the style of" piece on his work with Cream. The Cream period shows how blues isn't a single musical entity cast in granite; it can be modified and twisted to blend in with various other styles. There's a famous quote from Jack Bruce about Cream actually being a jazz group – it's just that neither he nor Ginger Baker told Eric about that! Listen to tracks like 'Sunshine Of Your Love' and 'White Room', though, and you're hearing one of the best rock bands of all time – it just goes to show that whatever category people put an artist in, it's the quality of the music that shines through.

I've based this tune around the standard twelve-bar blues progression, but in the spirit of what Cream were all about, I've made a couple of alterations to the chord sequence. All will become clear when you play (and listen to) the intro/main theme, as shown in the following example:

EX 1

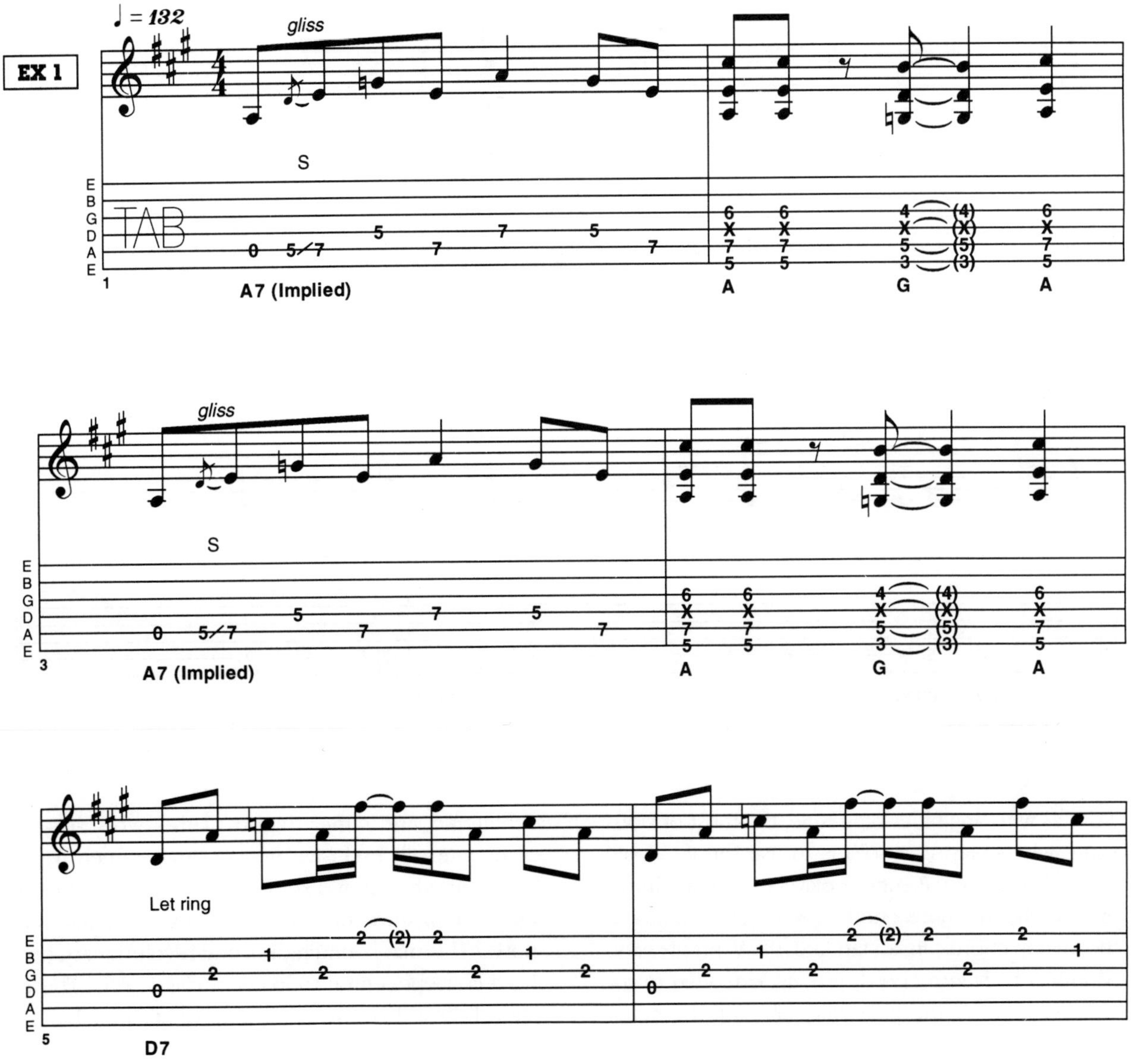

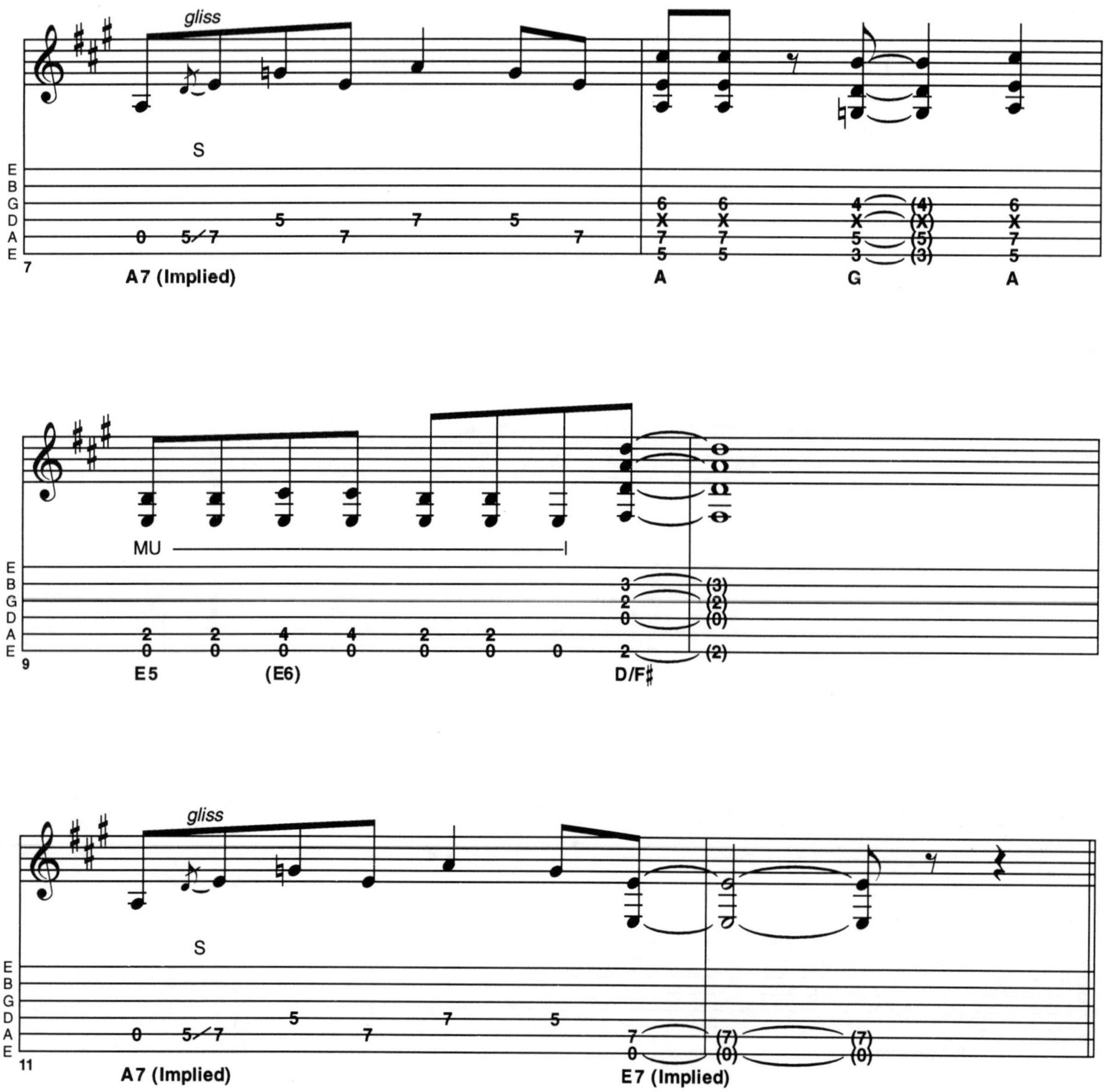

Now, as with any blues-type tune, the most obvious route when playing a solo is to use the good old minor Pentatonic. Plenty of players use that almost exclusively, and there's nothing wrong with that, but the major chords in a standard I-IV-V progression (dominant seventh chords are just extended major chords) indicate the possibility of using the major Pentatonic. And rather than treat the two scales as being mutually exclusive, why not move freely from one to another in mid solo, or even play licks made up of a mixture of major and minor Pentatonic notes? This may sound radical and revolutionary, but it's a concept central to loads of classic riffs. These short licks will give you a taste of what's possible...

EX 2

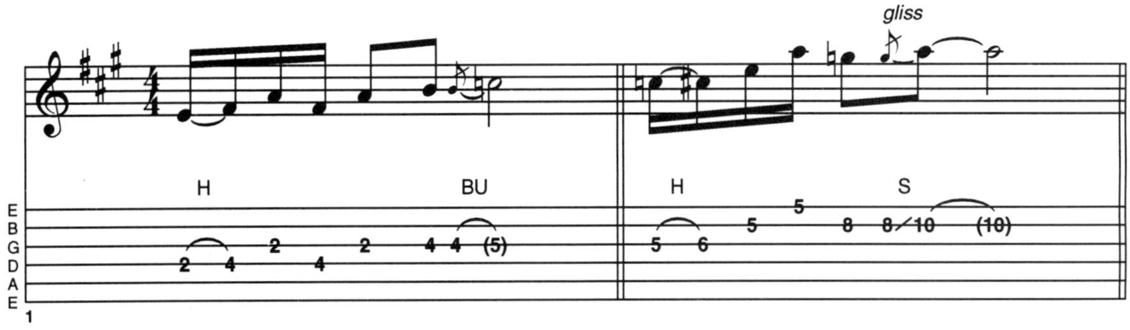

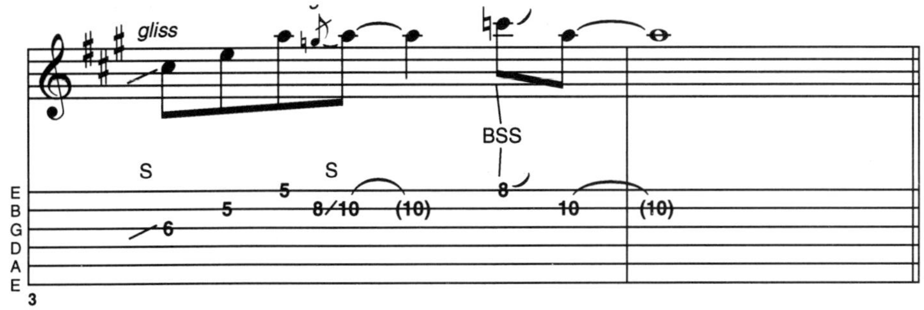

A MINOR PENTATONIC

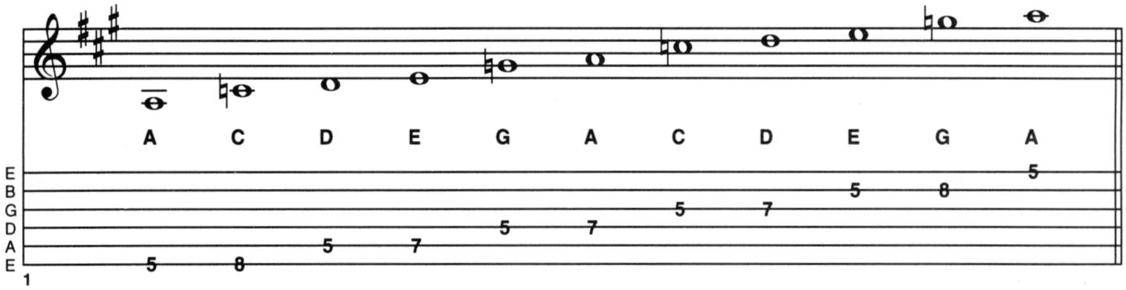

A MAJOR PENTATONIC

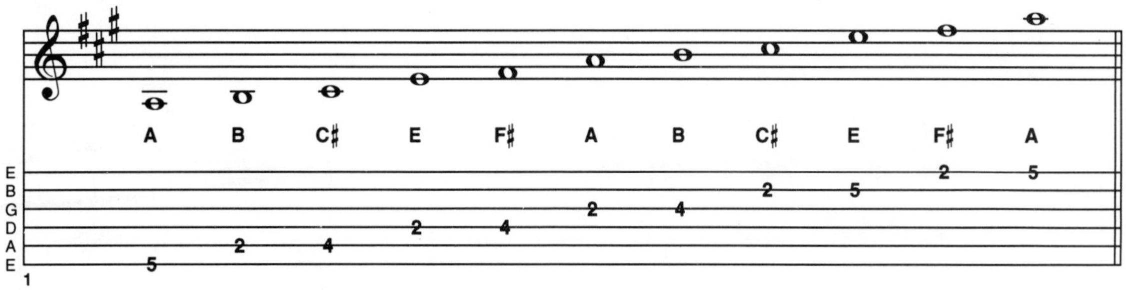

Here are the first twelve bars of the solo. Look out for licks using just the major Pentatonic, just the minor Pentatonic or a mixture of both.

EX 3

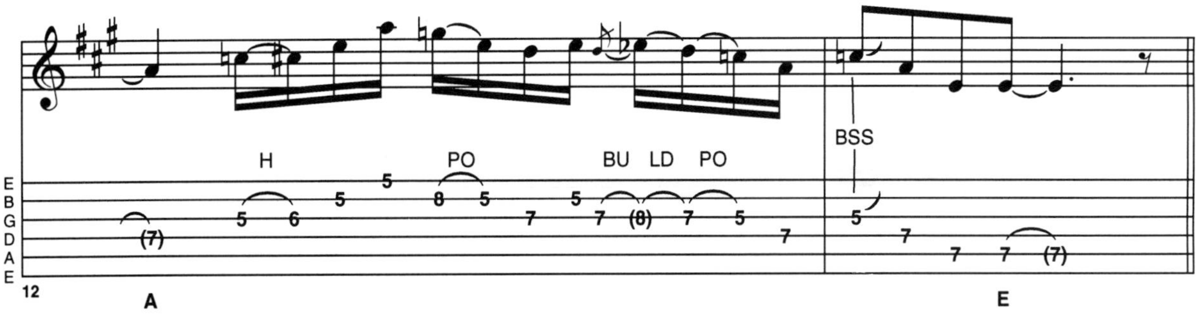

And another twelve bars' worth of solo. If you look carefully, you should be able to find plenty of Clapton trademarks here – the mammoth four-fret bend, the trick of playing the same note twice but on two different strings... Remember, Eric may be more of a singer-songwriter these days, making only occasional forays into standard blues territory, but back in the late sixties he was one of the hottest, most passionate players around. Listen to his playing on the album *John Mayall's Bluesbreakers Featuring Eric Clapton* – it's positively vicious!

EX 4

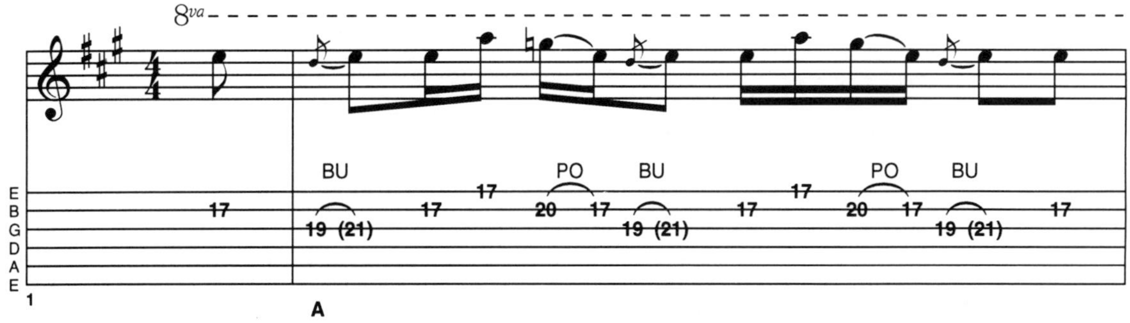

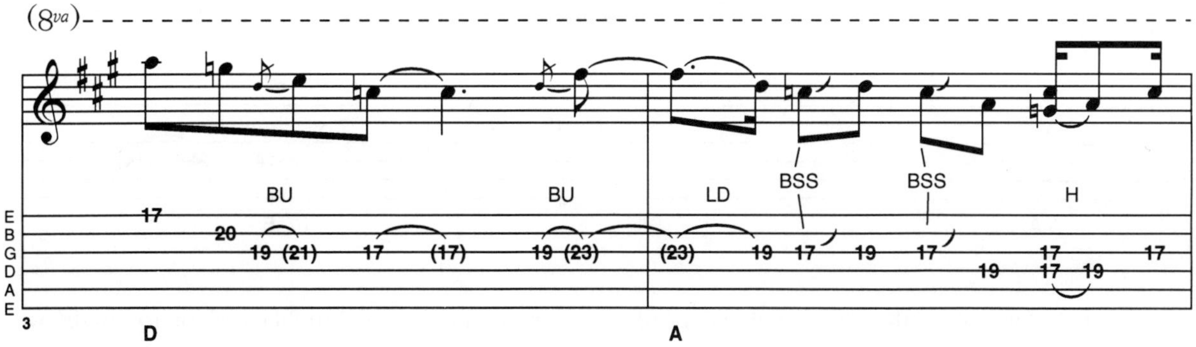

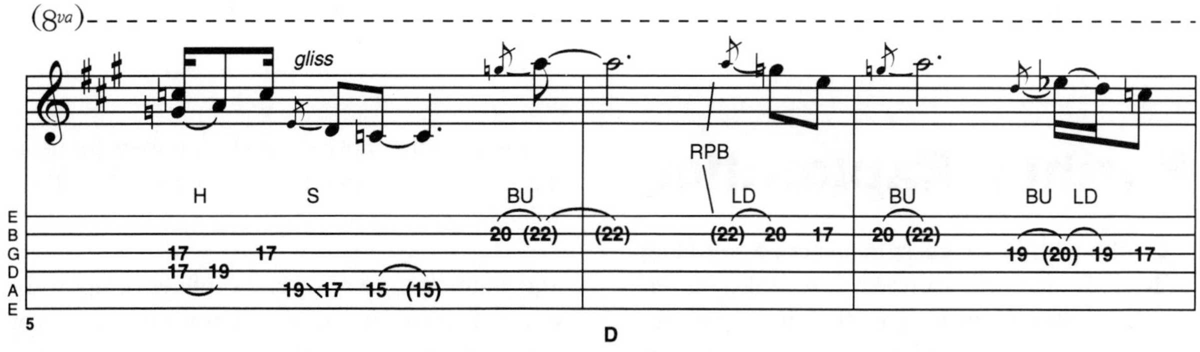

To round things off neatly, I repeated the head section (Ex 1) at the end. Admittedly, there are a couple of minor differences here and there the second time round, but I'll leave you to puzzle over those – I didn't use anything that we haven't already covered in this chapter!

Further Exploration

Although Eric's earliest influences were Buddy Holly and the early Elvis records, his life changed when he heard Freddie King. From then on, Eric became a full-time blues enthusiast, listening avidly to players such as Robert Johnson, Big Bill Broonzy, Blind Willie Johnson and Blind Willie McTell.

And as for the proof of Eric's influence upon the world of guitar... if you haven't noticed by now, you never will! Aside from the fact that he was a huge inspiration to his contemporaries in those heady days of the sixties, Eric is given as the primary reason why many younger players actually picked up the guitar.

If you yearn for Clapton-related info, the Eric Clapton FAQ should provide you with more than you could ever need – http://www.htwm.de/~suhlig/ec_faq.html

Or, for a more laid back approach, go to Eric Clapton's Page, a very well-written site which lives at http://www.kiss.uni-lj.si/~k4mf0026/eric_frame_index.html

CHAPTER 7
Kurt Cobain

biography

TRACK 24

BORN:
20 February 1967.

DIED:
8 April 1994.

CLAIM TO FAME:
Coming from Seattle and being left-handed had already been done by the time Kurt appeared on the scene (Hendrix, right?) so he went and invented grunge. That's what the trendy music media would have you believe, anyway, but in reality things were a bit more complex than that.

FIRST SPOTTED:
Hipper members of the student community (the ones with straggly beards, cut-off denim shorts and army boots – this was before Britpop, remember) were beginning to groove to the new sounds from the Pacific Northwest back in 1991, but most of us had to wait until 1993...

BIG BREAK:
Nevermind. No, I mean *Nevermind* – the multi-million-selling Nirvana album which established Kurt as a major character in rock history and gave the tabloid press another buzz word, complete with the attendant drink, drugs, messy hair and noisy music. "Grunge" had officially been born.

THE REAL BIG BREAK:
Butch Vig did a great production job on *Nevermind*, but its big rock sound doesn't really fit the grunge ideal. Nirvana's previous album *Bleach*, recorded for only $600, made a far more defining statement in terms of the anti-mainstream/lo-fi movement which followed.

THE GOOD BITS:
Tempted thousands of kids away from their turntables and expensive leisurewear, causing them to grow lank greasy hair and... learn to play guitar. Hence the reason for books like this and the fact that I have a fixed address.

THE BAD BITS:
Sleeping rough as a teenager, ridiculed by his father, mysterious stomach pains: it's no wonder Kurt injected so much anger into his songs and playing. And then there was the rather explosive end to it all...

THE REALLY BAD BITS:
Another great waste of a talent – Kurt shot himself in 1994, providing yet another Hendrix similarity – both died at the age of twenty-seven.

NUTS AND BOLTS:
The clumsy, idiot country cousins of the Fender back catalogue: Mustangs and Jaguars. Fender presumably couldn't decide which to reincarnate, so they produced a hybrid – the Jagstang!

VITAL VINYL:
Nevermind, without a doubt, simply because it contains most of the big hits. However, it is rather big and "metal", so for a rawer, more honest version of the Nirvana sound try *In Utero*. Although infinitely more polite, *Unplugged In New York* is a classic.

It all sounds a bit hackneyed these days, but back in the early nineties, everyone was getting all sweaty and excited over something as innocent as song structure. Yes, really – even advertising agencies had cottoned on to the fact that if you made a TV commercial featuring music which started deceptively quiet and then got loud and thrashy, young people would buy your product! Obviously it's not as simple as that, but plenty of Nirvana songs follow that sort of format, so let's borrow Kurt's approach for these examples.

Before we start, here's a useful tip: tune down! For the necessary "oomph", it's a good idea to tune your guitar one or two semitones lower than normal. For these examples I'm tuned one semitone flat, and in addition, I've tuned my sixth string down another two semitones. The result is like "dropped-D" tuning, but a semitone lower. One of the main advantages of this is that you can move power chords (the ones rooted on the sixth string, anyway) around more easily. Like this...

EX 1

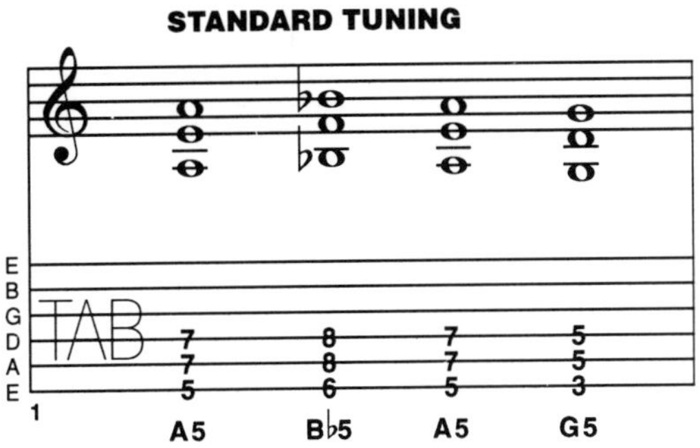

becomes

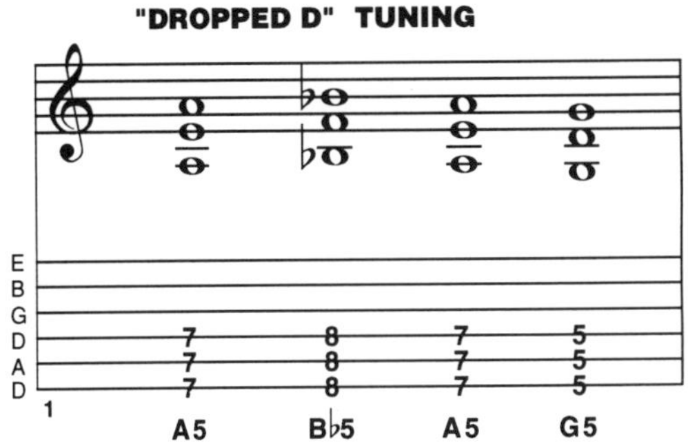

Right, now you know how that works, we can get on with some real music. If you're reading the standard notation (the "dots") as well as the Tab, don't worry, I've written all the pitches as if we were in standard tuning, or at least standard dropped-D. So let's start with a quiet bit. For the proper Nirvana sound, I'd be inclined to use this as both the intro and the verse.

EX 2

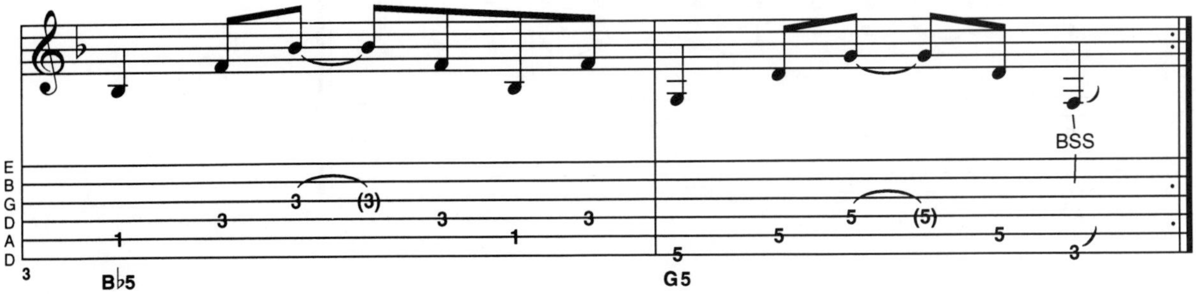

When trying to come up with your own versions of that sort of part, it's worth bearing a couple of things in mind. Firstly, Kurt wrote a lot of chord progressions with the same structure as I've used here – four chords, each lasting roughly the same amount of time (usually two beats or a bar). Secondly, he often used quite "angular" chord movements, so don't just stick to the old tried-and-tested routes. Let your fingers stray to some new out-of-key areas – you may like what you find! Oh yeah, and just to make the verse part stand out from the intro, I added a simple line using a flanger, just for a textural effect...

EX 3

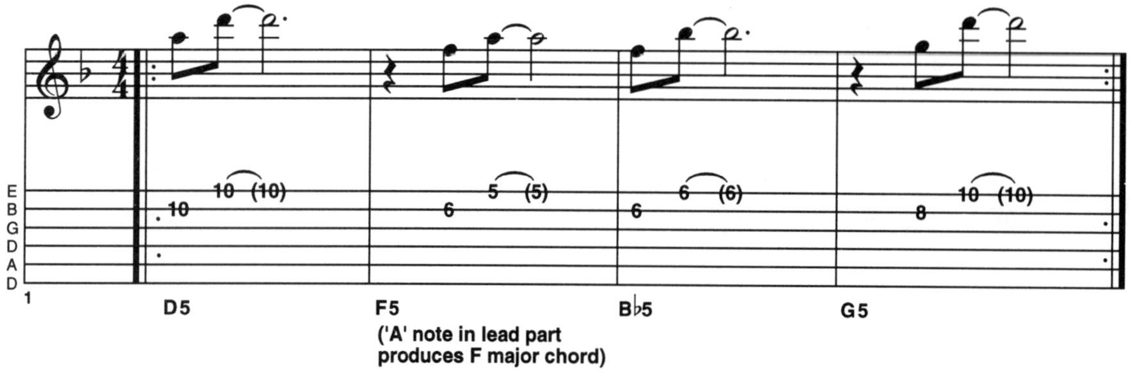

In the grand Seattle tradition, things are supposed to get loud here, so wind up that volume control, stomp on your new Satan's Lovechild XQJ-37 distortion pedal, and generally have a blast with the chorus part. Note that I brought in the distorted guitar part on the final chord of the verse – this helps to glue things together a bit better and make the change smoother.

EX 4

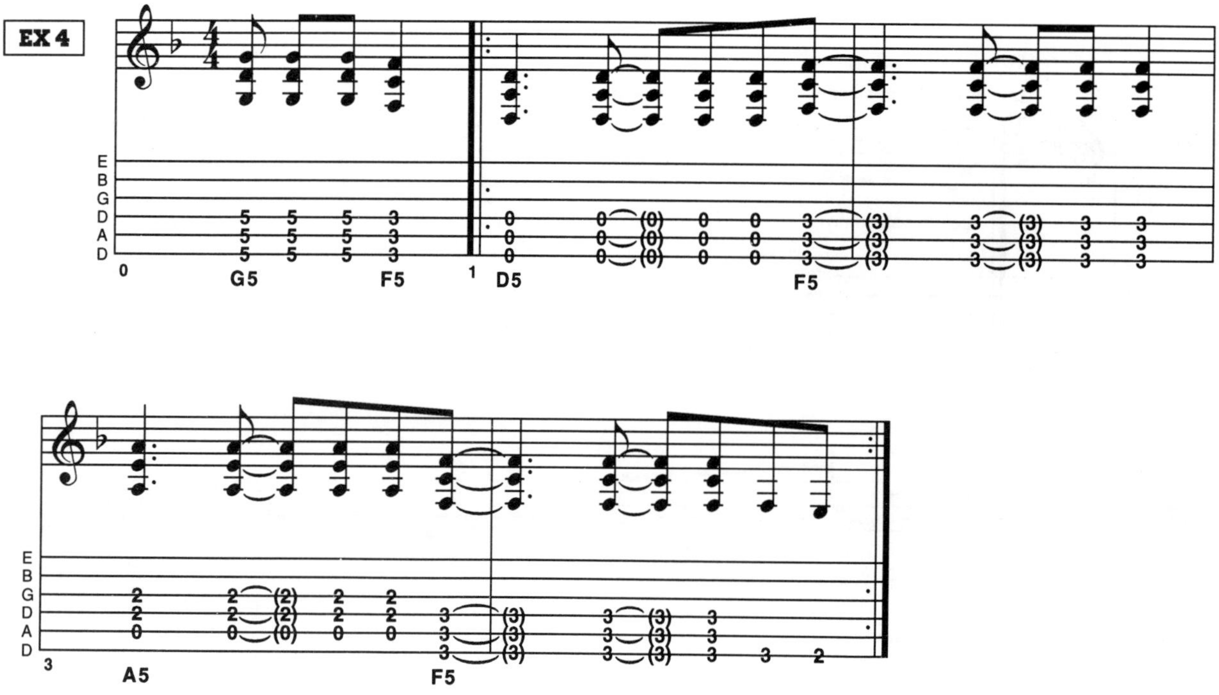

For the middle sections of some of his songs, Kurt used to strip things down even more, often going for a steady, pounding eighth-note feel. That's precisely what I've done here, and I've also doubled the speed of the chord changes (from once every four beats to once every two beats) to give a more insistent feel.

EX 5

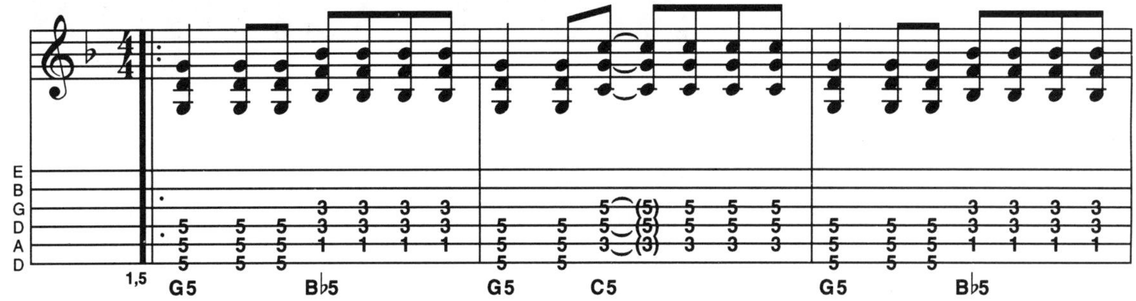

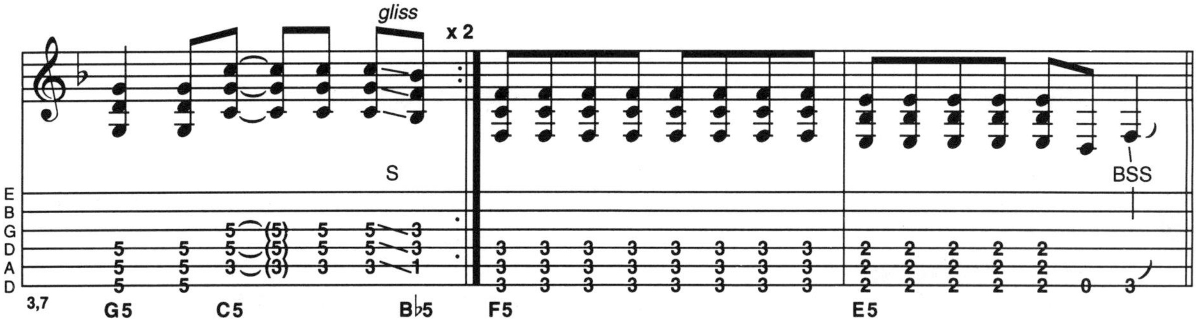

Things cool down a bit after that, because we're back to the verse part. As this isn't a real song, only a demonstration of a couple of ideas, I've ended it there, but in reality, you'd probably want to add an extra chorus or two and maybe even a repeat of the middle section. It's all entirely up to you. Take a leaf out of Kurt's book and do whatever you want to do, however unusual it may sound to other people – new trends have to start somewhere, you know!

Further Exploration

Kurt's earliest musical tastes included rock and metal bands, particularly Led Zeppelin, Deep Purple and Black Sabbath – one of his earliest musical goals was to be able to play 'Stairway To Heaven'. In time, he was also drawn to the aggressive sounds of English punk, especially The Sex Pistols, and American alternative bands such as The Melvins and The Butthole Surfers.

As Kurt's short but explosive career is still quite recent at the time of writing, it's probably far too early to accurately assess the sort of influence he has had or will have on guitar playing and rock music in general. Overall the whole "grunge" craze sparked off a renaissance in guitar-playing, as well as providing a "back to basics" antidote to all the shredhead antics of the late eighties, but regarding individual players... I'll keep you posted, folks.

As you'd expect, the Web is chock full of Nirvana-related stuff. If I have to read just one more sentimental teenage poem about how someone woke on that dark day in 1994, heard the trees crying and knew that Kurt was dead, I will scream! Luckily, there are some people prepared to take the time to construct something informative and worthwhile, like whoever was behind this website: http://seds.lpl.arizona.edu/~smiley/nirvana/history.html

CHAPTER 8
Steve Cropper

biography TRACK 5

BORN:
21 October 1941.

ORIGIN:
Memphis, Tennessee (somehow you just know it's not going to be somewhere like Basingstoke!).

OCCUPATION:
Mr Rhythm Guitar, the man who put the groove behind lots of the Stax soul classics.

FIRST SPOTTED:
Although his band The Mar-Keys had had a Top Ten hit in 1961, Steve's big career move came in 1962, when he formed Booker T And The MGs with keyboardist Booker T Jones, bassist Lewis Steinberg (later replaced by Donald "Duck" Dunn) and drummer Al Jackson.

SEEN IN THE COMPANY OF:
Okay, deep breath...member of crack instrumental/backing band Booker T And The MGs, who recently reformed to back Neil Young. Groovemeister supreme for the Stax label, where he played and often co-wrote with artists such as Otis Redding, Wilson Pickett and Eddie Floyd.

THE GOOD BITS:
Steve has come up with countless simple yet perfectly concise hooks. Somehow, even though every riff is stripped down to the bare essentials, they all still sound utterly huge.

THE BAD BITS:
As soul music isn't a traditional domain for huge, in-yer-face guitar sounds, Steve's fab rhythm parts tend to be too low in the mix.

NUTS AND BOLTS:
In the good old Stax days, Steve generally used a Fender Esquire or Telecaster through either a Fender Harvard or Twin Reverb amp. These days, he's become a loyal user and endorser of Peavey guitars.

SOUND ADVICE:
Switch off that distortion box! To get a tone similar to Steve's: use a clean, fairly bright amp sound, be precise and economical with your picking and strumming techniques and use a reasonably high action, so you can get a punchy attack without any extraneous buzzes.

VITAL VINYL:
For Steve's classic work on the Stax label, just get hold of one of the numerous sixties soul compilations available (especially since the film *The Commitments* was such a big hit) and all the great songs should be there: 'Dock Of The Bay', 'In The Midnight Hour', 'Green Onions', 'Soul Man', 'Knock On Wood'...

Whenever anyone talks about guitar heroes, chances are they're usually referring to people like Hendrix, Clapton, Van Halen and so on – players known for their breathtaking solos. It's an unfortunate fact that the handful of players who have made a major contribution to music primarily through their rhythm guitar skills rarely get a mention. When you think about it, these players ought to be given pride of place in the guitar hall of fame – being able to play a great solo is all very well, but most forms of music are based around at least some kind of preplanned "song" structure, so if you can't provide a suitable guitar accompaniment to carry a song... well, you're not gonna get many gigs, are you?

Enter Steve Cropper, one of the true geniuses of rhythm guitar. Steve's pithy riffs and hooks have driven many a great song, whether it's for the Stax label, the Blues Brothers band or Neil Young. Now I'll be the first to admit that I've probably tried to cram in more ideas here than Steve would usually allow to co-exist in a song, but we've only got a limited amount of space and I want to demonstrate as much as possible. To start with, here's a gentle intro...

EX 1

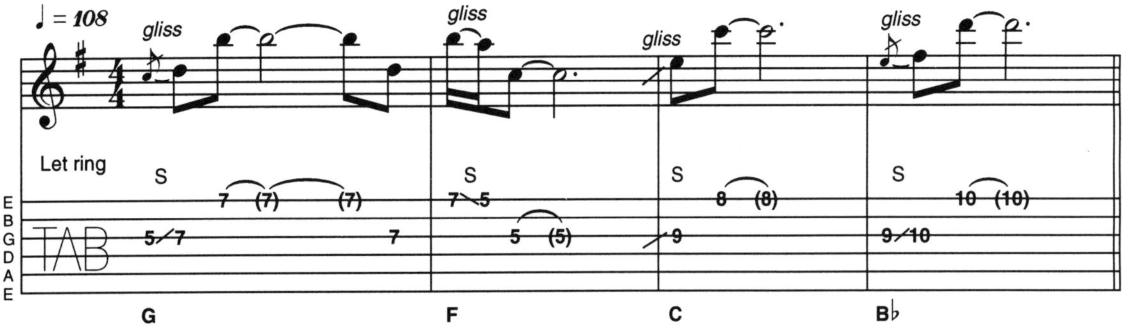

Notice how the sparse guitar part outlines the chord progression by using mainly notes from each underlying chords. Taking things up a gear, here's one of those dual guitar/bass riffs that Steve and "Duck" Dunn used to play so well together. Apart from the D7 chord at the end, all of these notes come from the G major Pentatonic scale (G A B D E G).

EX 2

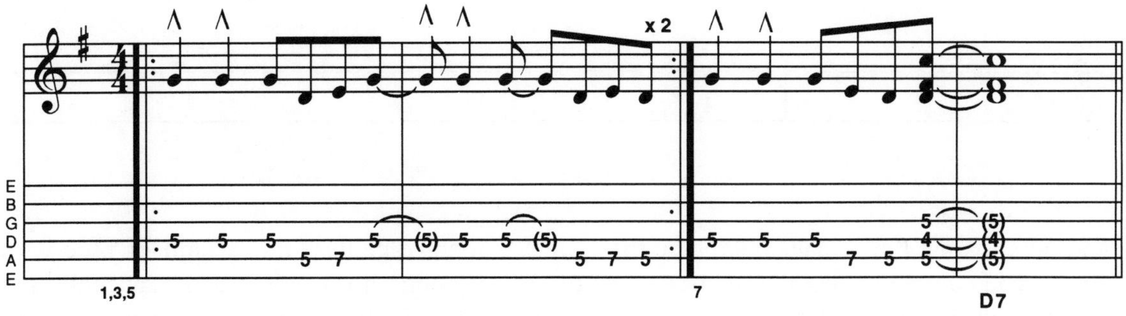

And for maximum coolness, it's a good idea – if you have the chance – to add a harmony part. This enters halfway through the previous example.

EX 3

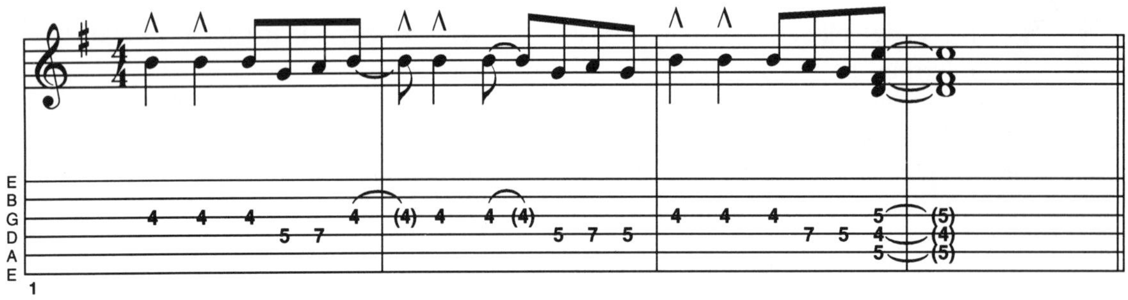

Now the main verse part. To make things clearer for you, I'll start by showing you the basic chordal framework. It's based roughly around a twelve-bar blues progression (in the key of G, as in the previous examples) except I've used a slightly different set of changes for the last four bars (the bit commonly known as the "Turnaround").

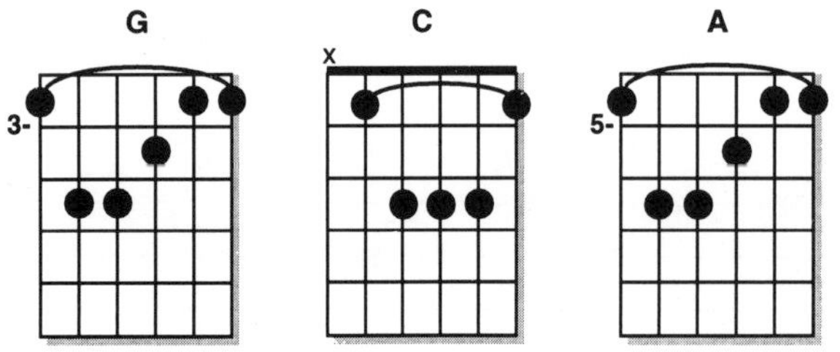

EX 4

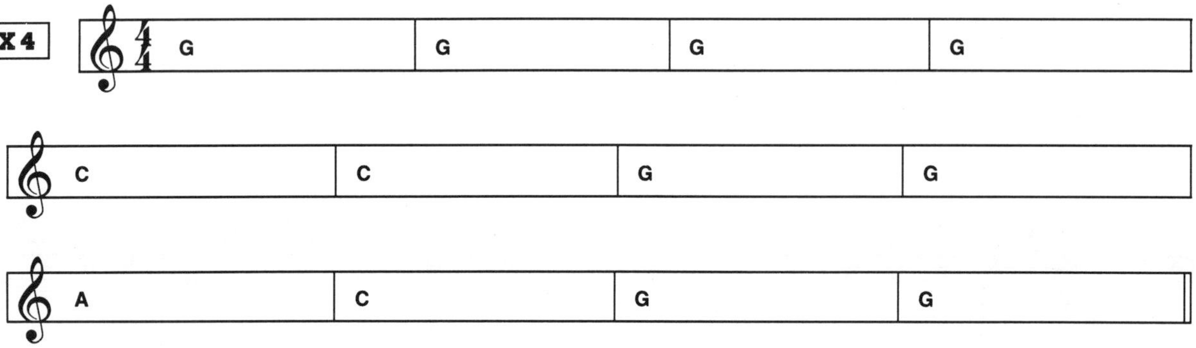

And here is what I'm actually playing on the CD. Since you already know the basic chord progression, I've used plenty of repeat signs to keep this example relatively uncluttered – just take note of how many times each bit repeats. For the G and C chords, I'm basically outlining two different voicings of each chord, and joining them together with a kind of bluesy-sounding passing chord. When you play funky sixteenth-note patterns like this, try to keep your strumming hand moving up and down constantly, muting or simply missing the strings on the beats where you don't want the notes to sound. Above all, relax!

EX 5

As a brief sort of chorus part, here's a simple little example built with chunky-sounding major chords, similar to the parts Steve played on 'Soul Man' and 'Knock On Wood'.

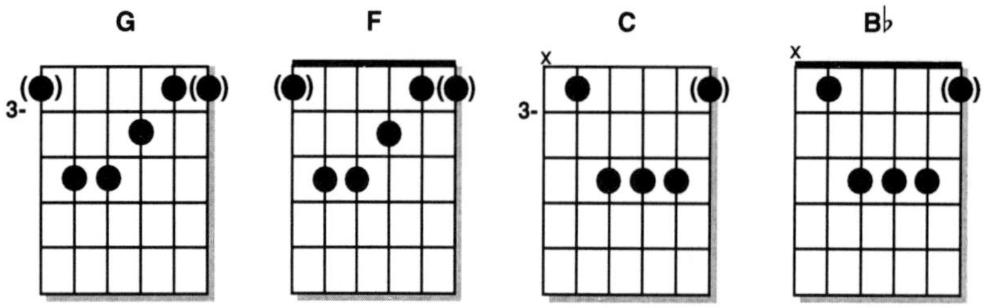

EX 6

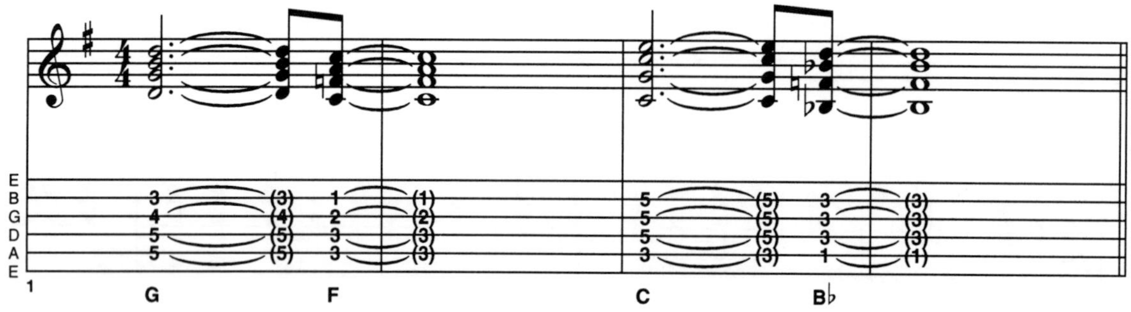

Right, that's all the basic material you'll need. All you have to do is repeat the verse and chorus again (Ex 5 and 6) followed by a repeat of the Pentatonic riff from the intro (Ex 2). In an attempt to get just one last, wafer-thin example of the Cropper style into this pastiche, here's what one of those two harmony guitars plays as a lead-in to the final G chord. This bluesy minor Pentatonic lick is vintage Cropper.

EX 7

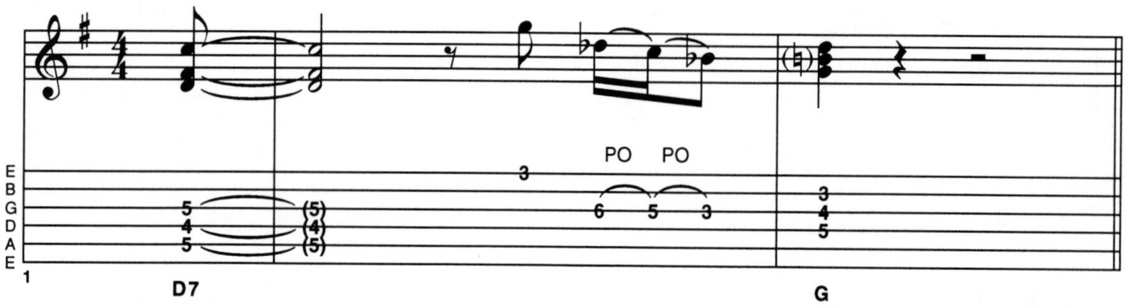

The other guitar just goes straight from the D7 to the G, by the way. Play a few parts like these once a day, and after just a short while, you'll start to develop a much more positive approach to life. Children will start to smile at you, stern old ladies will murmur "Yeah, man!" as you walk by, you'll even start dancing at weddings. You see, my friends, this is what happens when you discover the art of the GROOVE.

Further Exploration

As a young hopeful, Steve Cropper's main influences included Jimmy Reed, Chuck Berry, Scotty Moore, Chet Atkins, Tal Farlow, and Hank Garland, although he admits that he never achieved the level of sophistication heard in the playing of Atkins and Farlow.

Since the soul explosion of the mid sixties, Steve Cropper has become one of the most influential guitarists ever. Players to be touched by the mighty groove include Pete Townshend, Robert Cray, Jimi Hendrix and, more recently, Stone Gossard of Pearl Jam.

As one of the great sidemen in the world of guitar, Steve Cropper seems to have assumed sideman status on the Web, as the only references to him seem to be on sites devoted to other people. Shame.

CHAPTER 9
The Edge

biography TRACK 21

BORN:
8 August 1961 (as Dave Evans).

ORIGIN:
London.

FIRST SPOTTED:
In 1978 the Edge and his three schoolmates in the recently formed U2 won a talent contest sponsored by the Guinness brewery.

BIG BREAK:
The band's first EP, 'U2:3', topped the Irish charts in 1979, prompting Island records to sign them up at the double.

DISTINGUISHING FEATURES:
Deciding from an early age that the parrot-fashion blues licks and fast show-off playing of most well known players were not to his taste, Edge has spent his career concocting all those "other" guitar sounds, making extensive use of echo and reverb effects, drones and slide guitar.

THE GOOD BITS:
Of the handful of "interesting" players to emerge from the punk era, the Edge is by far the most experimentally-minded, moving from the sparse, echo-laden parts of the early albums, through a penchant for dark blues sounds to the heavily processed "is that a guitar?" riffs on the band's nineties output.

THE BAD BITS:
When a band becomes as huge as U2, individual musical talents have a tendency to be obscured in a sea of media hype, and through the majority of attention being given to the lead singer. Which is a pity, really, as the Edge's contribution to rock and pop guitar playing has been every bit as valid as that of Johnny Marr or Andy Summers.

NUTS AND BOLTS:
In keeping with his resolute "non-guitar hero" attitude, the Edge's choice of guitars has been eclectic and with sound as the utmost priority. He's used Gibson Les Pauls, a Gibson Explorer, Fender Telecasters and Stratocasters, a Rickenbacker twelve-string, Gretsch arch-tops, an Epiphone lap steel, Washburn acoustics... Amps have usually been Vox AC30s. I'm not even going to attempt to list all the effects he's used over the years.

VITAL VINYL:
The really big ones are *The Unforgettable Fire* (1984) and *The Joshua Tree* (1987) which show U2's progression from sparse post-punk to a more expansive approach, in keeping with their new-found ability to fill stadium after stadium. From the early years, try *War* (1983) and to hear how they've adapted their music for the high-tech nineties, gorge yourself on the multimedia experience of *Zooropa* (1993).

The Edge is the first to admit that he isn't a flash, technical player like most of the "guitar heroes" you're likely to come across. Despite his technical limitations, though, he's built up a very individual style by exploring a handful of relatively unusual musical techniques. His parts often make use of drones, chiming harmonics, muted sounds and delay effects. I've really gorged myself on layered sounds for this piece, so perhaps we should start by establishing the functions of the various guitar tracks.

Gtr 1: Harmonics with delay effect
Gtr 2: Main arpeggio rhythm parts with delay
Gtr 3: Overdriven power chords
Gtr 4: Slide guitar with liberal amounts of reverb and multi-tap delay
Gtr 5: Additional harmonics (see below)

The first sound you'll hear on the CD track is guitar 1, playing a natural harmonic with a touch of palm muting to keep the notes crisp. The delay unit is set to produce a single repeat after three quarters of a beat (402 milliseconds); if you play eighth notes, the delay fills in the gaps in between the notes, resulting in sixteenth notes (check out Albert Lee's 'Country Boy' or Nuno Bettencourt's 'Flight Of The Wounded Bumblebee'). The original signal is panned hard left, the delayed signal hard right.

EX 1

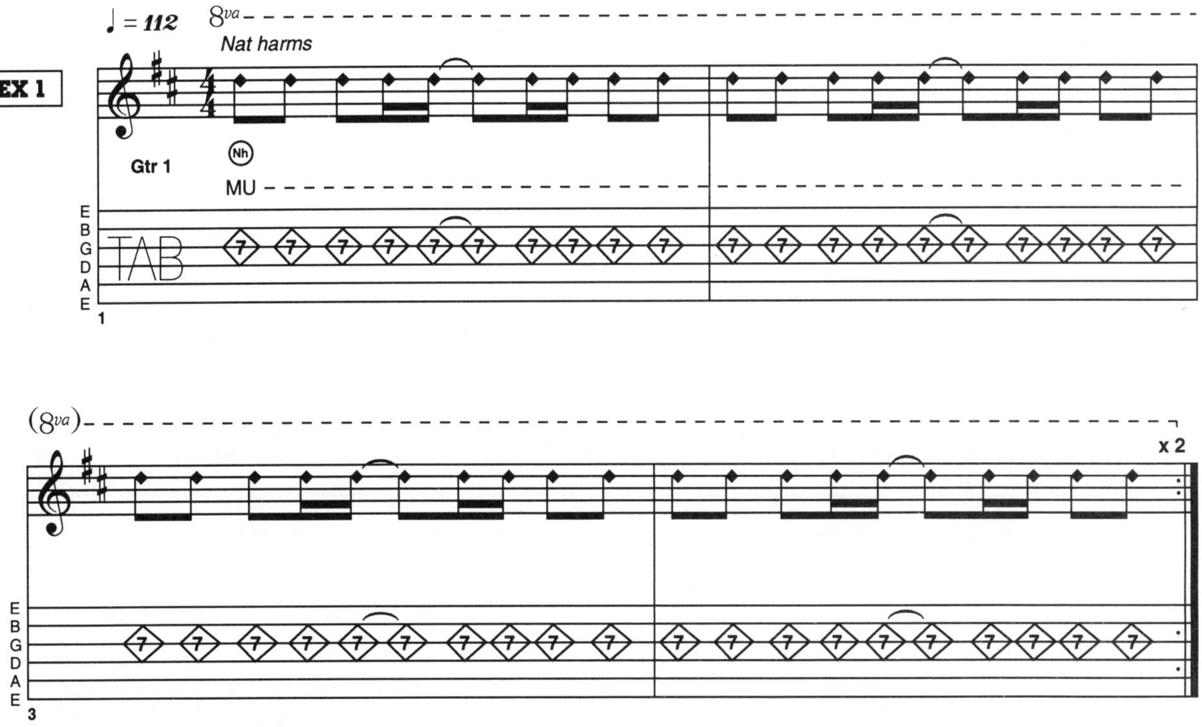

Guitar 2 enters halfway through the intro part with a high, repeating D5 arpeggio. This part also uses a delay but this time it's producing a single repeat with a delay time of exactly one beat (536 milliseconds).

EX 2

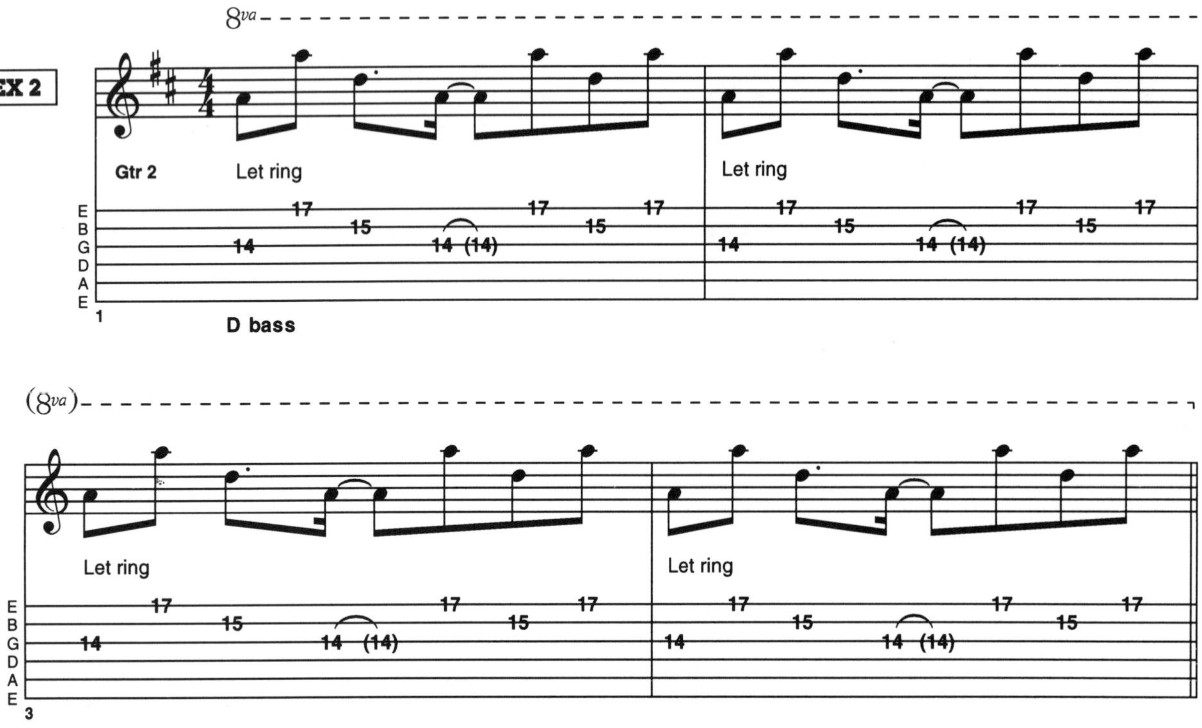

The verse part comes next, and the delicate arpeggios played by guitar 2 continue as follows...

EX 3

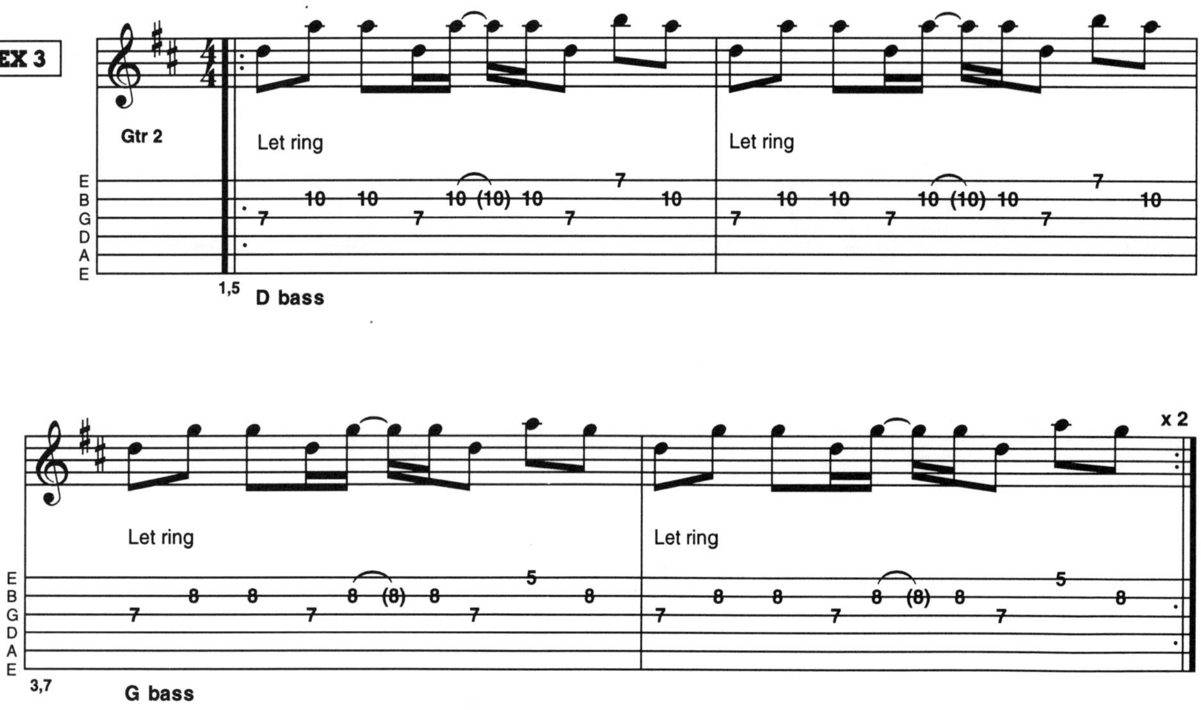

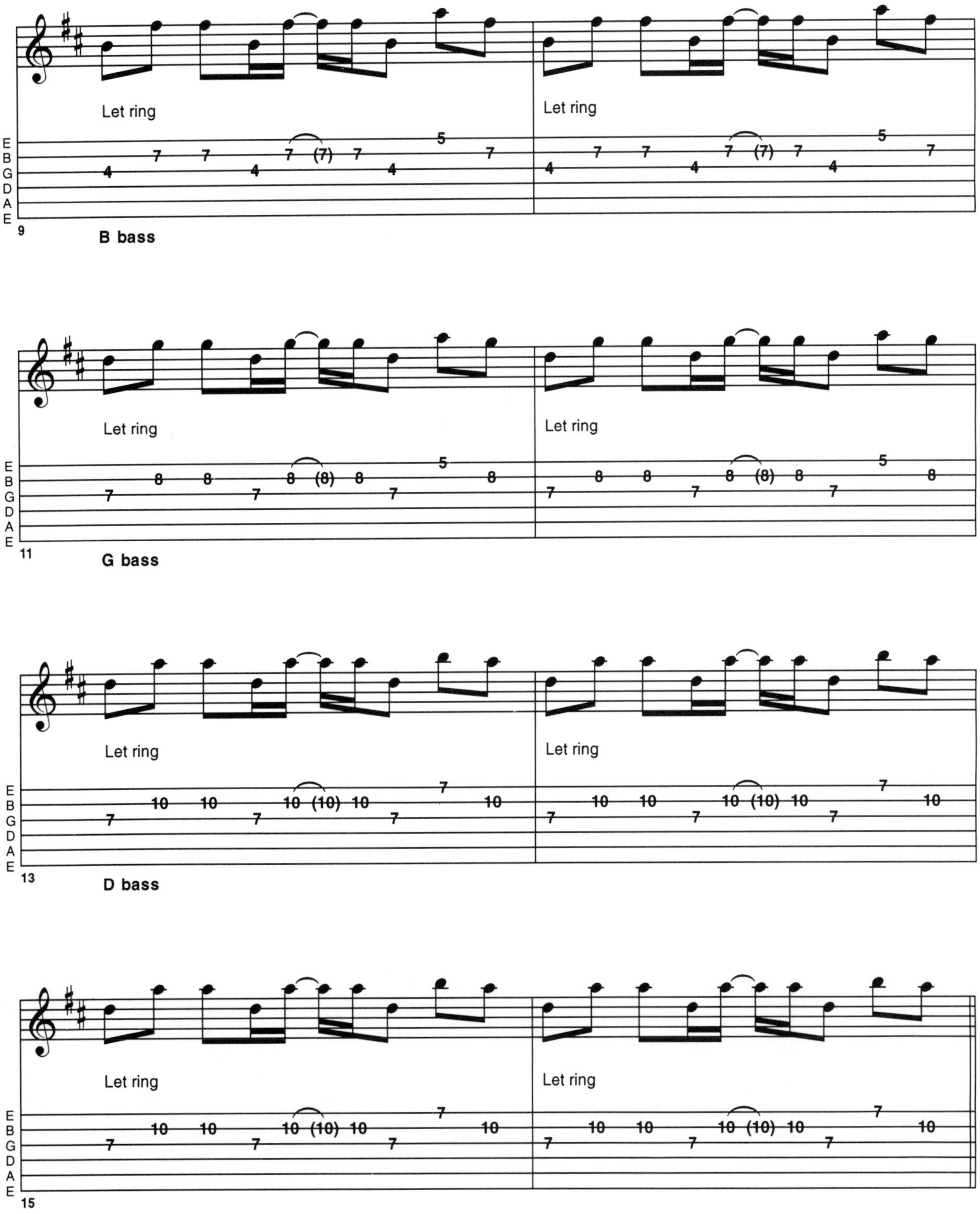

The harmonics continue, following the chord progression (Ex 4a) and we also see the entry of guitar 3, using a moderately overdriven sound to play sustaining two-note power chords (Ex 4b). For the last four bars of this section, I also added some random seventh fret harmonics (guitar 5) to increase the intensity.

EX 4A

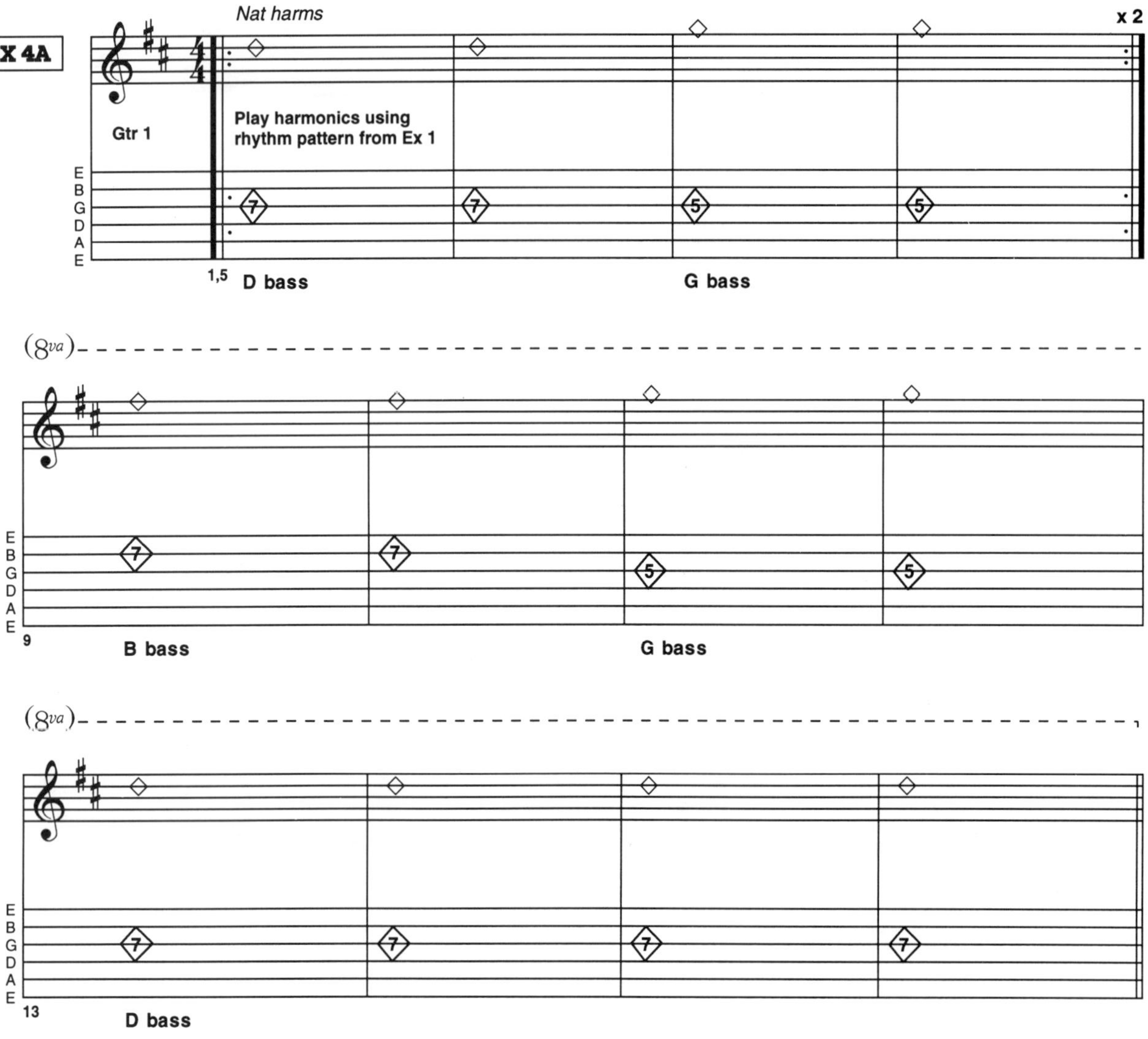
Nat harms
x 2
Gtr 1
Play harmonics using rhythm pattern from Ex 1
E B G D A E
7 7 5 5
1,5
D bass
G bass
(8va)
7 7 5 5
9
B bass
G bass
(8va)
7 7 7 7
13
D bass

EX 4B

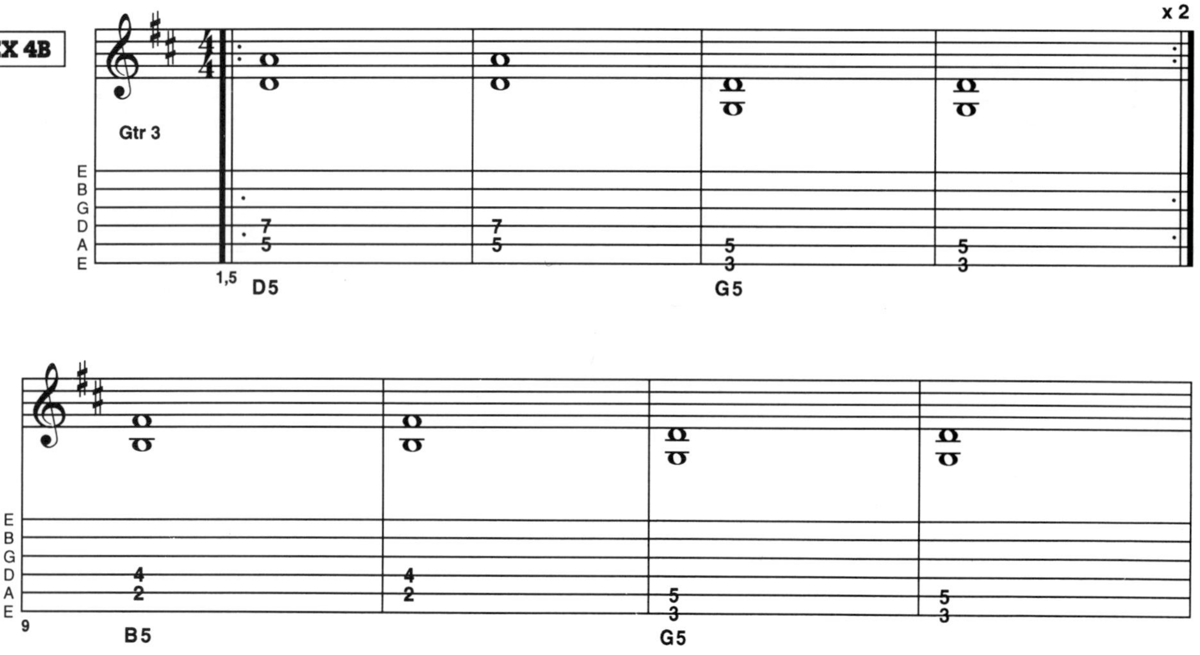
x 2
Gtr 3
E B G D A E
7 5
7 5
5 3
5 3
1,5
D5
G5
4 2
4 2
5 3
5 3
9
B5
G5

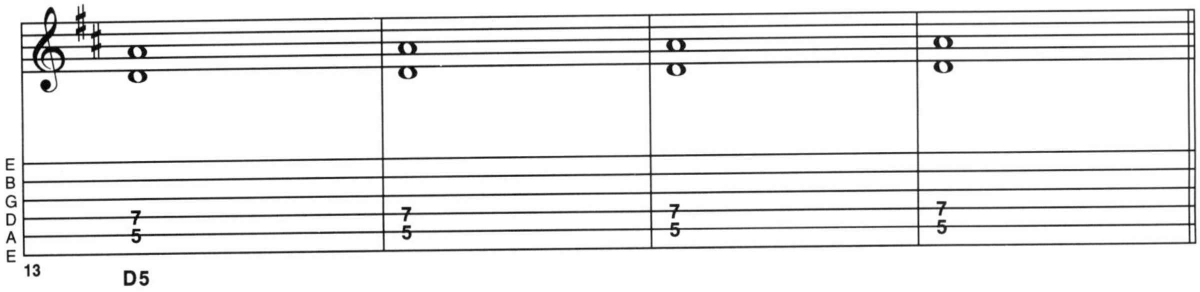

That sort of shimmering guitar pastiche is all very nice, but it can become rather bland if you go on for too long, so I've changed things round a bit for the chorus. The main rhythm part (guitar 2) starts strumming jangly chords instead of arpeggios...

EX 5

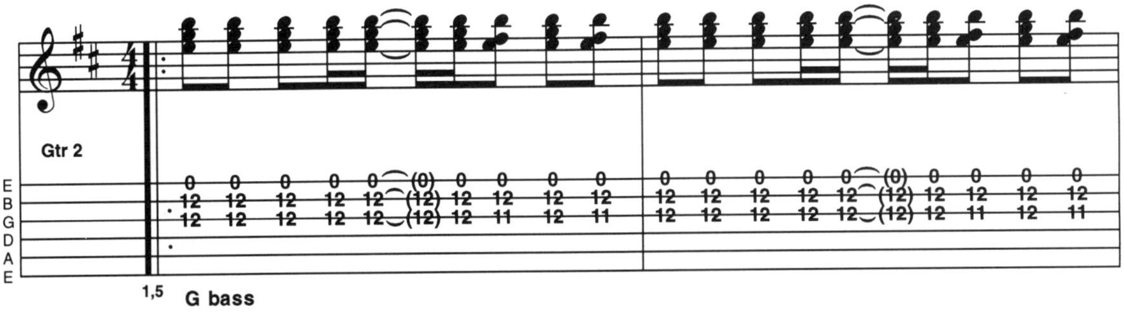

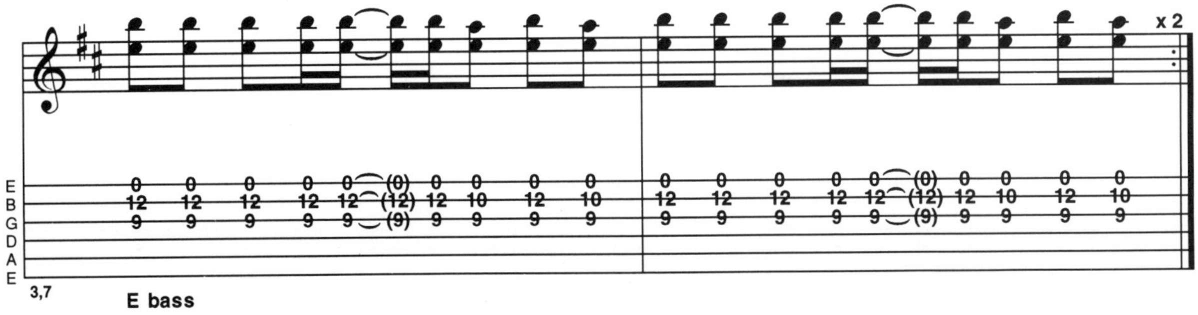

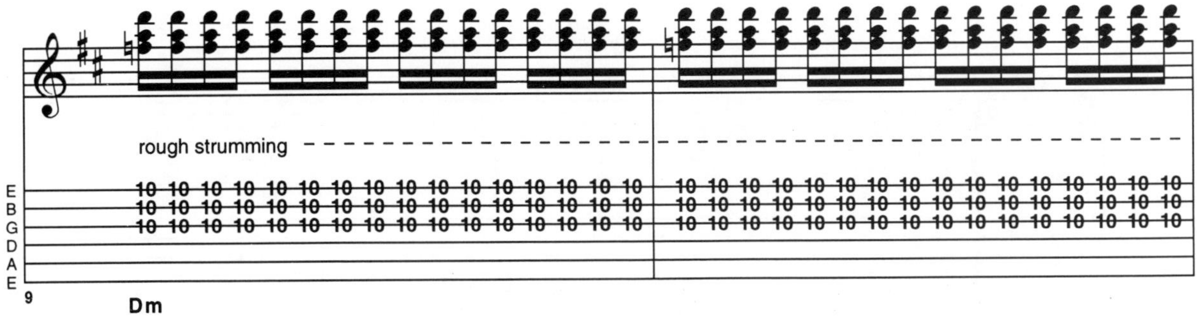

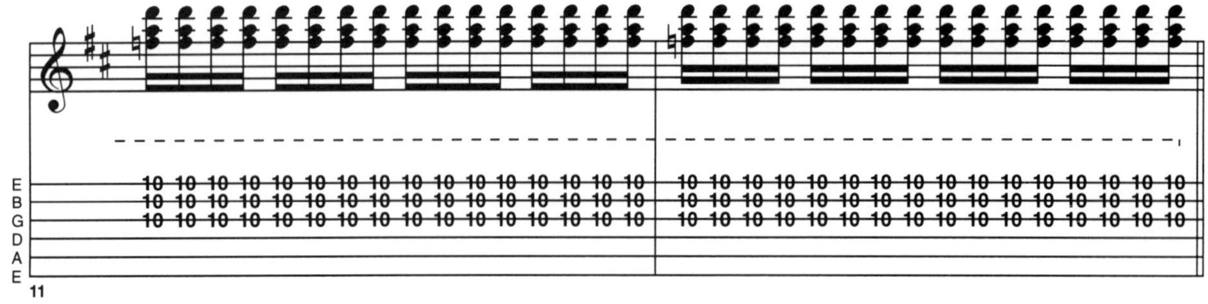

... and out go the harmonics, to be replaced by a big, expansive slide part. Don't worry if you're no good at playing slide guitar – you don't need to be for this! Just make sure you use plenty of ambient reverb and delay, and keep the sliding movements slow and smooth (Ex 6a). Guitar 3 continues with the power chords (Ex 6b) and I added a few more random seventh fret harmonics at the very end, just like in the verse part.

EX 6A

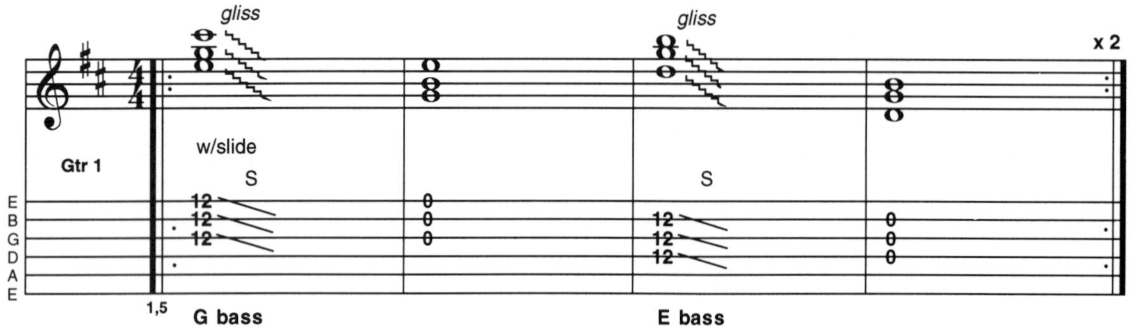

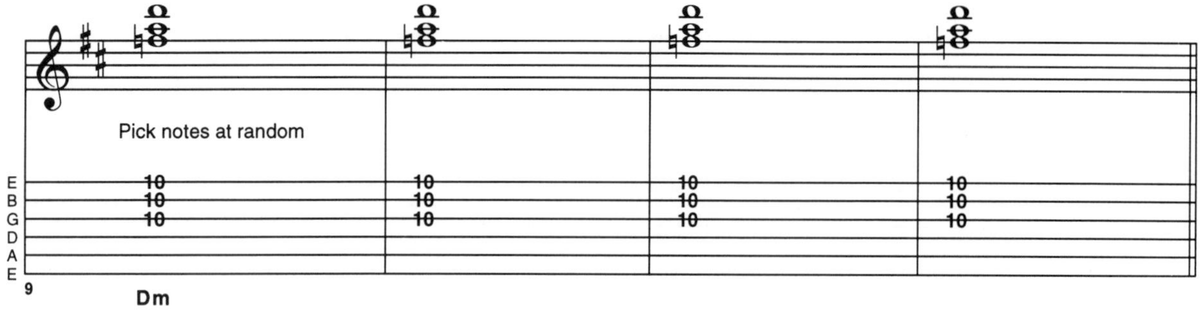

EX 6B

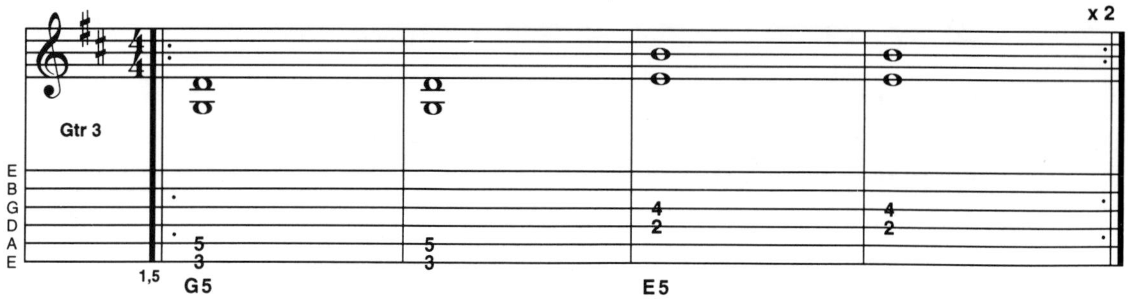

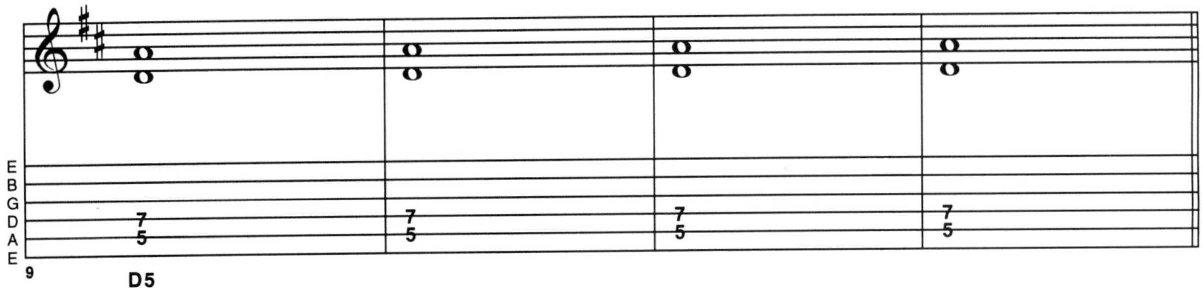

To give the whole thing more of a legitimate "song" feel, I repeated the verse and then went back to the second half of the intro (guitars 1 and 2 playing together) and repeated it into the fade-out.

Now, what about those delays? I bet you're wondering how I came up with those ultra-precise delay times, aren't you? Well, it's a very simple formula – you just need to know the tempo (that's the speed of the tune, for those of you not versed in musical Italian, and it's expressed in beats per minute – bpm).

If you want the repeat to come after a whole beat (as on guitar 2), start with the number 60,000 (the number of milliseconds in a minute) and divide it by the tempo. The tempo of this Edge-like tune is 112bpm, so the calculation goes: 60,000 ÷ 112 = 536.

For the harmonics played by guitar 1, I wanted the delays to come after three quarters of a beat, so this time we have to start with 45,000 (15,000 for every quarter beat of delay). This time the calculation is: 45,000 ÷ 112 = 402. Simple!

Further Exploration

When you listen to the Edge's playing, it's pretty obvious that he wasn't influenced by the traditional Hendrix/Beck/Clapton/Page quartet. More interested in sounds and tones than in learning specific licks, he gravitated towards the music of people like Lou Reed, Television, Patti Smith and Neil Young.

It's hardly surprising that the Edge's approach has been so widely copied since the post-punk days of the early eighties, as his style provided such a compelling alternative to the norms of the time. Countless guitarists have used harmonics, delay and other so-called "textural" effects (also influenced by Andy Summers) during the years since U2 broke onto the scene. Strangely enough, the Edge has often received his greatest plaudits from the more "traditional" players, such as Steve Cropper, BB King and Stone Gossard of Pearl Jam.

With U2's love of the potential of multimedia technology, you shouldn't have any trouble finding decent stuff on the Web. I found a particularly impressive site, Edge's U2 Page at http://www.geocities.com/SunsetStrip/Palms/4845/u2page.html

biography TRACK 18

CHAPTER 10
George Harrison

BORN:

25 February 1943.

ORIGIN:

Do you really need to be told where George is from? Here's a clue: 'Ferry 'Cross The Mersey' Still no idca? How about Cilla Black, Robbic Fowler, the Liver Birds... it's Liverpool, of course!

OCCUPATION:

The quiet one.

FIRST SPOTTED:

George was there from the very beginning, back when the band he formed with Paul McCartney and John Lennon was called The Quarry Men.

BIG BREAK:

The Beatles had plenty of pretty huge breaks over the years, but perhaps the most important one came in 1962, when having been rejected by Decca, their demo tape came to the attention of a certain George Martin, A&R man for EMI's Parlophone label. A fruitful association was to follow.

ANOTHER BIG BREAK:

Poor old George lived in the shadow of Lennon and McCartney for several years. Until, that is, he wrote the song 'Something' (from *Abbey Road*). "The most beautiful love song ever written," said Mr Sinatra. No doubt George could now walk the backstreets of Palermo without fear.

SEEN IN THE COMPANY OF:

Being a Beatle meant you got to hang out with lots of famous people. George has co-written with Eric Clapton, organised a massive charity concert (for Bangladesh) and formed a "supergroup" (The Traveling Wilburys) with Roy Orbison, Bob Dylan, Jeff Lynne and Tom Petty.

THE GOOD BITS:

Despite his rather unprolific status compared to John and Paul, George's Beatles-era output contains some great songs – the aforementioned 'Something', 'While My Guitar Gently Weeps', 'Taxman', 'For You Blue'...

THE BAD BITS:

His post-Beatles solo career has been patchy, despite occasional gems.

NUTS AND BOLTS:

George used a variety of guitars during his time in The Beatles, from Gretsch and Rickenbacker models through to the ubiquitous Stratocasters, Telecasters and Les Pauls.

VITAL VINYL:

Unless you happen to be a particularly big fan of George's solo career, start off with the entire Beatles back catalogue, and not just the songs George wrote – he played some pretty inspired guitar on plenty of Lennon-McCartney songs as well.

One of the difficulties in establishing just what constitutes the "George Harrison style" is that he's best known not as a solo artist, but as a member of a band (that's The Beatles, just in case you grew up in the sixties, and have therefore zapped your short-term memory with various chemical cocktails). So, although the guitar parts were all written with my George Harrison hat placed firmly on my head, the music as a whole has a kind of general Beatles-type vibe. Just thought you'd like to know.

The rhythm guitar part for the entire tune is very simple – lots of big, strummed chords. This progression is used for the intro and verse.

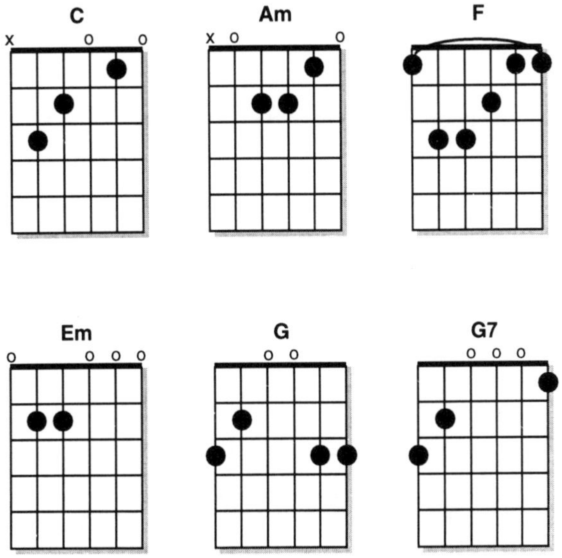

INTRO/VERSE

EX 1

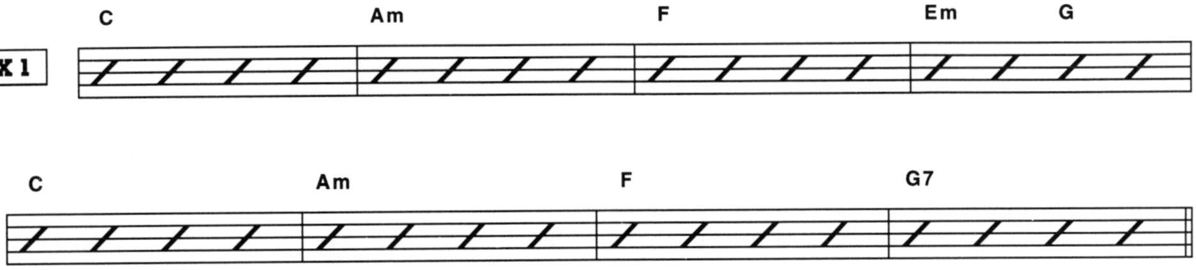

The lead part for the intro is made up of notes from the C Major Pentatonic scale (C D E G A C) with the exception of the final B, which I added to make the melody fit over the G chord (which contains a B note).

EX 2

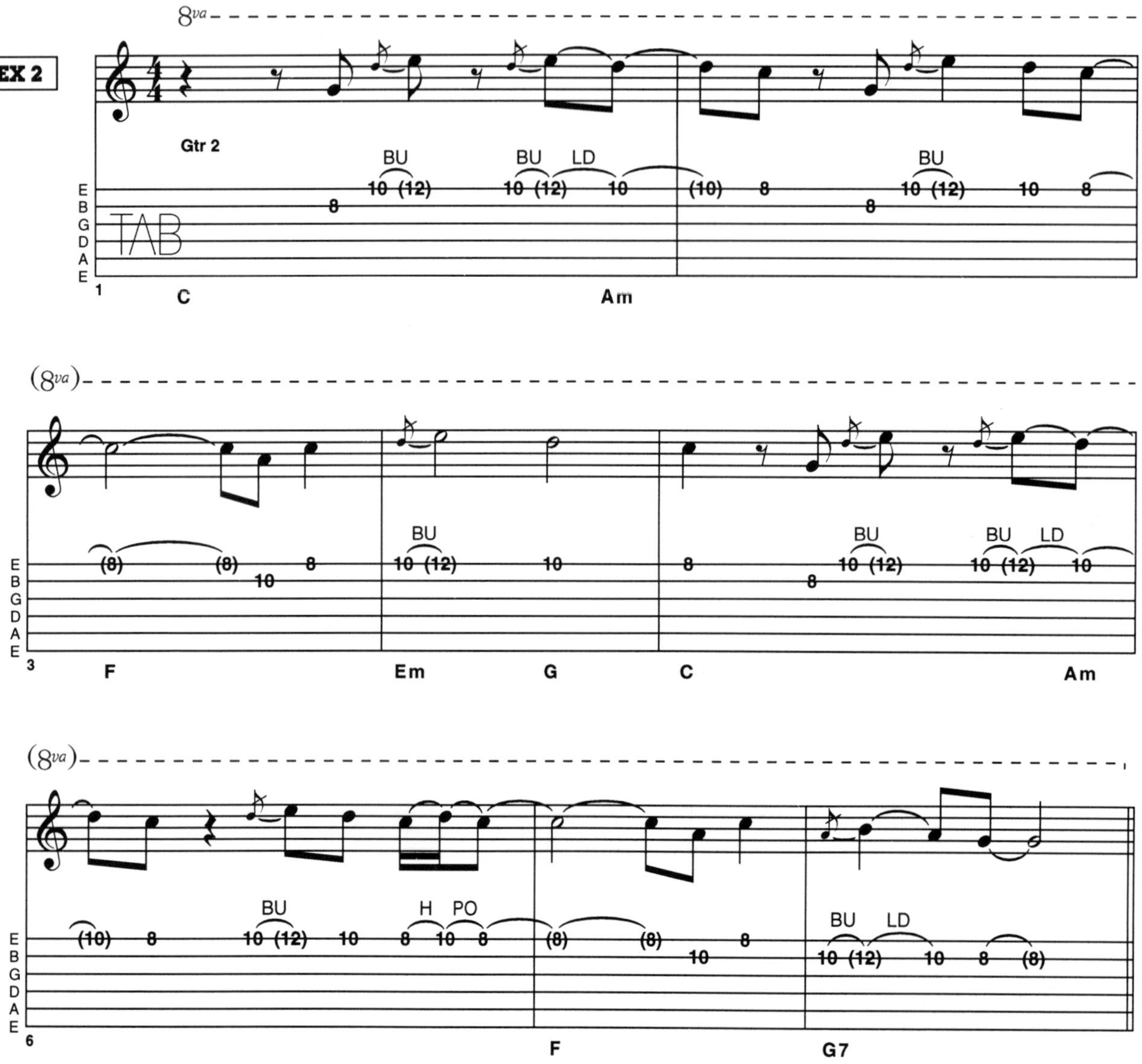

During the intro, there's another backing guitar featuring a tremolo effect. Not to be confused with the tremolo bar on your guitar (which correctly ought to be known as a vibrato bar – it was Fender who started calling them "tremolo" units years ago) tremolo effects are often built into amplifiers (especially older or retro-styled ones) and can also be found nowadays in pedal form. The effect produced is a regular oscillation of volume, and can be found on plenty of old rock 'n' roll, R&B and surf records from the fifties, as well as recent albums such as REM's *Monster*. Anyway, the tremoloed guitar is playing the same chords as the main rhythm part, but using smaller voicings...

EX 3

For the verse part, things become a bit more open, because – close your eyes and try to imagine here, folks – this is where you'd normally have someone singing, so you wouldn't want too many layered instrumental parts conflicting with the melody line (which, if you're aiming for hit success, is the most important thing to the majority of the record-buying public). In common with many of George's songs, though, I've added a short fill at the end of each line, and for a real Harrison effect, I've used twin-guitar harmonies for these fills. Not very helpful for live performance, I'm afraid, but it certainly works in the studio.

EX 4

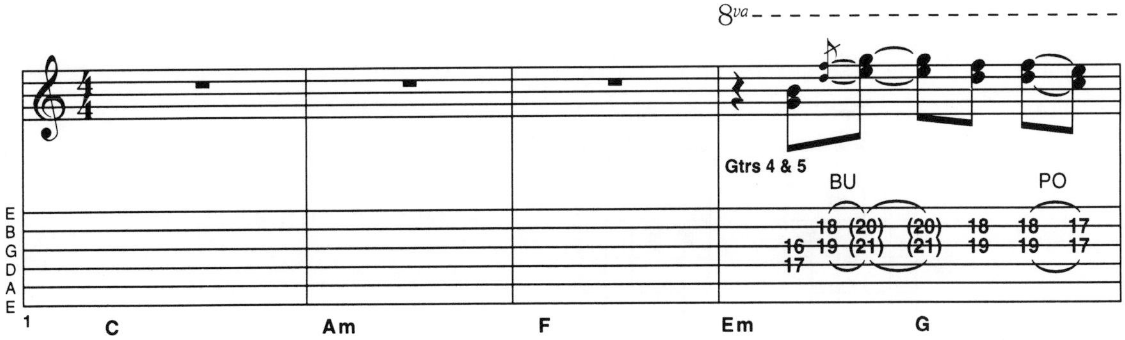

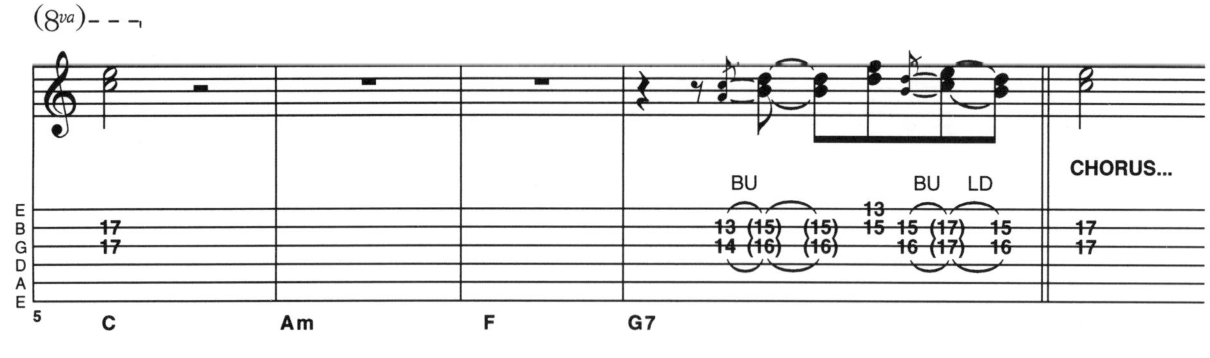

The chorus uses a different progression, again played using big, bold open chords as well as smaller tremoloed chords. Here's the progression... .

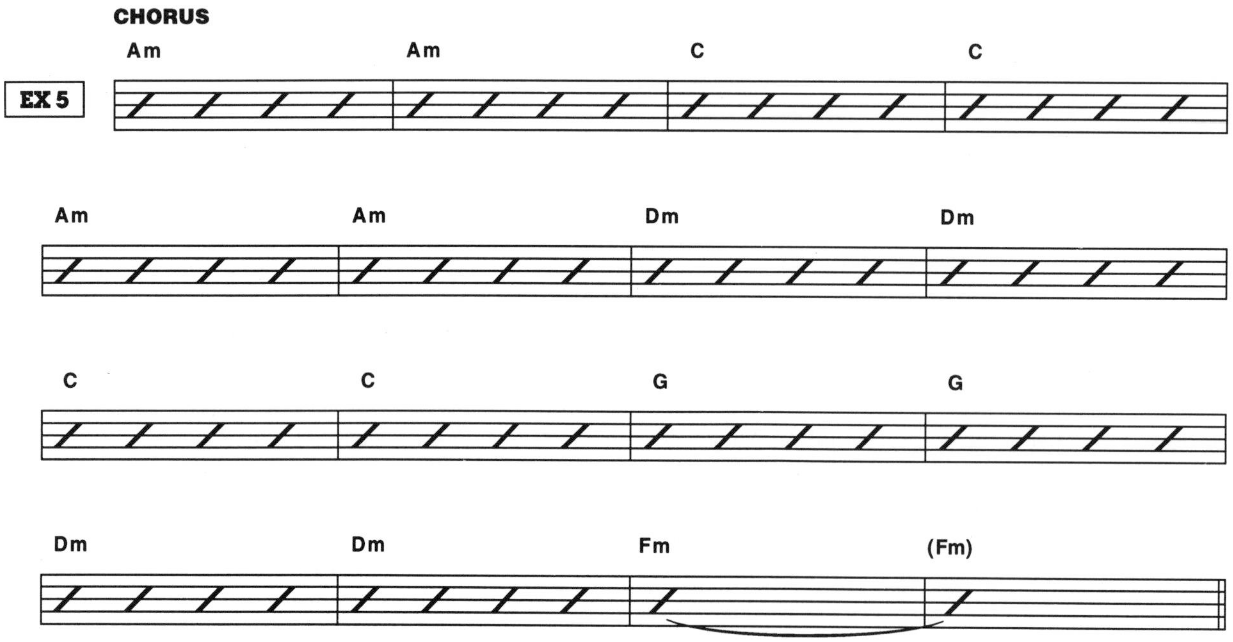

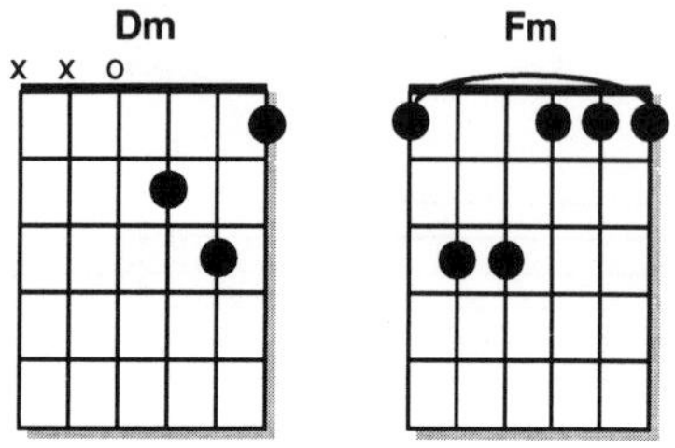

...and the tremolo guitar chords...

EX 6

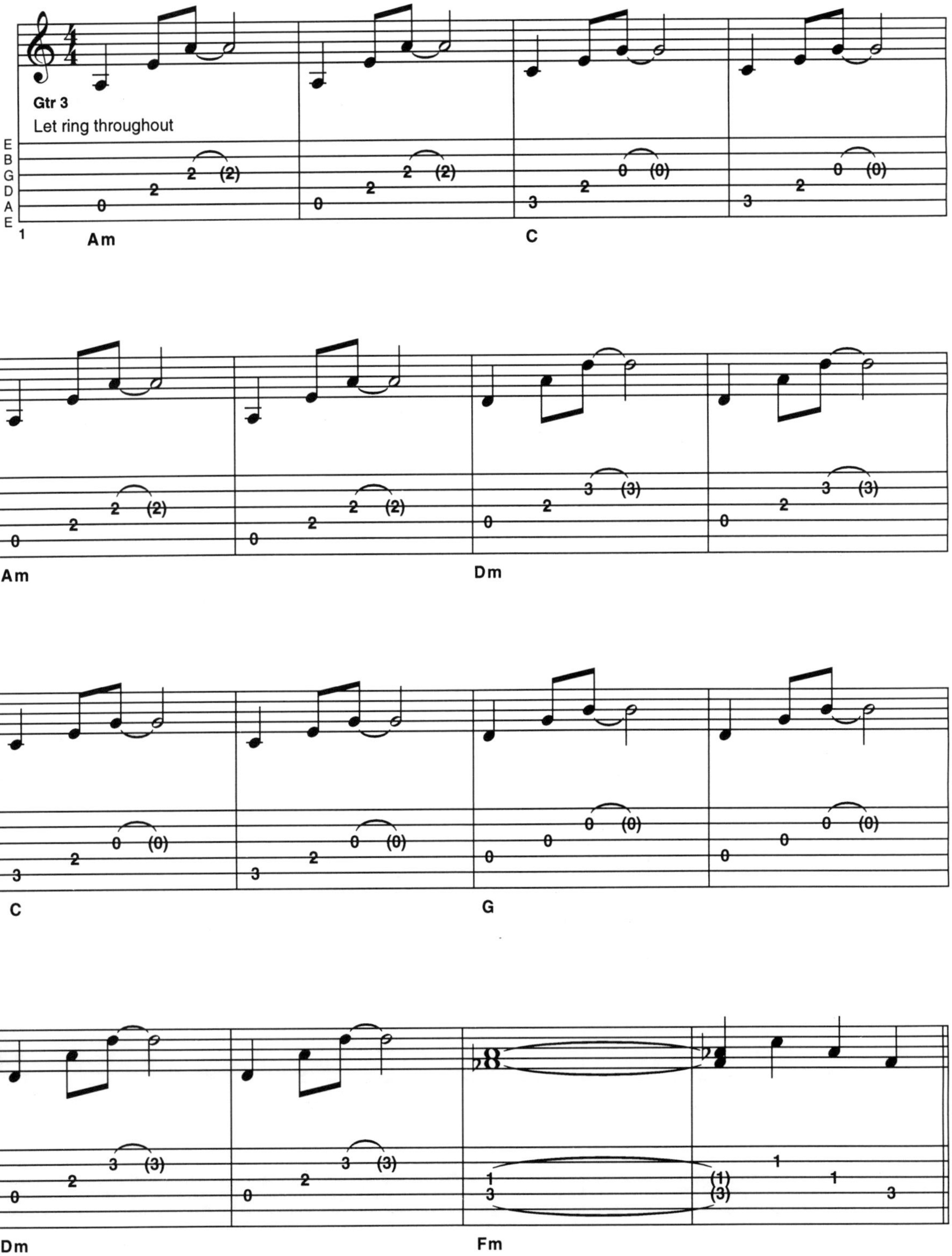

...and an extra part made up of arpeggios using relatively high chord voicings.

EX 7

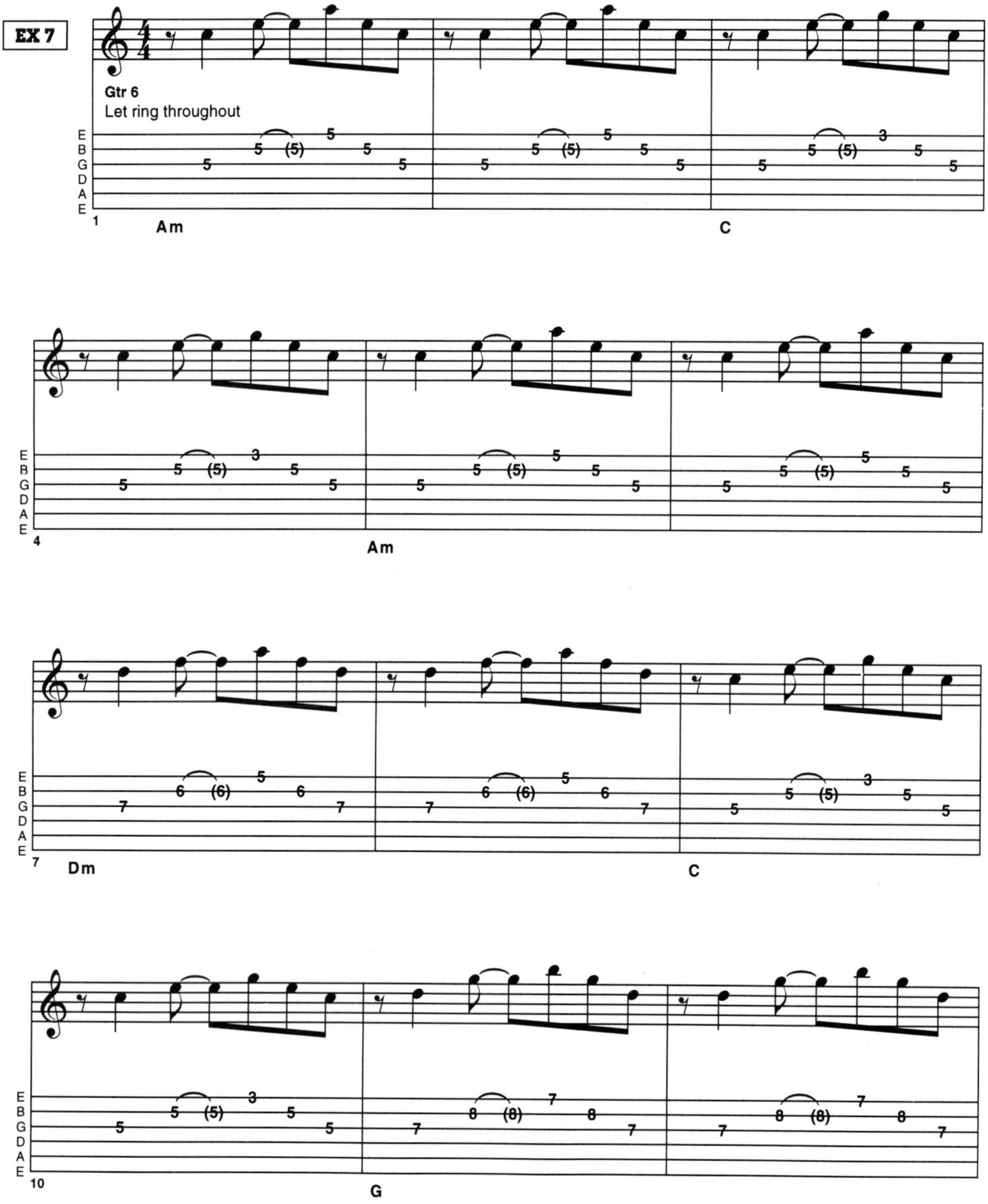

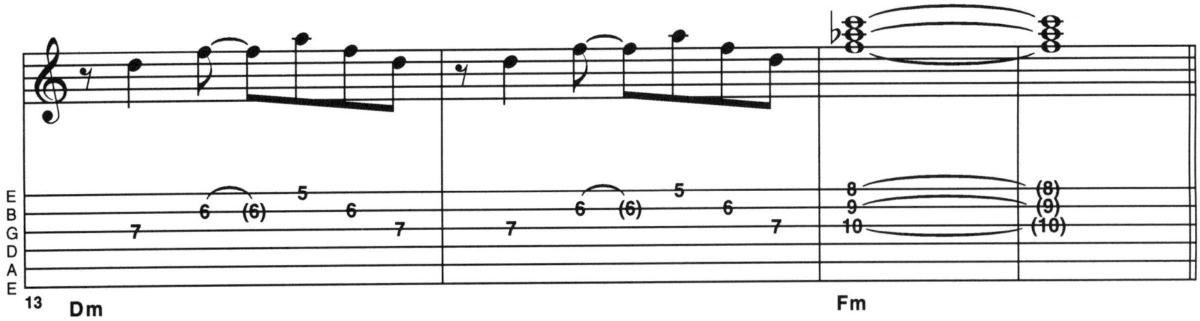

For the middle part of the tune, I've come up with one of those bendy country-tinged solos that George does so well. The backing part is just the first four bars of the verse progression, played twice.

EX 8

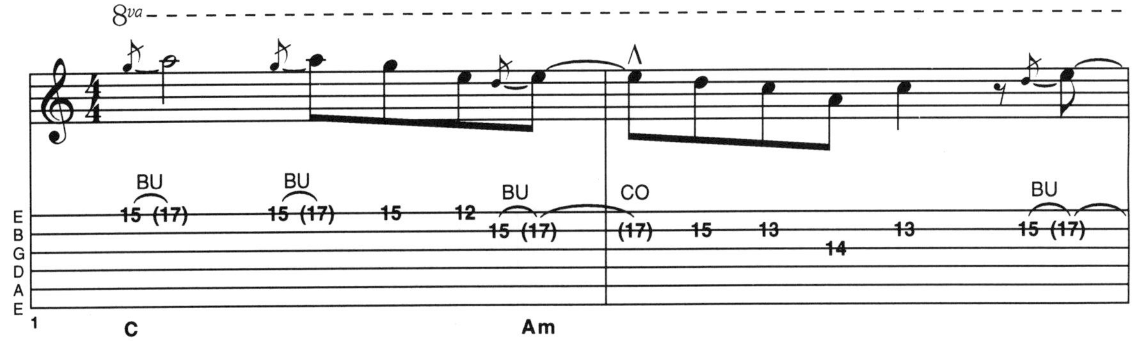

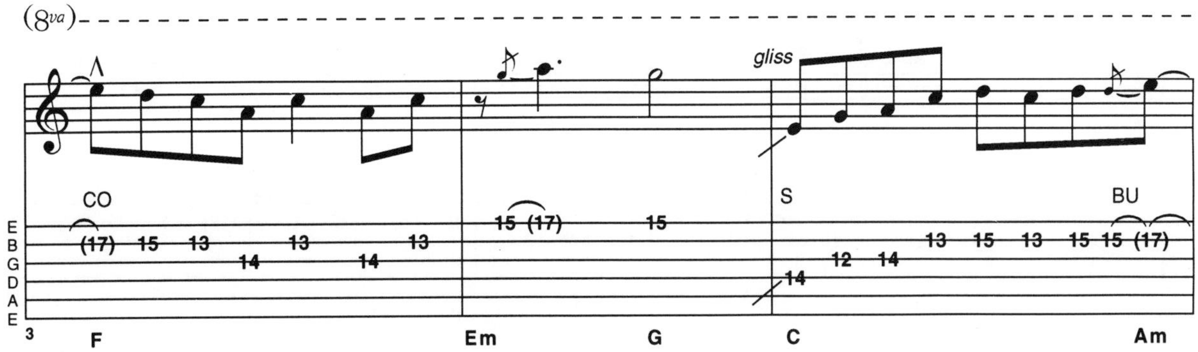

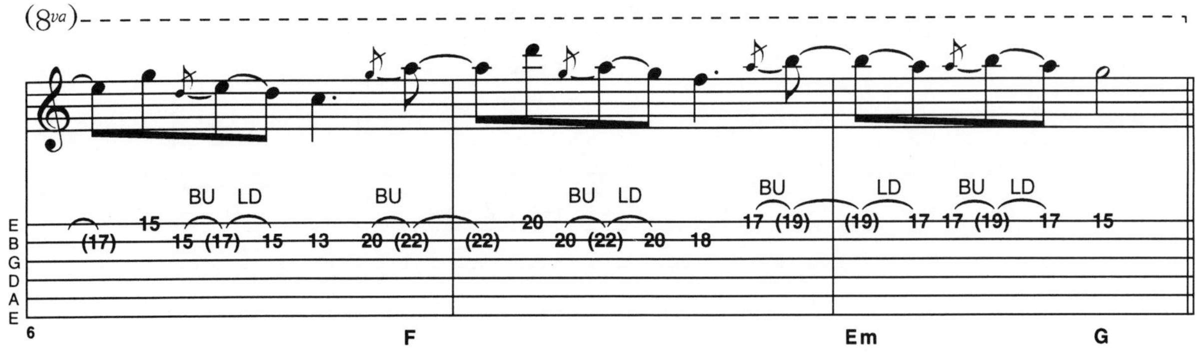

If you've ever heard George's most famous (and infamous, after the plagiarism case) hit, 'My Sweet Lord', you'll know about his penchant for slide guitar. When the chorus repeats after the solo, I decided it was high time for a bit of slide. By the way, all the slide stuff on this track is played using standard tuning, and with a standard set-up (ie my usual ten-gauge strings and low-ish action). I know a lot of people insist on using open tunings and having a separate guitar set up for slide playing but if, like me, you only want to dabble in slide technique, it's a good idea to get used to using your regular guitar. Believe me, it is possible!

EX 9

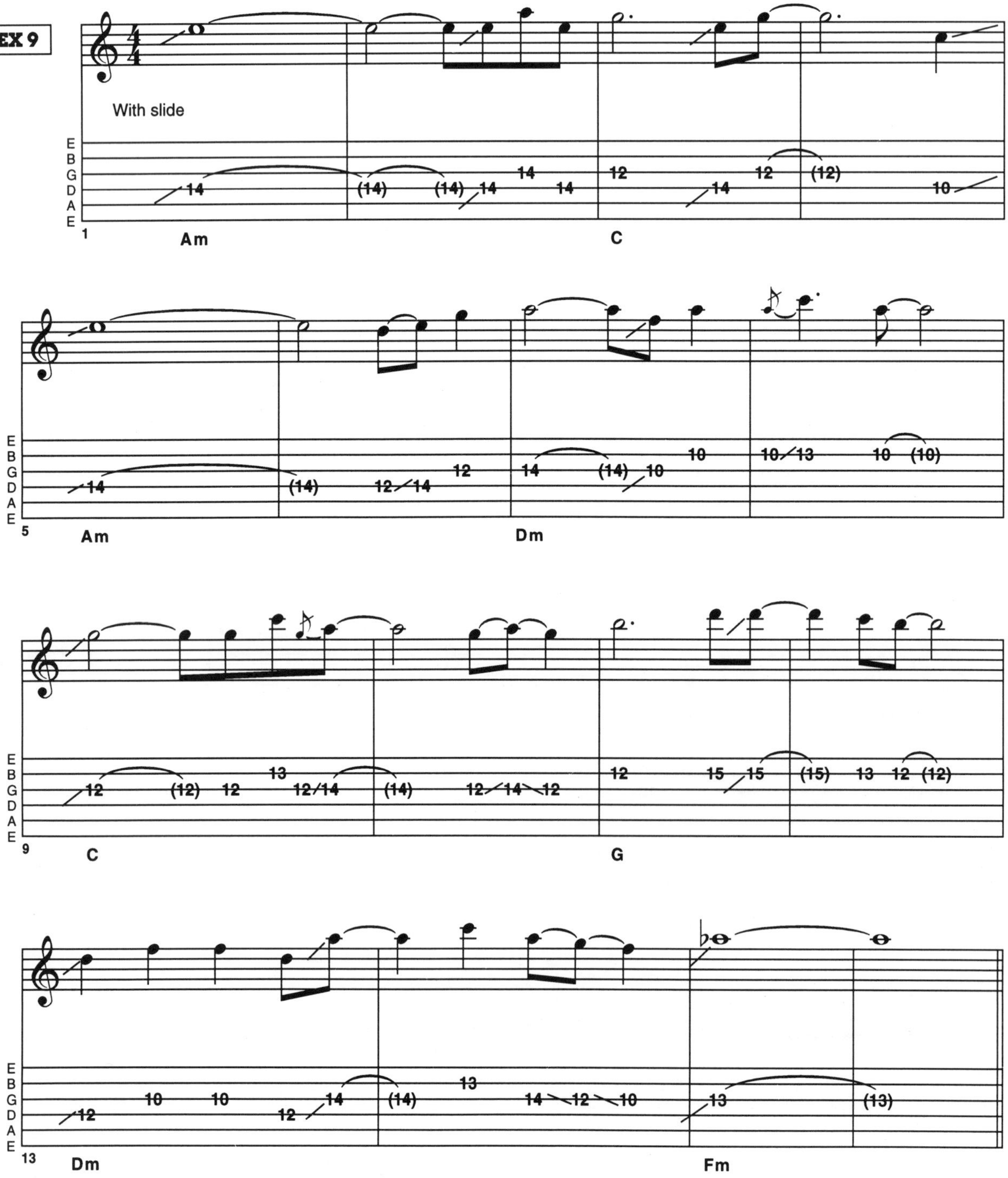

And that's all you need to know – just repeat the intro at the end, and you're done.

Further Exploration

The young George Harrison was originally turned on to the heady powers of pop by rock 'n' rollers Elvis Presley and Bill Haley, and the English skiffle star Lonnie Donegan. Once he started to play guitar, though, his earliest heroes were Duane Eddy, Carl Perkins and Chet Atkins.

It's hard to say whether George has been a major guitar influence in his own right, as the effect of The Beatles as a whole has been so all-consuming.

There are numerous George Harrison websites, but most of them seem to be made up of a couple of photographs and very little else, so your best bet is to go for the general Beatles sites. Try the "Obvious Moose Beatles Page" at http://www.moosenet.com/beatles.html – it's a high-quality piece of work, and some of my personal favourite webpages have come from Obvious Moose.

CHAPTER 11
Jimi Hendrix

biography
TRACK 15

BORN:
27 November 1942

DIED:
18 September 1970

ORIGIN:
Seattle, Washington.

FIRST SPOTTED:
Back in the early-to-mid sixties, on the southern US "chitlin circuit". Jimi played backing guitar for several soul and R&B artists: Little Richard, The Isley Brothers, Ike And Tina Turner, The Supremes...

BIG BREAK:
While playing in a club in New York City, Jimi's jawdropping playing and wild showmanship were spotted by ex-Animals bassist Chas Chandler. Upon being offered a trip to Swinging London™, our modest hero was apparently more excited about the prospect of meeting Eric Clapton than his own imminent breakthrough.

SEEN IN THE COMPANY OF:
The two incarnations of The Jimi Hendrix Experience and the short-lived Band Of Gypsys featured a total of only five musicians between them (including Jimi), but our man made up for that by jamming (often in the studio) with just about anyone you can name: Carlos Santana, John McLaughlin, Steve Winwood, Jack Casady...

THE GOOD BITS:
Well, despite the efforts of Beck, Townshend and Clapton, the guitar was still a bit too polite and clean-toned before Hendrix came along. He also acted as a great ambassador for eclecticism, showing how blues, rock, soul and free improvisation could be brought together.

THE BAD BITS:
Dying at the age of twenty-seven is always going to mess up your day, but one of the worst things for us is that we'll never find out just what he was really capable of. According to many accounts, just prior to his death he was growing increasingly disillusioned with his lot as a guitar hero and was planning a lavish project with jazz composer/bandleader Gil Evans.

NUTS AND BOLTS:
He liked Fender Strats, but I'm sure you knew that. More specifically, Jimi always used right-handed models, but reversed the strings so that he could play left-handed. (And yet, strangely enough, we don't really know for sure whether he actually was completely left-handed. A photograph exists which quite clearly shows Jimi writing some lyrics... with his right hand.)

VITAL VINYL:
Start off with the three studio albums released during Jimi's lifetime: *Are You Experienced?*, *Axis: Bold As Love* (both 1967) and *Electric Ladyland* (1968). Then try the live *Band Of Gypsys* (1970) and the two more experimental, posthumous releases *War Heroes* and *The Cry Of Love* (they're out of print, but many of the tracks can be found on *First Rays Of The New Rising Sun*). After that it's up to you, but remember that until recently, the flow of releases from the Hendrix archives was a little hit-and-miss.

There's a handful of players among the selection featured in these pages who can never be adequately summarised in a couple of rhythm patterns and a twelve-bar solo – even getting the right notes to fit with the right chords doesn't guarantee anything. So, it's with a certain amount of trepidation that I'm now going to show you how to play like Jimi Hendrix!

Rather than go through all the pyrotechnic-type stuff that originally attracted so many people to Jimi's music (let's face it, you can get a transcription of 'Purple Haze' just about anywhere) I'm going to focus on some of the more adventurous aspects of his songwriting, as shown in some of the later recordings. Here's an intro riff, based around the E minor Pentatonic (E G A B D E).

EX 1

Jimi Hendrix is often associated more or less exclusively with the minor Pentatonic, but plenty of his songs used major and Mixolydian-based tonalities, as well as major/minor combinations. He would often achieve the latter effect by taking a minor Pentatonic riff and harmonising it as if it were in a major key (as I've mentioned elsewhere in this book, the major/minor ambiguity is a vital component of the blues). Here's the harmony part that comes halfway through the first section.

EX 2

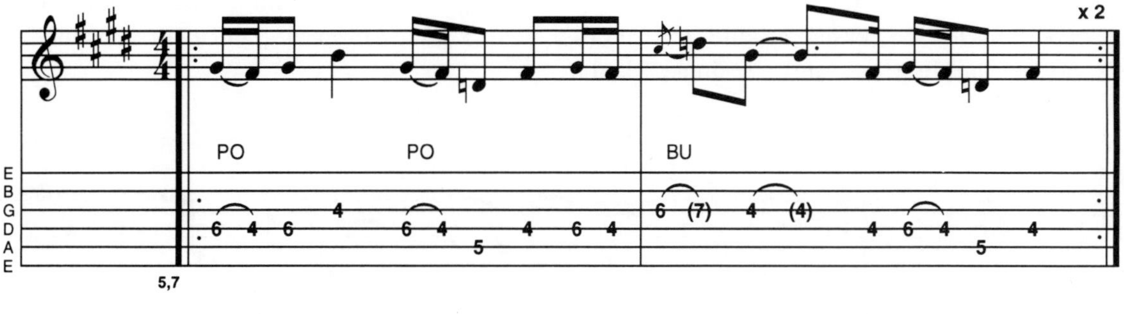

I've extended the intro a little bit further in order to include this melody part. This is more conventionally "major", being constructed using notes from the Mixolydian mode (in E: E F# G# A B C# D E).

LEAD PART

EX 3

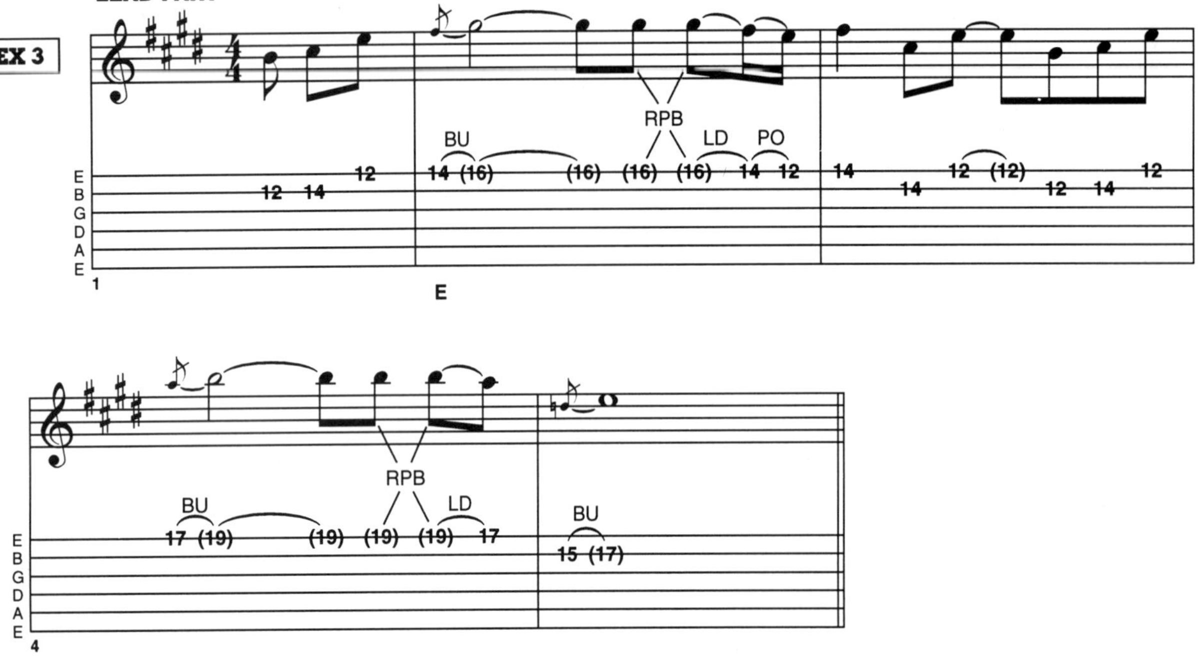

RHYTHM PART FOR MELODY ABOVE

EX 3A

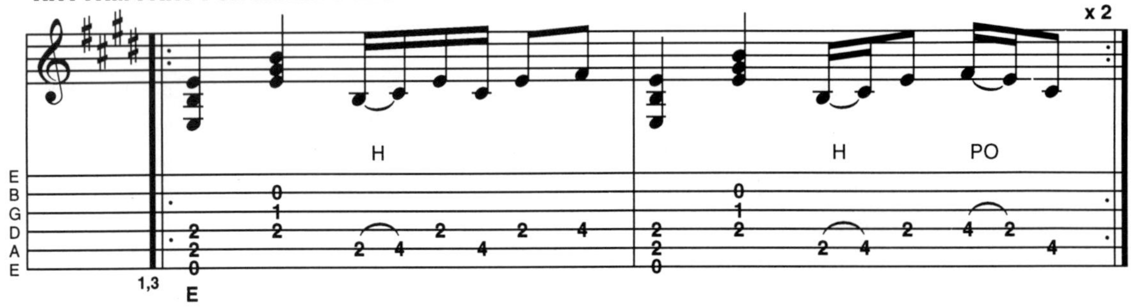

That leads on to the verse part. Using a progression loosely based around the chords found in 'Purple Haze' and the funky rhythm approach found on Jimi's later work, I've gone for a kind of universal "pan-Hendrix" result.

EX 4

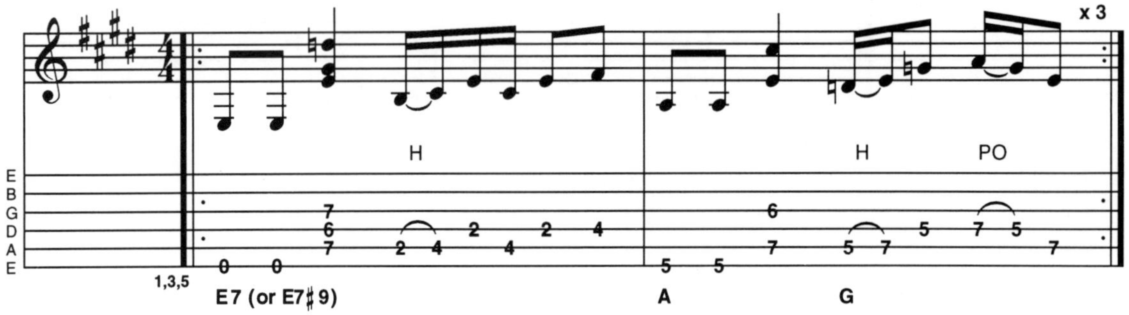

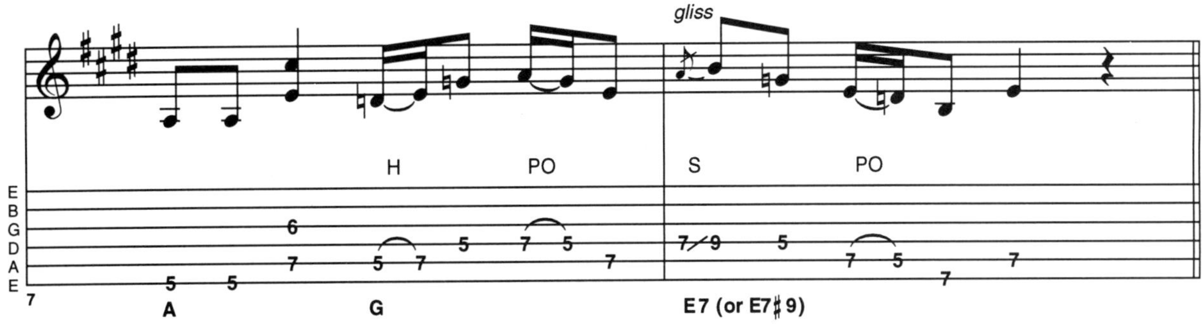

WAH-WAH GUITAR USES THESE CHORDS:

EX 4A

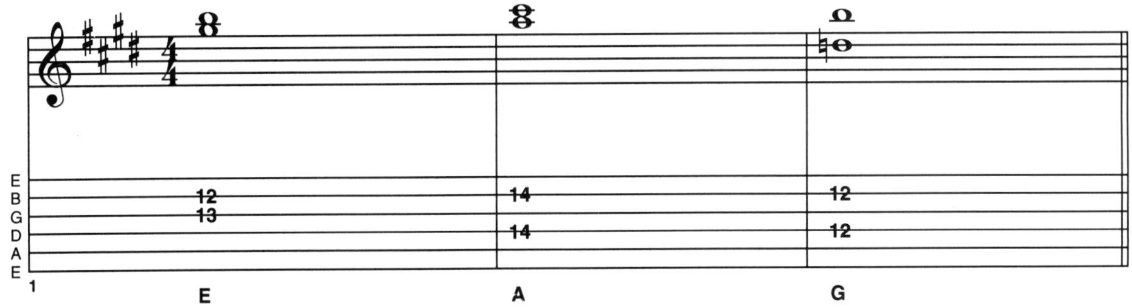

And the chorus part follows on from that. I realise that if you're just jamming along in your bedroom, woodshed or whichever part of the house your family banishes you to, you probably won't have access to all these overdubbed, contrasting guitar tones, but I've used lots of sounds to try to simulate the sonic creativity found in the music Jimi recorded in his state-of-the-art Electric Lady studio towards the end of his life. Well, I tried...

DISTORTED CHORUS GUITAR

EX 5

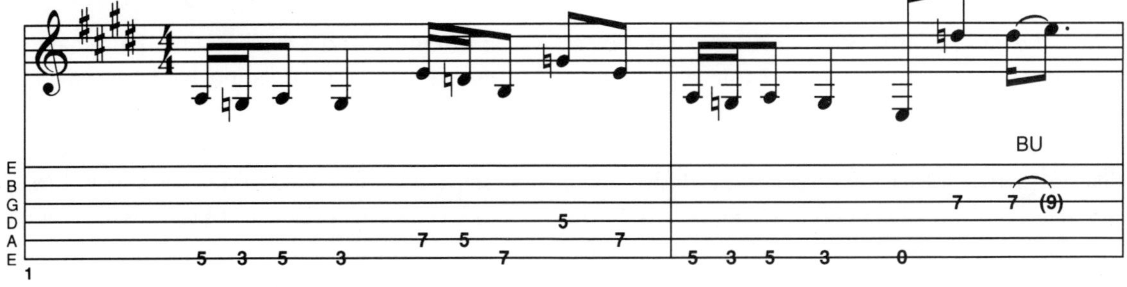

EX 5A

CLEAN CHORUS GUITAR

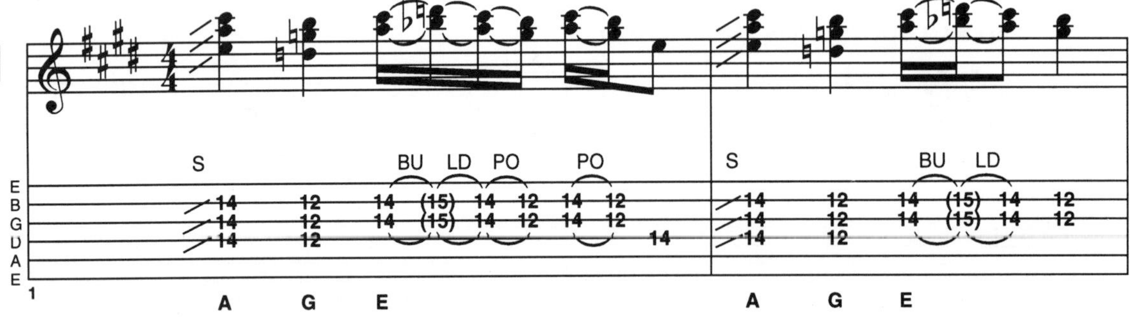

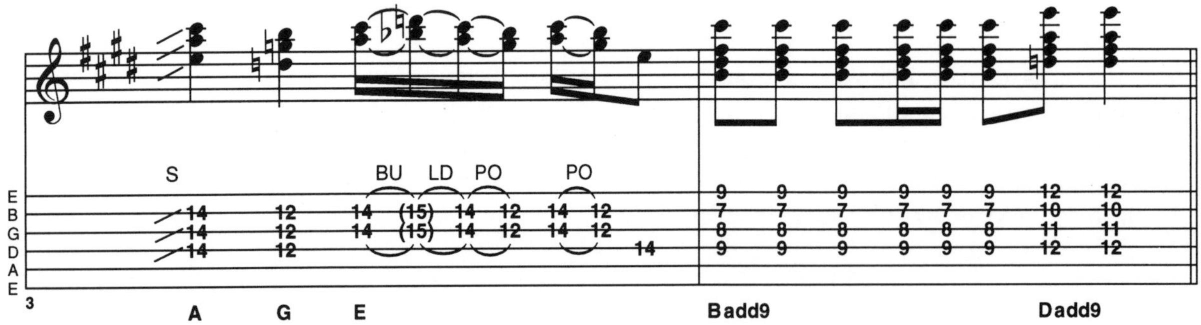

After the chorus, the very first intro riff (Ex 1) repeats, to lead us into the solo. If you listen to what the bass is playing behind the solo, you'll notice that it's an adaptation of the intro riff, but, like the actual solo, it's transposed up to the key of F#. Here's a useful tip: when changing key in the middle of a song (or "modulating", to use the correct term) it's usually a good idea to move upwards, as this gives a dramatic feeling of movement and development. This mainly applies when you're modulating by fairly small intervals (like a major second, as I've done here) and it's also more relevant when you're transposing a whole part, note for note, into a new key. Key changes between, say, a verse and a chorus are not usually as noticeable – the whole shape of the chord progression often changes. Anyway, here's the solo, using the F# minor Pentatonic (F# A B C# E F#)...

EX 6

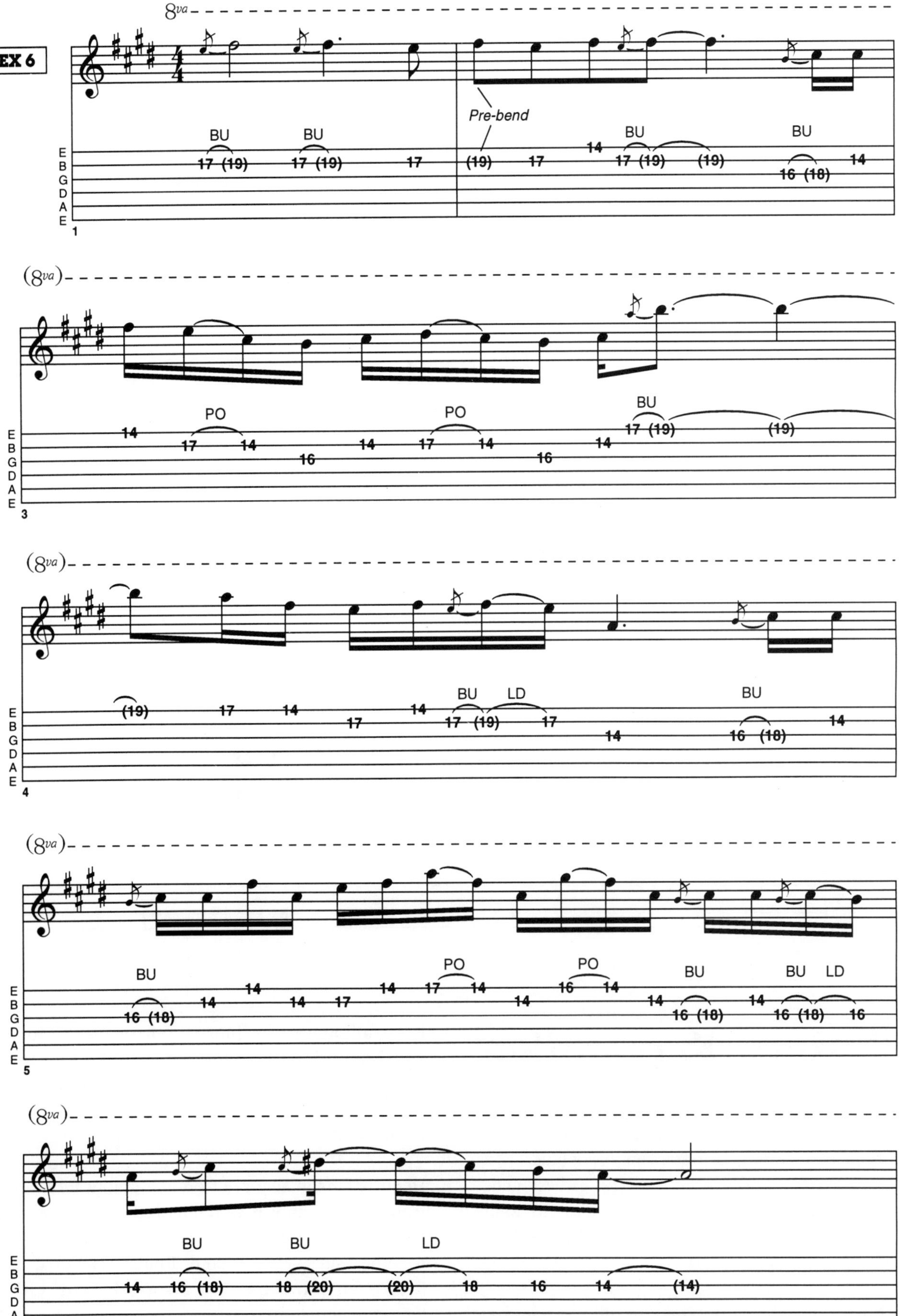

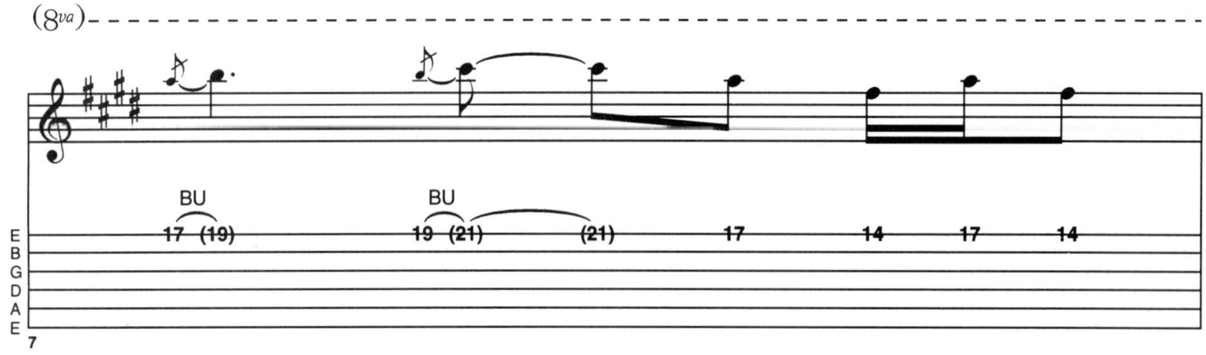

The chorus repeats after that, followed by a return to the intro section (the whole thing this time) and finally, this ending.

EX 7

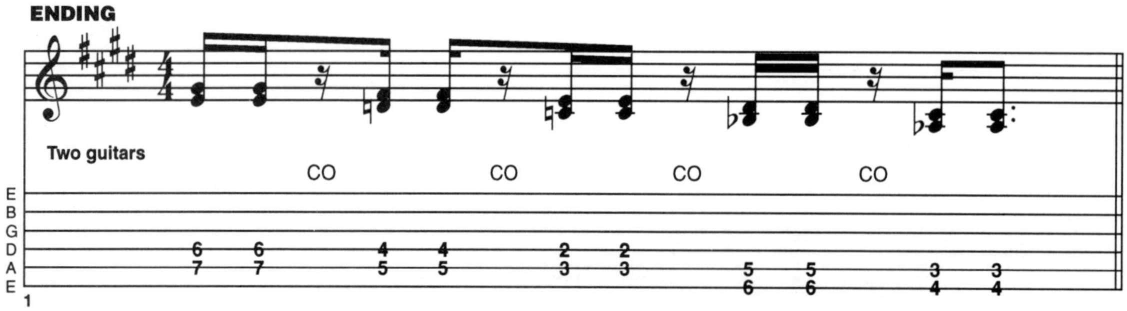

Further Exploration

As befits a player of such universal importance, Jimi Hendrix was interested in a broad range of music, including various examples of blues, jazz, classical and pop styles. Although his earliest guitar influences were blues players such as BB King, Howlin' Wolf and Robert Johnson, he later became a huge fan of Bob Dylan.

Now, do you really need me to tell you who has been influenced by Jimi Hendrix? Just to give you some food for thought: Steve Vai, Joe Satriani, Eric Johnson, Stevie Ray Vaughan, Robin Trower, Vernon Reid, Yngwie Malmsteen...

Hendrix fans in search of on-line gratification are truly spoilt for choice, with hundreds of websites to visit. One of my favourites, featuring plenty of links to other sites, is A Tribute To Jimi Hendrix, at http://cq-pan.cqu.edu.au/mc/lect/david-jones/jimi/jimi.html

CHAPTER 12

Albert King

BORN:

25 April 1923 (although other dates have been suggested).

DIED:

21 December 1992.

ORIGIN:

Indianola, Mississippi.

FIRST SPOTTED:

Albert's first solo recording, 'Bad Luck Blues' was released in 1953, although his recording career didn't really take off until 1961, when his single 'Don't Throw Your Love On Me So Strong' reached Number Fourteen on the R&B charts.

BIG BREAK:

Albert signed for the legendary Stax label in 1965, which guaranteed both a wider exposure for his music and the fact that Booker T And The MGs (featuring Steve Cropper) would be his session band.

SEEN IN THE COMPANY OF:

Albert never really did much performing or recording outside of his own successful career, but a couple of years before his death, he appeared on Gary Moore's *Still Got The Blues* album, guesting on the song 'Oh, Pretty Woman'.

THE GOOD BITS:

With his 6ft 4in stature, booming vocals and scalp-removing guitar licks, Albert King was one of the most powerful performers in the blues world. He had a huge influence on younger players such as Stevie Ray Vaughan and Robert Cray.

THE BAD BITS:

Despite being one of the finest blues guitarists of all time, Albert was often forced to live in the shadow of his namesake BB King.

SOUND ADVICE:

If you really want to get as near as possible to the Albert King sound, it might be an idea to use the same tuning as he did. Unfortunately, no-one seems to be entirely sure what this actually was. Steve Cropper, who played on many of Albert's early Stax sessions, reckons it was C B E G B E, low to high. Try it and see what you think.

NUTS AND BOLTS:

One of Albert's trademarks was his Gibson Flying V, nicknamed "Lucy", which he used from 1958 to 1974, after which he started using a custom made Dan Erlewine V-type guitar.

VITAL VINYL:

As with almost all of the great blues players, many of Albert's original recordings are now out of print, so you'll be limited to the various compilation albums on offer. Try to find one with plenty of the classic Stax recordings, for instance the hit song 'Born Under A Bad Sign'.

TRACK 17

biography

As I pointed out in the biographical section above, some of Albert King's best work was recorded for the Stax label, with those session masters, Booker T And The MGs providing the backing. For that reason, I've gone for a very relaxed R&B feel for the following Albert King-style piece of music. As with several of the players featured in this book, it's difficult to simulate Albert's approach exactly, as we don't have the luxury of vocals on these short tunes (and no, I won't bother singing, if that's all the same to you!). So... during the "verse" sections of the following tune, I've left gaps where the vocal lines would be, and played typical Albert-style fills in between. Make up some suitably miserable blues-style lyrics and sing along if you feel inspired (just don't do it round my house).

First off, let's start by having a look at the punchy single-note rhythm guitar riffs that act as a backing for the whole tune. You might notice that it's in the relatively guitar-unfriendly key of A♭ – Albert often used the "flat" keys, possibly because of the fact that he worked with a horn section, possibly because of that strange tuning. Who knows? The main scale used here is the A♭ minor Pentatonic, but to make it easier to read I've written the piece in the enharmonically equivalent key of G# (five sharps as opposed to seven flats!). The notes are exactly the same for the keys of G# and A♭, but they're named differently: G# B C# D# F# G# instead of A♭ C♭ D♭ E♭ G♭ A♭. To lead into this section, I also added a brief intro.

EX 1

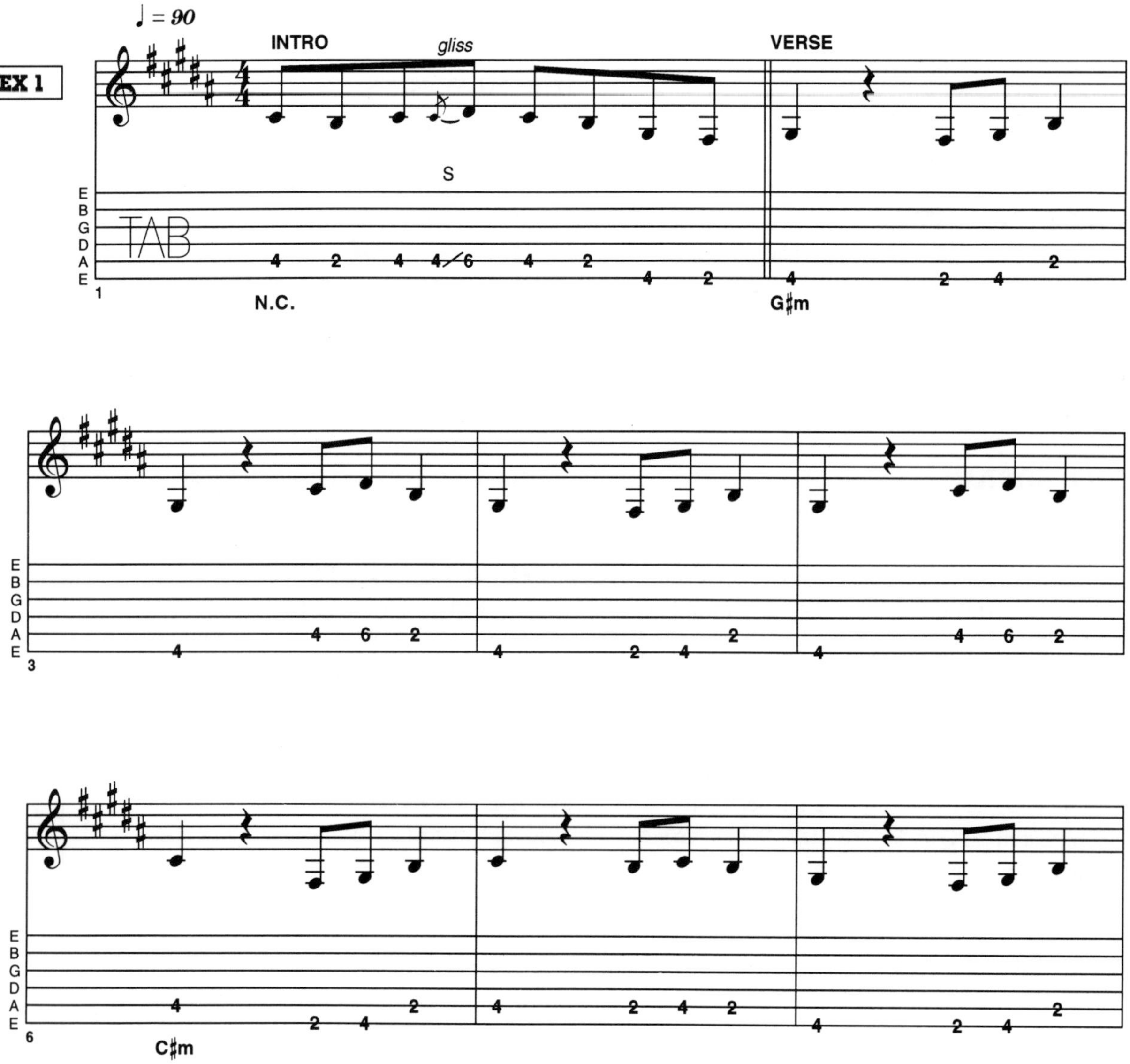

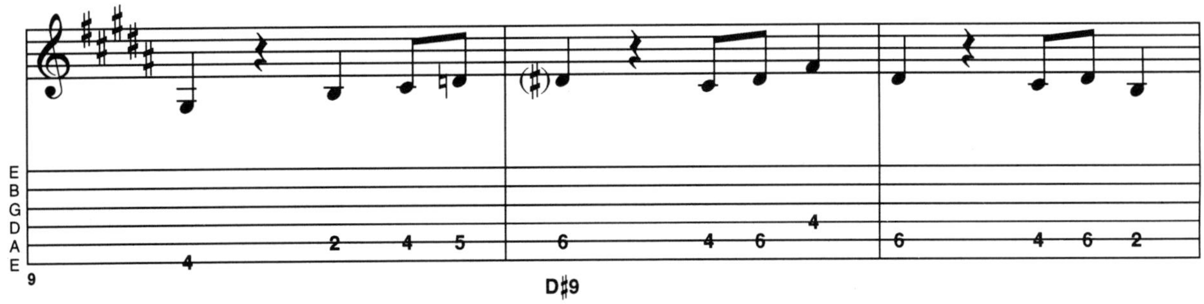

Now we'll turn our attention to the lead guitar. Here are two verses' worth of fills to fit in between our imaginary vocals. The main thing to bear in mind with this sort of thing is not to overplay – you'll end up either annoying your singer by obscuring his/her lines, or, if you're the singer in your band, making things difficult for yourself! So keep things simple and concise, and aim for that classic Albert King sting. (Hey, that rhymes...)

EX 2

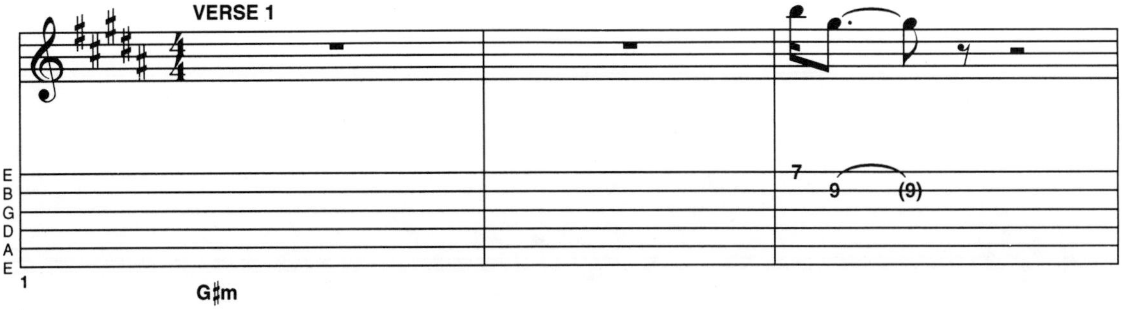

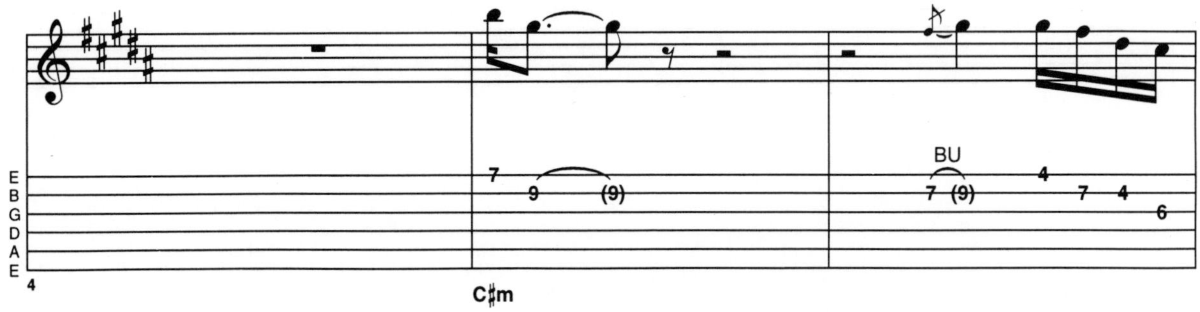

7
G♯m
D♯9
10
gliss
BU
S
G♯m
VERSE 2
13
16
BSS
C♯m

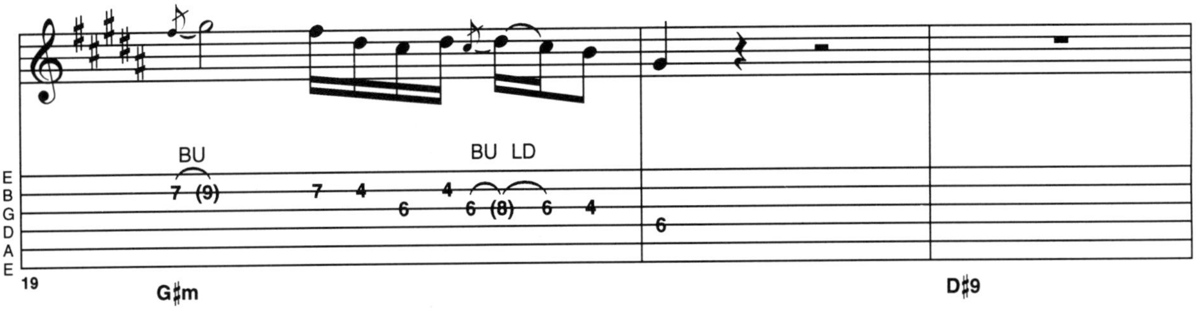

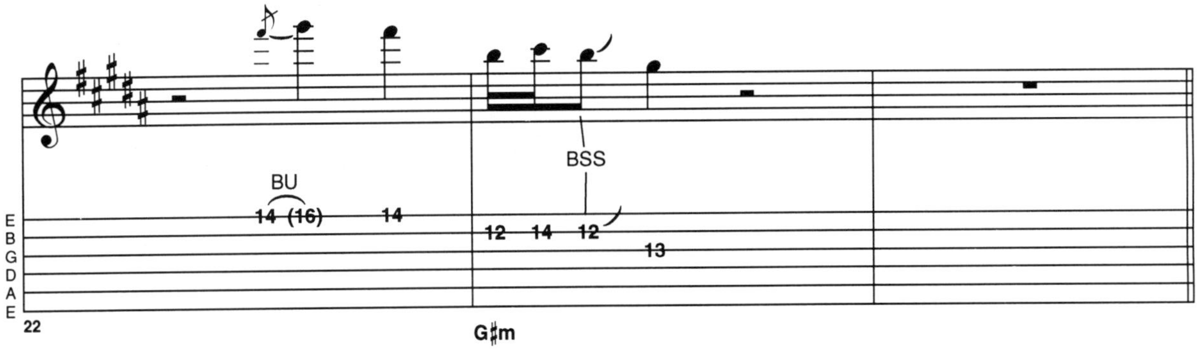

After showing such great reserve and self-control for twenty-four bars, your reward comes in the form of a couple of choruses' worth of solo. This is where you can stretch out a bit more, but remember that even in his solos, Albert still played in a smooth, relaxed manner, leaving plenty of breathing space between his licks.

EX 3

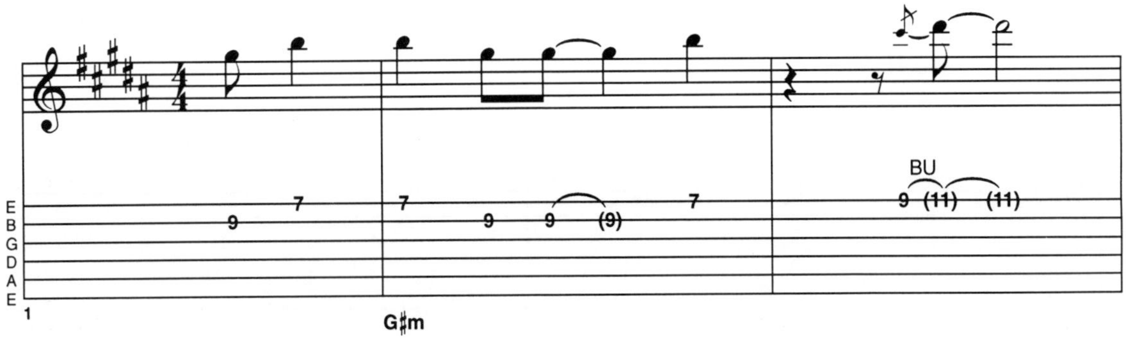

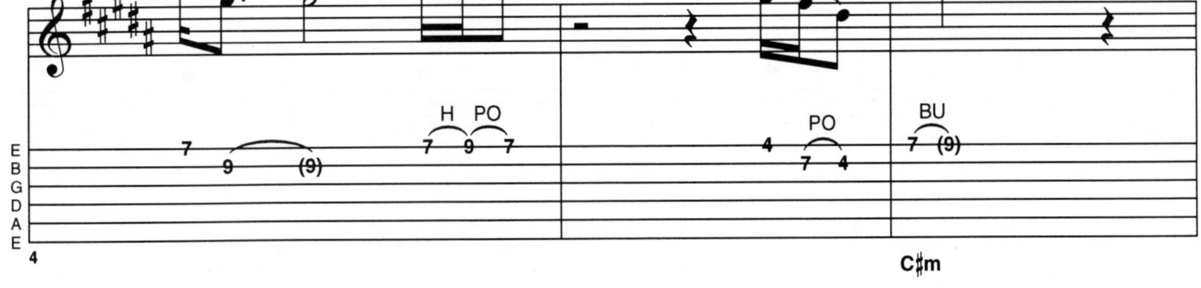

PO
CO
BU
LD
G♯m
gliss
S
D♯9
G♯m
gliss
G♯m

To finish off, I've repeated the verse section, with a few more fill-in ideas. Being able to play effective fills in between the vocal lines is a useful skill to master, and it's not restricted to blues. You can find plenty of songs in the worlds of jazz, rock, metal and country where the singer and an instrumentalist (or even two instrumentalists) use a "call and response" approach, with one playing or singing the main melody, while the other fills in the gaps. One of the easiest ways to learn this technique is to find the CD of a song you're already familiar with (preferably one without fills), and just go for it! With a bit of practice, you'll be able to respond to the singer, as well as anticipating the right length for your fills, so you don't impinge upon the next line.

Chords used within this chapter

G♯m

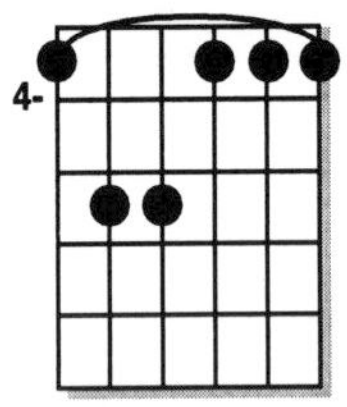

C♯m

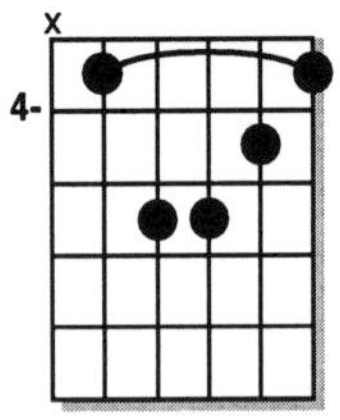

D♯9

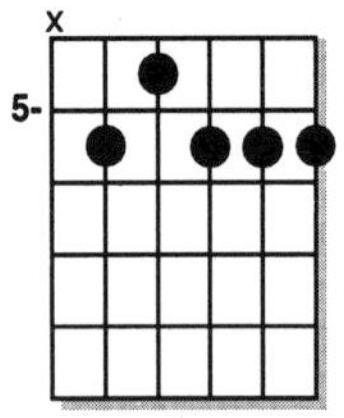

Further Exploration

As a young hopeful, Albert King was a broad-minded connoisseur of the blues, listening to Blind Lemon Jefferson, Memphis Minnie, Sonny Boy Williamson and Howlin' Wolf, among others.

Along with the other two blues-playing Kings, Albert was a major influence on the next generation of (mostly white) guitar heroes, with his band of acolytes including Eric Clapton, Gary Moore and Stevie Ray Vaughan.

Out of the three Kings, Albert is the least well represented on the Web. However, there is a reasonable amount of information about him – and loads of other blues musicians – at bluesnet, which resides at http://www.hub.org/bluesnet

CHAPTER 13
BB King

TRACK 20

biography

BORN:

16 September 1925.

ORIGIN:

Itta Bena, Mississippi.

OCCUPATION:

The most famous blues guitarist in the world.

DISTINGUISHING FEATURES:

BB never properly learned to sing and play at the same time, so he rarely plays standard rhythm guitar. Instead, he tends to sing a line and then respond to it with a phrase from his guitar. Also listen for that unmistakable, fast vibrato, which he developed in an attempt to imitate slide guitarists.

FIRST SPOTTED:

Apart from busking on the streets of Memphis, BB's real debut came in 1948, when he was invited to play on Sonny Boy Williamson's radio show on KWEM.

BIG BREAK:

In 1951 his cover version of Lowell Fulson's 'Three O'Clock Blues' went to Number One in the R&B charts. One of BB's most famous songs, the string-drenched 'The Thrill Is Gone' reached Number Fifteen on the US mainstream pop charts in 1969. Suddenly BB's music was no longer just for blues purists.

SEEN IN THE COMPANY OF:

BB has had some of the most enviable "guest artist" slots in music, appearing on albums by Miles Davis, Ray Charles and U2.

THE GOOD BITS:

Through his much-imitated playing, his high-energy live performances and his "Gentleman of the Blues" image, BB has probably done more to popularise blues music than just about anyone.

THE BAD BITS:

Well, I don't know about you, but I can't think of any, so let's have...

MORE GOOD BITS:

As well as being King of the Blues, BB has a healthy interest in many styles of music (I mean, how many other pension-age bluesmen would appear on stage with U2?) and has broadened his musical abilities to include piano, bass, drums, harmonica, violin and clarinet.

NUTS AND BOLTS:

Since 1959, BB King has been a loyal user of the Gibson ES355. He's always called them "Lucille", a tradition which dates back to the late 1940s when BB risked his life to save his guitar from a burning building. The fire had been started by two men fighting over a girl called... Lucille.

VITAL VINYL:

There are loads and loads of albums, but one of the best is *Live At The Regal* from 1965.

In the chapters on Kenny Burrell and Charlie Christian, we looked at two jazz players who have incorporated blues elements into their styles. With BB King, we'll do the opposite – the basic framework is unmistakably blues, but lots of his licks come from his love of jazz. BB often plays with a brass section, further adding to the jazz aspect of his music, and providing a greater level of harmonic sophistication than is generally found in blues music. Unfortunately we can't stretch to a brass section for the accompanying CD, but I've played the rhythm guitar parts using more ambitious chords and with a punchy, big-band feel. Here's the basic chord progression that I used throughout the piece.

EX 1

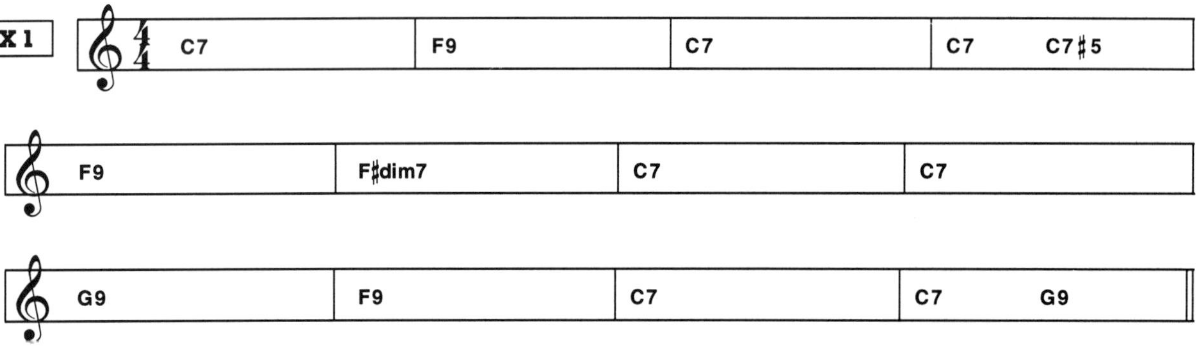

Whenever you're comping on this sort of tune ("comping" comes from the word "accompaniment" and is one of those jazz words that you can liberally toss into a conversation if you want to sound like you know what you're on about) it's a good idea to know several alternatives for each chord. Being able to vary the chords or their voicings prevents the rhythm part from sounding sterile. Here are some alternatives; try slotting them into the appropriate places in the previous example.

EX 2

C7 Shapes

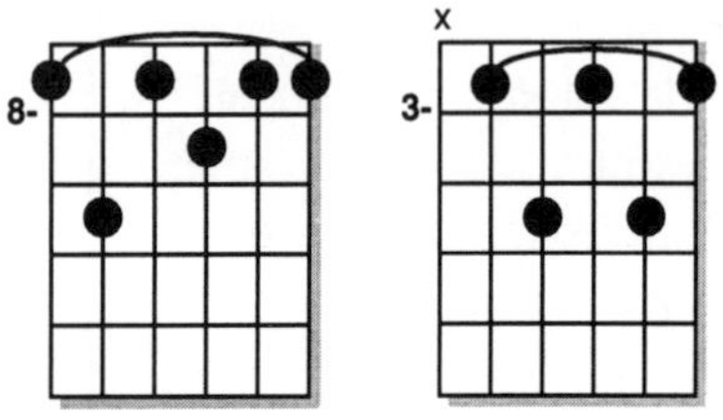

Alternatives

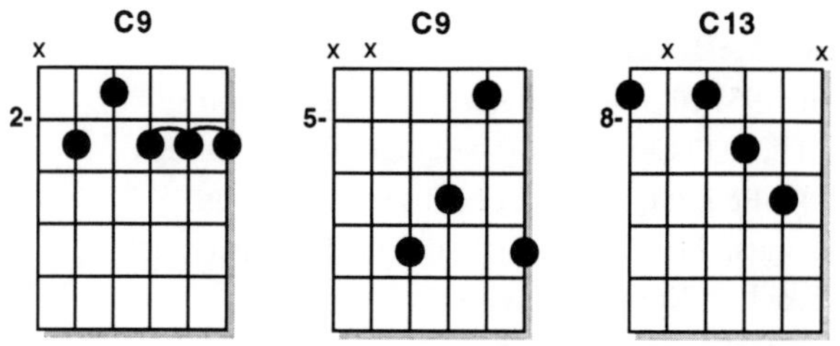

F9 Shapes

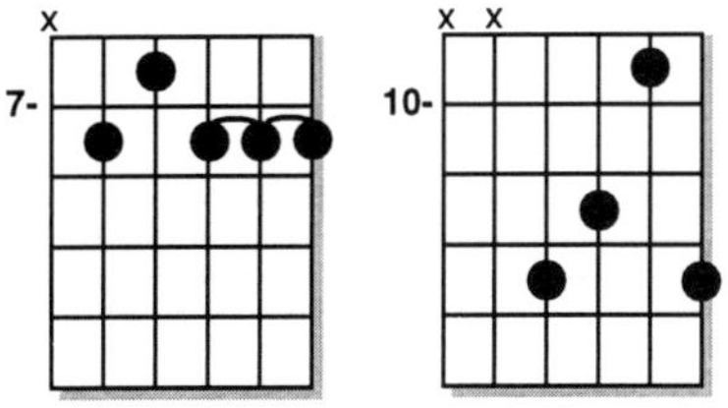

Alternative

F13

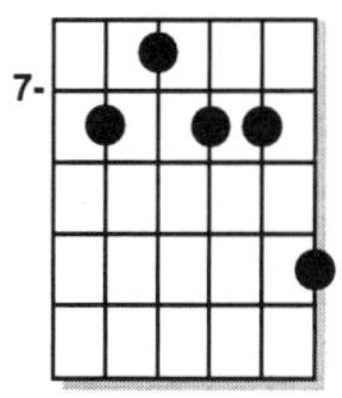

Other chords used

C7♯5 F♯dim7 G9

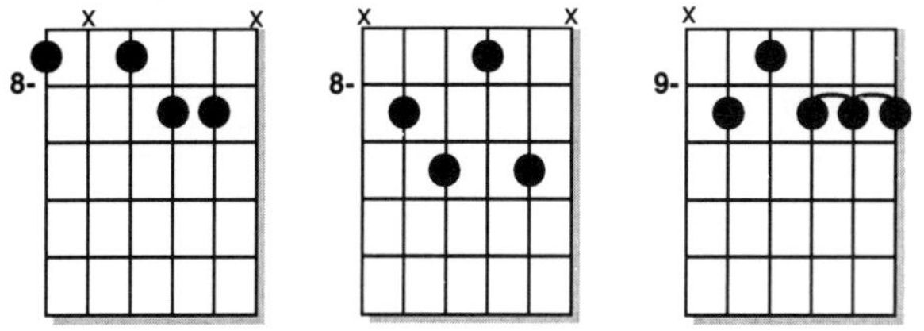

The next example shows the head section; as BB doesn't play many instrumentals compared to players such as his namesake Freddie, I've written this section as if it were part of a song with vocals. Therefore, the lead guitar is used to play fills in between the imaginary vocal lines. (I said "imaginary" – I wouldn't dream of inflicting my singing on you!) Here are some BB-style fills for a couple of verses.

EX 3

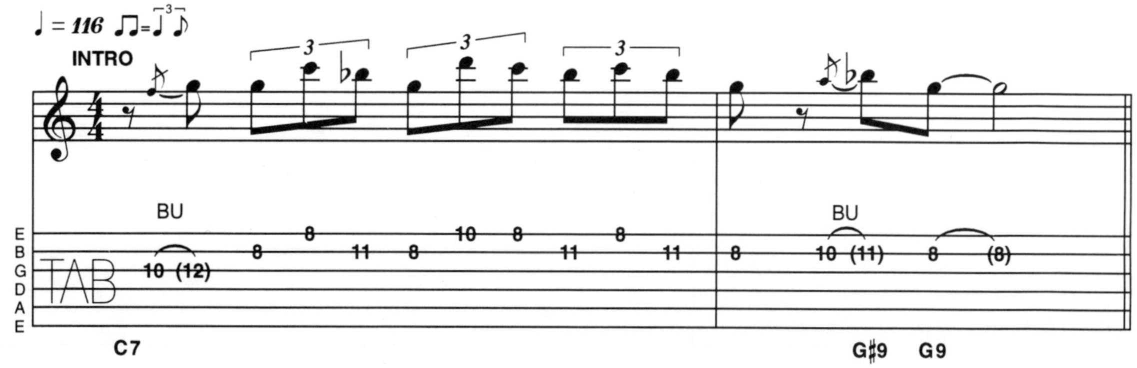

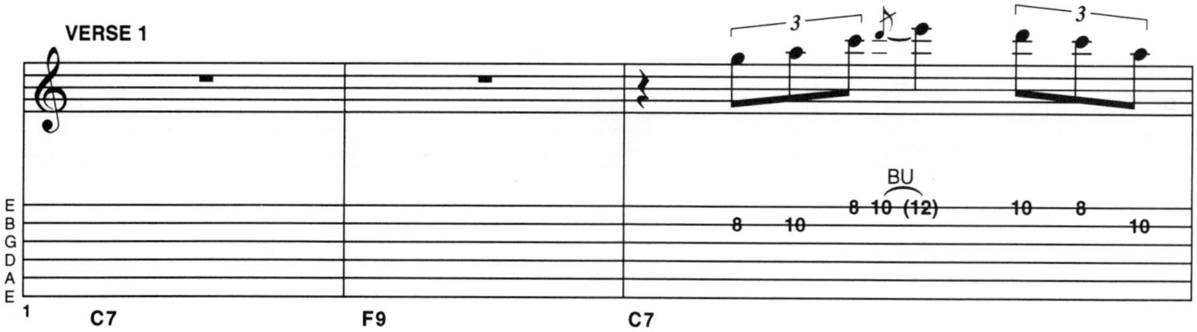

C7♯5
F9
F♯dim7
BU
C7
G9
BSS
BSS
BSS
F9
C7
G9
VERSE 2
C7
F9
C7
BU
BU
gliss
S
C7♯5
F9
F♯dim7

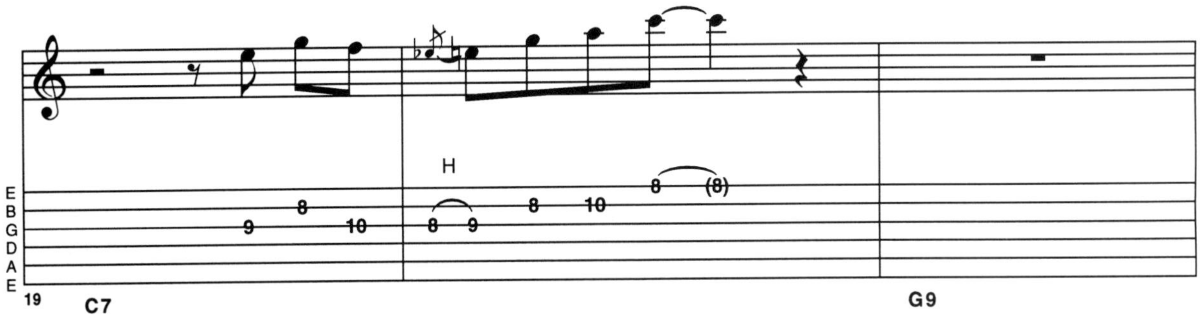

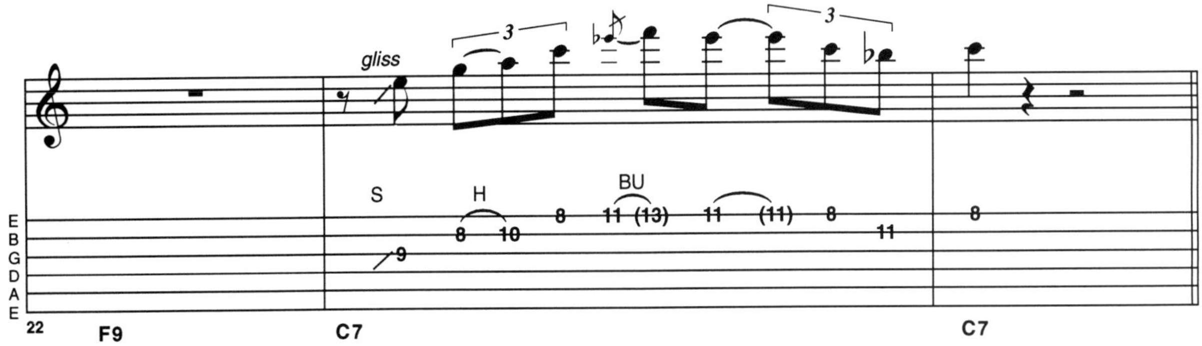

For the first chorus of the two-chorus solo, I incorporated some "stops" into the backing part. These serve to bring the guitar (or any other lead instrument, for that matter) to the forefront, and can be found in both blues, jazz and rock 'n' roll ('Blue Suede Shoes' springs to mind). The only trouble is that you need nerves of steel to do this sort of thing on stage – if you mess up, there are no loud, splashy cymbals to hide your bum notes! Here's the solo...

EX 4

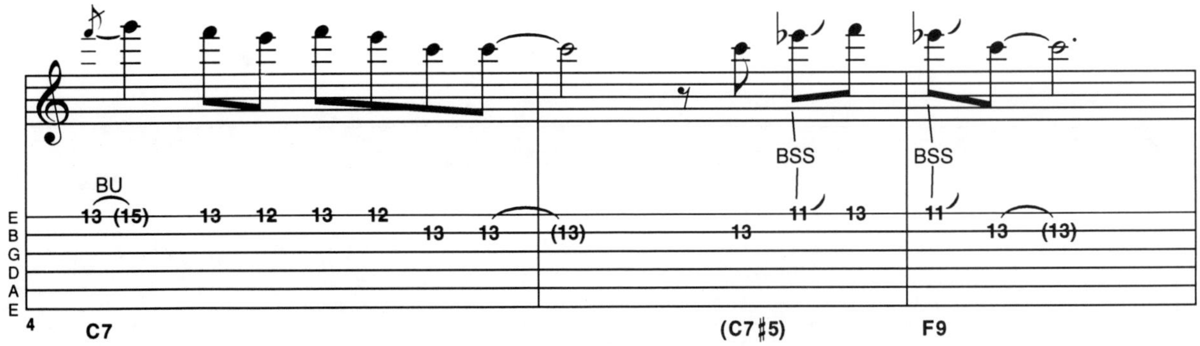

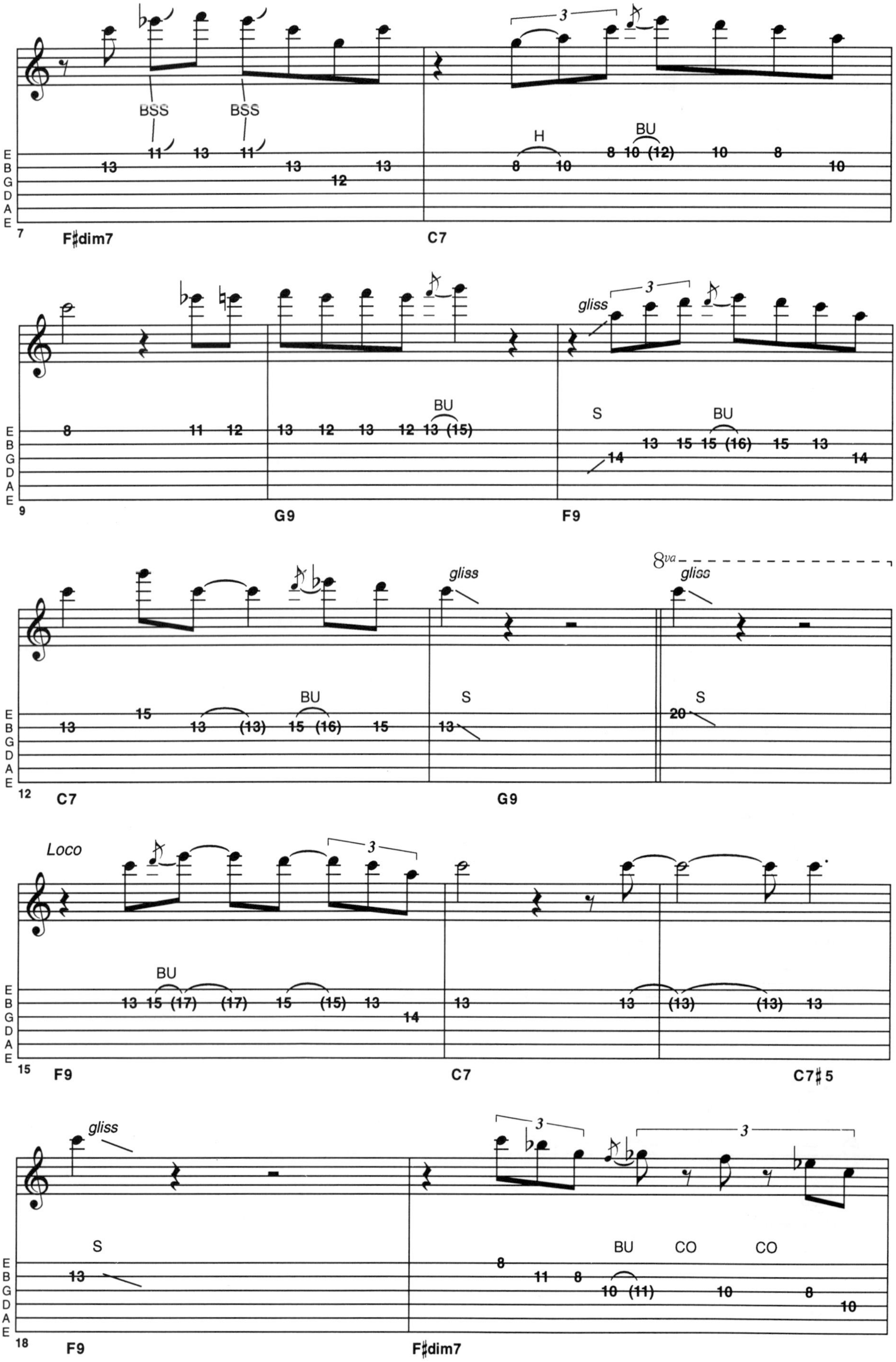
BSS
BSS
H
BU
F♯dim7
C7
BU
S
gliss
BU
G9
F9
gliss
8va
gliss
BU
S
S
C7
G9
Loco
BU
F9
C7
C7♯5
gliss
S
BU
CO
CO
F9
F♯dim7

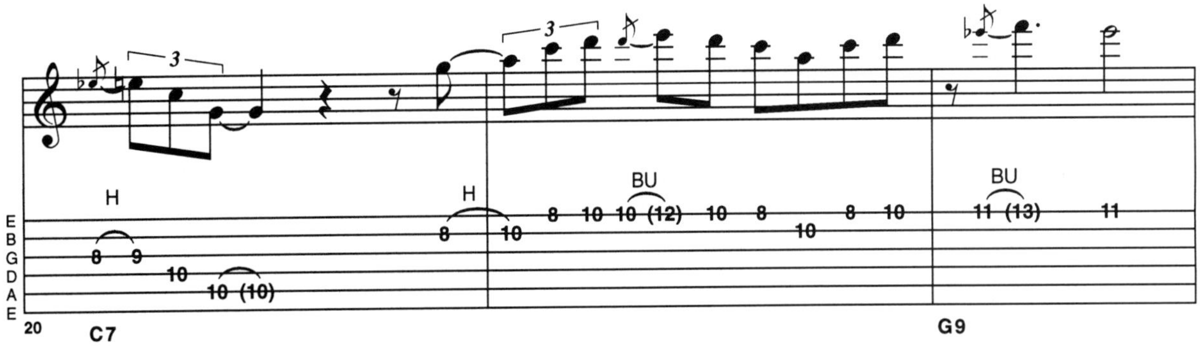

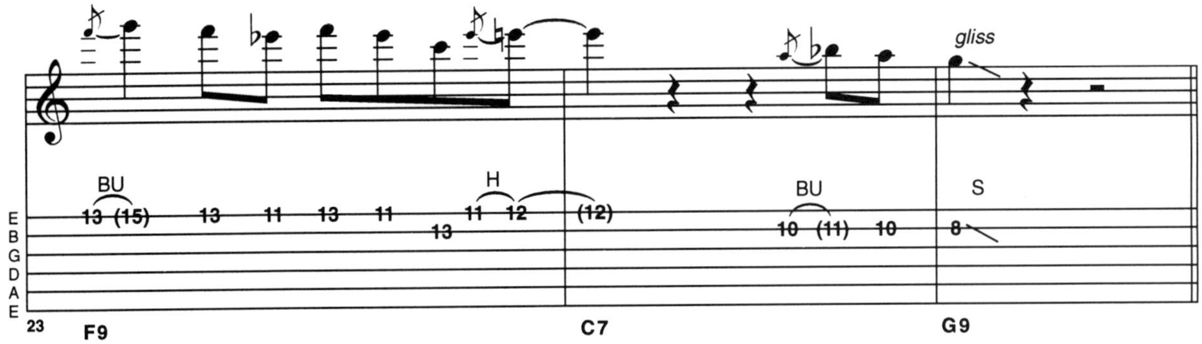

As for the notes and scales I used, it's that good old tried-and-tested combination of the major and minor Pentatonic scales. In the key of A (as used here) that gives you A B C# E F# A for the major Pentatonic, and A C D E G A for the minor. BB King tends to lean more towards the major side of the equation than other players; maybe that's why his playing always sounds so bright and positive.

At the end, I just repeated the head section with some different fills and added this ending. The final phrase is played "free-time" as there's no beat underneath to anchor the rhythms to.

EX 5

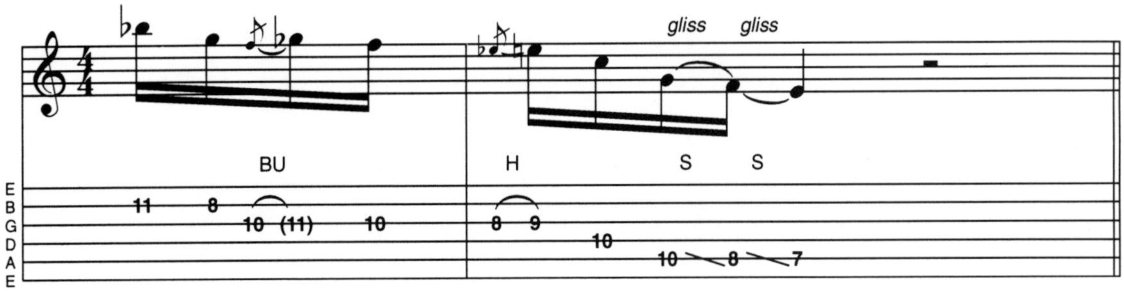

Further Exploration

Through his aunt's record collection BB received his earliest musical education. Some of his favourites were Blind Lemon Jefferson, Robert Johnson, Charlie Patton and Lonnie Johnson. He developed a love for jazz while in the army, especially Charlie Christian, Django Reinhardt and Kenny Burrell.

As one of the most popular blues players ever, BB has had an enormous influence on players of various styles: Stevie Ray Vaughan, Jimmy Page, Scotty Moore, Mark Knopfler, Jimi Hendrix, Eric Clapton...

My favourite BB King website is actually the official one, maintained by MCA Records. Featuring an "interactive biography", it can be found at http://www.bbking.mca.com

CHAPTER 14

Freddie King

biography

TRACK 1

BORN:
3 September 1934.

DIED:
28 December 1976.

ORIGIN:
Gilmer, Texas. Freddie moved to Chicago at the age of eleven.

DISTINGUISHING FEATURES:
Freddie was no purist, happily mixing together the blues styles of Chicago, Texas and the Mississippi Delta along with elements of country, jazz and pop. Although much of his playing was Pentatonic-based, he often added extra notes which resulted in a brighter, jazzier feel.

CLAIM TO FAME:
Out of all the great blues players, Freddie King was one of the first to find success with a more mainstream pop audience, due mainly to catchy, upbeat instrumentals such as 'The Stumble' and 'Hideaway'.

FIRST SPOTTED:
Having played in Chicago clubs for several years, Freddie released his first record, *Country Boy*, on a local label in 1957.

SEEN IN THE COMPANY OF:
Freddie worked with some of the biggest names in blues: Muddy Waters, Howlin' Wolf, Little Walter and Eric Clapton.

THE GOOD BITS:
Those cheery, catchy instrumental hits make Freddie one of the most listenable of the great blues players, especially those new to the genre. Next time you're down at your local blues club on "jam night" and you see one of those people who seem to think "blues" is just a matter of wailing endlessly and discordantly with the E minor Pentatonic, point them in the direction of a few Freddie King albums.

THE BAD BITS:
It's that same sad old story again. Freddie died of pancreatitis at the age of forty-two.

NUTS AND BOLTS:
Freddie recorded most of his earlier hits on a Les Paul Gold Top, but later moved to Gibson ES355s, which he used up until his death.

VITAL VINYL:
As is often the case with blues and jazz musicians, the original Freddie King albums are almost impossible to find; they're rarely reissued on CD, and vinyl copies tend to be collectors' items (at collectors' prices!). So it's the old compilation method again, but do beware of the plethora of horrendously recorded budget-price CDs on the market.

Freddie King was the master of the blues instrumental. He had far more Top Forty success than most other blues guitarists, possibly because of the catchy nature of many of his tunes, for example 'Hideaway' and 'The Stumble'. If you're really serious about developing your blues chops, it'd be well worth spending some time studying Freddie's playing – you'll see how the good old Pentatonic scales can be used to construct memorable melody lines as well as blazing solos.

Now, one of the best ways to get that bright, cheerful sound you hear in some of Freddie's tunes is to use the major Pentatonic scale. Although often associated with country music, this scale works perfectly well with blues, and if you're careful, you can actually use it in conjunction with the more common minor Pentatonic. Here's how to play it...

Chords used in this chapter

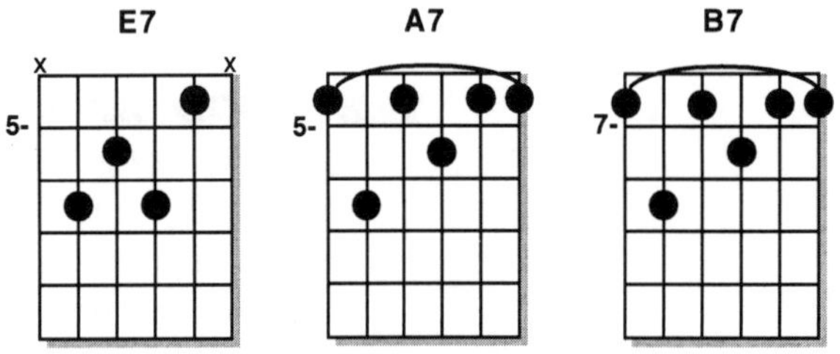

EX 1

E MINOR PENTATONIC

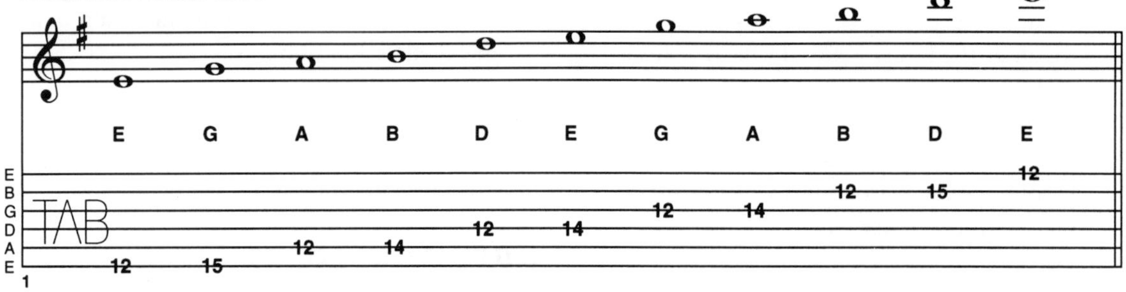

E MAJOR PENTATONIC

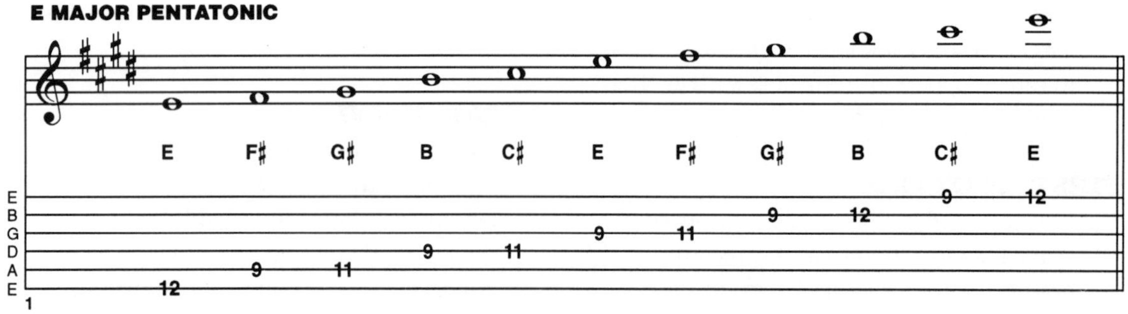

As you can see, a simple formula for finding any given major Pentatonic is to take the minor Pentatonic (presuming you already know that) and move the box pattern down three frets. Obviously there's more to a scale than just a single box shape, but that's a good starting point to orientate yourself from. Next let's use a combination of the two scales for our main melody.

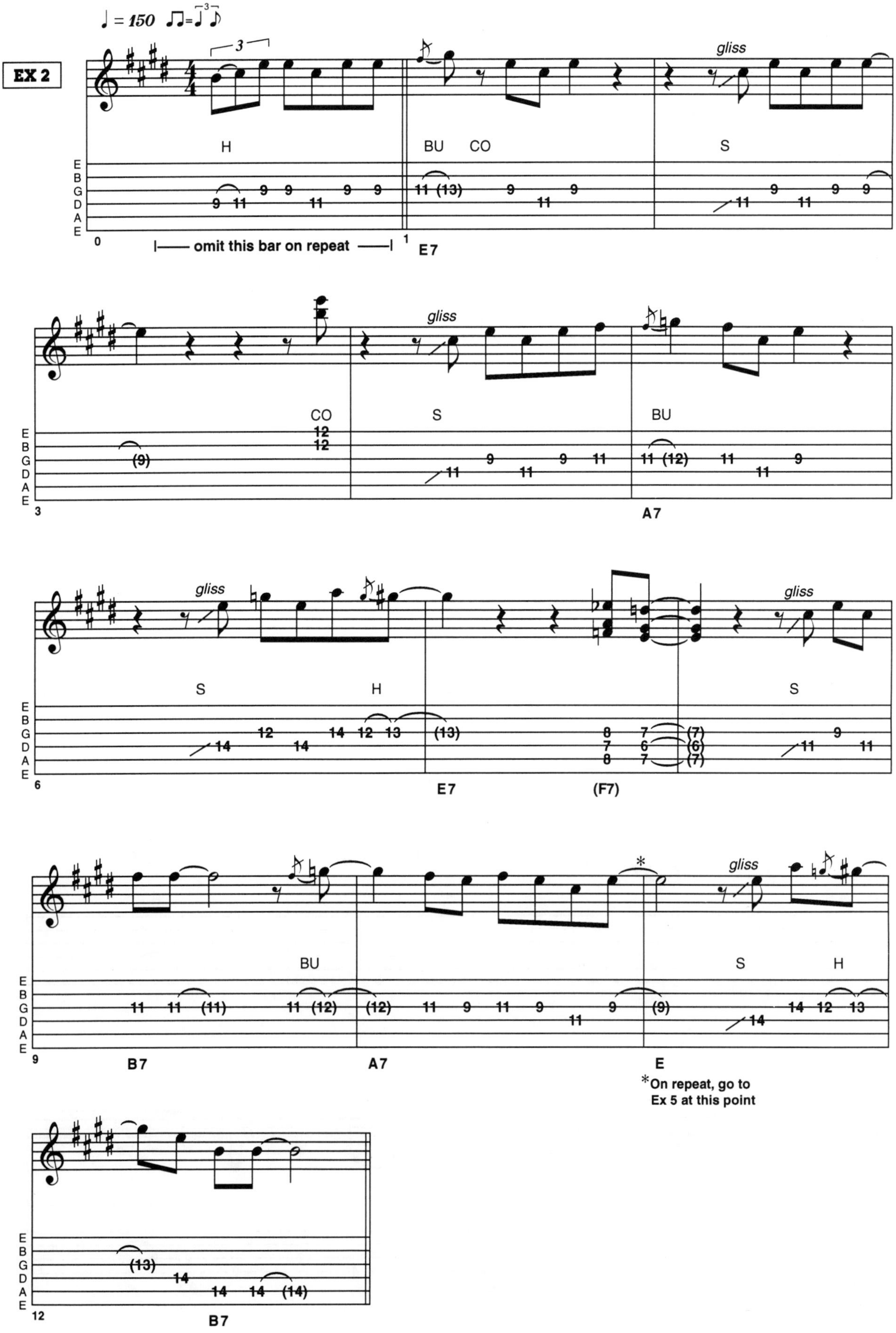
EX 2
♩ = 150
gliss
H
BU CO
S
omit this bar on repeat
E7
A7
(F7)
B7
E
*On repeat, go to Ex 5 at this point

In true Freddie King style, I decided to break up the feel of the tune by cutting to a bass-string riff, similar to the sort of thing he does in 'Hideaway'. Notice how I've taken the first riff (over the E chord) and transposed it exactly to fit over the A chord, but used a slightly different pattern over the turnaround. Don't ask me why it works, or why numerous blues players do that sort of thing – just remember that it sounds cool!

EX 3

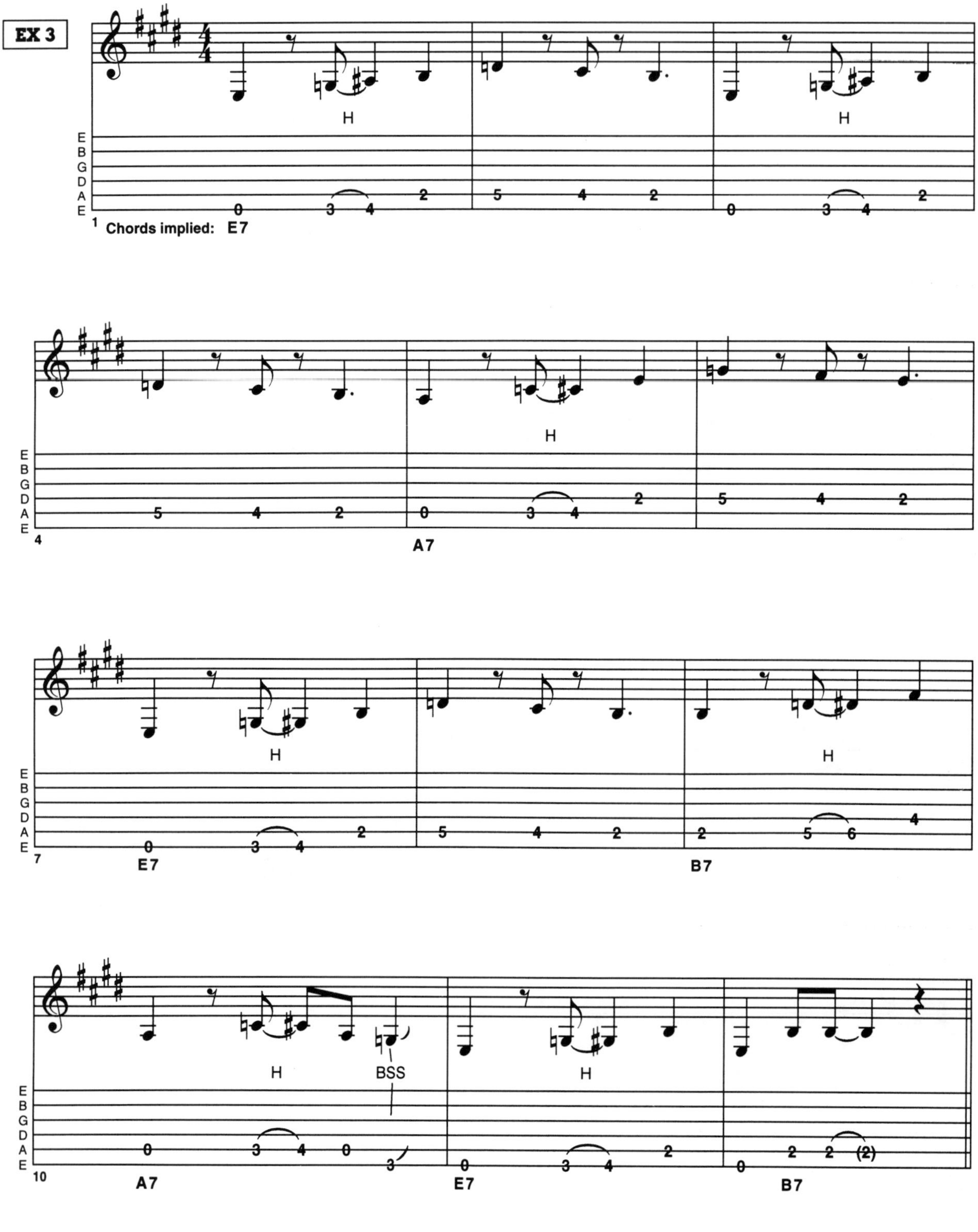

The attention-grabbing effect of those low riffs provides a perfect entrance for the solo. The solo is two choruses long, allowing for some very Freddie-like "stops" in the middle.

EX 4

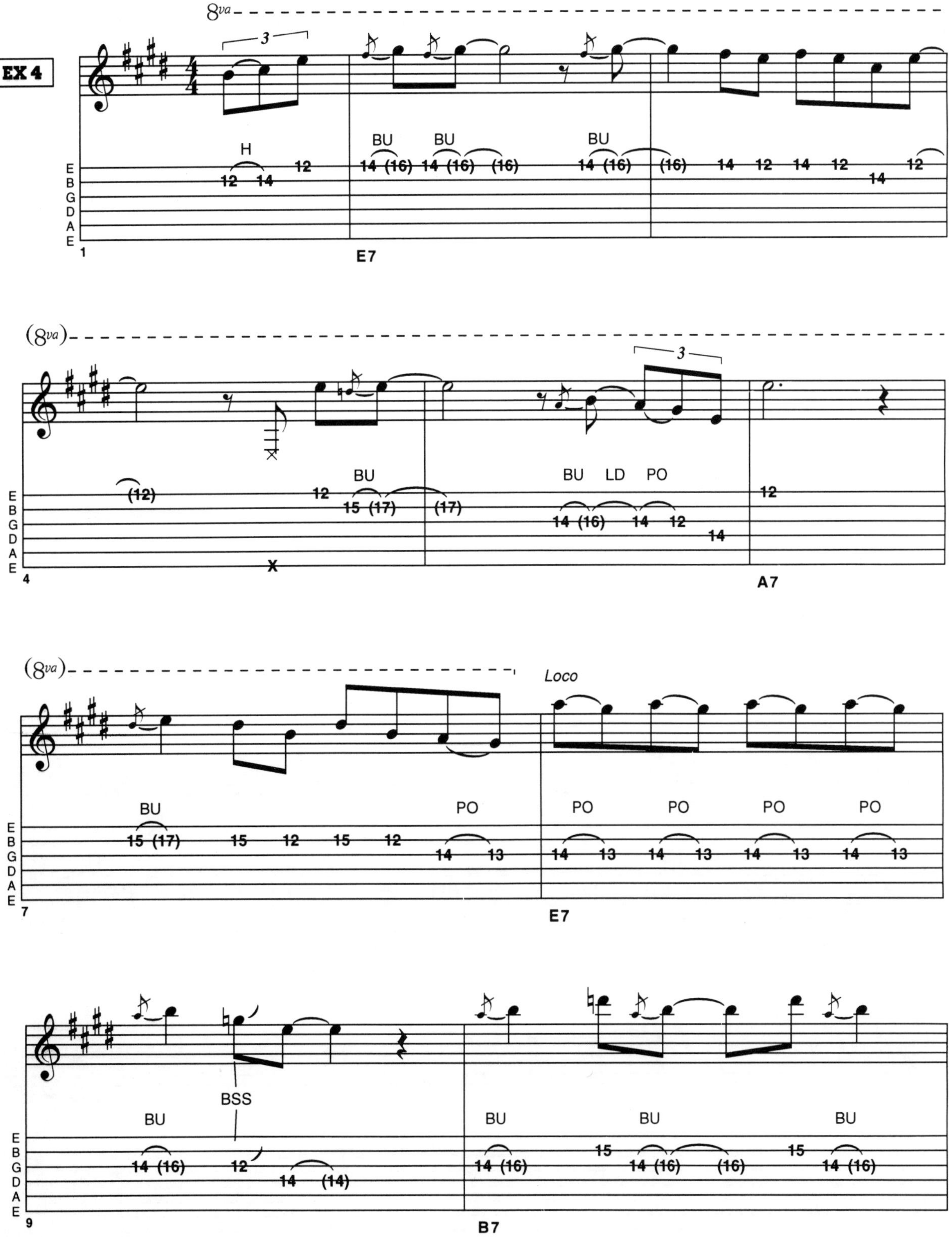

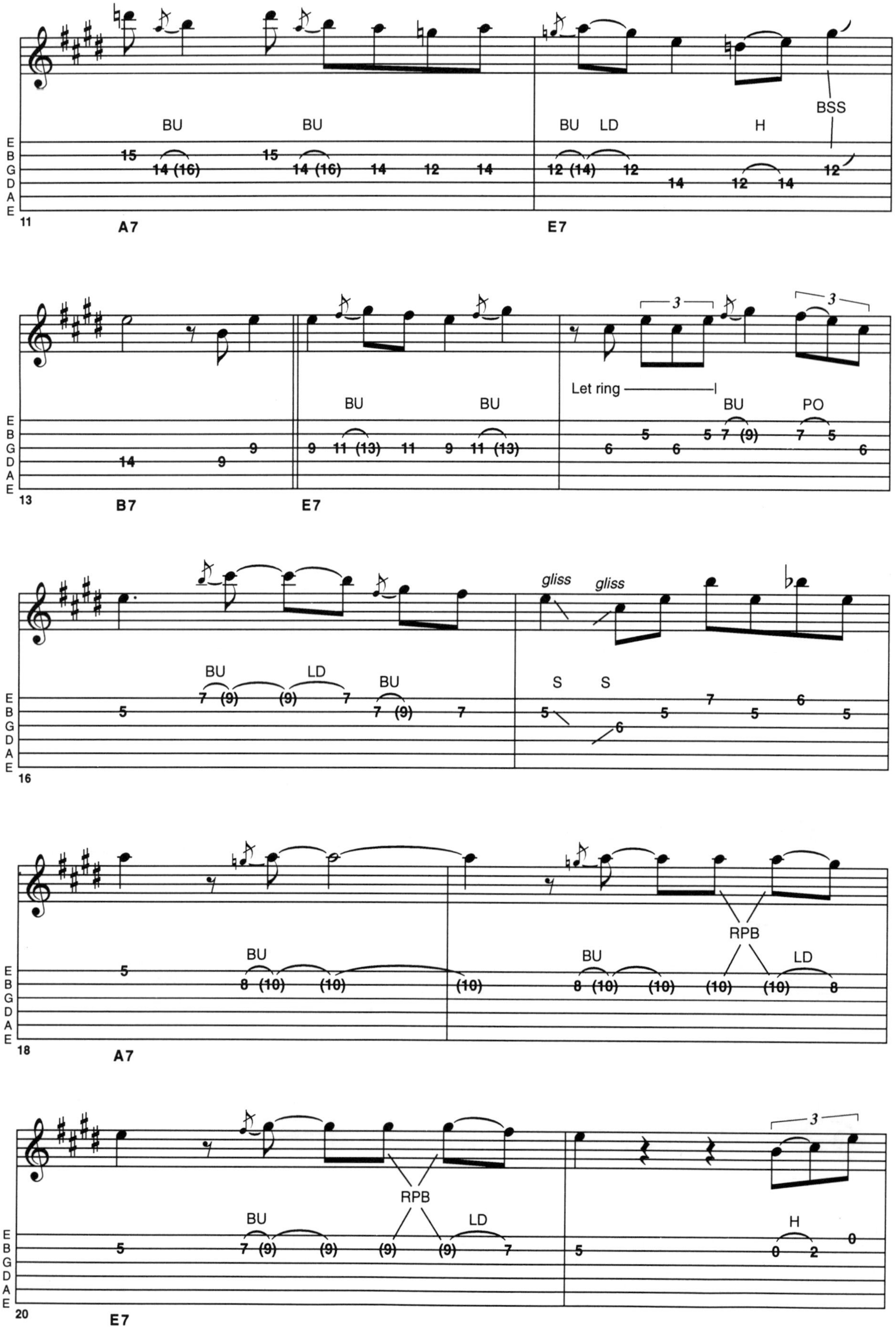

BU
BU
BU LD
H
BSS
11
A7
E7
BU
BU
Let ring
BU
PO
13
B7
E7
BU
LD
BU
gliss
gliss
S
S
16
RPB
BU
BU
LD
18
A7
RPB
BU
LD
H
20
E7

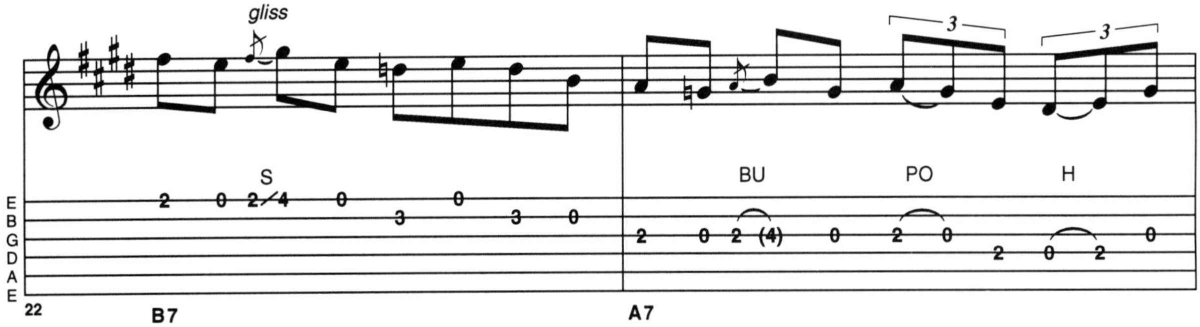

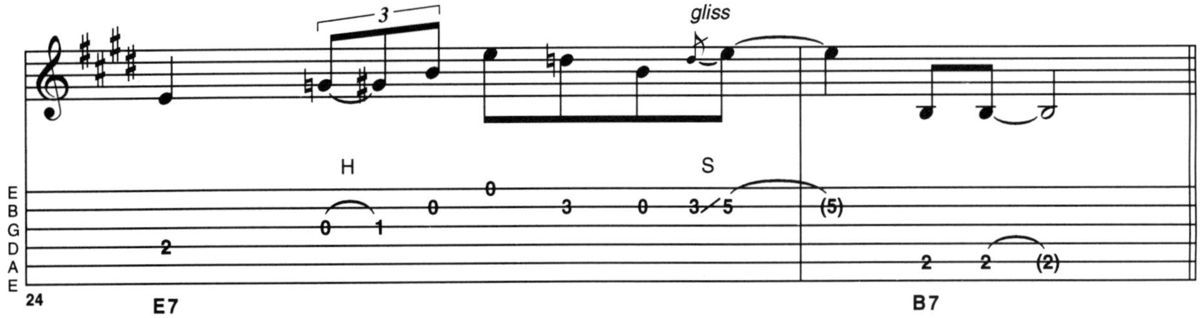

To round things off, I just repeated the "head" section (that's the correct term for the main theme, boys and girls) and added this little ending. These double stops are based on the interval of a sixth (some are minor, some major, depending on their position within the scale) and perhaps the best way to play them is to use your pick for the notes on the G string and your middle finger for the high E string. Of course, if you're going for the last word in authenticity, you'll already have donned your metal thumbpick and fingerpick (for your index finger) and you'll have found an even easier way of playing the double stops!

EX 5

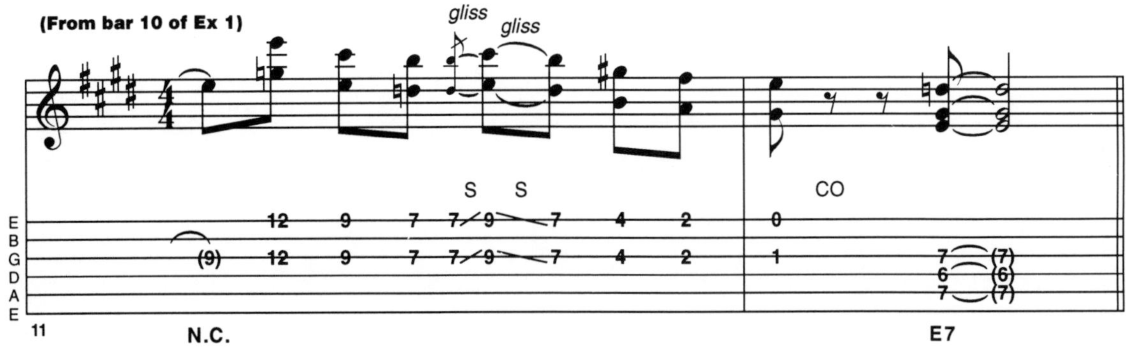

Ta-daaah! A short blues instrumental like this (and many of Freddie's originals) may look rather easy, especially compared to something like 'Surfing With The Alien', but don't forget that what you see on paper is never the full story. Things like vibrato and nuances of phrasing can never be accurately represented by written symbols, so get used to listening in detail! By the way, Freddie's vibrato was big, fast and mean, so take a deep breath before launching into this tune!

Further Exploration

Having spent time in both rural Texas and urban Chicago, Freddie learnt from a mixture of blues styles. His biggest influences were Lightnin' Hopkins, BB King, Muddy Waters and T-Bone Walker.

Back in the big British blues boom of the mid sixties (try saying that after seven pints of lager!) Freddie King, with his enormous stage presence and in-yer-face guitar playing, was one of the most popular Americans to be emulated. Eric Clapton and Peter Green recorded covers of his instrumentals during their tenures with John Mayall's Bluesbreakers, and Freddie also had a great influence on Mick Taylor, Jimmy Page, Jeff Beck and Dave Edmunds, as well as white American players such as Billy Gibbons and Stevie Ray Vaughan.

The very impressive Freddie King Web Page – http://www.mazeppa.com/fking.html – should be your first stop for Freddie-related surfing, and you could also try the comprehensive Bluesnet (see the Albert King chapter for the address).

CHAPTER 15
Brian May

BORN:
19 July 1947.

ORIGIN:
Twickenham, Middlesex.

DISTINGUISHING FEATURES:
Apart from the towering stature and those ever-present clogs, Brian May has one of the most recognisable guitar sounds around, characterised by a thick, singing tone and frequent use of layered, multiple harmony parts.

SIGNIFICANT EARLY EVENT:
In 1963, Brian and his father set about making an electric guitar, with the intention of combining the best aspects of contemporary guitar design along with a few ideas of their own. Armed with part of an old fireplace, assorted motorcycle bits, a handful of pearl buttons and three handwound Burns pickups, they created the Red Special.

THE GOOD BITS:
Apart from being one of the most pleasant-natured and modest guitarists in the rock world, Brian is also a great player (that's why he's in this book). As well as filling numerous Queen albums with his fluid, melodic solos, he's done plenty of sonic experimentation, introducing the world to the delights of layered guitar harmonies.

THE BAD BITS:
Freddie's death, obviously. Although Brian May is a great musician in his own right, there was something uniquely special about the way those four people worked together.

NUTS AND BOLTS:
The Red Special. Probably the most famous electric guitar ever made, not least because it's homemade and completely unique. Brian's not the only guitarist to have used a homemade axe in a top-flight professional music career (there's also Eddie Van Halen) but he's one of a very rare breed. What's even more amazing, is just how well-made it must be to survive over thirty years in the hands of one of the biggest names in rock guitar. And just look at the specs – a knife-edge trem that never seems to suffer from tuning problems, a twenty-four-fret neck, handwound pickups, tuners aligned to give the strings a straight path through the nut... blimey! Combine that with a wall of Vox AC30 amps, and that's as close to the Brian May sound as you're ever going to get. (Oh go on, Brian, lend us your guitar... please?)

VITAL VINYL:
There's a wealth of quality music in the entire Queen back catalogue, as their endless stream of hits will show, but somehow I can't help feeling that the first six or seven albums (with their proud claim of "no synthesizers") are where the classic stuff can be found. *Queen II* is the ultimate in overblown prog-rock, *Sheer Heart Attack* and *News Of The World* can out-rock just about anything you care to name, and *A Day At The Races* and *A Night At The Opera* showcase Brian, Freddie and Co at their eccentric best.

TRACK 8

biography

As you may have realised on your way through this book, some guitarists are easier to sum up than others. That may sound dismissive and derogatory, but I'm not saying that the "easier" guitarists are any less profound in their musical statements than the others; it's just that the surface elements of their styles are easier to understand. For instance, it's no problem for me to show you what notes to use when concocting BB King-style licks as he has such a consistently recognisable style. However, his touch and vibrato are so subtle and unique that you might spend years trying to copy them and still never come close. Then there are the players whose styles provide problems right from the start... enter Brian May, who seems to reinvent himself for just about every song. Sure, the thick tone and layered harmonies are usually there, but there's just so much more!

One of Brian's most famous techniques is his use of an echo unit on 'Brighton Rock'. By playing in time with the single repeat, he was able to create an instant two-part harmony effect ideal for onstage use, where his huge orchestra of guitar parts was impossible. In time, Brian started using a modified echo unit in order to produce two repeats, thus enabling him to play three-part harmonies and making his live 'Brighton Rock' extravaganza even more ambitious. Using a delay unit set to produce two repeats (at 857 and 1714 milliseconds, panned hard right and left) I've come up with an unaccompanied intro part to this piece. Here's the basic part...

EX 1

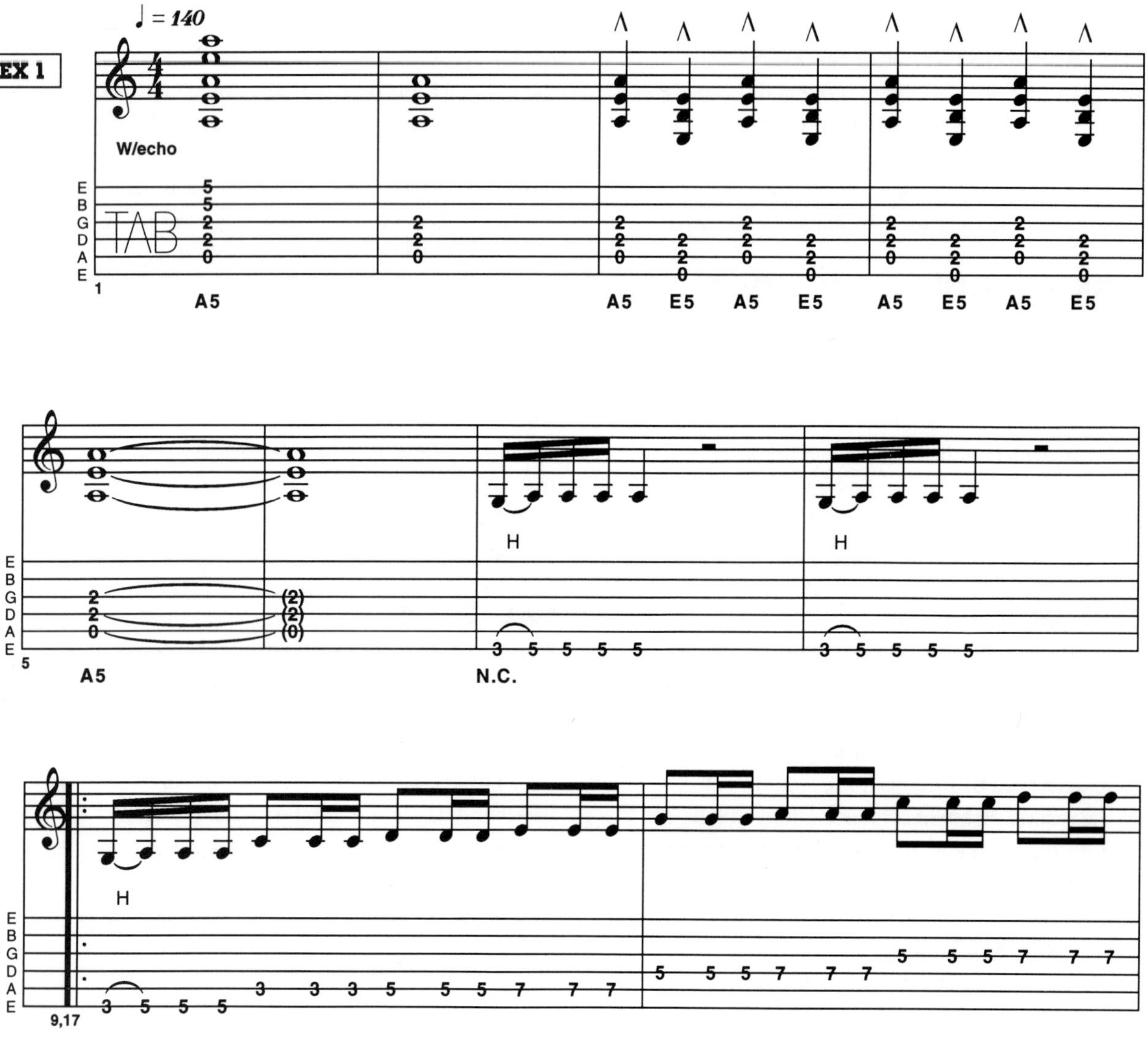

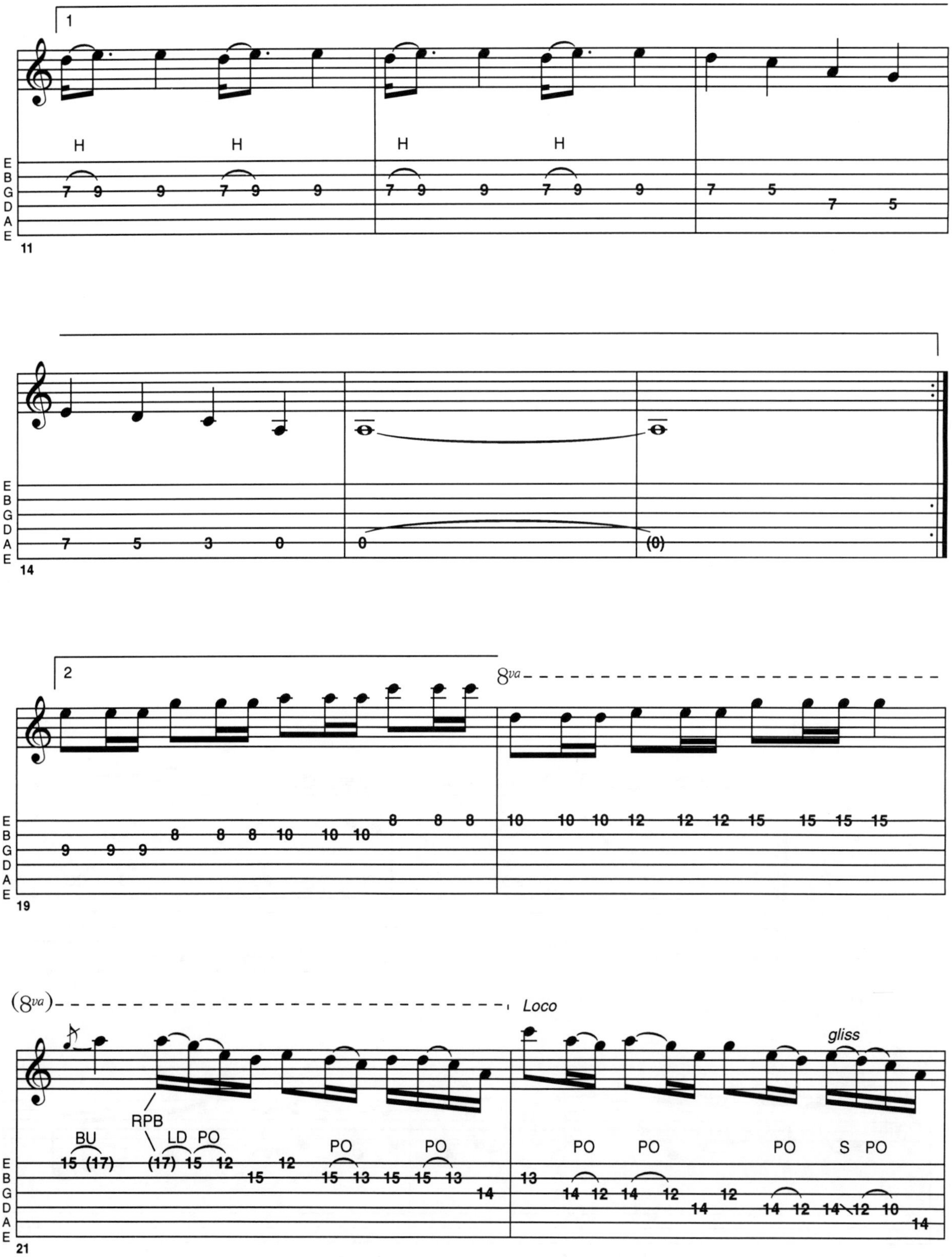
1
H H H H
E B G D A E
11
E B G D A E
14
2
8va
E B G D A E
19
(8va)
Loco
gliss
BU RPB LD PO PO PO PO PO PO S PO
E B G D A E
21

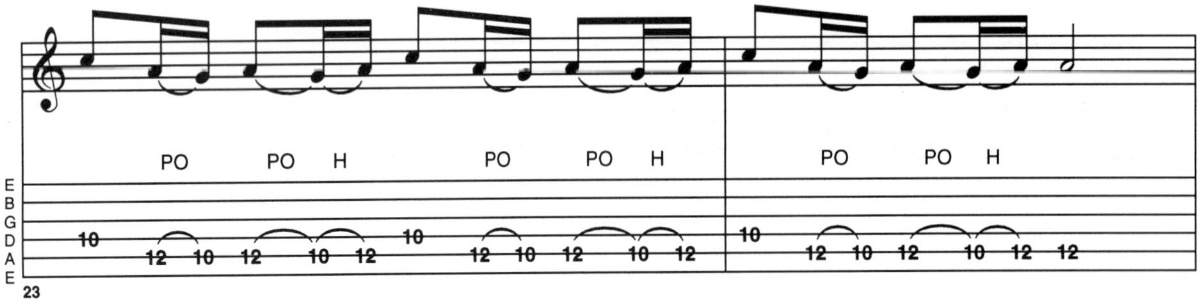

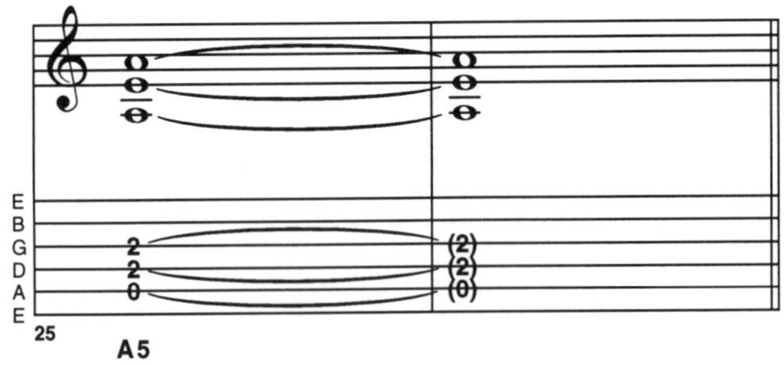

The main riff of the second section follows immediately on from that. The tempo's pretty quick, so be careful to keep those sixteenth notes nice and accurate. The main scale being used here is the E minor Pentatonic, but I also added the common additions of B♭ and F# (the flat fifth and major second respectively).

EX 2

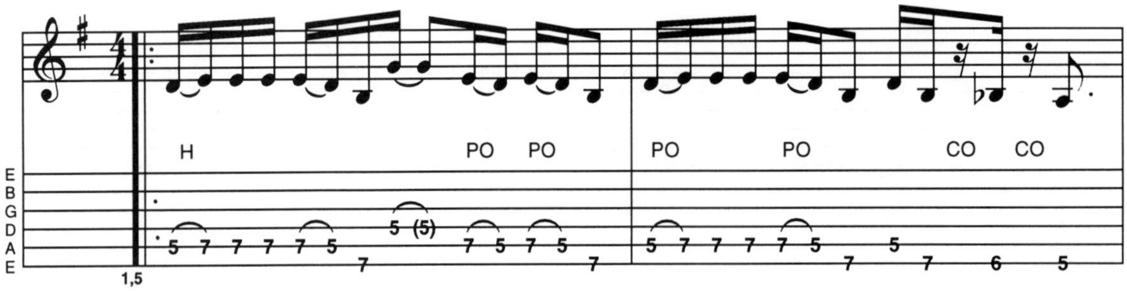

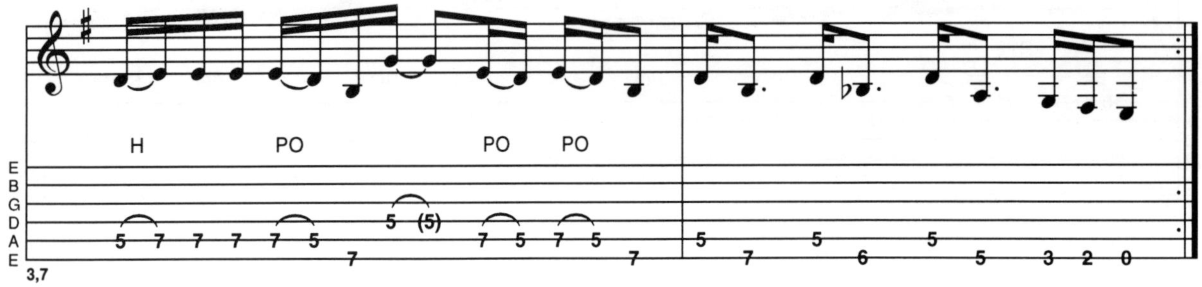

Now the verse part. In the following example, I've combined the main rhythm guitar part with the lead guitar fills which fit over the G5 chord. Even though I recorded these bits on two separate tracks for a more authentic layered effect, it should be possible to play this as a single, live part.

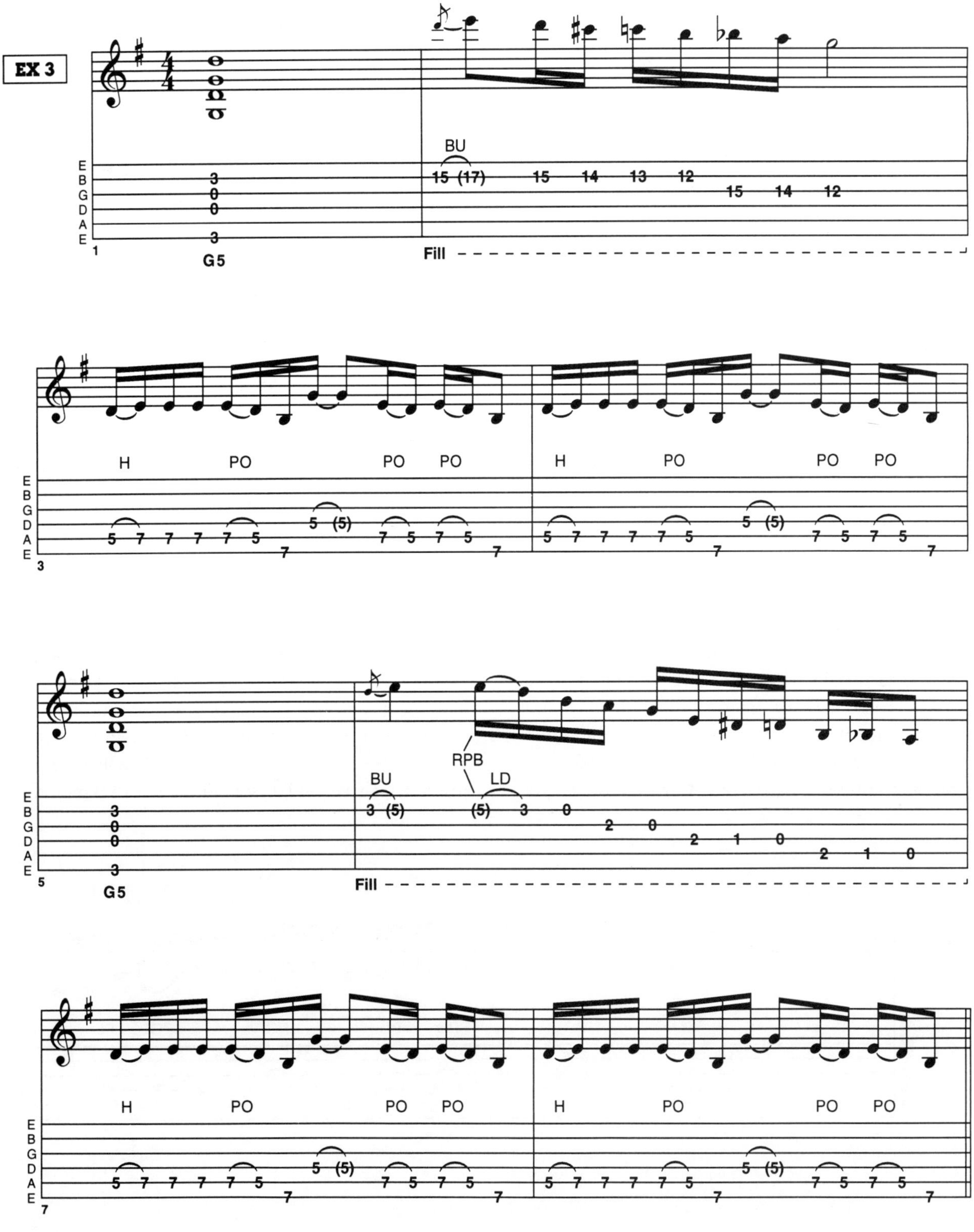

In order to bring in a contrasting feel for the chorus part, I dispensed with the pounding sixteenth notes and used a more sustained approach.

EX 4

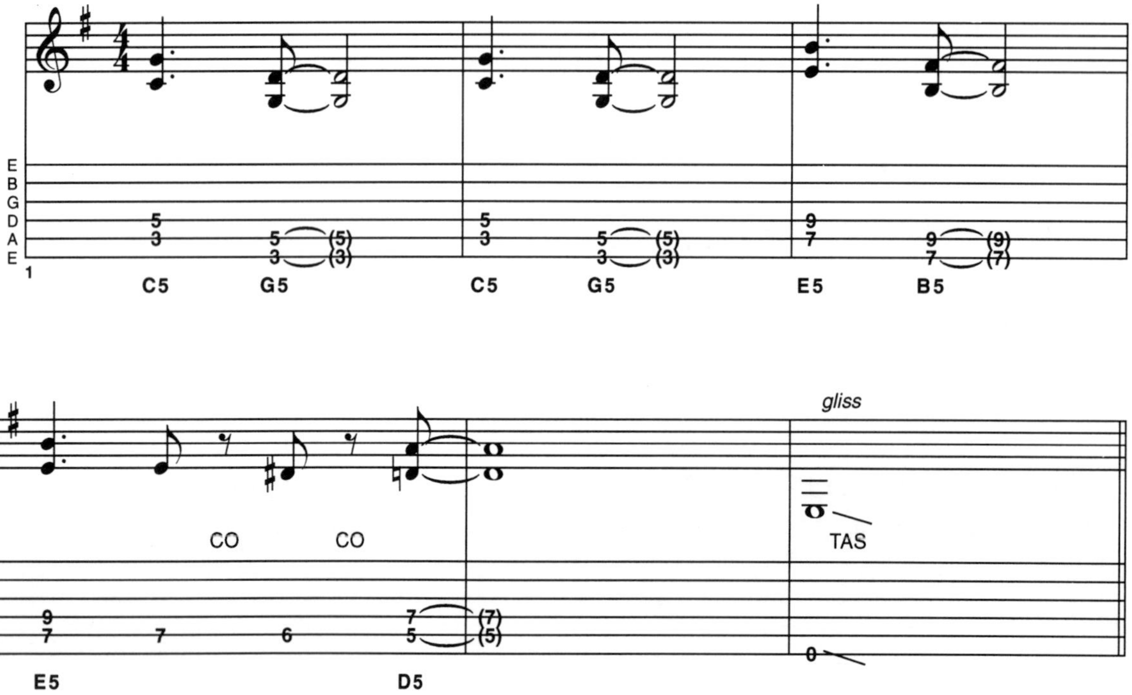

As you may have noticed, the musical information used so far in this piece is relatively simple; it's the "classic rock" fare of minor Pentatonic riffs and power chords. To my mind, one of the most compelling aspects of Queen was their ability to combine raucous hard rock with Chopin-esque romanticism and a bit of old-fashioned English camp – listen to the album *A Night At The Opera* for shining examples of all three categories. To introduce a few complexities into our Brian May-style piece, here's a two part solo section. The first part is just a standard eight-bar solo in the key of B minor...

EX 5

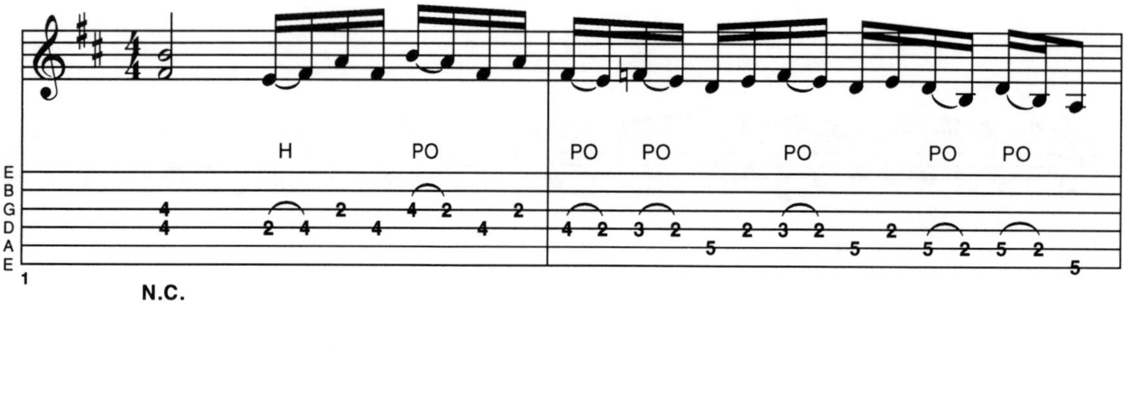

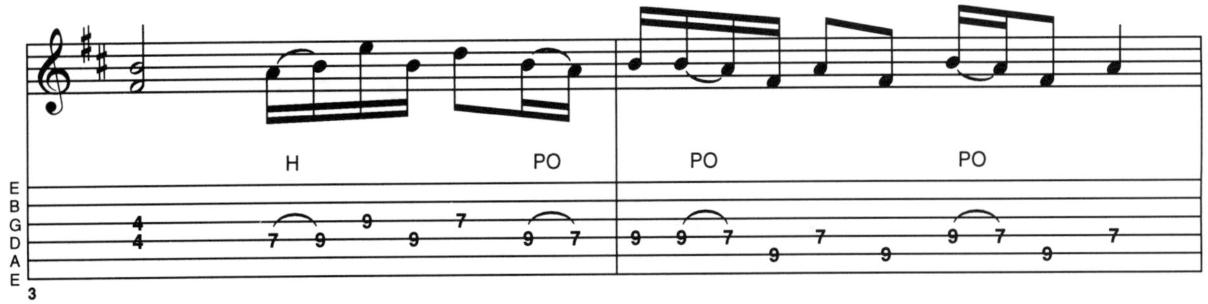

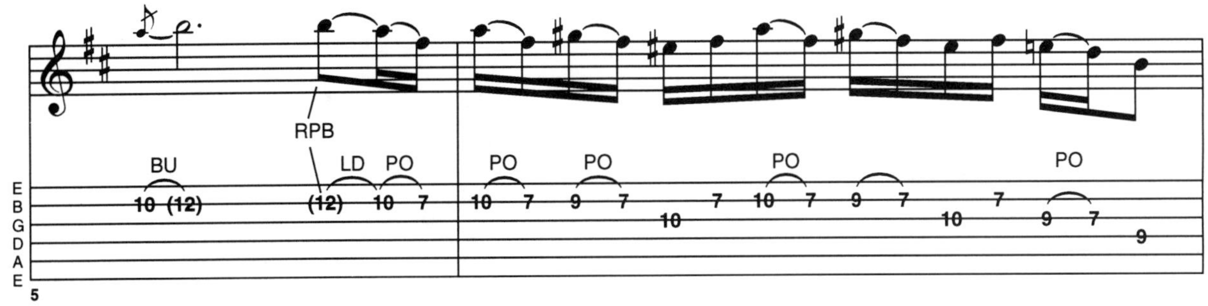

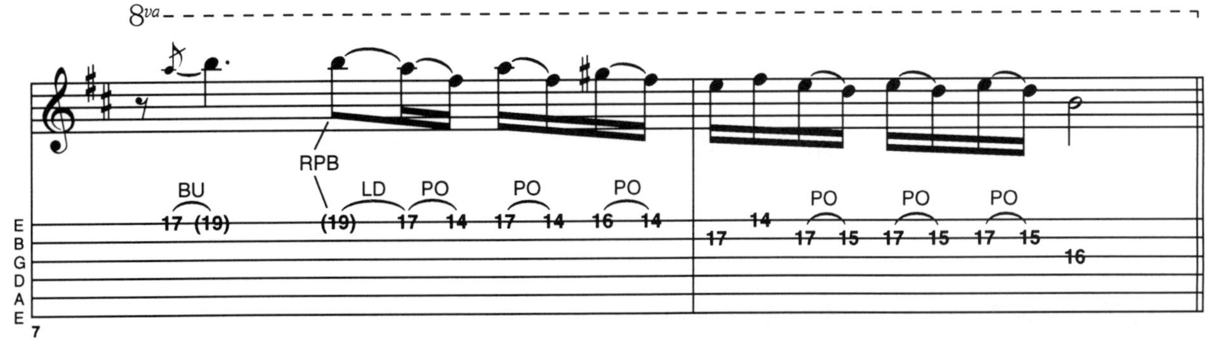

...while the second part, in the relative key of D major, introduces another of Brian's trademarks: those guitar harmonies. Explaining the various methods for writing harmonies would take up most of this book, so I'll just provide you with the transcription of what I played by way of an example. If you are interested in pursuing the matter further, there are plenty of books on basic harmony. They're usually fairly dry and deal mostly with classical music, but then again, most of Brian's parts seem to adhere to traditional theory. Here's the full guitar score...

EX 6

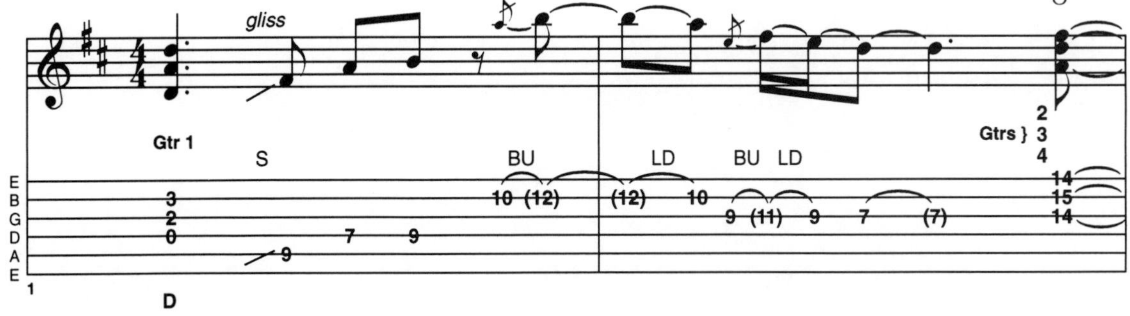

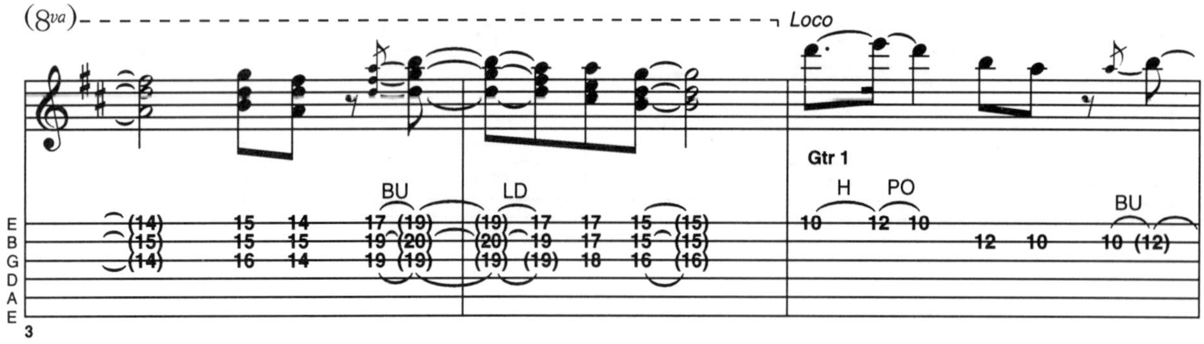

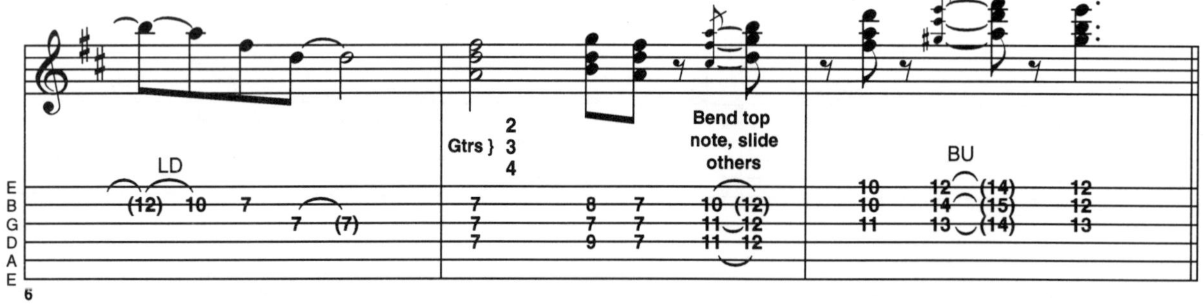

If you think that was complex, you obviously haven't heard just what Brian is capable of! After all that, I repeated the chorus and intro parts, before ending on an E5 chord.

Further Exploration

Back in his short-trousered days, Brian was a big fan of The Beatles, with Jimi Hendrix and Jeff Beck having the biggest effect on his guitar playing.

Every time you hear the sound of layered harmony guitars, you can bet your life that the person playing has spent several hours dissecting the complex parts found on Queen albums. Among the best-known players to give the musical nod in the direction of the world's favourite clog-wearer are Nuno Bettencourt, John Petrucci and Steve Vai.

Forget the unofficial Brian May sites – for the best in online Queen-related fun, get yourself along to the award-winning http://queen-fip.com where you'll find sounds pictures and even a game.

CHAPTER 16

Roger McGuinn

BORN:
13 July 1942.

ORIGIN:
Chicago, Illinois.

FIRST SPOTTED:
McGuinn was a bit of a teenage prodigy, with a successful career in folk music during the early sixties. He worked in New York for a while as a session musician and songwriter, before moving to California (with impeccable timing, seeing as certain parts of that state were shortly to become somewhat popular).

SEEN IN THE COMPANY OF:
Mainly just The Byrds – Roger proved to be the only constant in a frequently mutating band that also featured David Crosby, Gram Parsons and Clarence White at various times.

DISTINGUISHING FEATURES:
The unmistakable jingle-jangle of an electric twelve-string; in fact, the Rickenbacker 360/12 has become almost synonymous with Mr McGuinn.

CLAIM TO FAME:
Somehow, Roger managed to be there at the very genesis of some of the main developments in popular music during the sixties (he was more or less single-handedly responsible for a couple of them). Folk-rock, psychedelic pop, country-rock, making Bob Dylan songs listenable... our Roger had a hand in all of them.

THE GOOD BITS:
If only everyone who had a couple of blockbusting hits in the sixties had gone on to experiment with musical styles as much as Roger McGuinn, instead of thrashing away on the reunion tour circuit, desperately trying to ignite the flame.

THE BAD BITS:
It's a shame that a band with such a huge and varied back catalogue will be remembered primarily for just two songs: 'Mr Tambourine Man' and 'Eight Miles High'. Mind you, they're cracking songs.

NUTS AND BOLTS:
That old Rickenbacker 360/12. But I think you'd already gathered that.

VITAL VINYL:
Mr Tambourine Man and *Turn, Turn, Turn* (both 1965) are probably the definitive folk-rock albums; *The Notorious Byrd Brothers* (1968) features some of their best writing from a transitional period; *Ballad Of Easy Rider* (1969) is the band's country-rock classic.

I've already mentioned Roger's musical eclecticism and bemoaned the fact that most people only know The Byrds through a couple of big hits, so you're probably going to think I'm a bit of a hypocrite here. For the musical examples, I must admit I've leaned rather heavily on the styles and techniques found in 'Mr Tambourine Man' and 'Eight Miles High', not because the other stuff isn't valid, but for the simple reason that these aspects of Roger's playing live on in the sounds of so many other bands. Also, before we start, don't worry if you haven't got a twelve-string guitar. Obviously you won't get the exact sound, but that doesn't matter – Peter Buck of REM regularly plays McGuinn-style parts on a six-string. And remember the aim of this book? We're learning to interpret and be creative here; not to copy verbatim.

So... let's start with a pleasantly jangly, arpeggio-based intro. This is basically in the key of D major, so if you've learned your theory, you'll probably be wondering why there's a rogue C major chord in there, right? Well, er... I liked the sound of it! You'll find this sort of thing in literally thousands of major-key songs – adding a major chord built on the flattened seventh gives a much more hip and groovy sound than if you use the straight major scale/key. It also implies the way-cool Mixolydian mode (check out the Theory Primer if you're confused).

Chords used in Ex 1 & 5

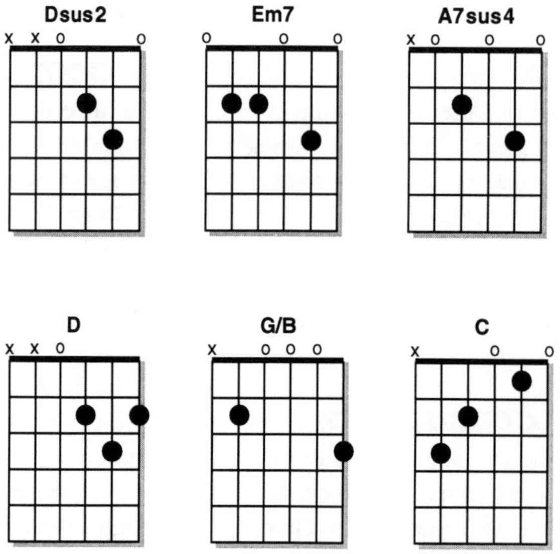

EX 1

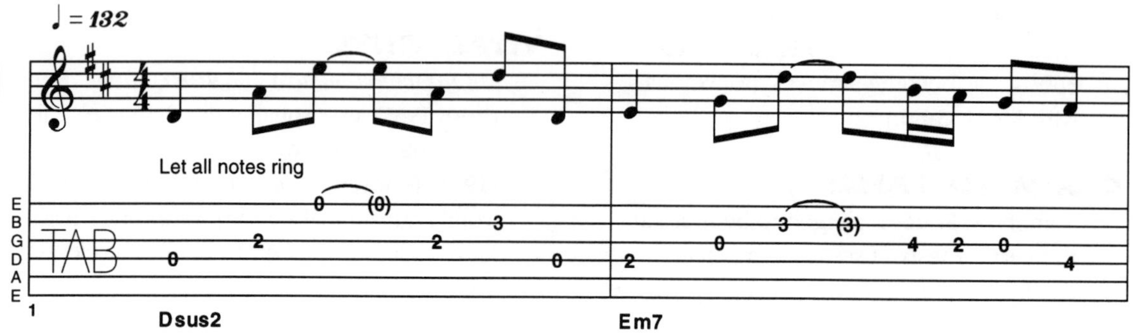

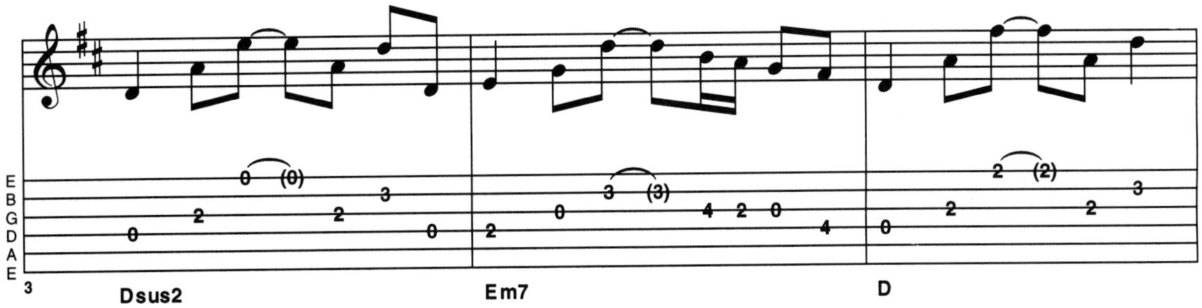

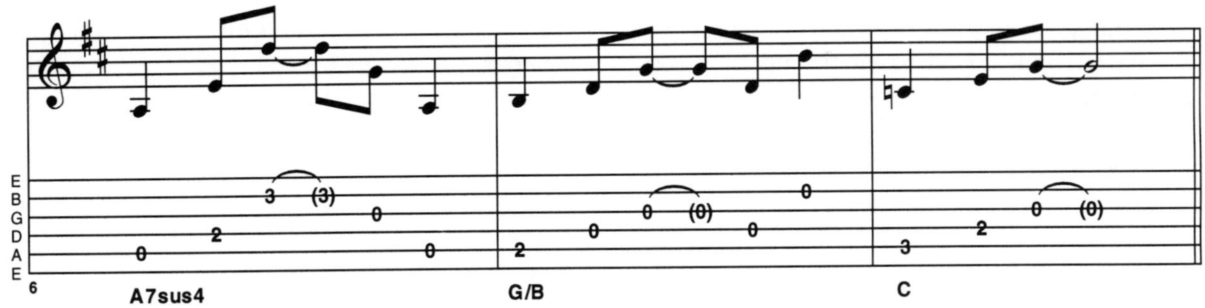

That's enough jingle-jangle-jingle for the moment, because it's time to get a bit spaced out (I was actually referring to the musical style, so please stop rummaging around in your parents' medicine cabinet). The next thing you'll hear on the CD is rhythm guitar #1 pounding away on a low open E string; after four bars this is joined by the more interesting rhythm guitar #2...

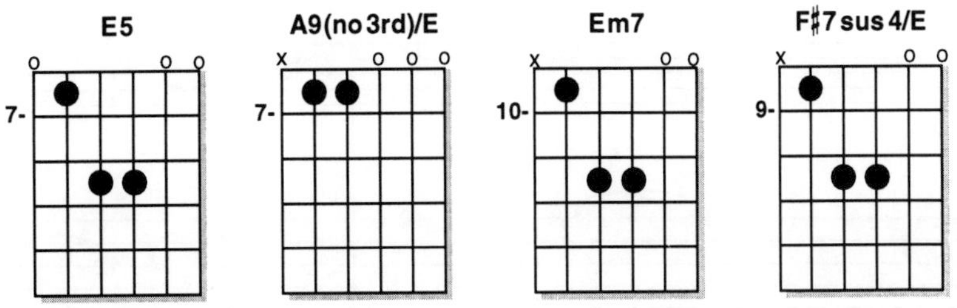

EX 2

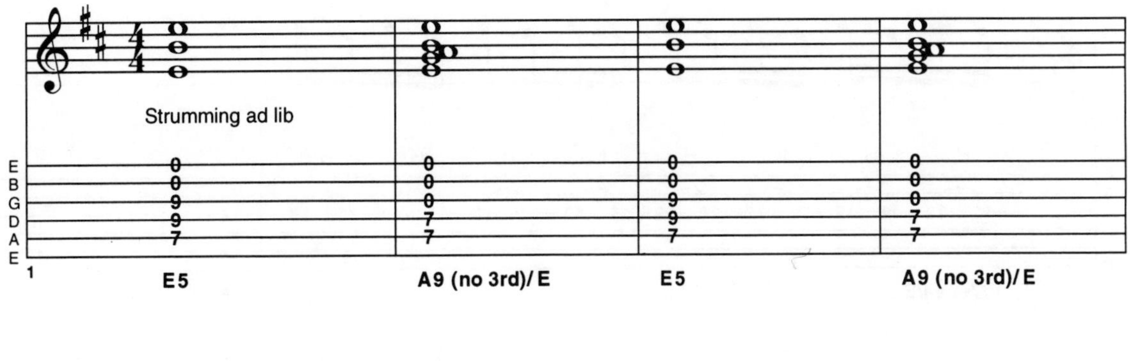

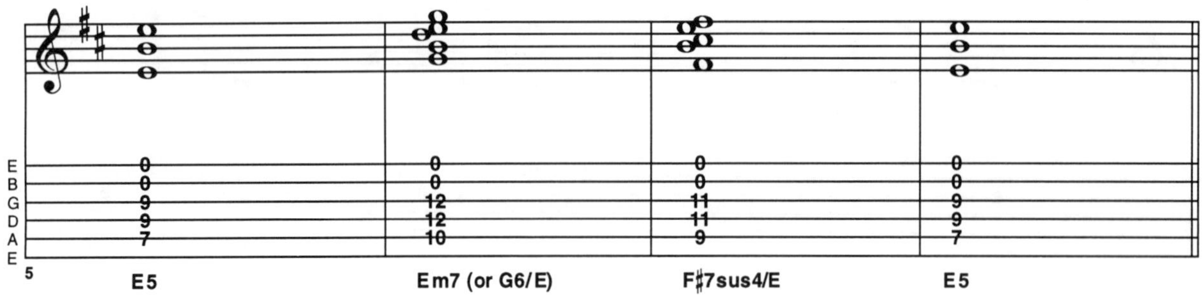

Even though all of those notes are from the key of D, the fact that it's all based around an E root means that we're using the E Dorian mode (E F# G A B C# D E – notice how it's just the D major scale seen from an E point of view). You can ignore all that technical stuff and just take my word for it if you like, or you could read the section on modes in the theory primer. Still using the E Dorian, I improvised a bit of a Coltrane-via-McGuinn-style solo...

EX 3

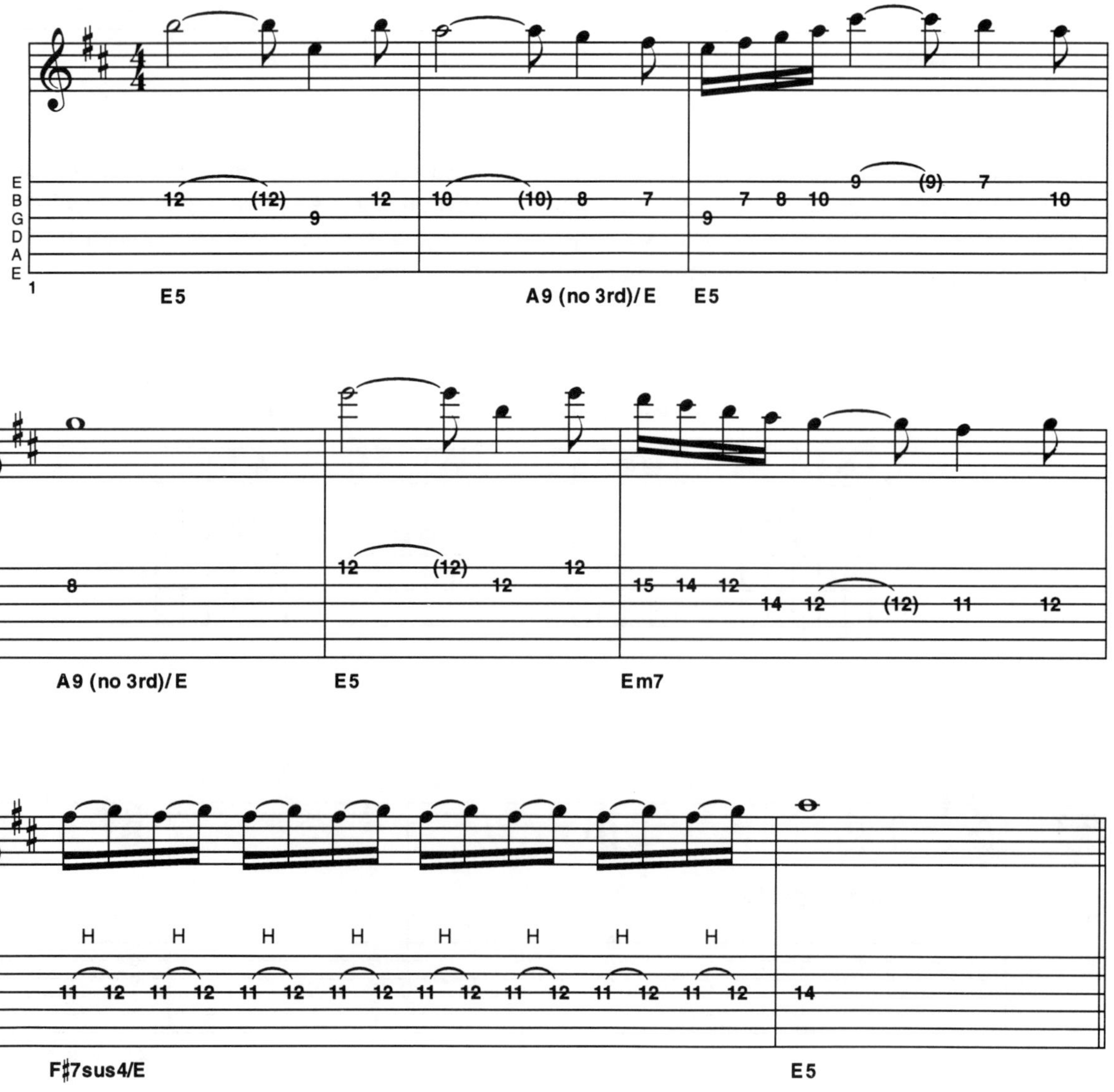

You and your friends can practise your three-part harmony vocals over the next couple of sections, if you like. Go on, have a go – I've always thought there was a certain ethereal beauty about the sound of dying cats. Anyway... here's a verse part.

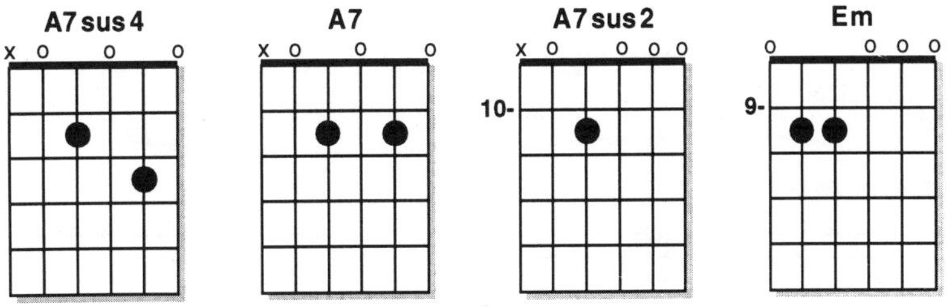

EX 4

And after the verse, you gotta have a chorus. In a fit of thematic-continuity-itis, I thought it would be nice to use those original intro chords for the chorus. (It also means I can clear off to the pub twenty minutes earlier.)

EX 5

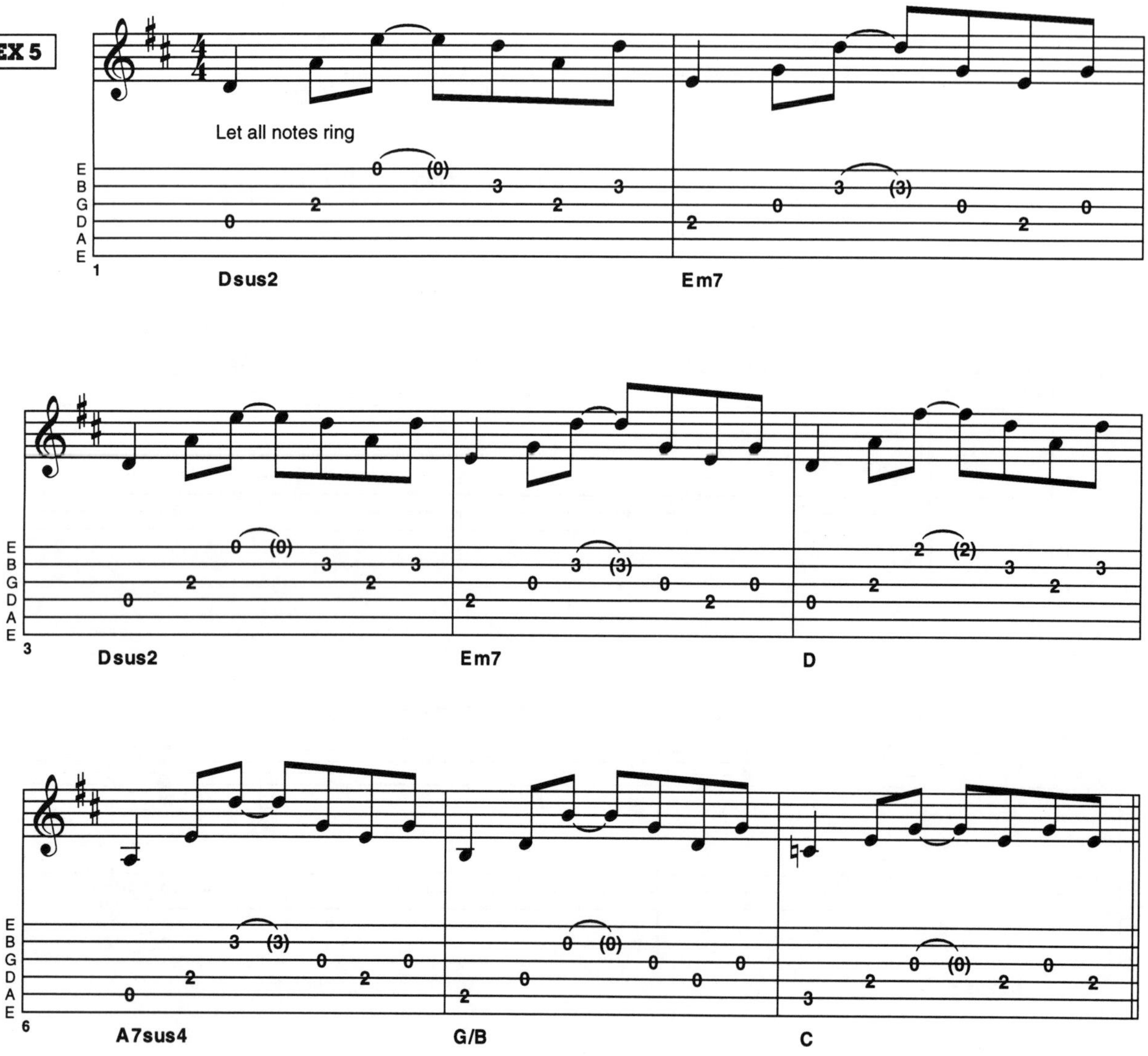

After that, I did another trippy solo. Unfortunately (for you) I'm not going to transcribe this one – instead, I'll give you the raw melodic material (the E Dorian mode) and leave you to figure it out yourself or just practise improvising your own solos. It's not as hard as you think!

EX 6

D MAJOR SCALE

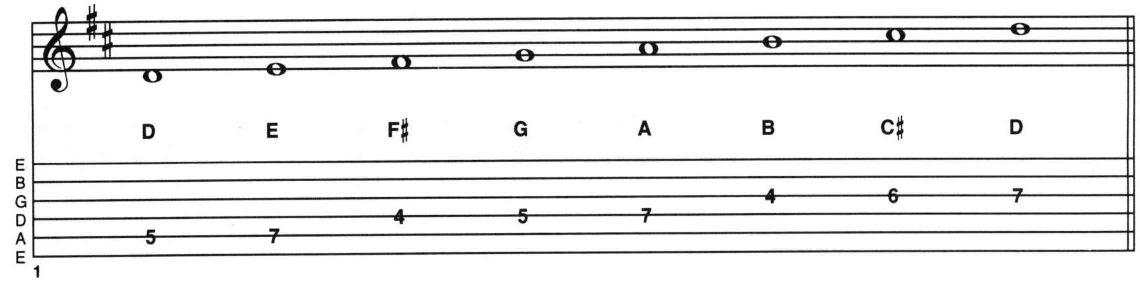

E DORIAN MODE

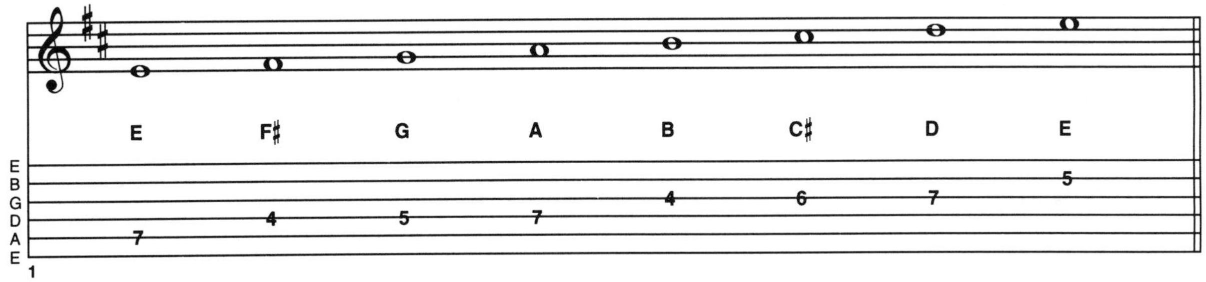

The main part of the tune then fizzles out as it began, with that hypnotic, low-E pedal tone. Just make sure you spend some time coming back down to earth before attempting to drive or operate machinery.

Further Exploration

It's difficult to be certain about who influenced Roger McGuinn's style, as it came about at a very fertile and experimental point in pop/rock history. Presumably the early sixties coffee-bar folkies were a major influence, in particular a certain Bob Dylan.

The other way round, things are much clearer. Just listen to anything by REM or Tom Petty for an example of how influential Roger has been.

In the cyberworld, Roger McGuinn/Byrds fans should count themselves lucky, as there's a lot of high-quality, well-written stuff out there. Start off by checking out http://mcguinn.com where you'll find loads of links, including one to the utterly fabulous Folk Den (or just go to http://www.uark.edu/~kadler/rmcguinn/FolkDen/index.html). The Folk Den is designed to maintain the traditional oral aspect of folk music (a noble aim in this sterile age), and the site contains plenty of sound files for you to listen to. Then, for even more fun, try http://pw2.netcom.com/~mcguinn/mars.html which actually seems to be written by Roger himself! I think we like this man, don't we?

CHAPTER 17

Scotty Moore

biography

TRACK 10

BORN:
27 December 1931.

ORIGIN:
Gasden, Tennessee.

FIRST SPOTTED:
While working at a cleaning plant in Memphis, Scotty met record producer Sam Phillips and was invited to become a session guitarist at the legendary Sun studios.

BIG BREAK:
Two years later, in 1954, Scotty and bassist Bill Black worked on some recordings backing a talented young singer from Tupelo, Mississippi...

CLAIM TO FAME:
Scotty's biggest contribution to popular music history was his playing on Elvis Presley's landmark "Sun Sessions". Music would never be the same again.

SEEN IN THE COMPANY OF:
Apart from his work with Elvis during the fifties and sixties, Scotty has kept a relatively low profile. He actually retired from music in 1968, but since his comeback in 1976 has done a handful of blues/rock 'n' roll sessions.

THE GOOD BITS:
Scotty occupies the same sort of place in guitar history as, say, Charlie Christian or Jimi Hendrix in that his playing was vitally important in defining a whole musical approach. His rapid-picked double stops, low-string boogie riffs and bluesy phrasing were influential, both on his contemporaries and on the young fans who learned from his playing, for example Jeff Beck, Jimmy Page and Robert Fripp.

THE BAD BITS:
Scotty tends to be very under-rated – they hadn't invented the concept of the "guitar hero" back in the fifties; even if they had, what chance would a member of Elvis Presley's backing band have of stealing the show?

NUTS AND BOLTS:
Scotty used a variety of archtop electrics with Elvis. For the earliest sessions he played a Gibson ES295; a year later he started using an L-5, which was then followed by a Super 400.

VITAL VINYL:
Most of the early Elvis Presley sessions have been remastered, repackaged and re-released ad nauseum (Elvis was rather famous, in case you hadn't realised) so you ought to be able to find some of Scotty Moore's playing simply by swinging a large fishing net around your head in a record store. To get a more complete picture, though, there are two compilations: *Elvis – The King Of Rock 'N' Roll: The Complete Fifties Masters* and *The Complete Sun Sessions*.

As I mentioned above, Elvis Presley's "Sun Sessions" turned out to be one of the high points of Scotty's career – one of the high points in the entire history of rock music, in fact. There was something about that high-energy mix of honky-tonk, blues and country that captured the imagination of the optimistic post-war America.

You only have to listen to Elvis's voice to realise that the blues formed a major part of his musical style, and this is reflected by the fact that many of those early songs are built around the standard twelve-bar I-IV-V progression. However, if you then add Scotty Moore's country- and jazz-influenced guitar lines to the stew, you get something totally original. For our Scotty Moore-style piece, I've used the I-IV-V in the key of A, as I'm sure many of you are already familiar with that progression. Here's the first verse (that's right – there's no intro, they kept things lean and mean in those days).

Chords used in this chapter

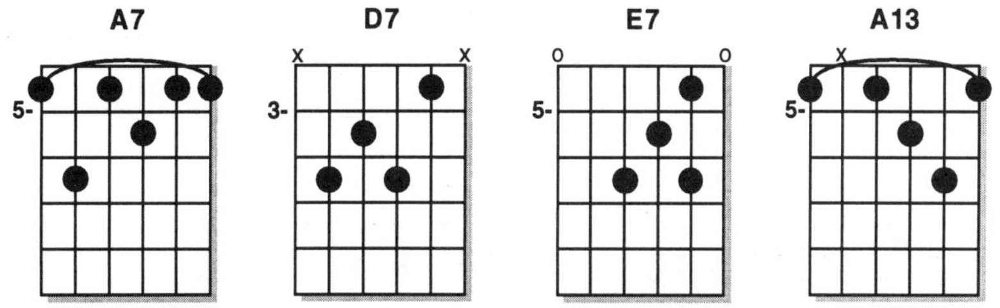

EX 1

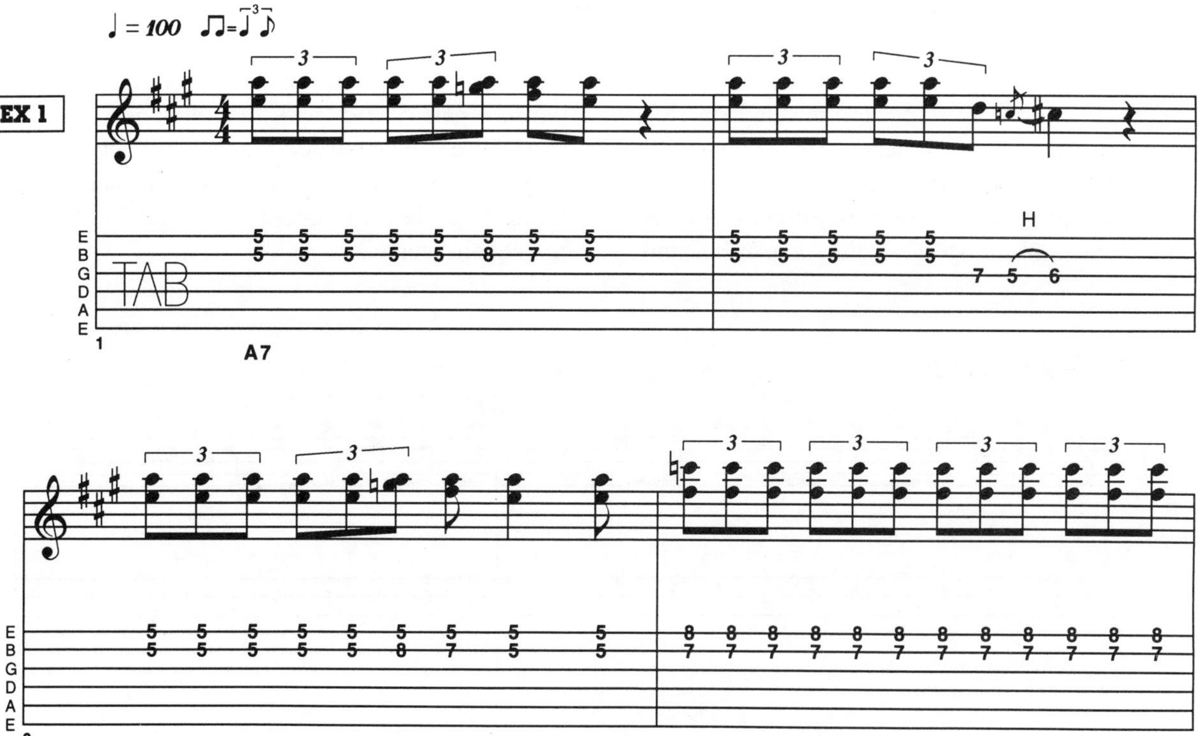

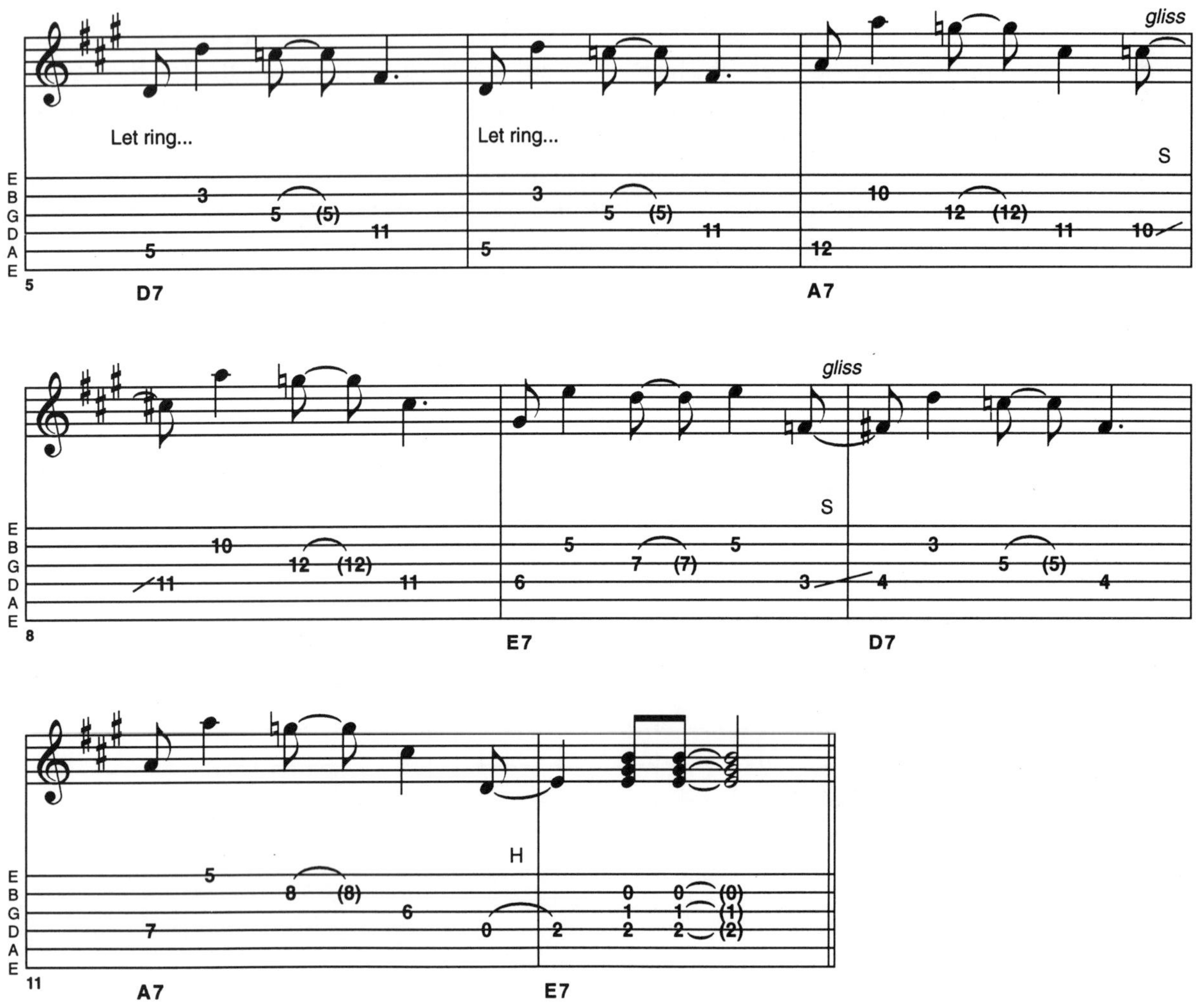

Just to give you a bit of background information on what was going on there... for the first four bars, I used a lot of double stops (playing two notes at once). This aspect of Scotty's playing had a major influence on younger players, and became part of the "rock 'n' roll style". For the rest of the twelve-bar sequence, I basically played through the chords, but using a laid back arpeggio style reminiscent of rockabilly. Here's the second verse...

EX 2

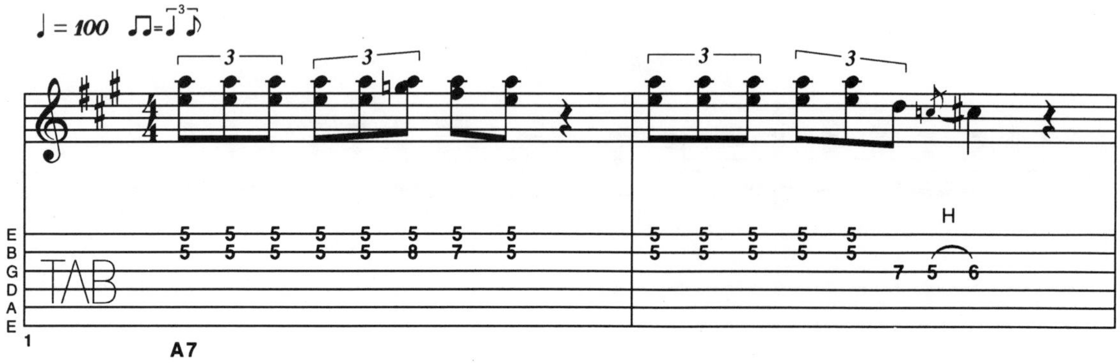

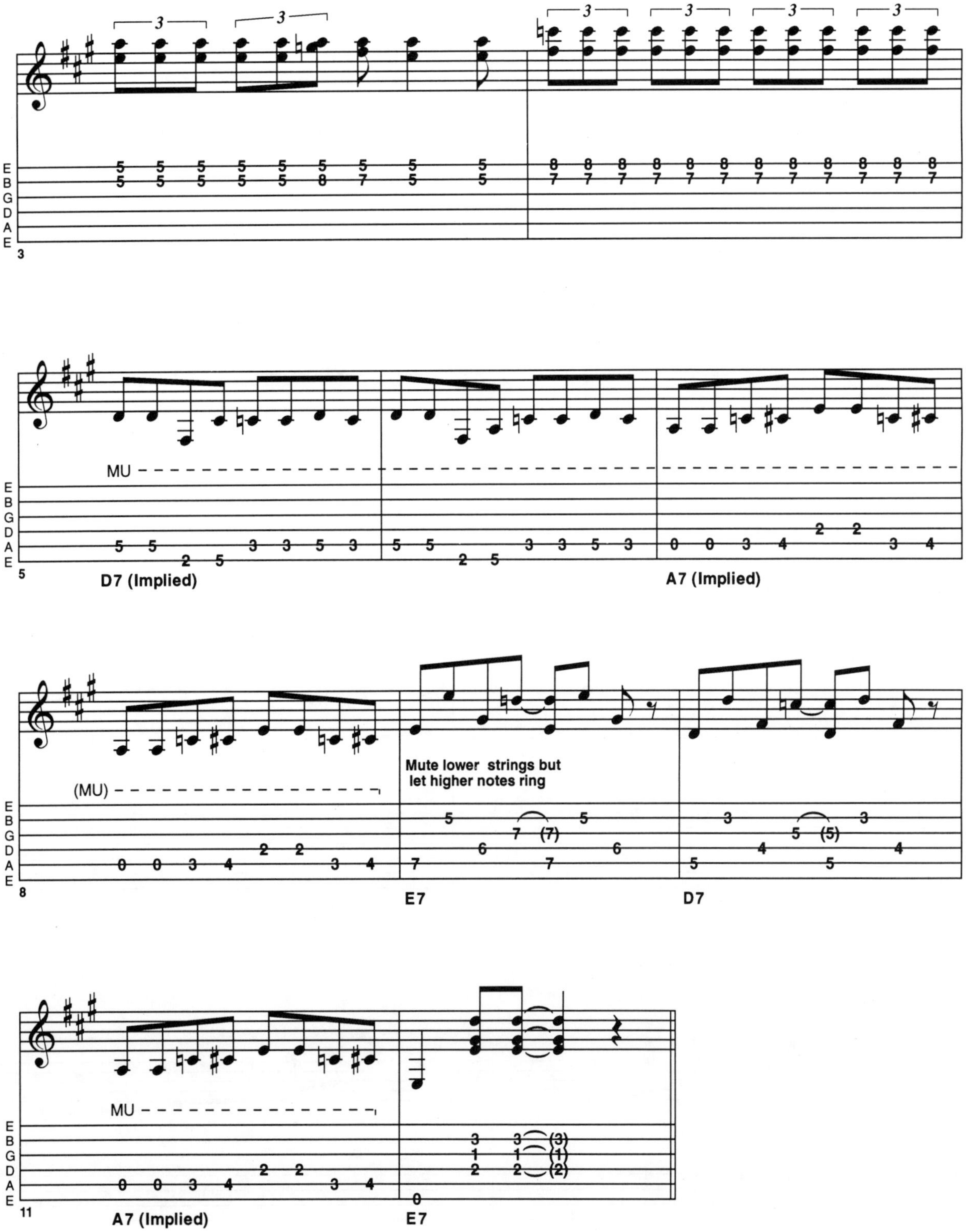
MU
D7 (Implied)
A7 (Implied)
(MU)
Mute lower strings but
let higher notes ring
E7
D7
MU
A7 (Implied)
E7

Although I started in the same way, by using double stops for those four bars of A, I went off on a couple of tangents after that. First, I used some muted bass-string runs – perfect for suddenly introducing a tighter feel. Then, for the turnaround section (that's the E – D – A bit at the end) I played the chords using a bit of rockabilly-style fingerpicking. To avoid having to put down my pick, though, I used "hybrid picking" here – using my pick along with my second and third fingers. Give it a try, it works almost anywhere as a substitute for standard fingerpicking. Time for a solo, I think...

EX 3

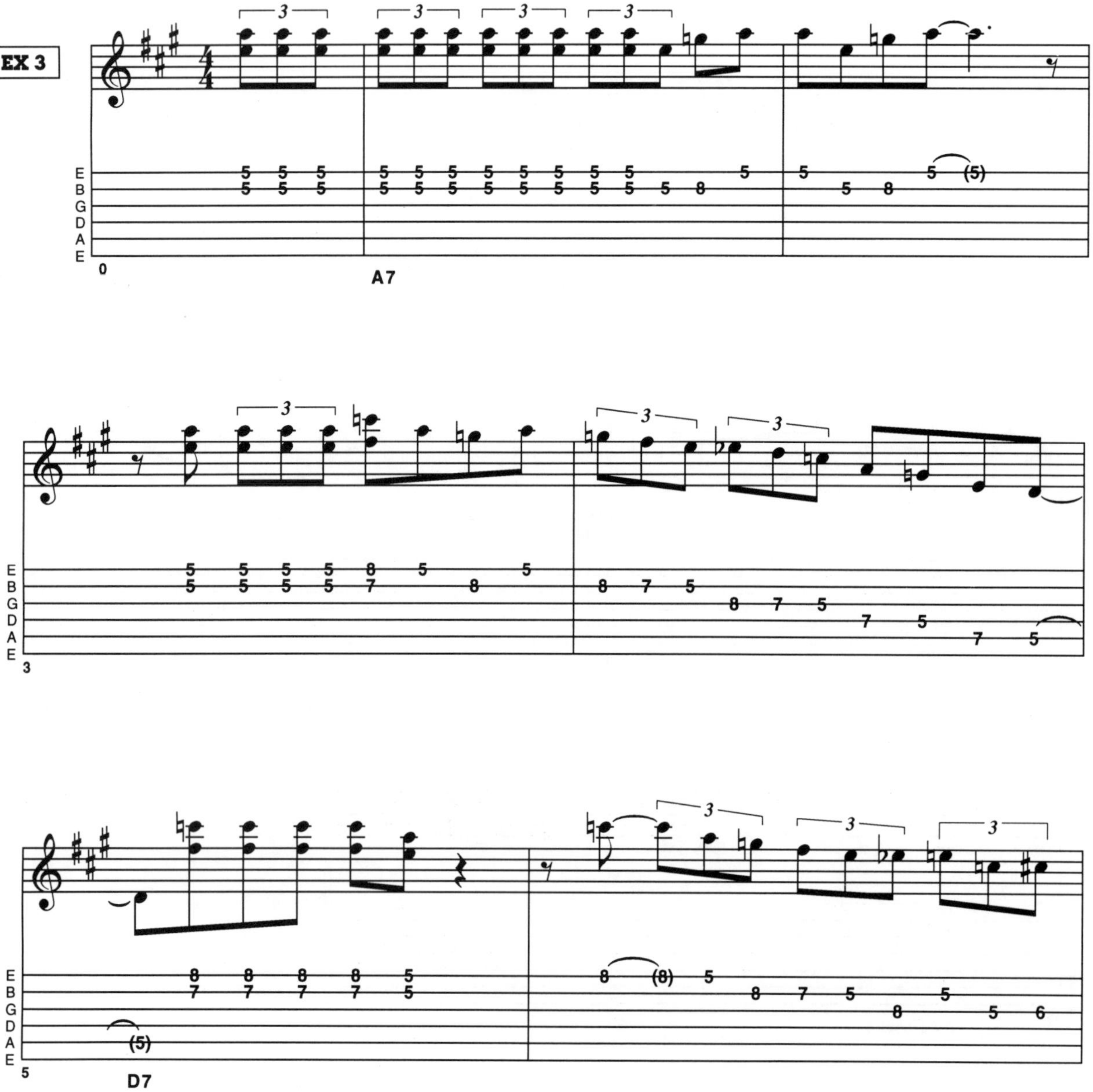

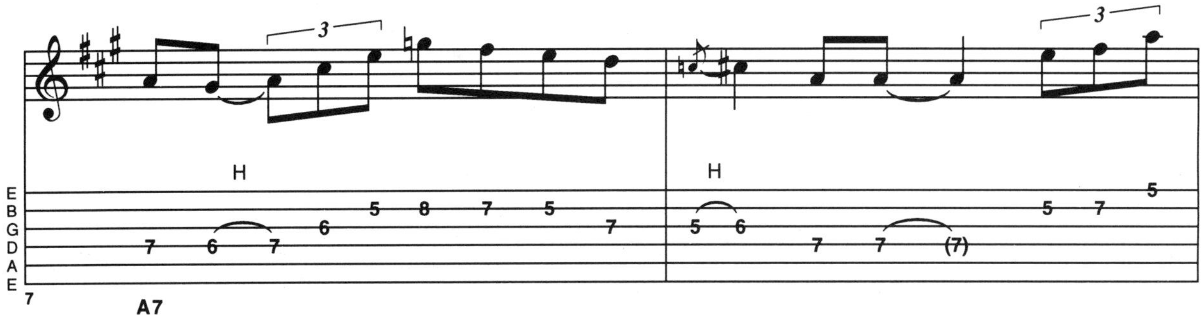

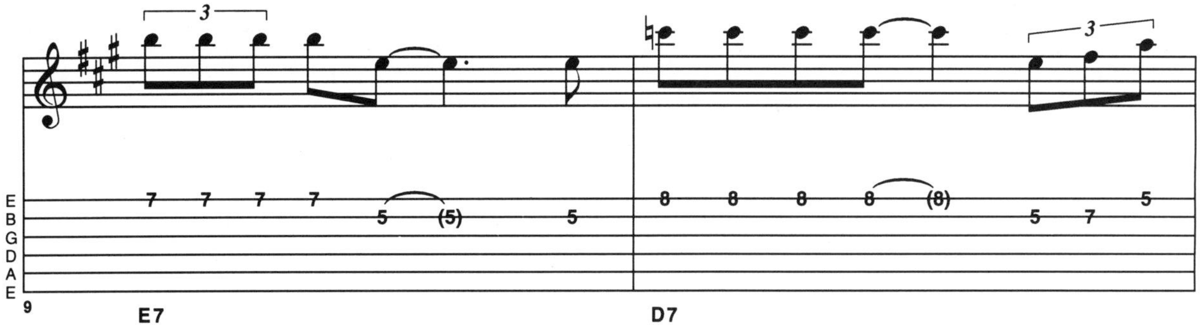

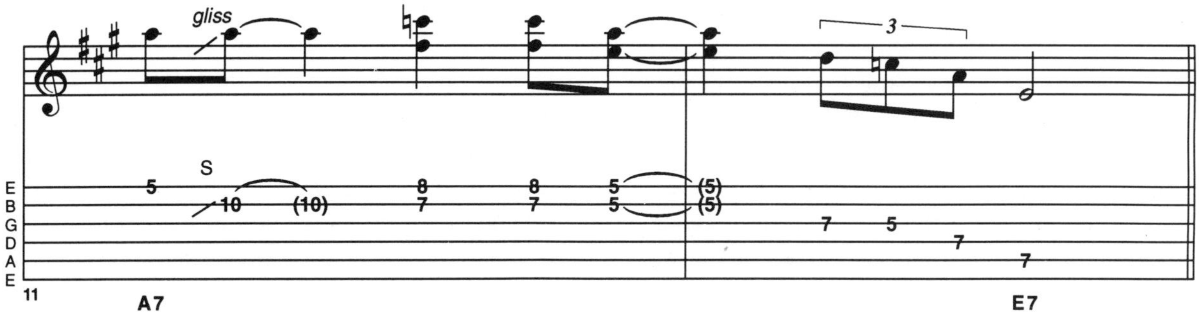

If you've only ever played blues-type solos using the plain old minor Pentatonic, you'll probably be surprised at the amount of extra notes there. Don't forget, though, that Scotty had a background in country and pop as well as blues, and his note choices often reflect this. The scale used here is a kind of hybrid – by combining the notes of both the A minor Pentatonic (A C D E G A) and the A major Pentatonic (A B C# E F# A), you get something like this...

EX 4A

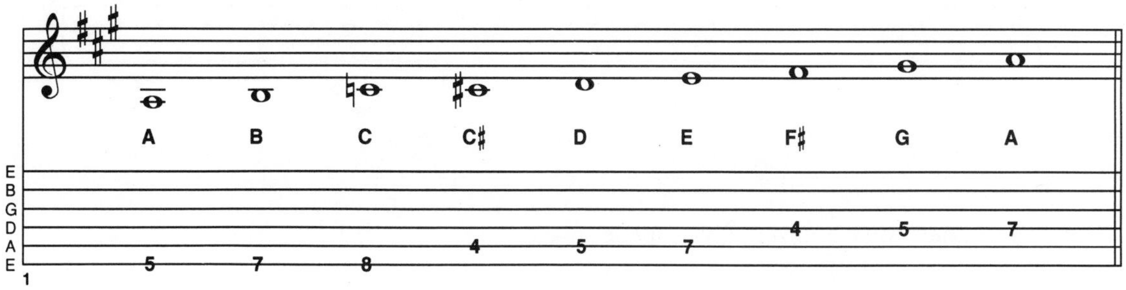

And by adding the bluesy "flat 5" note (in this case E♭) you get the following:

EX 4B

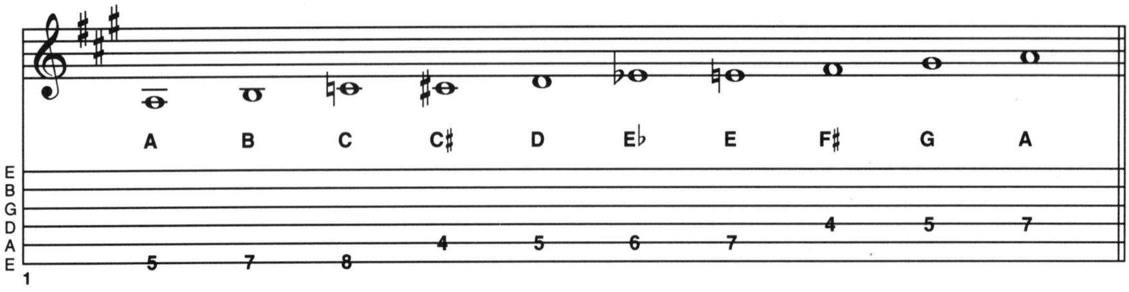

Now, you wouldn't use that to play long scalar melodies as you would with a standard major or minor scale, as not all the notes will work everywhere in the twelve-bar progression. Instead, it's the perfect scale for extracting cool licks from. For instance, the C to C# hammer-on is especially effective over the A chord, as in bar 8. If you play standard minor Pentatonic licks but replace all the G notes with F# notes, you get a cheery country-type sound that fits both the D and A chords. There's loads more so just experiment and see what comes out. By the way, if you're wondering why I haven't mentioned the rogue G# in bar 7... well, it's not really theoretically correct, but Scotty used it on his 'Hound Dog' solo and it sounds good, so what the hell!

For the final verse, I simply mixed together a few of the techniques and approaches from the first two verses – see if you can figure out what I did. There is one part where I departed from the previous pattern; over the last two bars of the progression, I played this little ending.

EX 5

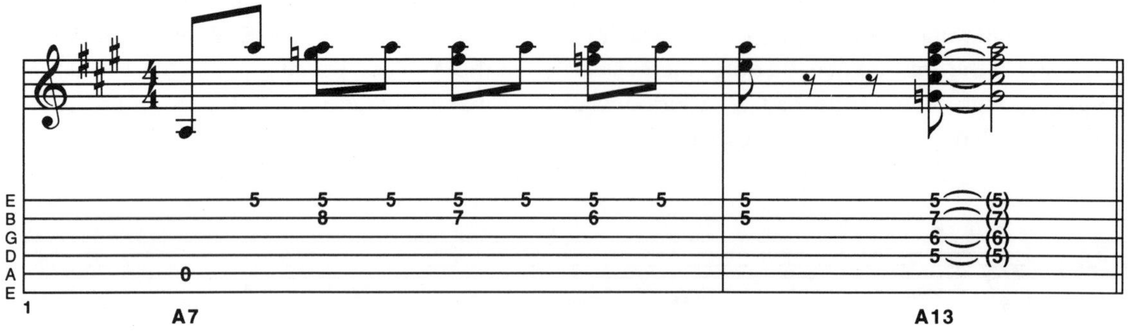

There. All you need now is a pair of blue suede shoes.

Further Exploration

Scotty was influenced by a wide range of musicians: country pickers Merle Travis and Chet Atkins, blues players BB King and Muddy Waters, jazzers Tal Farlow, Johnny Smith and Barney Kessel... but he has always attempted to take these styles and add his own spin to them, rather than just copying them outright. A lot of this, he admits, is due to his own limitations, but I think we can all learn from that attitude, can't we, folks?

Playing guitar behind the one and only King Of Rock 'N' Roll™ guarantees a certain amount of prime-time exposure, and Scotty's six-string approach to this new musical style provided the initial germ of musical inspiration for countless young listeners: Jeff Beck, Jimmy Page, Keith Richards and Robert Fripp, to name a few.

Unfortunately, one of the most important guitarists of all time doesn't seem to be particularly well-represented on the Web. Looks like you'll have to try scouring through the boundless stream of Elvis sites – you're on your own with this one!

CHAPTER 18
Jimmy Page

biography TRACK 16

BORN:
9 January, 1944.

ORIGIN:
Heston, Middlesex.

FIRST SPOTTED:
Jimmy joined Neil Christian's Crusaders, in 1960. This was his first real band, but within a few years, he had become one of Swinging London's most prolific session guitarists, playing on hit records by artists such as Van Morrison and Them, The Kinks, Donovan and Burt Bacharach.

SEEN IN THE COMPANY OF:
Just in case you're really, really new to the world of guitar, Jimmy Page's most famous playmates were Robert Plant, John Paul Jones and John Bonham, the foursome going by the name of Led Zeppelin. Just prior to forming Led Zep, Jimmy had played bass and later guitar in the final Yardbirds line-up (also featuring Jeff Beck for a time). In the post-Zeppelin years, Jimmy has worked on a variety of projects: The Firm (with Paul Rodgers), the *Coverdale/Page* album and the ambitious Page/Plant reunion, to name but a few.

THE GOOD BITS:
Like Steve Howe of Yes, Jimmy is often the victim of generalisations made on the basis of Led Zeppelin's assumed "category". If you think Led Zep were a heavy metal band, listen to the enormous helpings of folk, country, blues and Indian music in Jimmy's playing. Also, Jimmy Page is possibly the greatest arranger/producer rock music has ever known – all of the Led Zeppelin albums are masterpieces of tone and texture, light and shade. Listen very carefully to them if you don't believe me.

THE BAD BITS:
With such a lot to live up to, the post-Zep career has never shown a similar spark. Then again, there's no reason why it should have to – Jimmy did more for rock music in eleven years than most people could do in a lifetime.

NUTS AND BOLTS:
Jimmy's perhaps best known for his sunburst Gibson Les Paul Standards, but he's also spent a lot of time with a Fender Telecaster in his hands – the famous 'Stairway To Heaven' solo was played on a Tele. Apart from that, there's the good old Gibson ES1275 double-neck and the Danelectro used for live performances of 'White Summer/Black Mountainside'. Amps tend to be Marshalls.

VITAL VINYL:
Simple. Just listen to all the Led Zeppelin albums. Every single one contains some fine examples of guitar playing, songwriting, arranging and production.

Apart from being a genius songwriter, producer and arranger, Jimmy Page came up with some unforgettable guitar riffs – 'Black Dog', 'Houses Of The Holy', 'The Ocean' and 'Good Times, Bad Times' being just a handful of his best. And now you're sitting there, expecting me to come up with something of similar stature, right? Oh dear. Here's something which hints at Jimmy's style on the later Led Zeppelin albums – I just hope your drummer's up to the task!

If you disregard the chords at the end of bar 2, this part could easily sound like one of those meaty Les Paul-plus-Marshall riffs from the earlier Led Zep records, but the more complex harmonies reflect some of the sounds Jimmy was using on the albums *Houses Of The Holy* and *Physical Graffiti*.

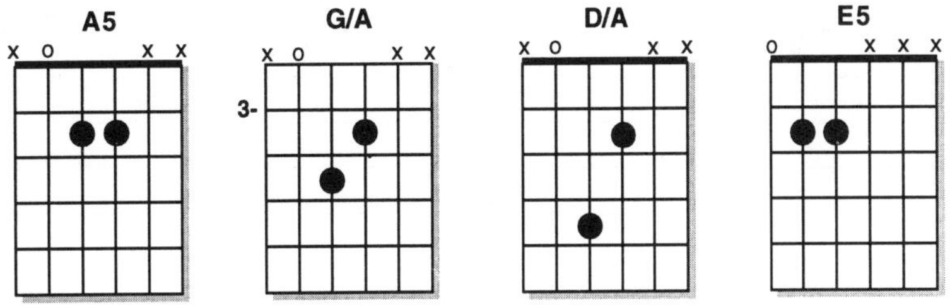

EX 1

For the chorus part, I've smoothed things out a little by using some dreamy, open-string-laden chords and a much cleaner tone. If you're ever stuck for an interesting-sounding chord, there's a great deal of mileage to be had from taking a boring familiar old chord shape and adding a couple of open strings here and there. Unless you really know your theory, you'll have to use a bit of trial and error, but hey, that's all part of the fun! For instance, the first two chords on each line actually started life as standard "E-shape" barre chords, but I let the E and B strings ring open, added an open A string as a pedal bass and nixed the low E string altogether. Most of the other chords are just mini shapes played over more droning bass notes.

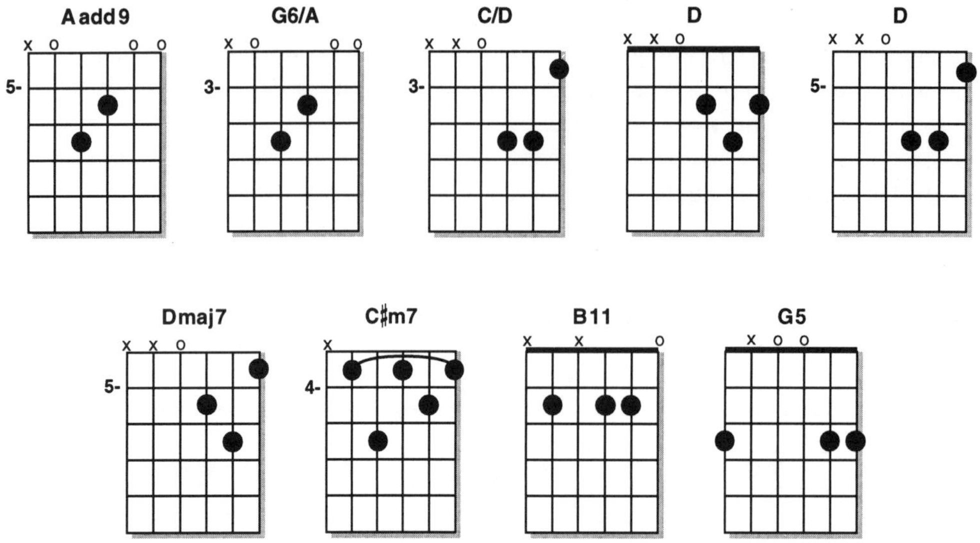
Aadd9
G6/A
C/D
D
D
Dmaj7
C♯m7
B11
G5

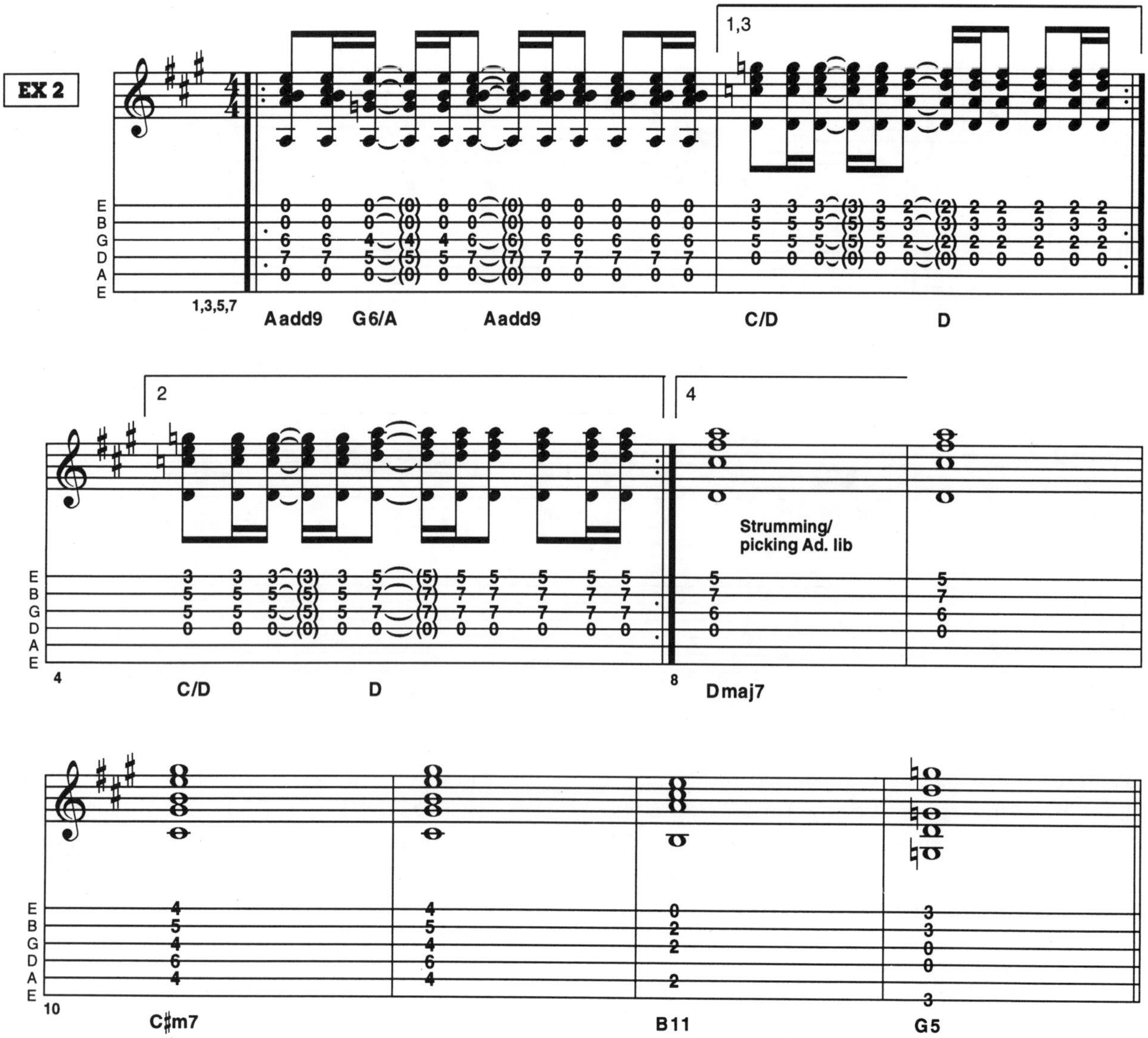
EX 2
1,3
2
4
Strumming/
picking Ad. lib
1,3,5,7
Aadd9
G6/A
Aadd9
C/D
D
C/D
D
Dmaj7
C♯m7
B11
G5

The great thing about using lots of open strings like this is that they stay constant, so as you move the chord shapes around, the relationships between the fretted notes and open notes are constantly changing, resulting in some quite unexpected sounds.

Next here's a Jimmy Page-style solo for you to get your teeth into. One of the most enduring features of Jimmy's playing is the way he often uses notes from both the major and minor Pentatonic scales. There are two ways of doing this: if you add the occasional major Pentatonic note to a primarily minor Pentatonic line – especially the major third and sixth (C# and F# in the key of A) – you'll be doing something that countless blues players have done for years – it's all part of making a largely minor-based melody fit over major chords. If you do the opposite, starting out with the major Pentatonic as a basis and sneaking in the occasional minor Pentatonic note – usually the minor third or minor seventh (C and G in the key of A) – the result will be more reminiscent of country playing. Maybe it's got something to do with the countless sessions Jimmy played in the mid sixties, I don't know, but you can find examples of both approaches in his playing.

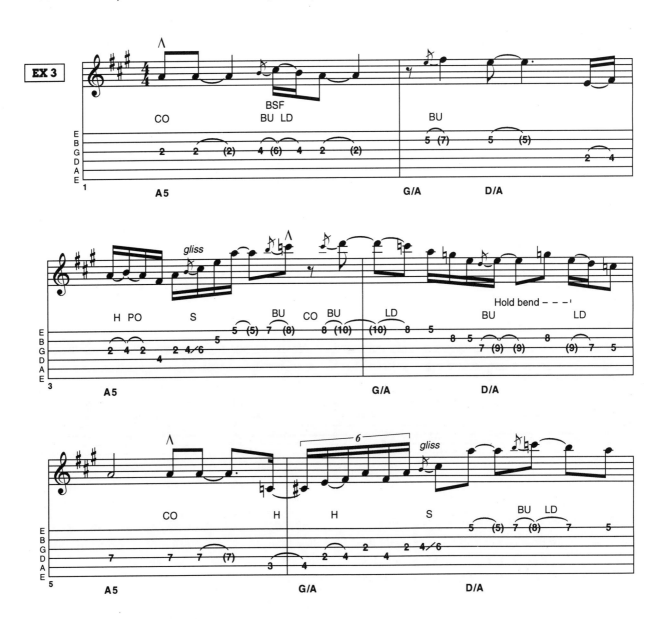

EX 3

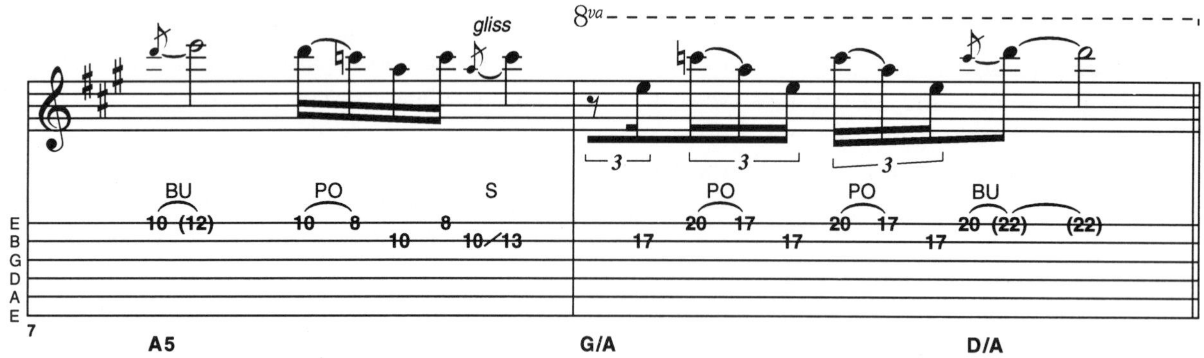

To help you get used to this method of combining both major and minor Pentatonic scales, here are some practice ideas...

First of all, you need to know the basic box positions for both scales. The easiest way is to use the same shape for both, with the major version being positioned three frets below its minor equivalent (shown here in the key of A).

EX 4A

A MINOR PENTATONIC

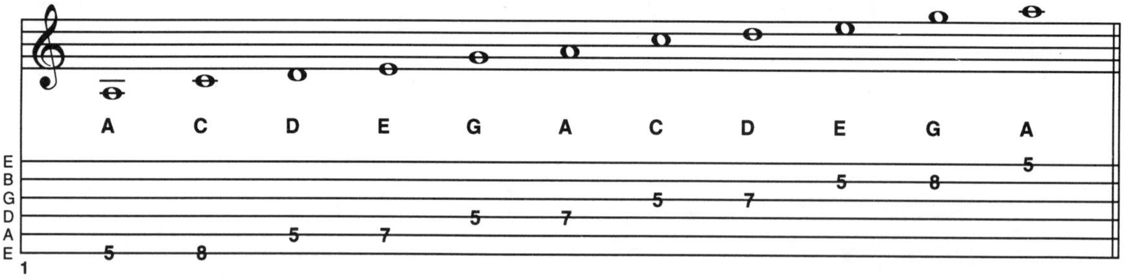

A MAJOR PENTATONIC

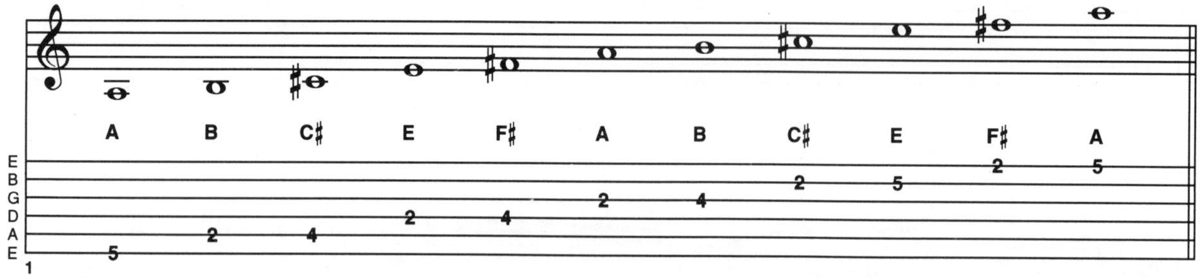

Then, work out how you can add to each scale the extra notes borrowed from the other scale. (I've just concentrated on the four main notes listed above, but if you work out where all of the other notes lie, you'll have a whole new fingering for each scale).

A MINOR PENTATONIC, WITH MAJOR 3rd AND MAJOR 6th ADDED

EX 4B

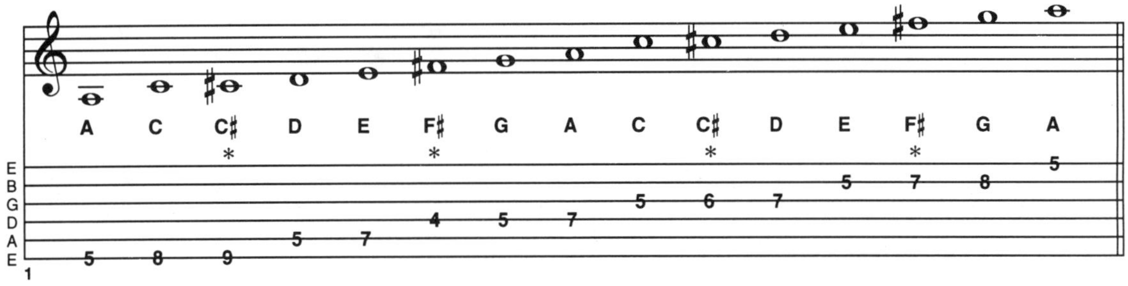

A MAJOR PENTATONIC WITH MINOR 3rd AND MINOR 7th ADDED

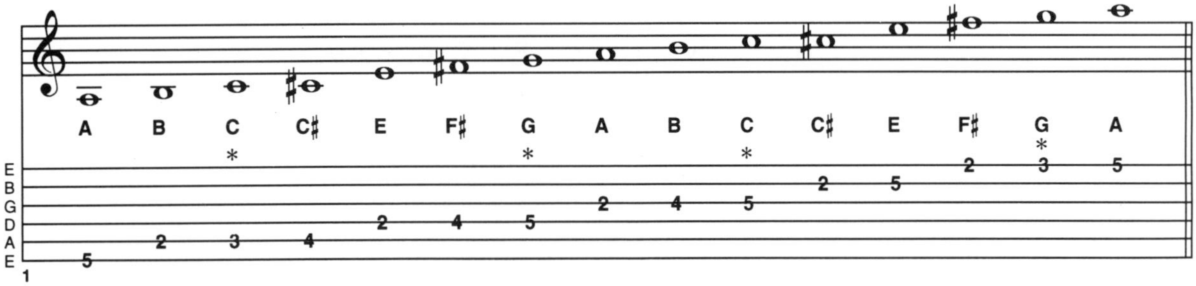

All you have to do now is work out a few cool licks!

Getting back to our Jimmy Page-style tune, here's the slightly different chorus part I used right at the very end. Although songs usually end on the tonic chord (that's the chord built on the root note) I decided to end on the F chord, for a less predictable effect.

FINAL CHORUS ONLY

EX 5

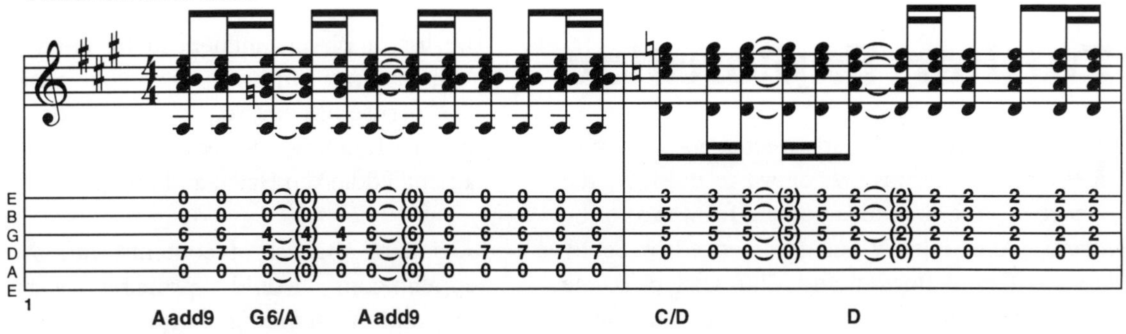

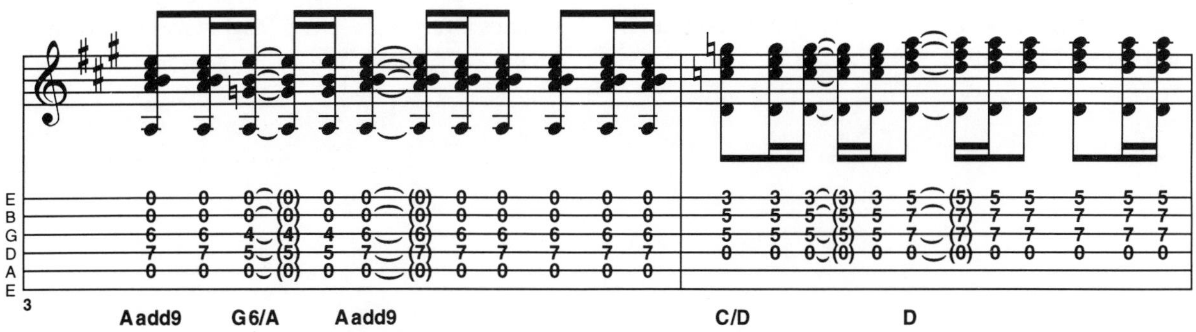

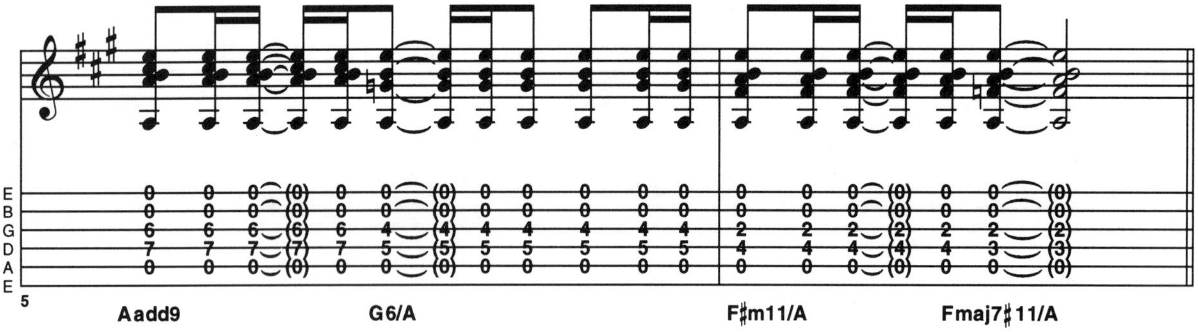

Chords mostly as Ex 2 except:

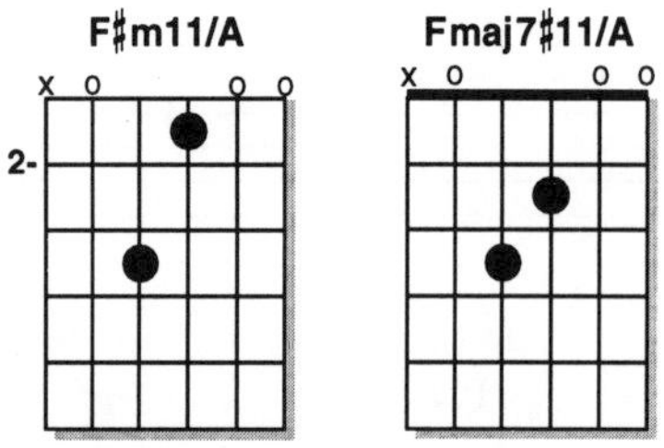

And there you go. Hey, those sequinned bell-bottoms really suit you.

Further Exploration

In common with many teenagers in 1950s Britain, Jimmy was first drawn to music by the new rock 'n' roll sounds coming from across the Atlantic. After initially being influenced by Scotty Moore, James Burton and Cliff Gallup (Gene Vincent's guitarist) he broadened his listening to include studio genius Les Paul, blues players Hubert Sumlin, Otis Rush and the three Kings, and acoustic fingerpickers Bert Jansch, John Renbourn and Davey Graham.

The list of players influenced by Jimmy Page is staggering, not surprising when you consider how his expertise has covered so many fields. The best known of Jimmy's followers are Steve Vai, Joe Satriani, Eddie Van Halen and Slash.

Judging by the list of contents, http://www.led-zeppelin.com would probably leave the competition standing, with its promise of biographies, pictures, sounds, rare videos etc. That is, it would if I could get into it – my computer crashes every time I try. Maybe you'll have more luck.

CHAPTER 19

Joe Satriani

BORN:

15 July 1956.

ORIGIN:

Long Island, New York.

FIRST SPOTTED:

Joe first came to our attention with the credit card-funded 1986 album *Not Of This Earth*. There had also been a self-titled EP the previous year (all sounds played on guitar) but that remained unknown to all but the sort of people who scour *Guitar Player* magazine's record reviews looking for interesting oddities (ahem!). Fear not, though, as four of its five tracks can now be found on the *Time Machine* compilation.

CLAIM TO FAME #1:

While most of us struggle to bring even a hint of potential fifteen-minute-ness into our sad, dull lives, Joe Satriani has done two things which place him firmly in the guitar history books. First, he taught a teenaged Steve Vai many of the techniques and musical concepts that can still be heard in Vai's playing (he also taught other now-famous players: Kirk Hammett, Larry LaLonde, Alex Skolnock and Charlie Hunter).

CLAIM TO FAME #2:

Not content with that, he then completely revolutionised and repopularised rock guitar in the eighties, becoming a New Messiah for the instrument (as had Hendrix in the sixties and Van Halen in the seventies).

THE GOOD BITS:

Honestly, have you not listened to a single word I've said? He's a master of melody, harmony and song structure; he's never afraid to keep pushing the boundaries of his own musical style; has a command of theory and technique that can send shivers down your spine and, more importantly, never uses those abilities merely to show off.

THE BAD BITS:

Er... can't think of any. Oh all right, in the interests of impartiality, the songs featuring vocals are never quite as good as the instrumentals. (They're not bad, though.)

NUTS AND BOLTS:

Joe is a long-time endorser of Ibanez guitars. He was using the new Radius and Power models (from the RG540 range) back in 1987, but as time went on, the Radius started its journey of many mutations, producing various JS models. A recent prototype sported a mahogany body and two P90 pickups. Amps vary, being most commonly Marshalls, but for the *Joe Satriani* album sessions he used a seventeen-watt Wells valve head.

VITAL VINYL:

For an unforgettable lesson in mainly instrumental rock guitar, buy 'em all: *Not Of This Earth* (1986), the groundbreaking *Surfing With The Alien* (1987), *Dreaming #11* (1988 – a mostly live EP), *Flying In A Blue Dream* (1989), *The Extremist* (1992), *Time Machine* (1993 – a double live/studio compilation of rare and unreleased stuff) and *Joe Satriani* (1996 – a new approach for Satch, but still excellent).

TRACK 13

biography

Out of all the players I've covered in this book, Joe Satriani was bound to prove the most difficult to sum up in such a short musical excerpt. Much like his great friend and one-time pupil Steve Vai, Joe has an incredibly deep, complex and ever-expanding musical personality; it seems sacrilegious to write about his playing with the old "Here are some cool Satch-style licks..." approach. However, it has to be done (bravely facing up to responsibilities here... my parents will be so proud of me) so let's dive in. As it is, you'll notice that the relevant track on the CD for this chapter is longer than any of the others, and I assure you I've had to miss out loads of potential ideas!

Despite the obviously sophisticated nature of much of Joe's playing, he has an ear for great "classic rock" riffs, you know – the sort of thing with lots of big, bold power chords and lots of energy. Here's a little something I concocted...

Chords used in this chapter

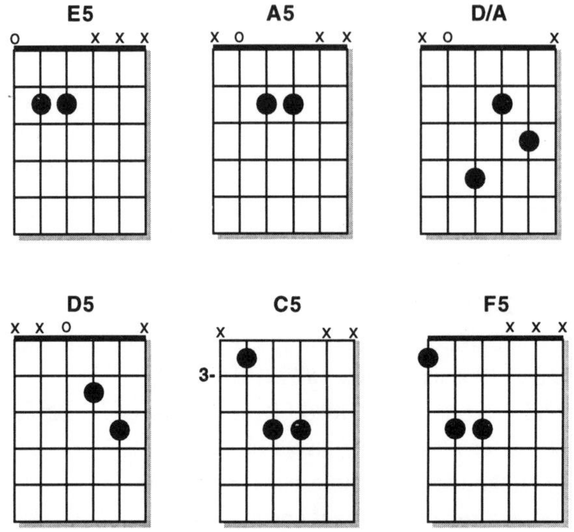

EX 1

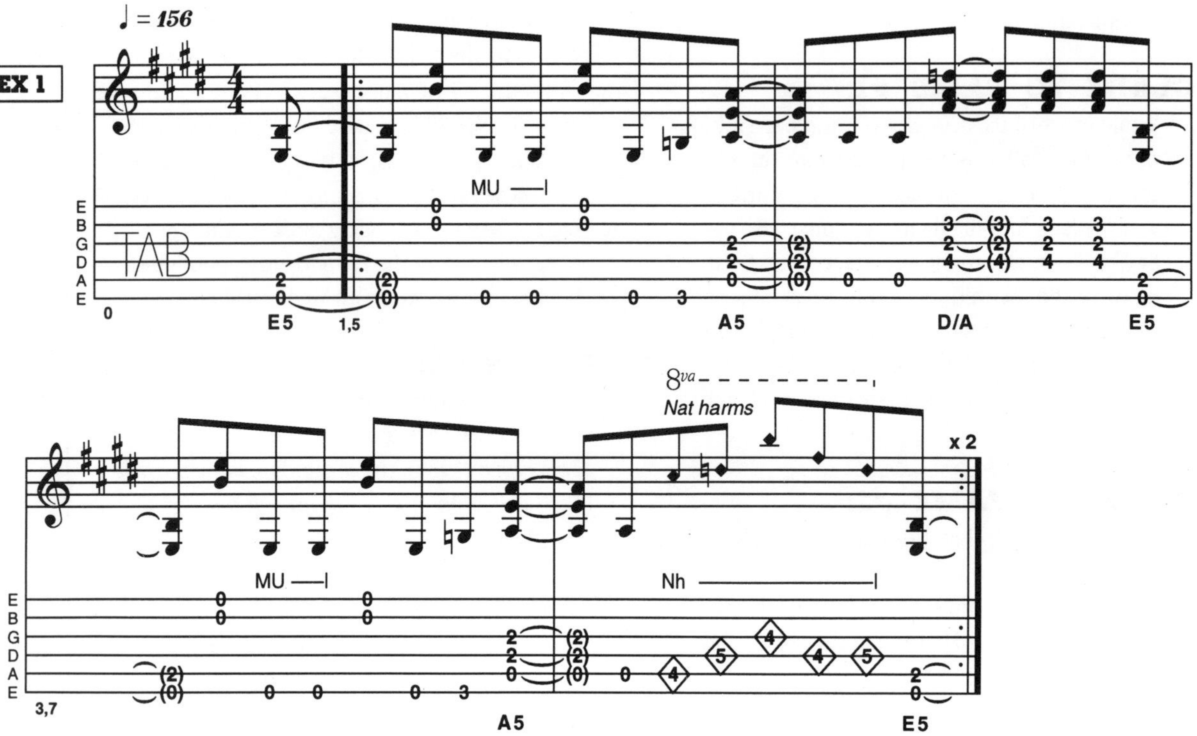

Right, that's the intro – although you need to go at it with a certain amount of abandon, you do have to be careful with the harmonics, especially the ones at the fourth fret. Try to keep any extraneous open-string sounds to a minimum.

Now we need a verse melody. One thing to bear in mind is that Joe never really had an awful lot in common with the late eighties "neo-classical" craze, so the melody lines need to be fairly simple. You should feel the urge to whistle along, not hit the floor with your lower jaw and go "Whoo... cool sweep-picked sextuplets". I've used the same three chords from the intro, plus a couple of others to vary the sound...

EX 2

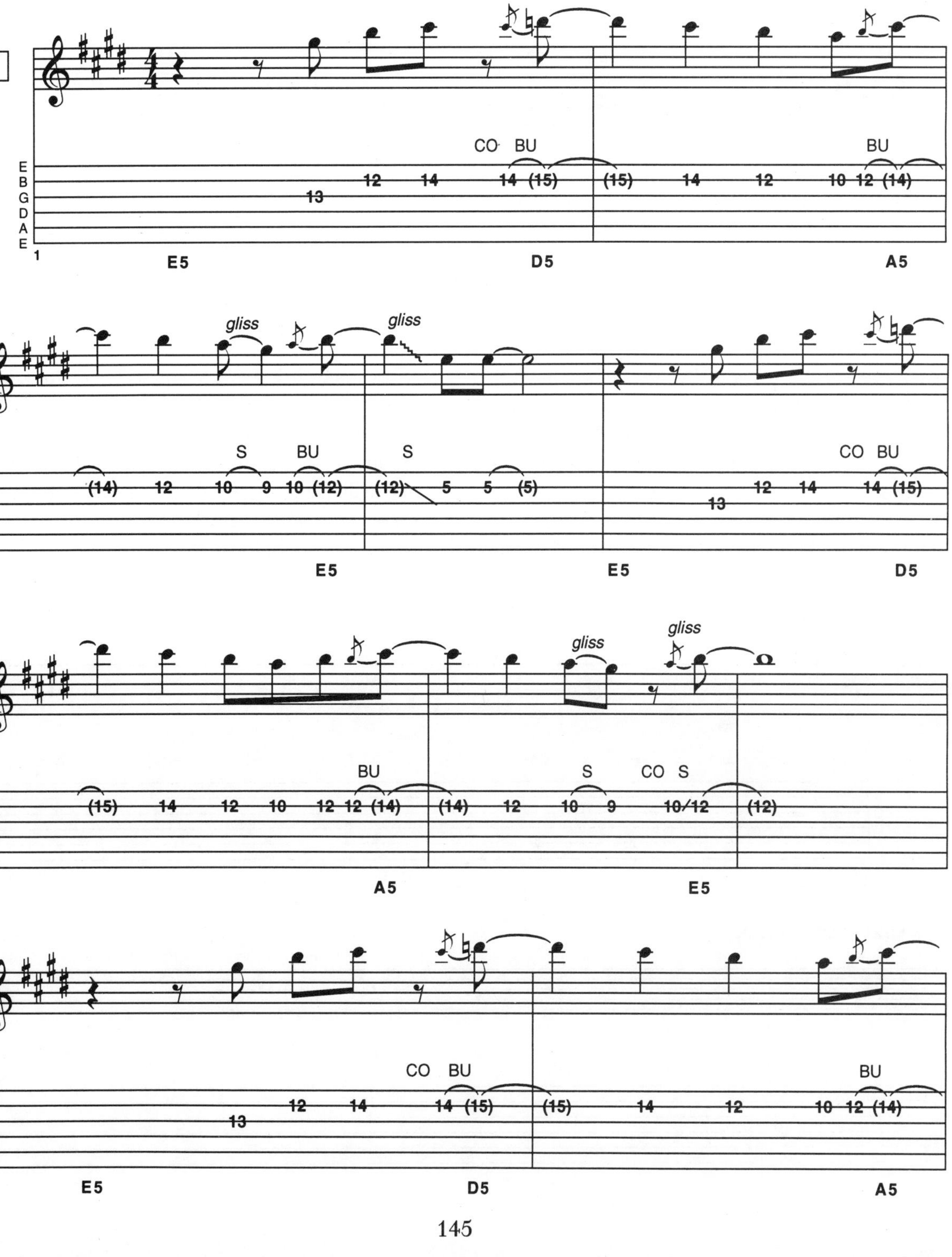

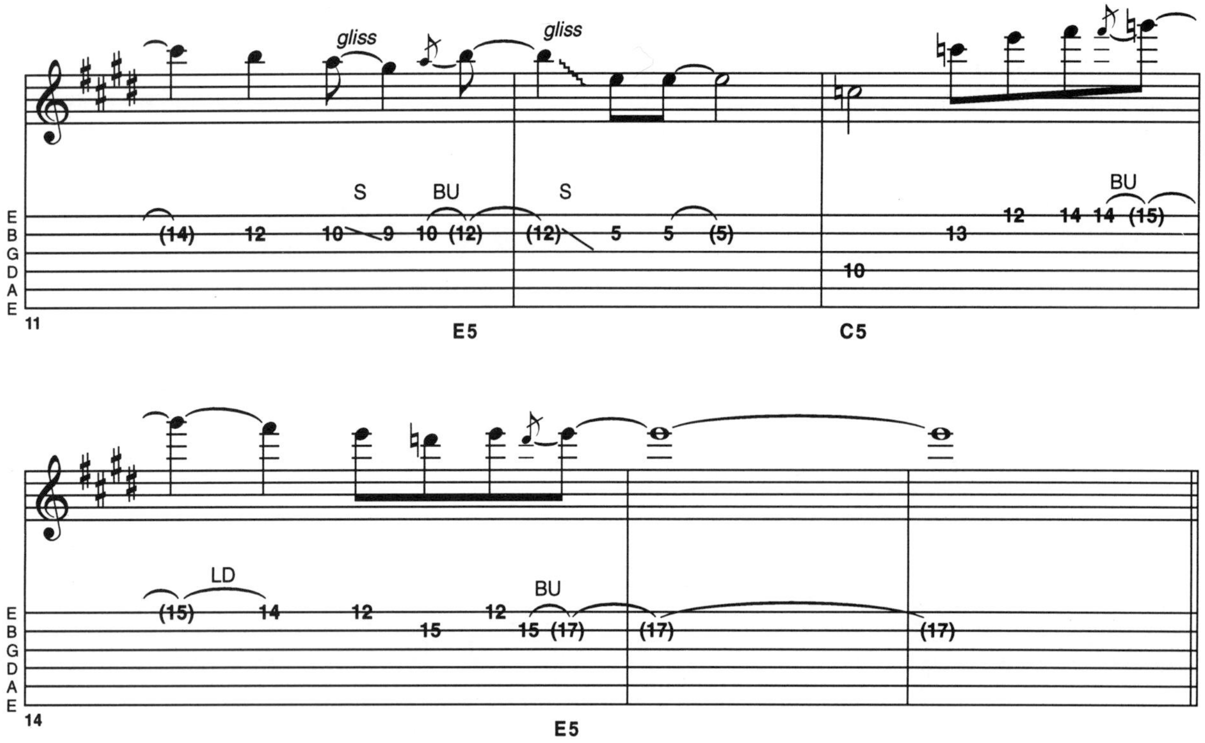

Now, before we go any further, let's talk about scales... (I know that can be a distressing concept, especially if you belong to a Weight Watchers club as well as playing guitar, but just be strong for me, okay?)

The simplest way of playing over the E, D and A chords is to use the A Major scale, as the key of A major contains all three of these chords. However, the whole verse part has a feeling of being rooted around E, so that means we're actually using the E Mixolydian mode (E F# G# A B C# D E: same notes as A major but based around E). Got it? Here's what it all looks like...

A MAJOR SCALE

EX 3A

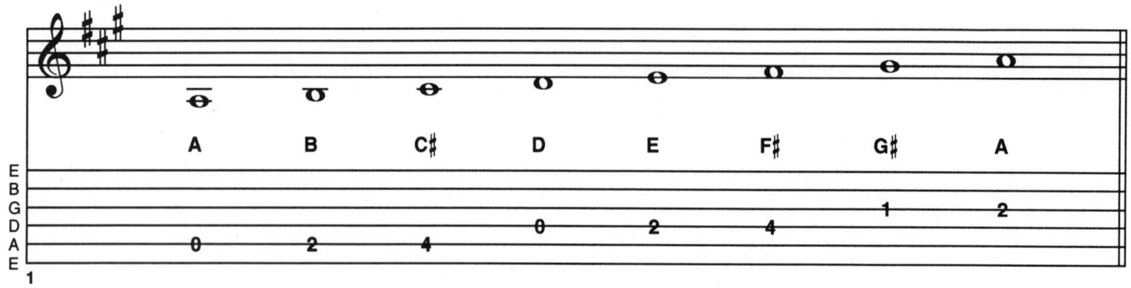

E MIXOLYDIAN MODE

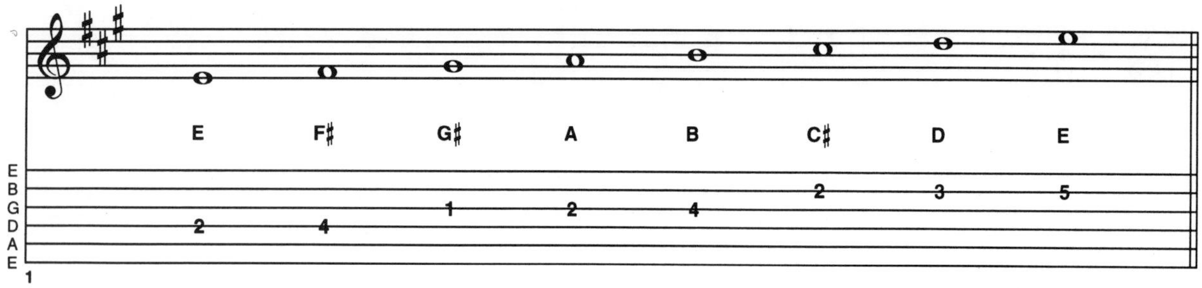

The C chord doesn't actually come from the key of A major, so I went for the nearest possible scale (ie the one with the most notes in common with A major) which turns out to be G major. And when you root the G major scale around C, the result is... C Lydian! If all this modal talk is confusing you, check out the section on modes in the Theory Primer.

G MAJOR SCALE

EX 3B

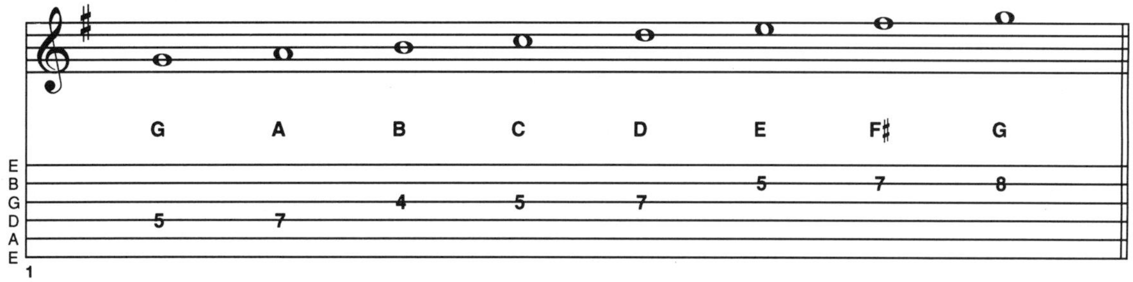

C LYDIAN MODE

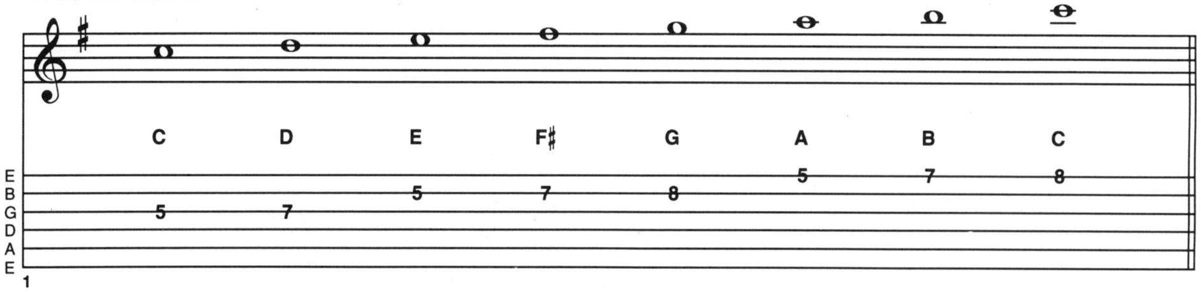

When you play totally instrumental guitar music, you have the disadvantage of not being able to use lyrics to distinguish one verse from another, so you have to think up lots of tricks to prevent things from getting boring. One possible method is to play the second verse an octave higher...

EX 4

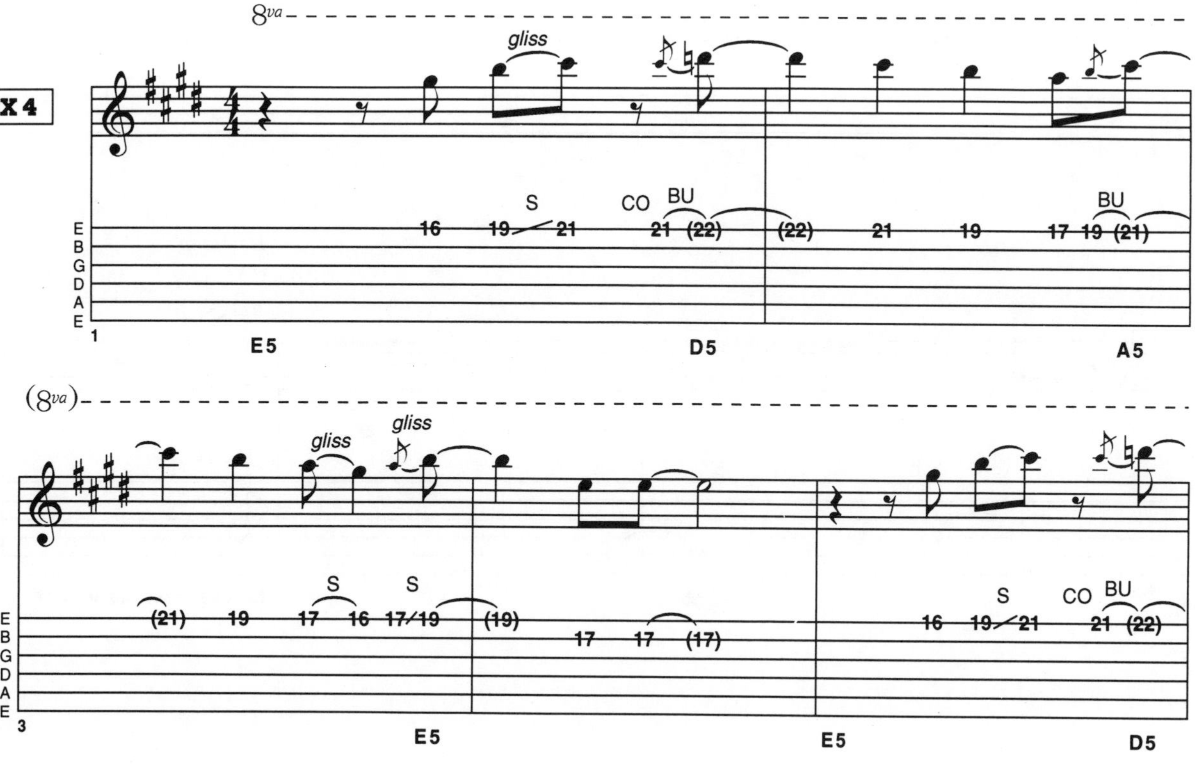

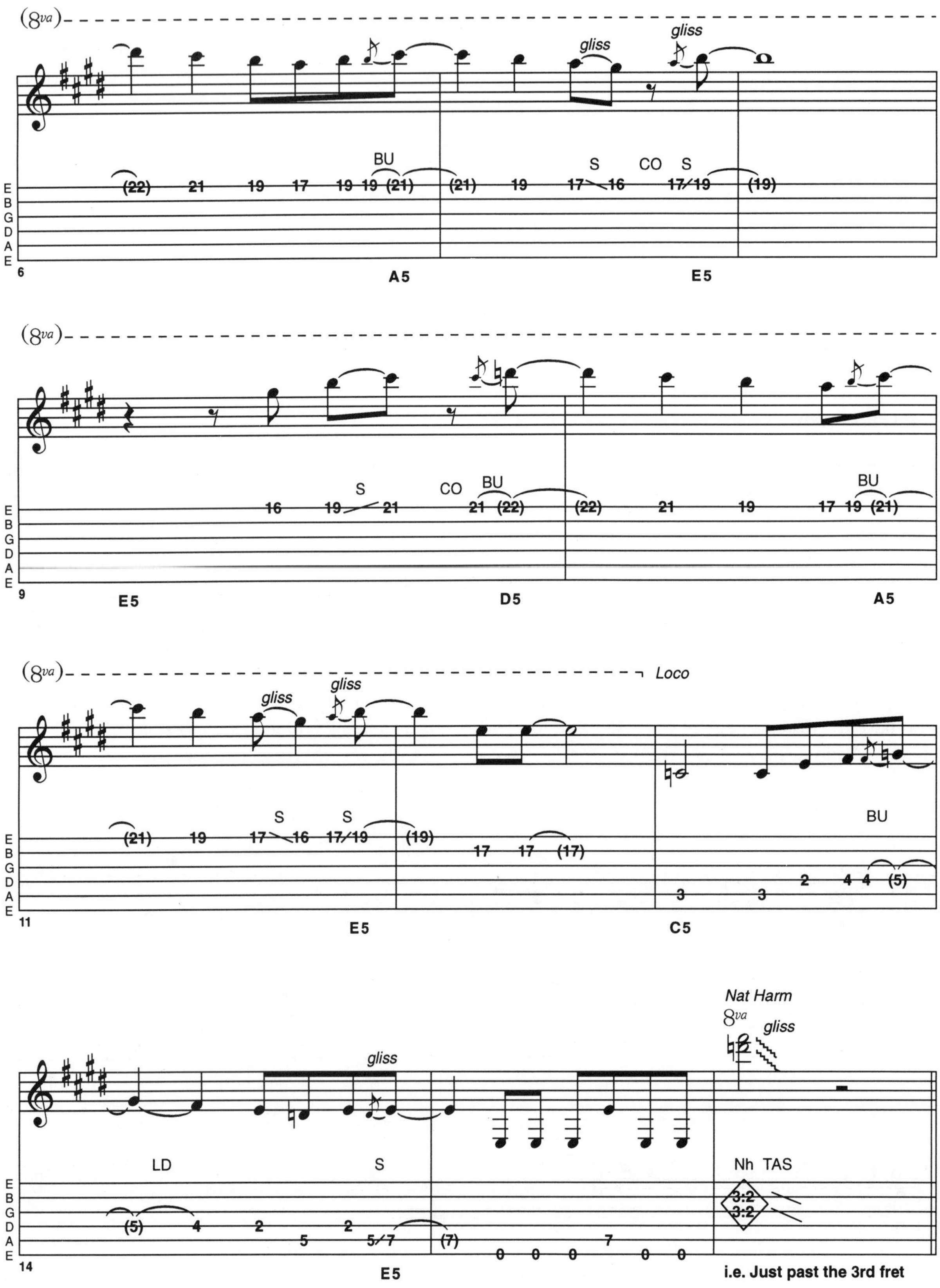
(8va)
gliss
gliss
BU
S
CO S
(22) 21 19 17 19 19 (21) (21) 19 17 16 17/19 (19)
E B G D A E
6
A5
E5
(8va)
S
CO BU
BU
16 19 21 21 (22) (22) 21 19 17 19 (21)
9
E5
D5
A5
(8va)
Loco
gliss
gliss
S S
BU
(21) 19 17 16 17/19 (19) 17 17 (17) 3 3 2 4 4 (5)
11
E5
C5
Nat Harm
8va
gliss
LD
S
Nh TAS
(5) 4 2 5 2 5/7 (7) 0 0 0 7 0 0 3:2 3:2
14
E5
i.e. Just past the 3rd fret

Did you spot the cunning change I made there? Although I raised most of the verse part by an octave, I actually lowered the last bit, to stop things from getting predictable.

Joe has a great talent for bringing a feeling of drama to his tunes, often by means of a sudden, unexpected key change or the introduction of a different sonic texture. Unfortunately, I don't have anything like that sort of talent, but in a brave attempt to impress you, I've come up with a chorus part featuring a change of key as well as some harmony parts to provide a change of texture.

EX 5A

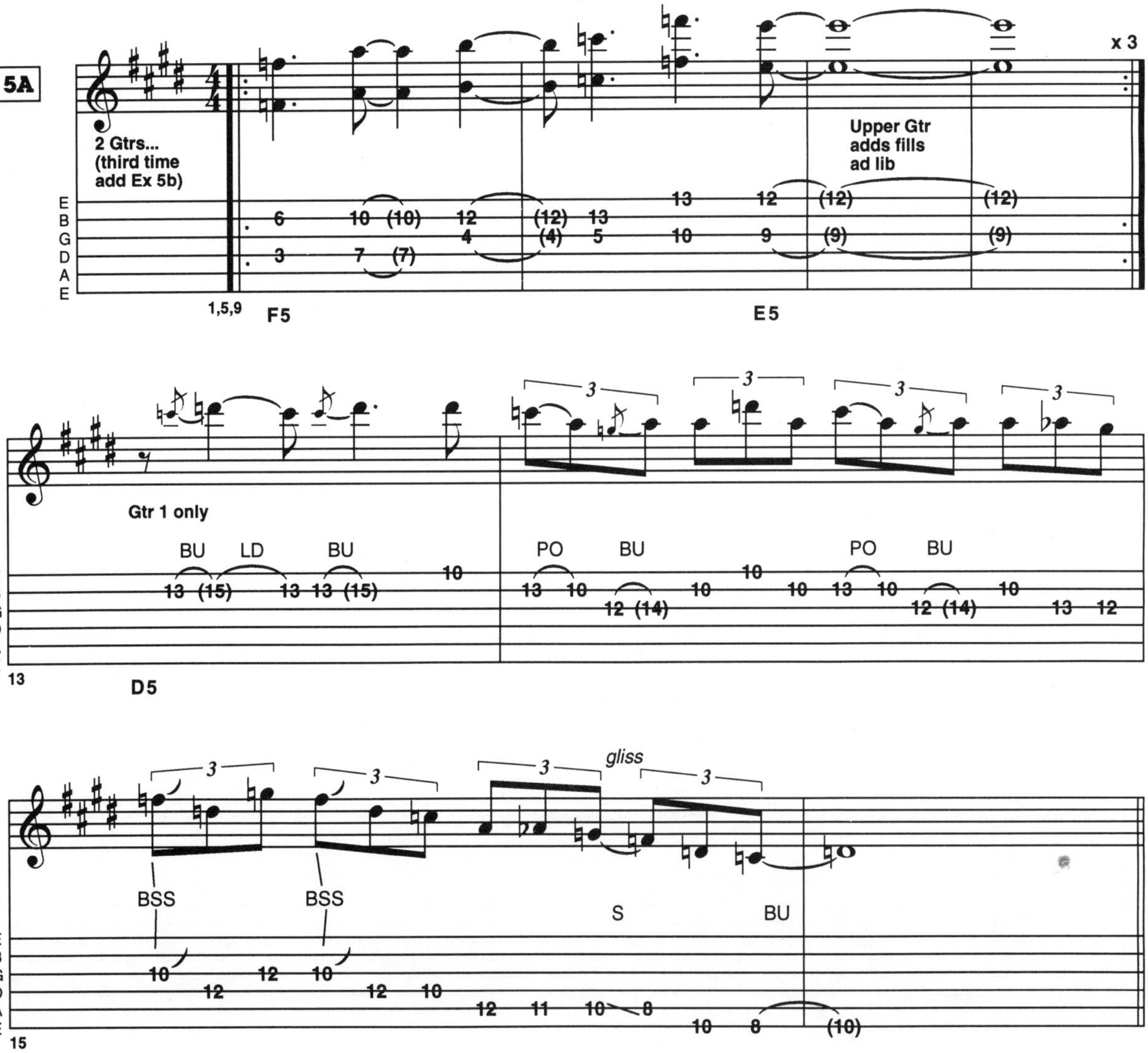

EX 5B

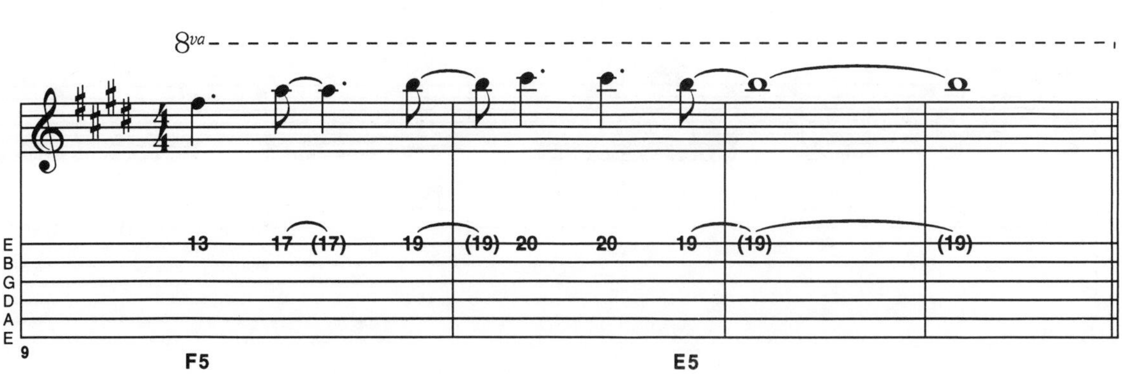

So just what the hell was going on there, Adrian? Well, the first twelve bars of Ex 5 are made up of a melody (using F Lydian, if you're interested: F G A B C D E F, same as C major) played three times by two guitars an octave apart. The third time, another guitar appears (Ex 5b) playing what initially seems to be the same melody an octave higher still, but right at the end, this guitar diverts and introduces a couple of harmony notes – both taken from the underlying chords. After that, things cool down a little over the D chord.

To keep you on your toes, let's dive straight into the solo. I've put some key changes in here to break the solo up into sections and, therefore, to prevent it from getting boring. The first section is in our original key of E, but since the backing is just an E5 (power chord) with no major or minor restrictions, I've decided to use the Dorian mode for a "bluesy minor" sound. The second section sees the key centre move up to F#, and I've decided to copy Joe's penchant for exotic-sounding scales by using the Phrygian Dominant (see the Ritchie Blackmore chapter for more information). Finally, we move up to an A root, and for this third section I've used the Mixolydian mode, which introduces a "bluesy major" sound (heightened by the fact that I've used a few partially bent C notes, which don't quite reach the C#). Even if you learn nothing else, you'll see that changing key, or "modulating", in an upward direction is a great way of adding drama to a song.

EX 6

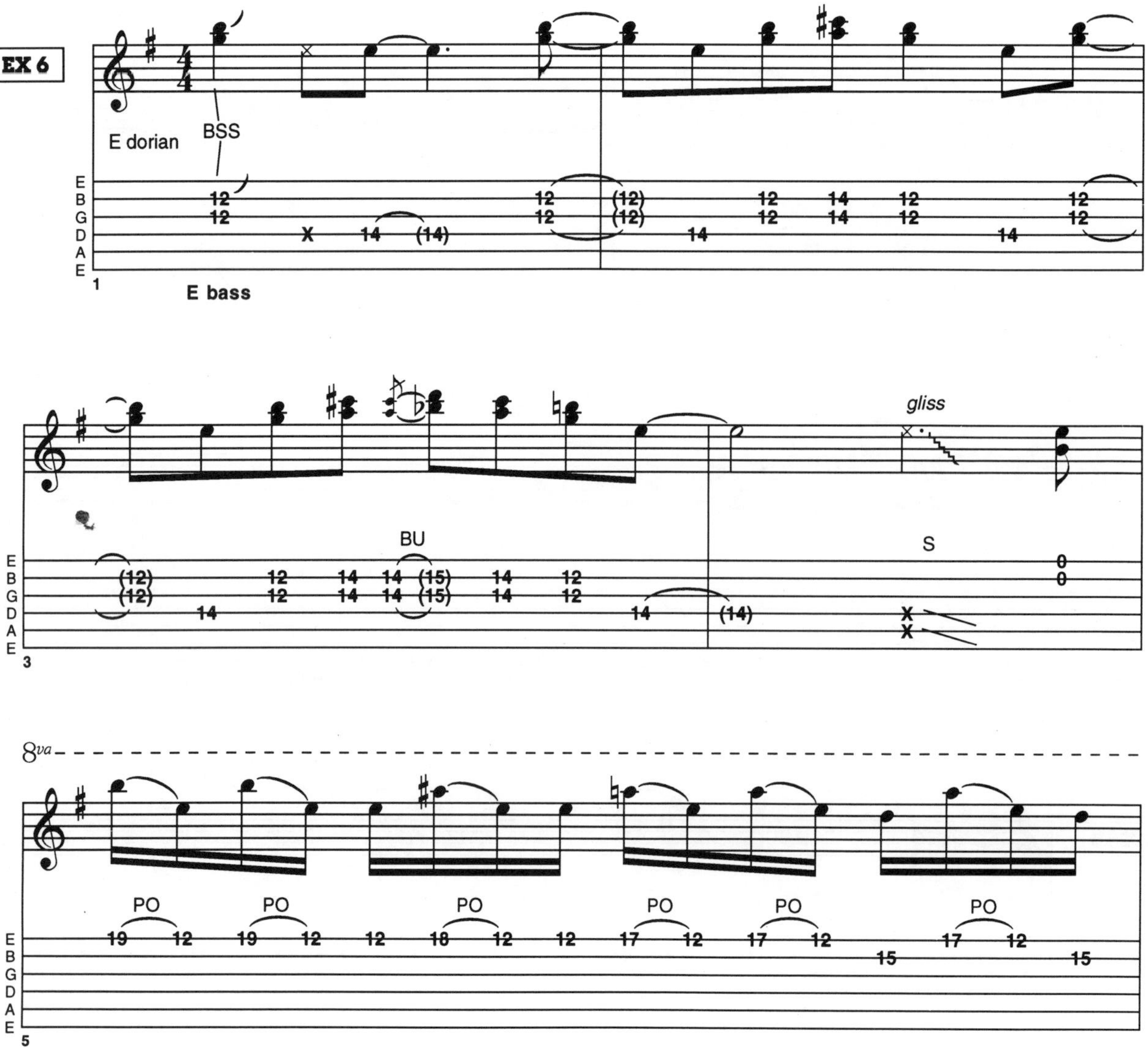

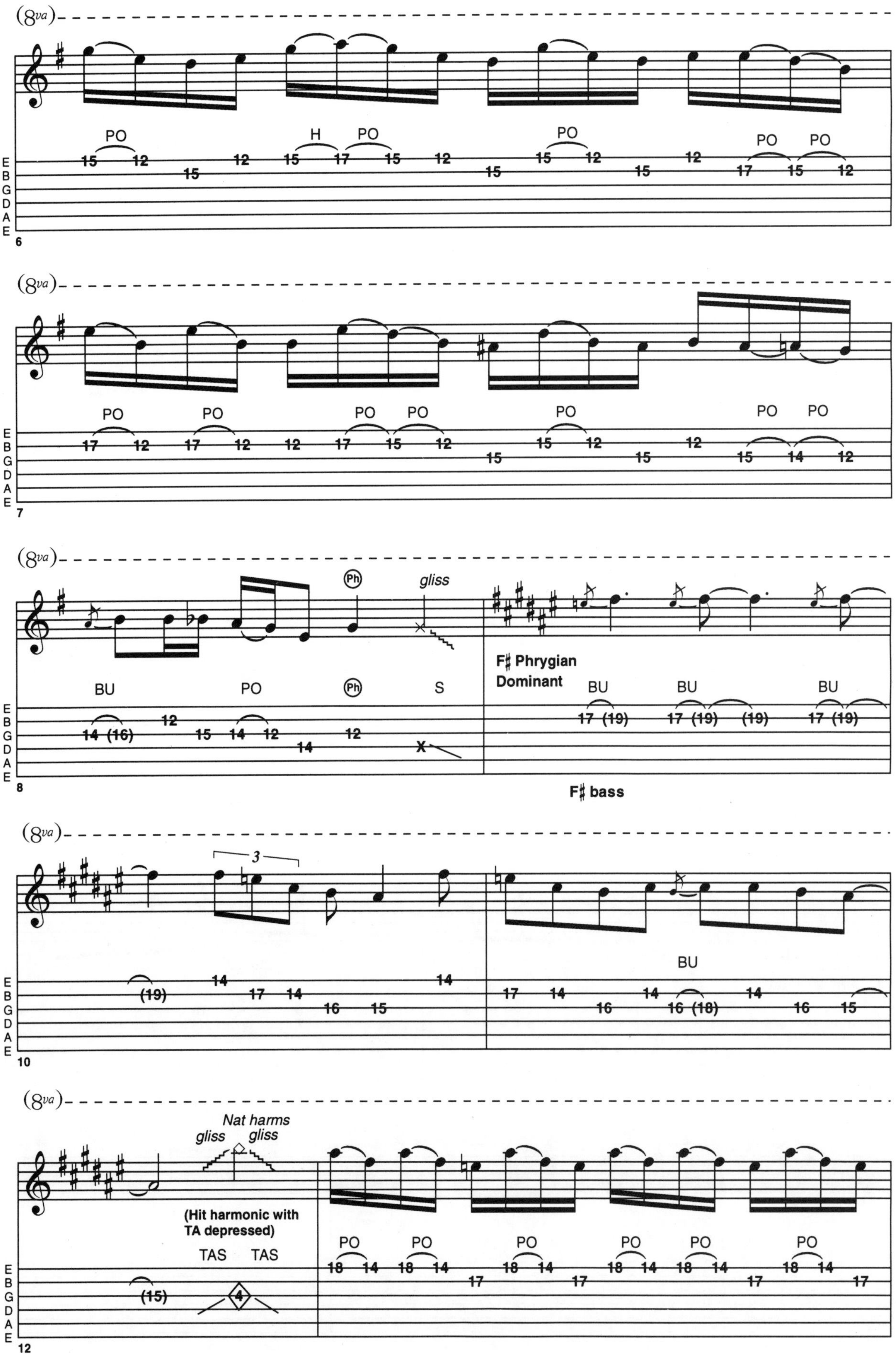
(8va)
PO
H
gliss
F♯ Phrygian Dominant
BU
S
F♯ bass
Nat harms
(Hit harmonic with TA depressed)
TAS
E
B
G
D
A
E

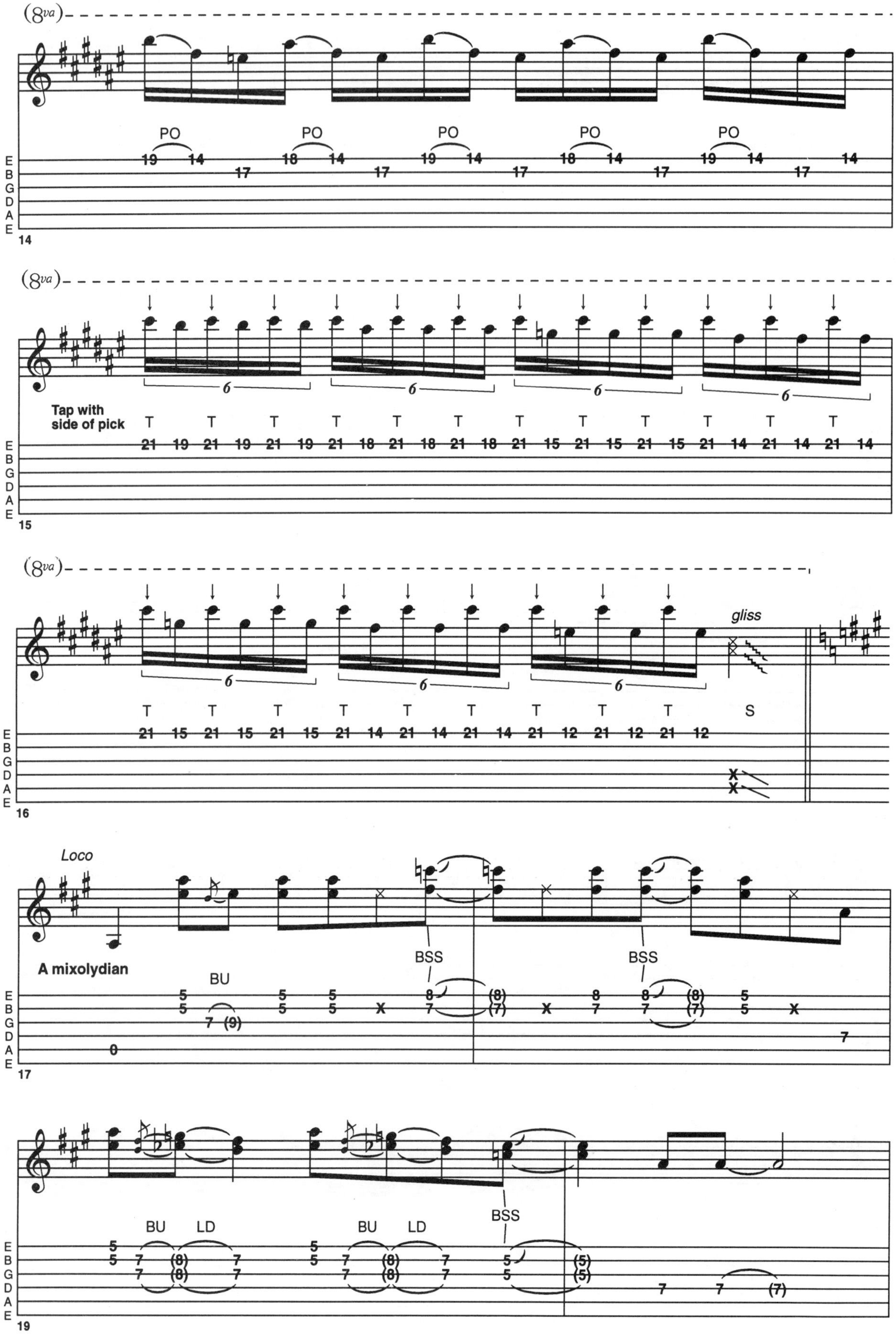
(8va)
PO
E B G D A E
14
Tap with side of pick
T
6
15
gliss
S
16
Loco
A mixolydian
BU
BSS
17
BU LD
BSS
19

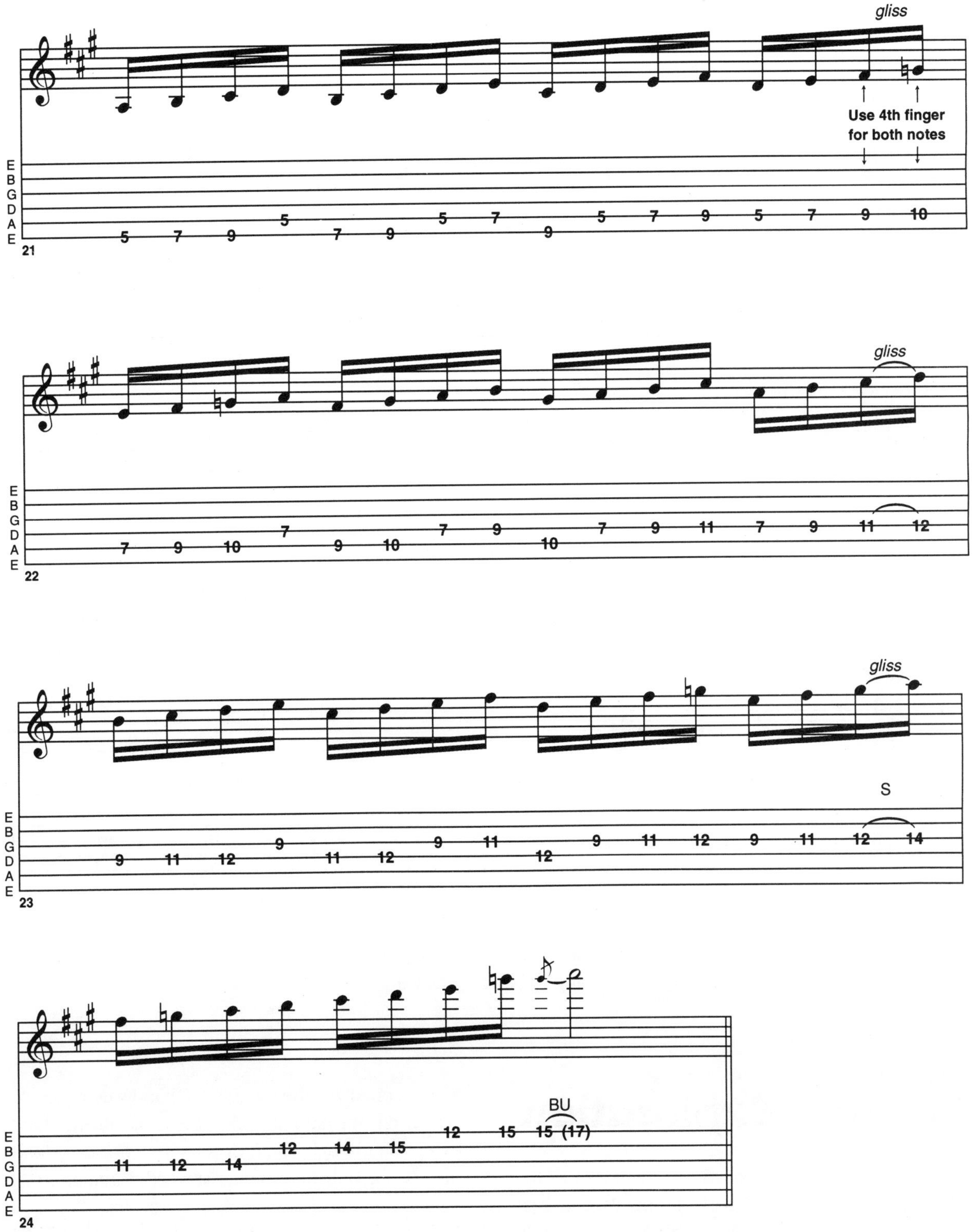
gliss
Use 4th finger
for both notes
E
B
G
D
A
E
21
gliss
22
gliss
S
23
BU
15 (17)
24

Just to help you with your own improvisations and experiments, here are the three scales I used in the solo.

E DORIAN

EX 7

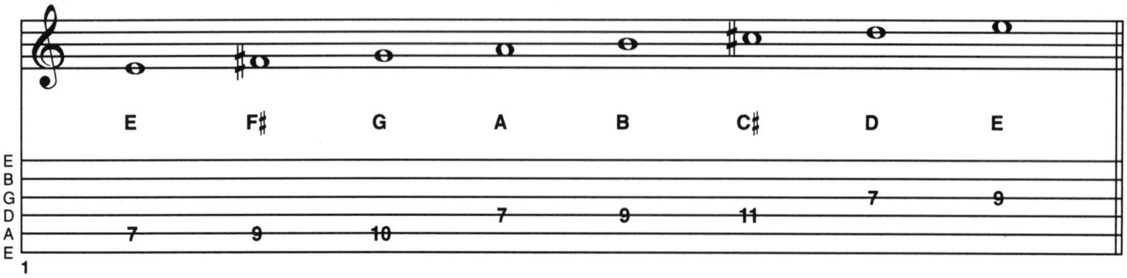

F♯ PHRYGIAN DOMINANT

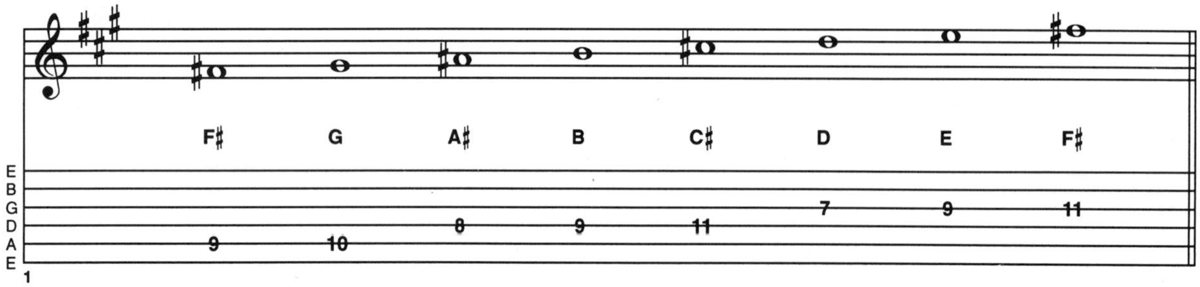

A MIXOLYDIAN

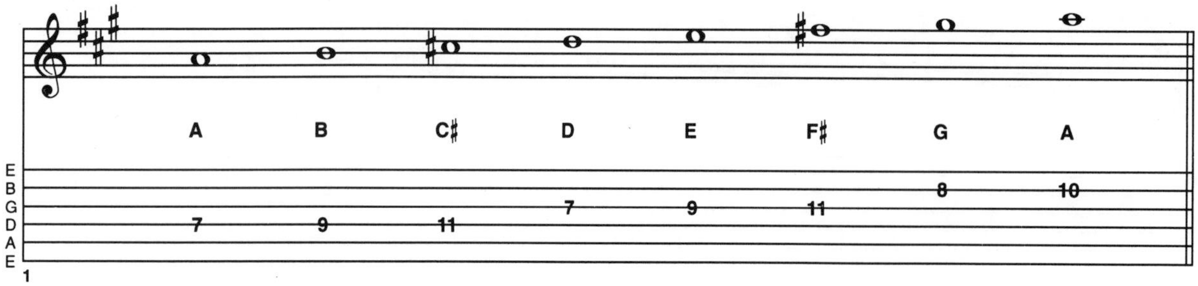

There you go, you can sit down, make yourself a cup of tea and have a well-earned rest. What? Did I say it was going to be easy? Did I?

Further Exploration

To hear where Joe got his earliest kicks from, start with Jimi Hendrix and Jimmy Page. Other than that, Joe seems to have such a broad range of musical interest that it's impossible to pin things down any further; maybe you should just follow Joe's lead and listen to as much as possible.

In the other direction, the detritus of the late eighties instrumental rock orgy contains plenty of guitarists who hopped on the Satch-style bandwagon before falling off through a lack of similar talent. One exception, though, is Jan Cyrka – Joe once described him as "the only other guitarist worth listening to".

For online Satch-related fun, start from the official homepage at http://www.satriani.com and follow the numerous links from there (there's a great message board where, at the time of writing, Joe regularly responds to questions). Closely linked to this is another site, Cybersatch, which can be found at http://www.cybersatch.com

CHAPTER 20

Andy Summers

TRACK 7

biography

BORN:

31 December 1942.

ORIGIN:

Blackpool, England.

THE PRODUCT OF:

Starting from an early age as a jazz guitarist, playing R&B in the sixties, studying classical guitar and twentieth century composition at university in the early seventies and following all that with four years of intensive sitar study. Presumably the concept of spending a relaxing Sunday morning eating croissants and reading the papers would be lost on Andy.

BIG BREAK:

Forming The Police in 1977 with Stewart Copeland and Sting, and conveniently taking advantage of the sudden rise in popularity of both reggae and snappy, no-frills songwriting.

THE GOOD BITS:

Provided an interesting link between the angry young punks and the boring old dinosaurs they were trying to kick out – Andy and the boys could actually play their instruments, just like Yes and ELP! Between the punch-ups, The Police wrote some fantastic short, snappy songs, featuring some of the most intriguing pop/rock guitar playing of all time.

THE BAD BITS:

For every innovator, there's always a bandwagon crammed full of clones. The mid-eighties British (and no doubt US) pop scene was awash with the sound of muted add9 arpeggios played with a clean tone and lots of chorus, flanger and delay pedals.

MORE BAD BITS:

To play a lot of Andy's parts correctly, you're going to need to do some pretty mean stretching with your fretboard hand. Start warming up now, while you're reading this!

NUTS AND BOLTS:

Andy played various guitars with The Police, but he was most often to be seen with a Fender Telecaster Custom, equipped with a Gibson humbucker in the neck position. He's also used various models from the Roland guitar synth range, and most recently seems to have settled for one of Steve Klein's custom electrics, also used by Henry Kaiser and Bill Frisell.

VITAL VINYL:

All of the Police albums are vital in understanding Andy's style – *Outlandos D'Amour*, *Regatta De Blanc*, *Zenyatta Mondatta*, *Ghost In The Machine* and *Synchronicity*. From his solo career, the most interesting are his collaborations, with John Etheridge on *Invisible Threads* and with Robert Fripp on *I Advance Masked* and *Bewitched*.

As you can probably tell, Andy Summers has had quite a varied career, covering a number of musical bases, so with the limited space we have here, I'll just concentrate on his playing with The Police, as this is probably what he's most famous for. The main characteristics of Andy's playing on Police records were: sparse, minimal chord parts, very few solos, ambitious use of chorus, flange and delay effects and... those wonderfully chimey chords. Mostly, these came from the category known as "sus" or "add" chords. Here's a brief run-down:

1. The building block for most chords is the triad. To build a major triad, you take the first, third and fifth notes of the appropriate major scale (eg C E G for a C major triad) and to build a minor triad, you do the same but flatten the third (eg C E♭ G for a C minor triad).

2. To form a "sus" chord, you have to replace the third with either the second or fourth note of the parent scale (giving sus2 and sus4 respectively). Since the third defines a chord's major/minor nature, a sus chord can be neither major nor minor.

3. For an "add" chord, you retain the third but still add the second or fourth note (which, due to certain music theory conventions, now have to be called the "ninth" or "eleventh" respectively). As the all important third is still present, four different chords can be generated: Cadd9 (C E G D), Cmadd9 (C E♭ G D), Cadd11 (C E G F) and Cmadd11 (C E♭ G F).

Clear as mud? Don't worry – just spend a happy half hour messing about with these shapes.

EX 1

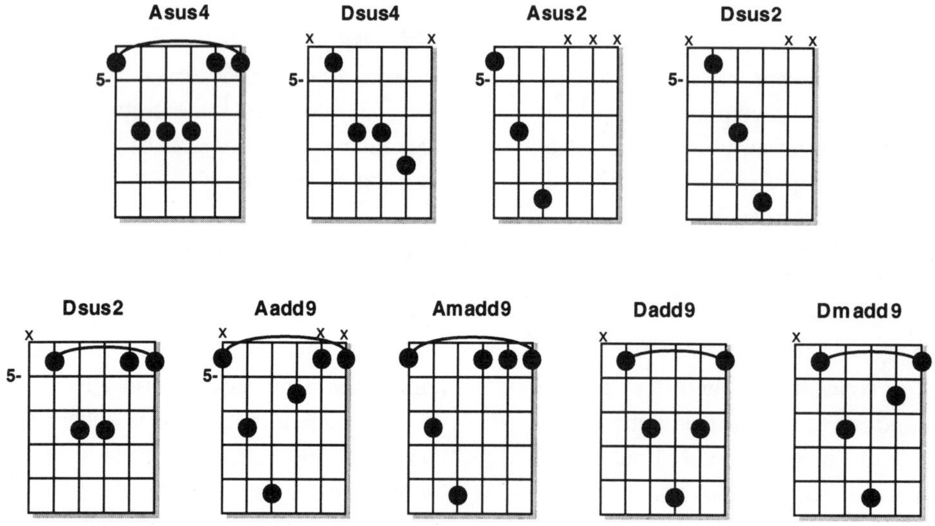

There. You may recognise the sound of some of those chords, and not just from Andy Summers' playing – they've been used by Alex Lifeson, Steve Vai, Joe Satriani and many others.

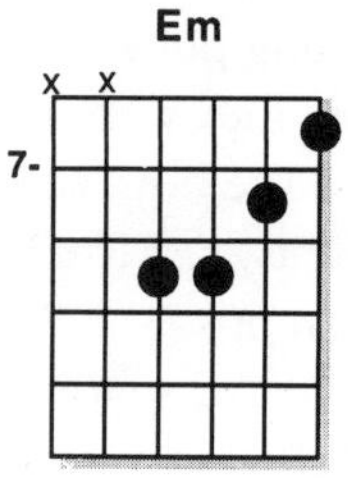

Now let's get down to business. This intro part uses a standard Em chord, but notice how I've restricted it to just the high notes – another feature of Andy's Police-era playing.

EX 2

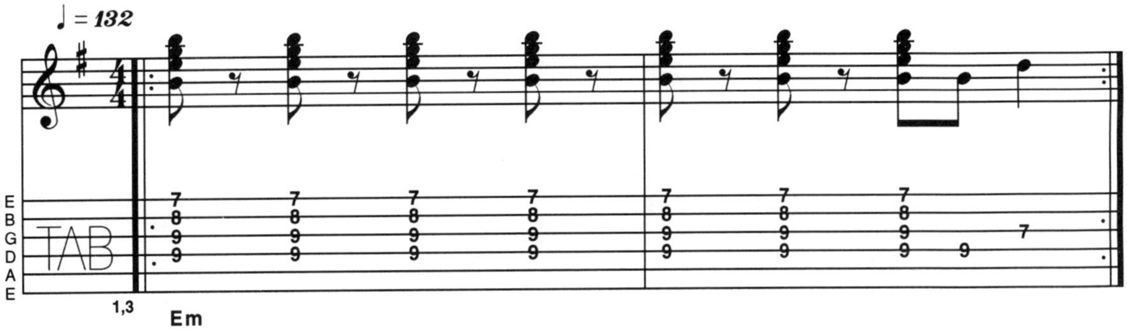

The verse continues in much the same vein, except I've added a B minor chord as well. Make sure you keep those chords abrupt and snappy by releasing the fingers of your fretboard hand almost as soon as you've struck the strings with your picking hand.

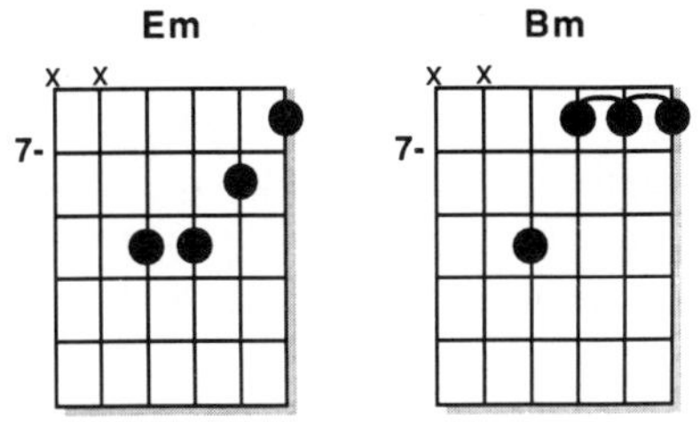

EX 3

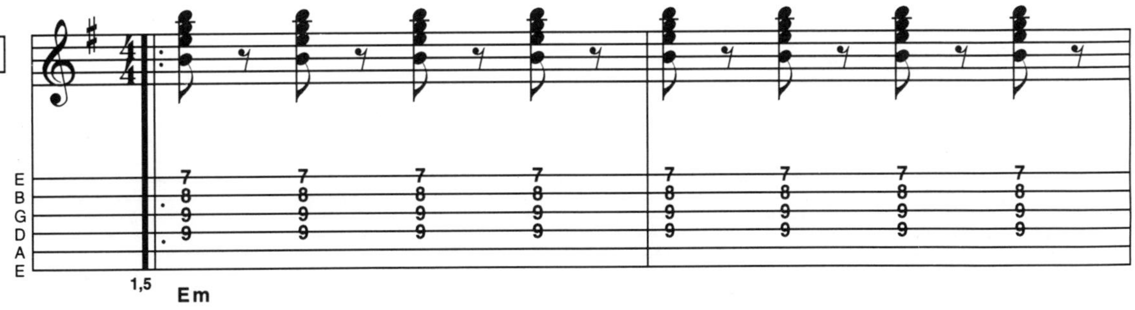

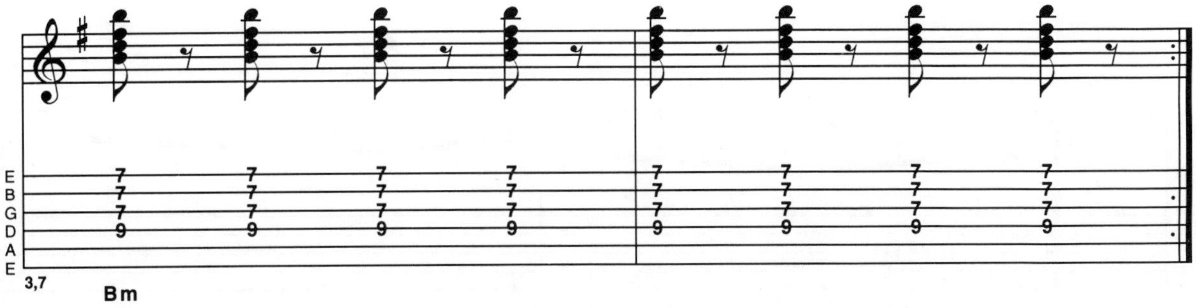

That sort of choppy sound can only go on for so long if you want to hold the interest of your listeners, so now's the time for a contrasting part. I've used a couple of sus2 chords and a couple of standard major chords to make a bridge section between the verse and chorus. Hit 'em hard and let 'em ring.

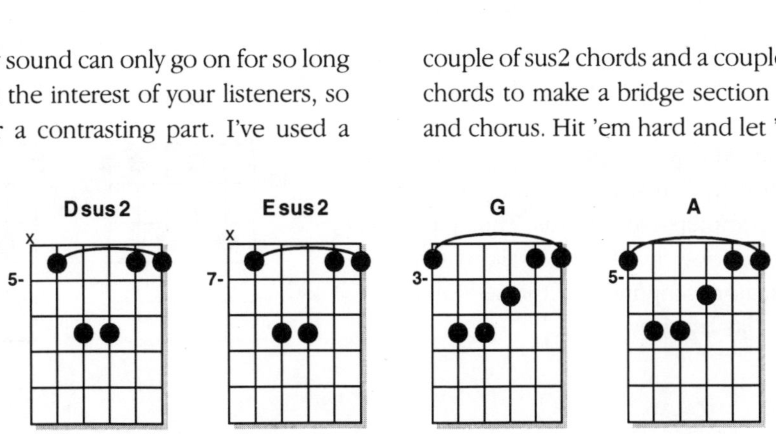

EX 4

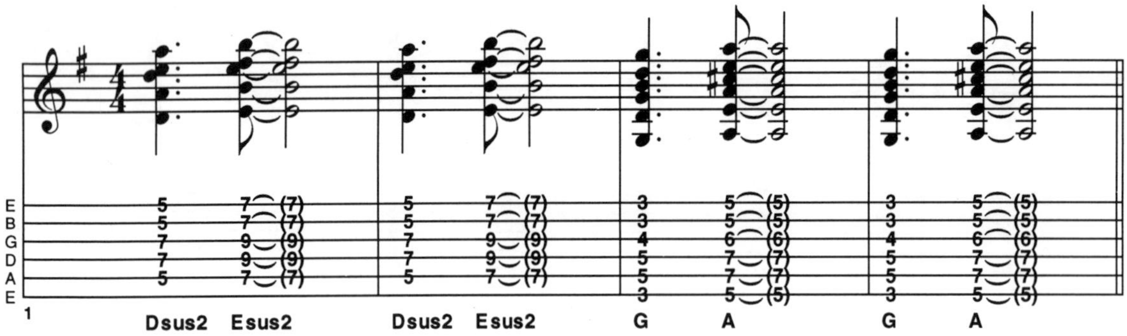

For the chorus, I've gone all out for the sus2 chords, but this time I've used the sparser (and more difficult) fingering. This is played four times; for the last two times I added a parallel harmony part, pitched a perfect fifth (seven semitones) higher than the main part. Although I physically played the harmony part on another track, there's no reason why you couldn't use a harmoniser.

EX 5

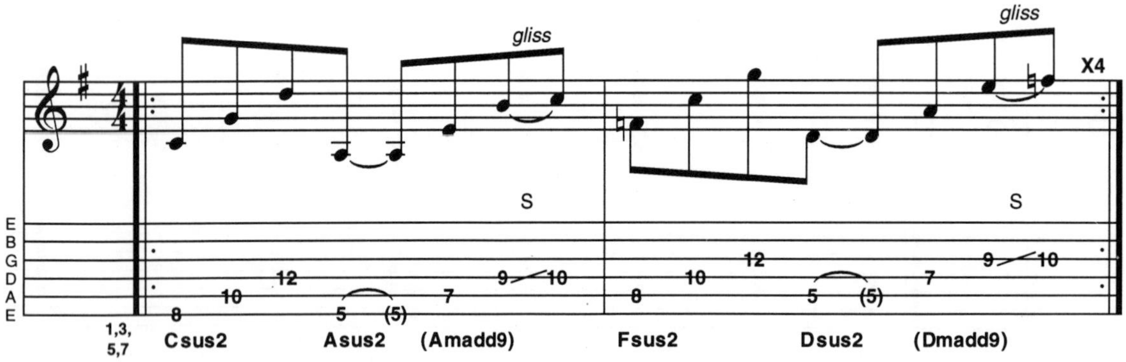

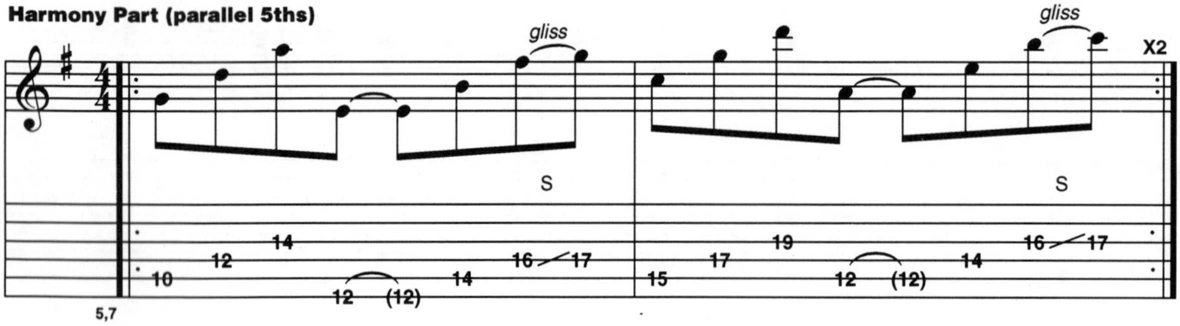

After a repeat of the verse part, I shifted down a gear by adding a more "textural" middle section, built on a couple of typically Summers-type chords. The first one – the Dm11 – is that famous chord from 'Walking On The Moon'. The other major component of this section is the liberal use of delay (lay-lay-ay-ay-y).

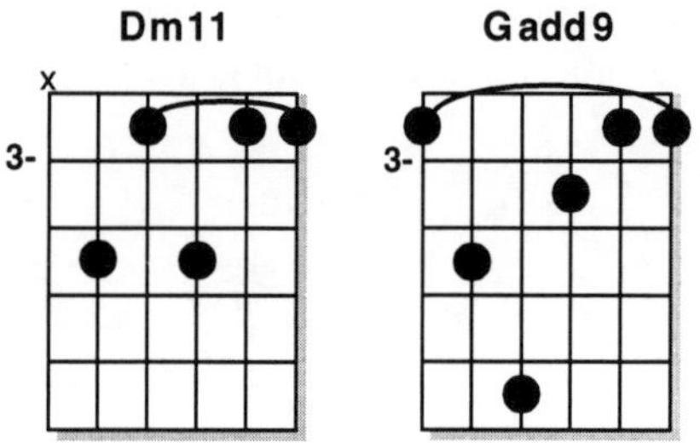

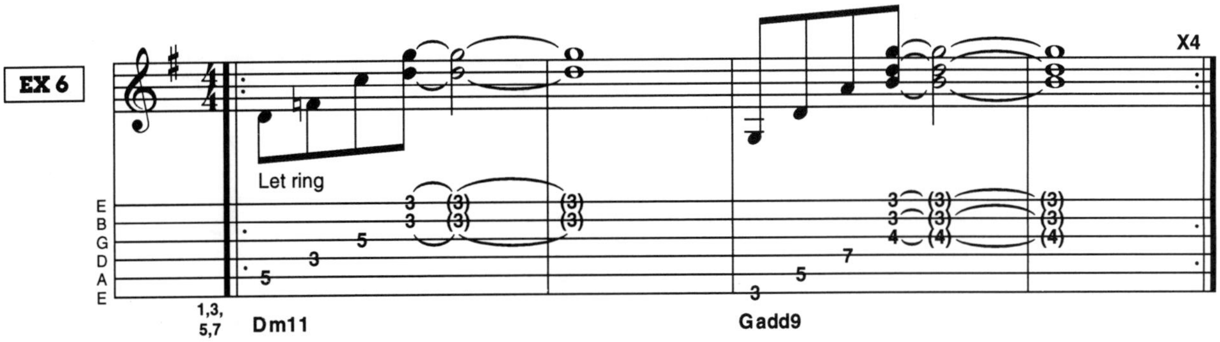

And that's it! The bridge and chorus sections are repeated at the end, just to round things off. The great thing about these jangly suspended chords is that their very nature makes them eminently compatible with ambient effects (delay and reverb) and modulation effects (phaser, flanger, chorus) so when you're experimenting with chord ideas like this, build a bit of extra breathing space into your riffs, and try thinking about how you can work with your guitar sound to create a fuller effect.

Further Exploration

Andy's list of influences covers a wide range of musical styles: jazz (Django Reinhardt, Kenny Burrell, Charlie Parker), R&B (Ray Charles, Otis Redding, Jimmy Nolen), classical (Bartok, Messiaen, Stravinsky), traditional Indian and Middle Eastern music and of course rock, with Jimi Hendrix as a major inspiration.

Andy's non-traditional approach with The Police had a major effect on many guitarists eager to find an alternative to the blues-rock excesses of the seventies. Listen to the sparse, minimal chords and frequent use of delay and chorus effects on hundreds of pop/new wave songs from the early eighties, and you can hear the influence of Andy Summers.

Personally, I'd have thought that there'd be reams of Police-related stuff on the web, with at least a handful of links to sites specifically related to Andy Summers. Unfortunately, all I could find was a site maintained by his record company, CMP Records. A bit official, maybe, but beggars can't be choosers! It's at http://www.move.de/cmp-records/cmphone.html

CHAPTER 21
Pete Townshend

biography

TRACK 11

BORN:
19 May 1945.

ORIGIN:
Chiswick, London.

DISTINGUISHING FEATURES:
Lots of big, vibrant power chords, windmilling right arm, onstage trail of destruction...

FIRST SPOTTED:
'I'm The Face', the debut single by The High Numbers, appeared in 1964. By the following year this promising young band had changed its name to The Who, and the rest... need I say more?

SEEN IN THE COMPANY OF:
Apart from a few isolated guest appearances and sessions (most notably Eric Clapton's post-heroin Rainbow Concert) Pete has remained loyal to two causes: The Who and his own, rather more literary minded solo career.

THE GOOD BITS:
One of the best songwriters in the entire history of rock/pop music, Pete's skills have meant that The Who's songs have endured lyrically as well as musically – even the ones written during the flower power era! As a guitarist, Pete practically set the scene for what powerful rock rhythm playing would be in the late sixties and seventies.

THE BAD BITS:
The solo career has just never lived up to expectations, and to make matters worse, The Who gradually fizzled out after numerous reunions. "Just another bunch of rock dinosaurs," they said.

NUTS AND BOLTS:
Pete's broken – sorry, played – quite a number of guitars during his long career. Most of those classic late sixties and early seventies shots show him with the famous Gibson Les Paul, but there have also been Rickenbackers, Fender Telecasters and Schechters. Pete, like Keith Richards, has always been a fan of acoustic rhythm guitar, and can often be seen with a Takamine in his hand.

SOUND ADVICE:
From the point of view of your guitar, use the heaviest strings you can stand. Sets with a nine- or ten-gauge top E are not really enough; for those big powerful chords you ought to be using an 11-52 gauge set. Amp-wise, use much less gain than you think you're going to need, as high gain settings tend to even out the dynamics. With the amp on a "mild overdrive" setting you can now use sheer strumming power to overdrive the amp when necessary.

VITAL VINYL:
For a good Who overview, get hold of *The Who: 30 Years Of Maximum R&B*, as this contains all the classic songs. Regarding specific albums, *Live At Leeds* is considered to be one of the finest rock albums of all time; the cream of the band's studio output can be found on *My Generation*, *Who's Next* and *Quadrophenia*.

Why don't you all f-f-f-find a guitar and learn to play these Townshend-style examples? You'll probably notice that there's a considerably higher proportion of rhythm guitar techniques here than in some of the other chapters, but that's not really surprising given Pete's reputation as a veritable riff-monster. You might also be surprised at how much I've used the acoustic guitar, even when there are quite heavy electric parts going on as well, but Pete's always been a big fan of acoustic rhythm guitar. Like The Rolling Stones, The Who often used the acoustic to provide a propulsive rhythmic and harmonic backbone in a song, to which the rest of the arrangement could be anchored.

To start with, here's a little solo intro, based loosely around the 'Pinball Wizard' intro, and making similar use of pedal point. "What's that all about?" I hear you ask. Well, a pedal point is basically any note or group of notes which stays constant (either by repeating or sustaining) while other parts above or below it are changing. In this example, the pedal point is the open D string, which stays constant despite the changing chords above it.

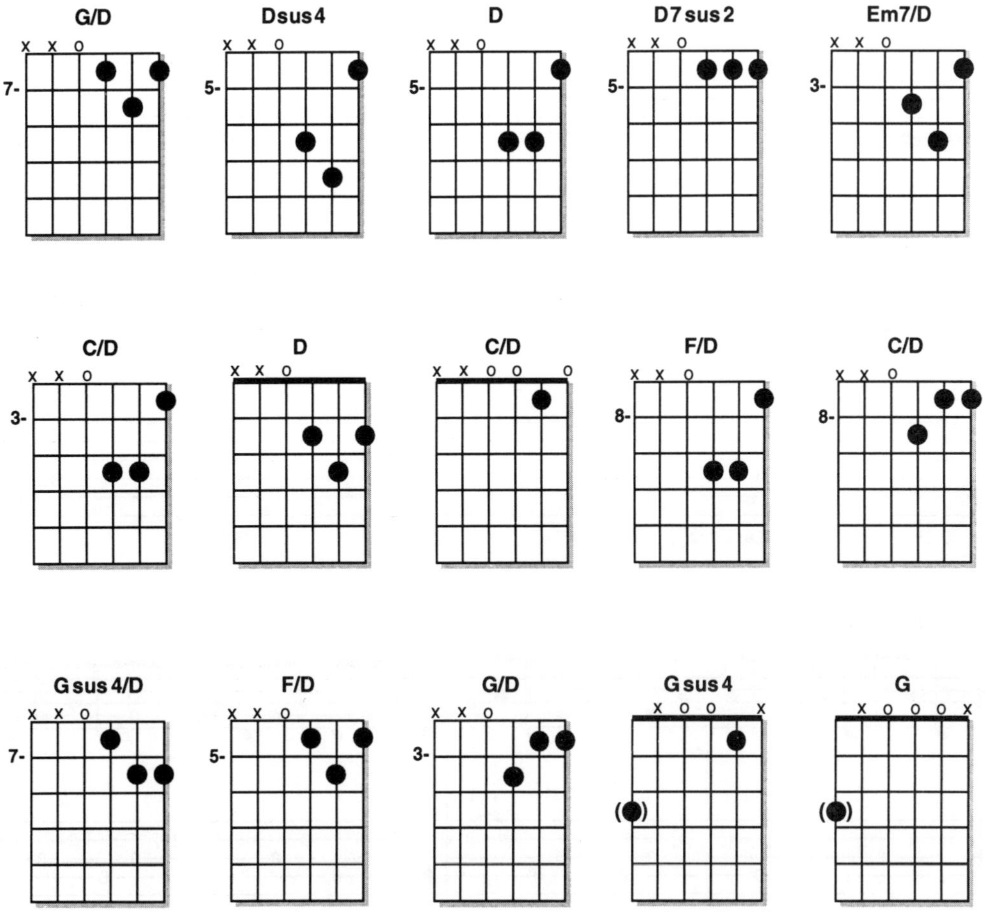

EX 1

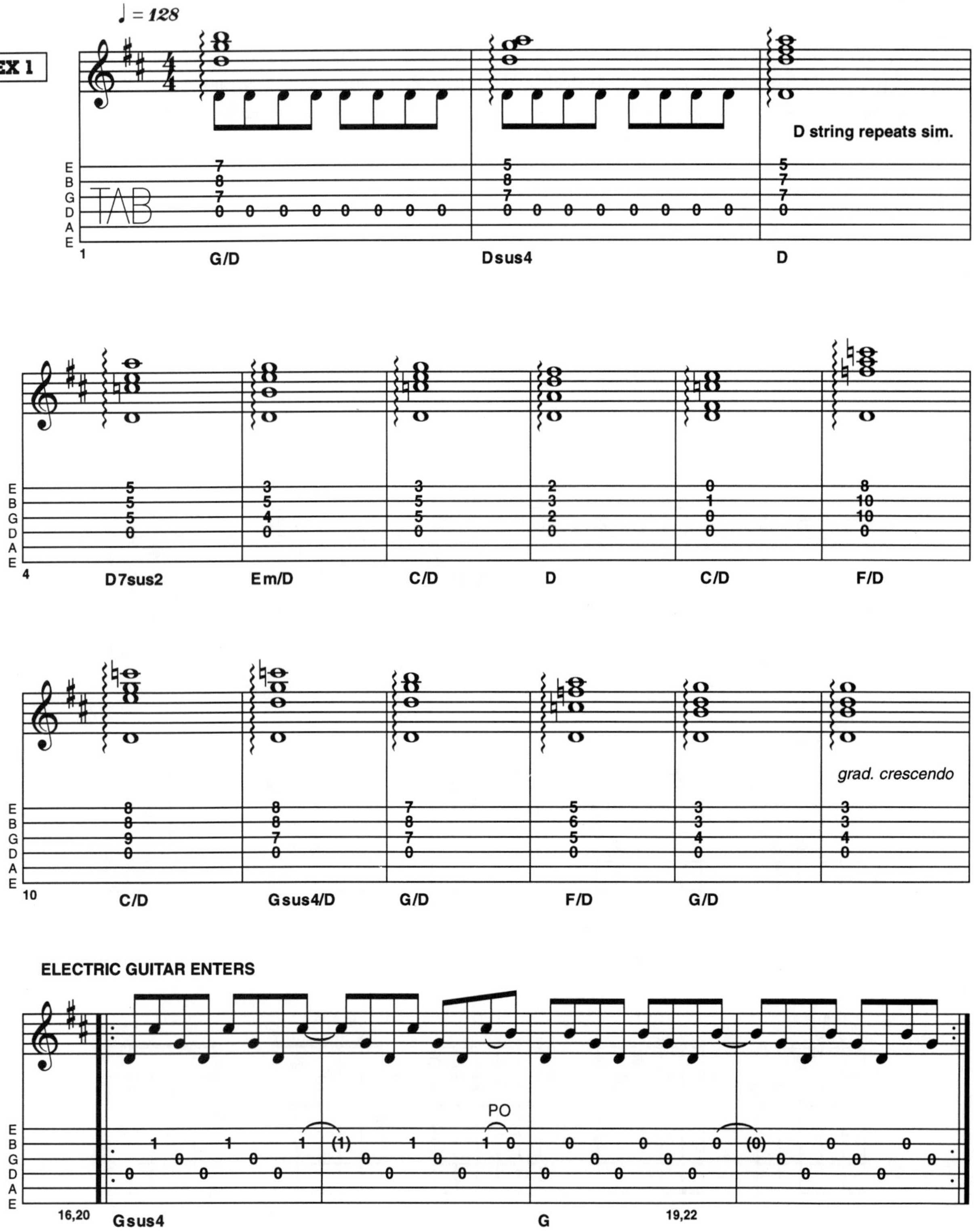
♩ = 128
D string repeats sim.
G/D
Dsus4
D
D7sus2
Em/D
C/D
D
C/D
F/D
C/D
Gsus4/D
G/D
F/D
G/D
grad. crescendo
ELECTRIC GUITAR ENTERS
PO
Gsus4
G
16,20
19,22

At the point marked "electric guitar enters here" in Ex 1, the electric guitar part does, surprisingly enough, enter. Instead of just whacking these big G5 chords, rake your pick more gradually through the notes for the maximum amount of "Brrranggg!" (listen to the CD and you'll hear what I mean).

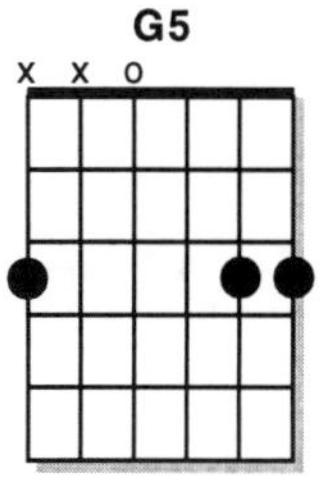

EX 2

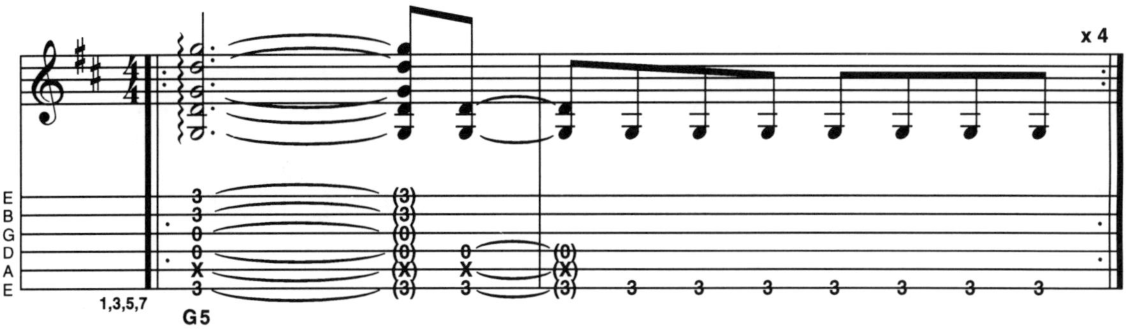

Just electric guitar for the verse, folks, but if you've been playing the other parts on an acoustic and don't want to change guitars, don't worry – this bit will work just as well on an acoustic. As you can see, there's nothing particularly unusual about these chords – you've probably played similar progressions in hundreds of songs. What's important, though, is the fact that you can trace the roots of this meaty, typical rock rhythm approach right back to the work of Pete Townshend on the first few Who albums.

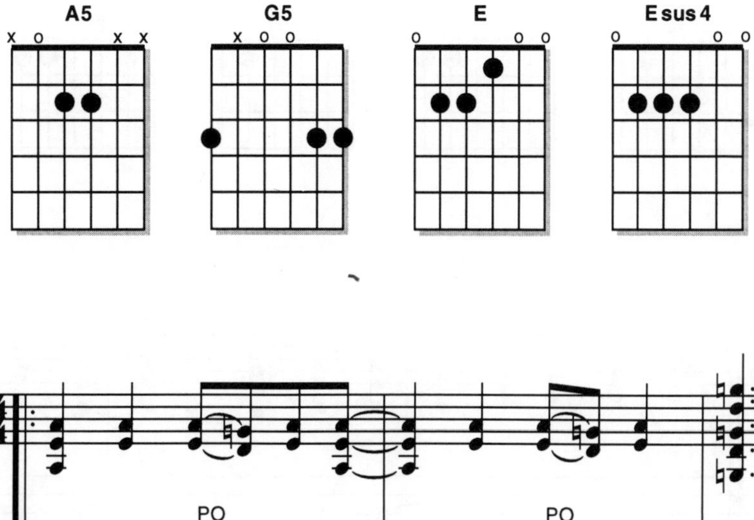

EX 3

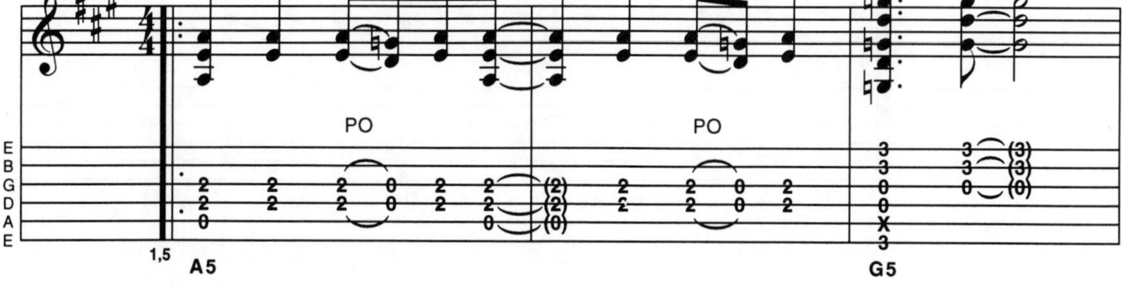

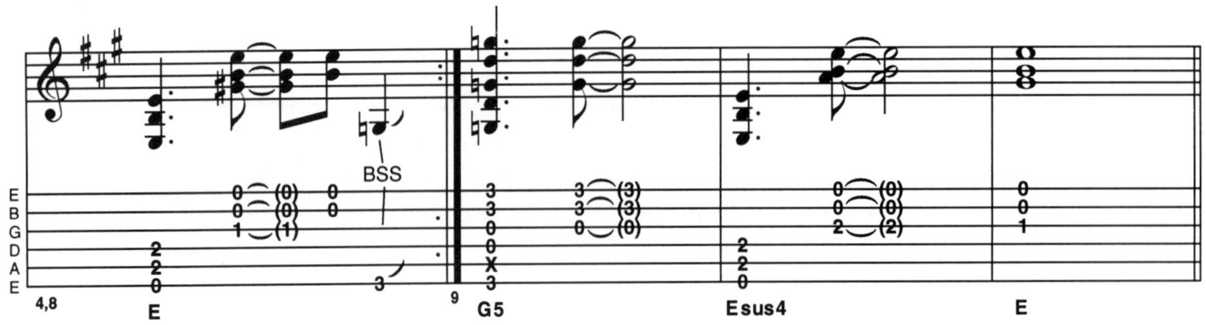

Another clue to the Townshend style can be found in the Esus4 chord at the end of the last example. Apparently, the presence of so many of these chords (often accompanied by a resolution to the equivalent major chord, ie Dsus4 – D) in Pete's songs is due to his love for the music of Henry Purcell (an English composer from the Baroque period). Pete was introduced to Purcell's music while writing songs for the first Who album, and found the 300-year-old suspensions and resolutions particularly inspiring. There's more of that sort of thing in the chorus...

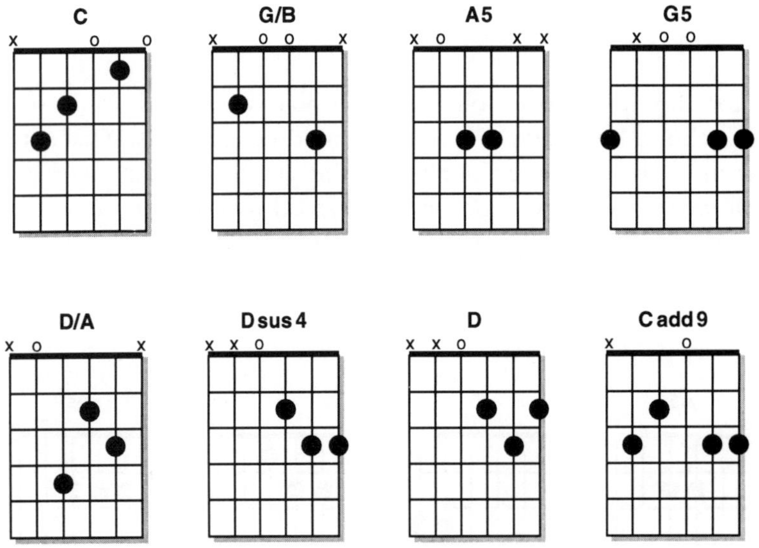

EX 4

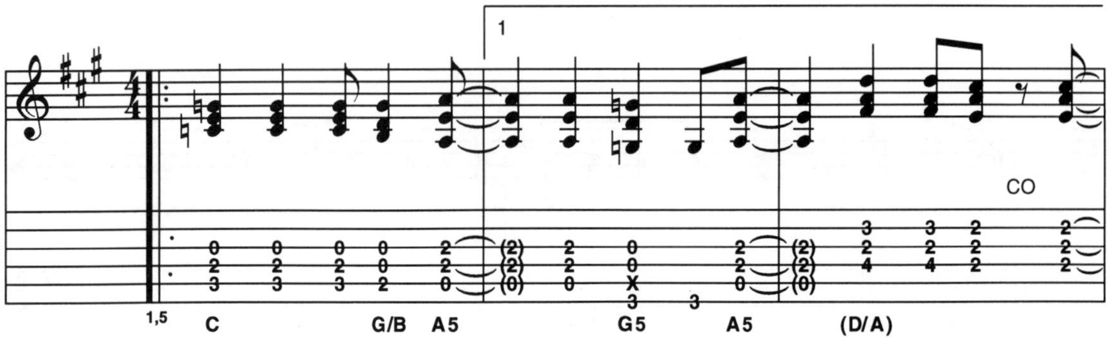

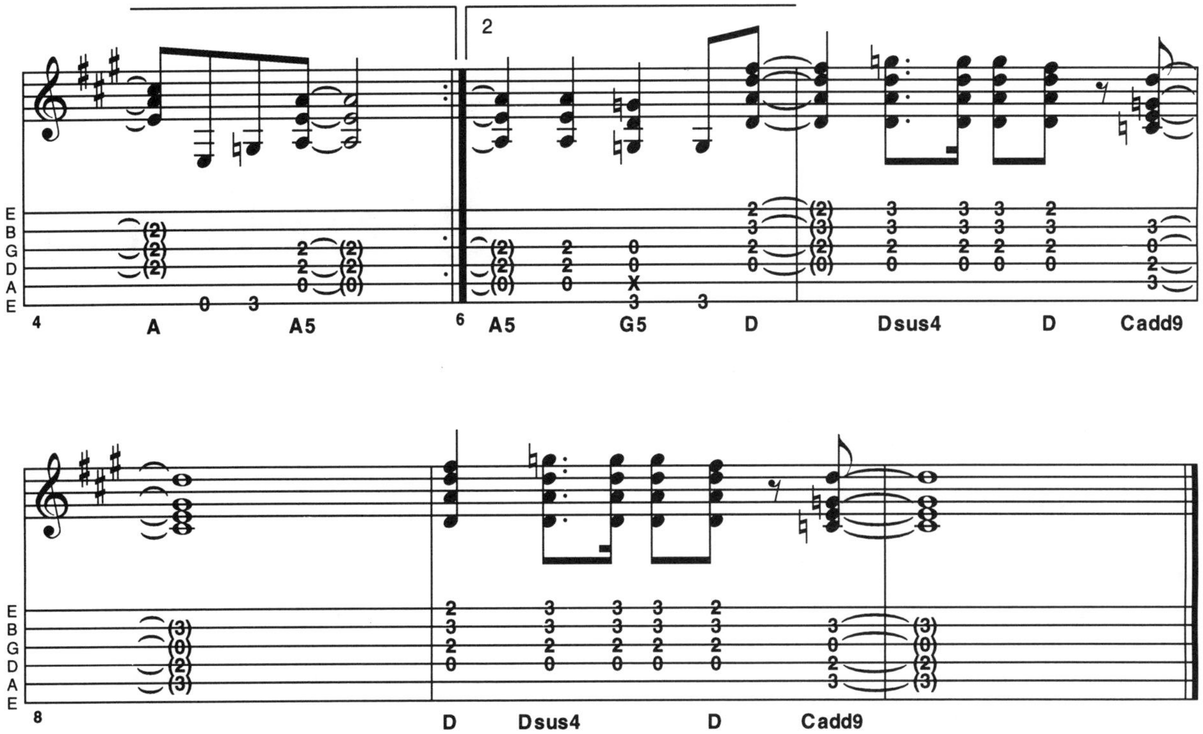

The chorus part notated above is the one played by the electric guitar; for the acoustic part all you really have to do is play the same chords but use fuller voicings. For instance, the first chord played by the electric guitar in the chorus is basically a shrunken-down version of the good old standard open C shape, so for the acoustic part I simply used the full-sized version.

After that, the verse (Ex 3) and the second part of the intro (Ex 2) repeat. As there's only a limited amount of CD time available for each chapter I've had to condense things considerably, so when writing your own Who-type songs try elongating some of the sections and adding more verses and choruses for the true epic effect.

Further Exploration

In common with many of the great British rock musicians of the sixties, Pete grew up on a steady diet of blues, jazz and R&B, his enormous list of influences including Muddy Waters, John Lee Hooker, Steve Cropper, Chet Atkins and (of course) Hank Marvin.

Fittingly, given the range of Pete's musical influences and listening habits, the Townshend effect can be heard in plenty of younger players: Peter Buck (when he's not doing the jangly McGuinn-style stuff), Paul Weller, Steve Jones of The Sex Pistols and... Brian May (come on, where else did he get those huge suspended chords from?!).

As you'd expect from a band with a large and loyal following, most of whose members are over thirty, there's plenty of high-quality Who-related info on the Internet. The Pete Townshend And Who Web Page – http://www.cybernet.net/~kmoon/ – is a typically professional example, but if you object to waiting ages for largely picture-based sites to download, you may be disappointed. If that's the case and you crave a little bit more in the way of text and solid information, try http://ucsub.colorado.edu/~golman/pt_g.html/ for a plethora of links to other sites, both official and unofficial.

CHAPTER 22
Steve Vai

biography TRACK 12

BORN:
6 June 1960.

ORIGIN:
Long Island, New York.

FIRST SPOTTED:
As a twenty-year-old in Frank Zappa's 1980 tour band. Steve had already been working for Frank as a transcriber since 1978, but secured a regular place in the band on account of his extraordinary guitar ability. (Steve is variously credited on Zappa album covers for "impossible guitar parts" and "Strat abuse".)

SEEN IN THE COMPANY OF:
Steve gained a bit of a reputation as a hired gun during the 1980s, appearing on rock albums by David Lee Roth, Whitesnake and Graham Bonnet's Alcatrazz, not to mention the more unusual projects with Shankar and Public Image Limited. More recently, his most important collaboration came in the shape of G3, the tour with Eric Johnson and Joe Satriani.

THE GOOD BITS:
One of the most intriguing players around today, Steve is constantly developing his style and adding more and more to his already impressive playing and composing abilities. Despite his ridiculous technical ability, there's never a feeling that Steve's showing off or going through the motions – he really suffers for his art!

THE BAD BITS:
Sex And Religion, the ill-fated "I want to be in a proper rock band" album. It just sounded clumsy, and maybe Steve shouldn't have tried to do mainstream US rock – somehow he's always best at the weird stuff.

ECCENTRICITY QUOTIENT:
An effortless hundred per cent – in his youth, Steve would put in mammoth twelve-hour practice sessions, he regularly fasts when recording solos, he used to transcribe Zappa's spoken-word parts... and then double them on guitar! Then of course there are the animal noises, the flower-pattern guitars, the blue hair (yes, it was a long time ago, Steve, but how could we let you forget?)...

NUTS AND BOLTS:
Steve's been endorsing and using Ibanez guitars for years – the various incarnations of the Jem model and the Universe seven-string. Amps tend to be a bit more variable, with VHT, Bogner, Laney and Marshall coming into the sonic equation somewhere or other.

VITAL VINYL:
From the solo career, *Passion And Warfare* is a masterpiece as well as a landmark in rock guitar history, but be sure to check out the wacky and wonderful *Flex-able* (get the one with extra tracks) and the non-stop, in-yer-face mini-album *Alien Love Secrets*. From the Zappa days, *Volume 6* of the live retrospective set *You Can't Do That On Stage Anymore* features some great work by Steve – how did he play that stuff!? Finally, for a great example of how Steve can transform a straightahead rock outing, get David Lee Roth's *Eat 'Em And Smile*.

It's difficult to know where to start with Steve Vai. His playing is so utterly unique and so seamlessly an extension of his personality, that trying to establish just what makes up the "Vai sound" is like attempting to gain entrance to an exclusive restaurant wearing T-shirt, shorts and a "kiss me quick" hat. The stuff on the inside looks deliciously tempting, but all entrances are barred to you. Don't despair, though – there is plenty to learn from Steve's playing, as well as his attitude to the study of music; you just have to be patient and prepared to put in lots of practice time.

For a change, I haven't written a proper introduction for this piece; we'll just dive in with the verse part. This is based entirely around alternating A and F chords. For the A chords, I've kept things very simple, and therefore ambiguous – is it major, Mixolydian or Lydian? With the F though, I've used one of Steve's favourite modes, the Lydian (in F this is F G A B C D E).You may have realised that there's no way both of these chords could have come from the same key, but that doesn't matter – Steve often uses quite "surprising" chord progressions in his tunes.

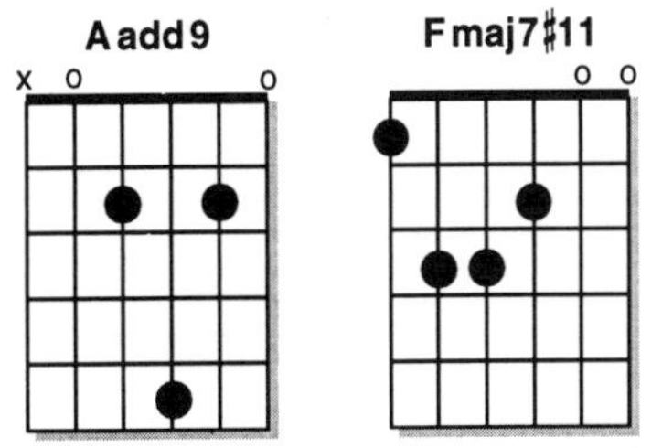

EX 1

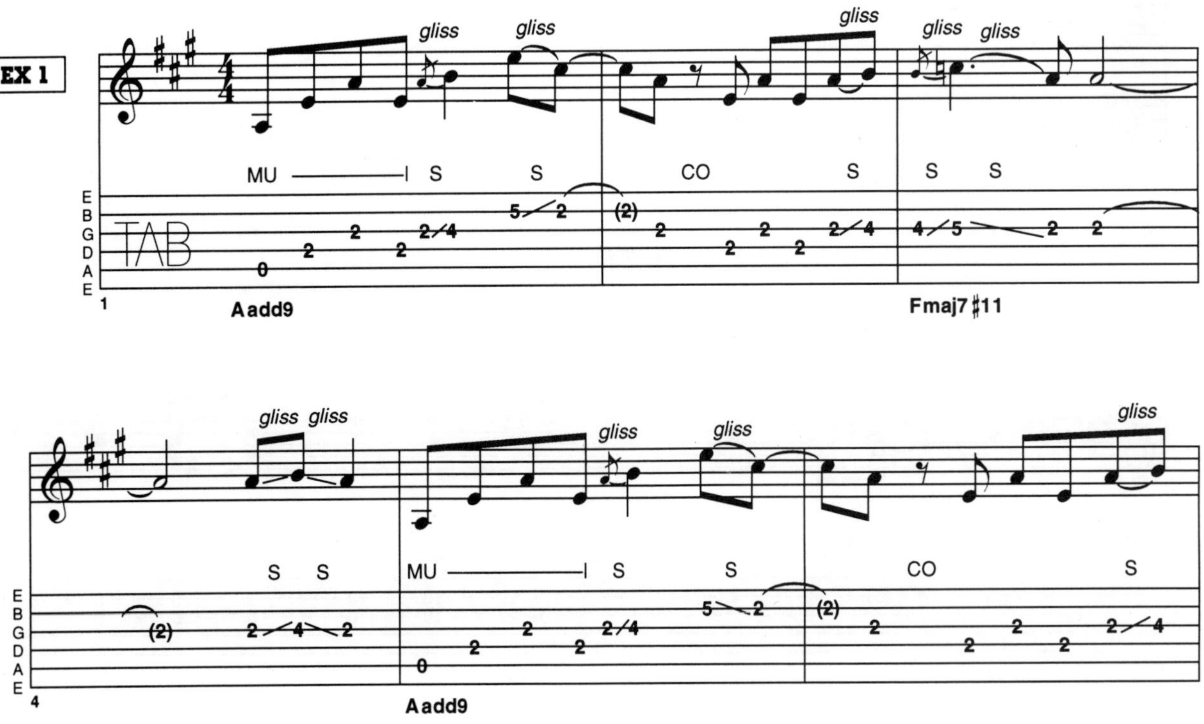

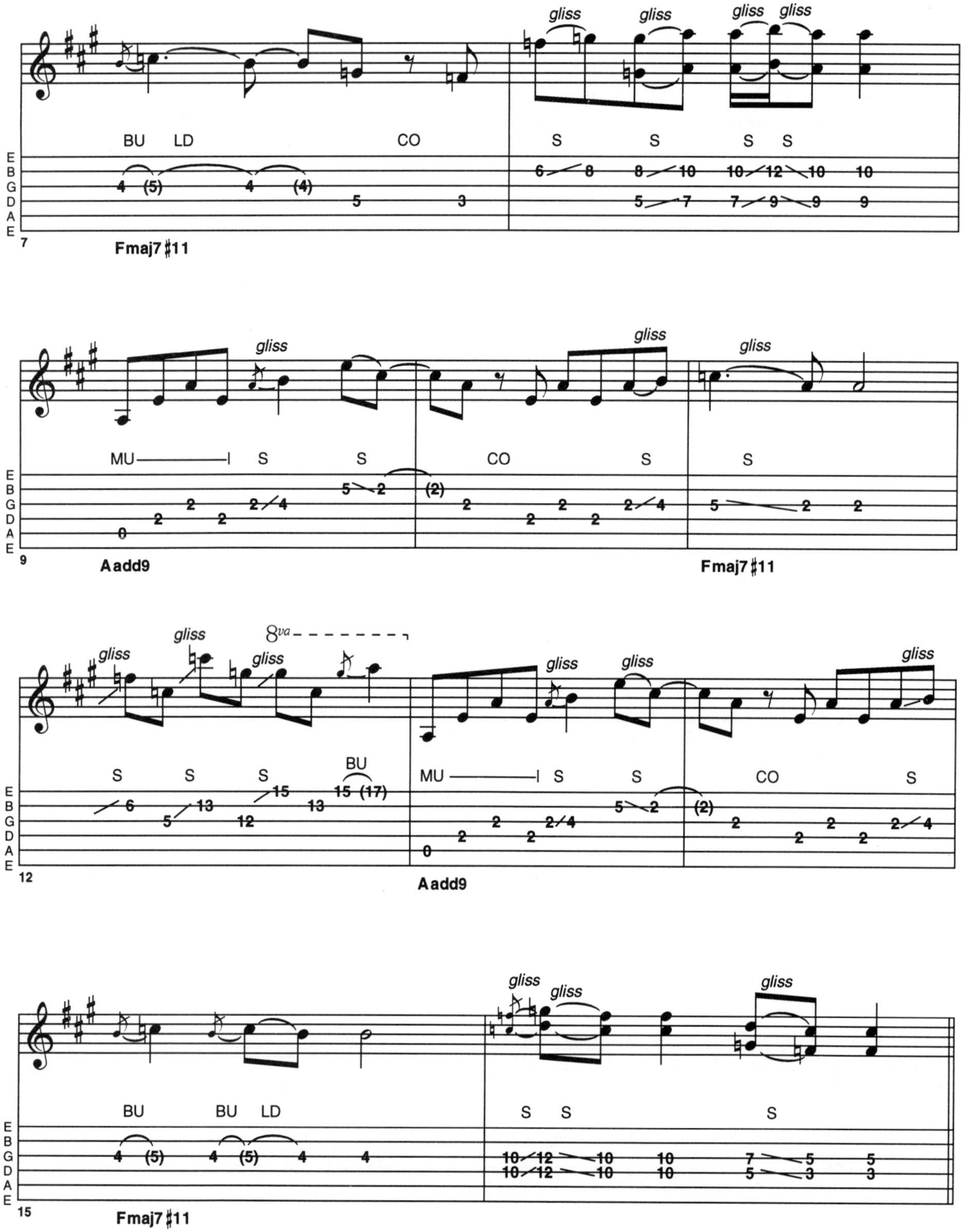
gliss
BU LD CO S
Fmaj7♯11
MU S CO
Aadd9
8va
15

Another of Steve's favourite compositional devices is something known as reharmonisation. Look at Ex 2. I've used a simple three-note melody (which happens to be the first three notes from 'Three Blind Mice'!) and harmonised it in five different ways. You can try this with any melody, and remember: the chord changes don't have to follow every note of the melody. In most cases, a given melody note can be found in the underlying chord – for instance, you might harmonise a C melody note with A minor (A C E), C major (C E G) or D7 (D F# A C) – but this is one of those rules that can easily be broken. Just experiment and see what comes out!

MELODY

EX 2

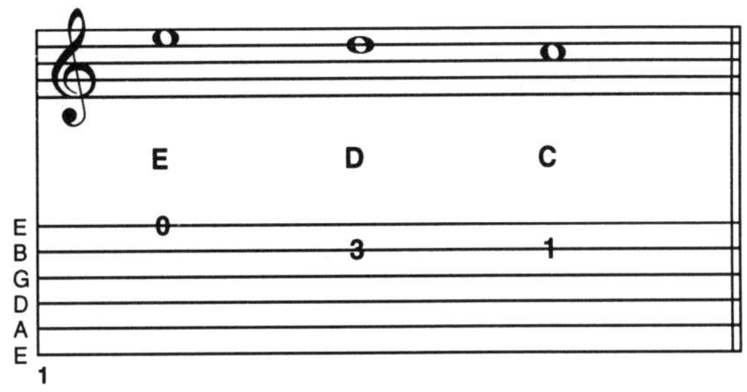

HARMONISATIONS

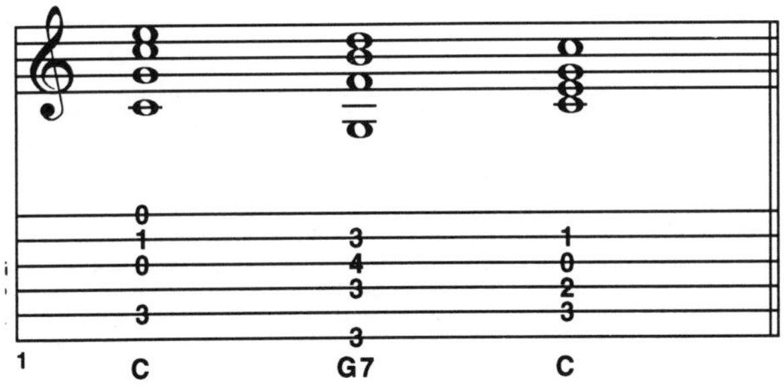

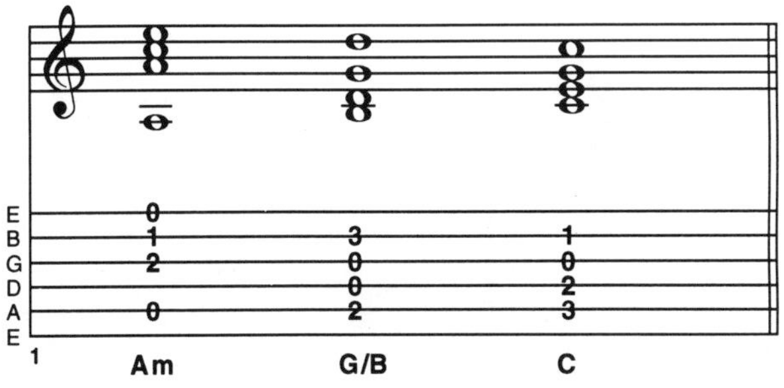

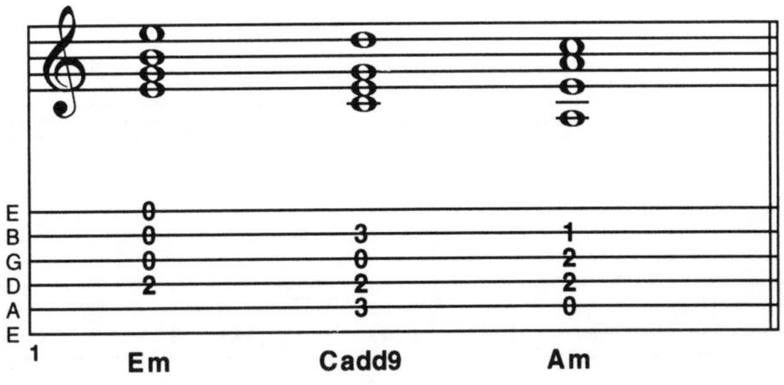

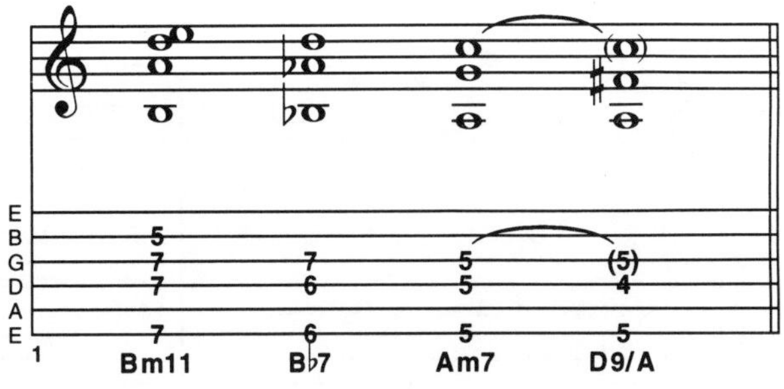

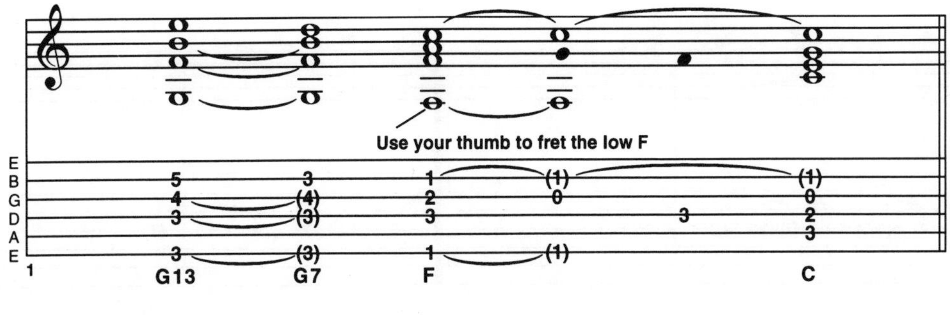

Here, to give you a more usable example of reharmonisation, is the chorus part. Each two-bar chunk features a variation on the same melodic phrase, but I've expanded upon its basic sound by harmonising it with a variety of possible chords. This section is basically in the key of E minor (E F# G A B C D E – the relative minor of G major) but since I avoided the F# note, it actually works over the otherwise impossible Fsus2 chord. By restricting the melody in the final bar to just A and D notes, I was also able to play over the potentially dodgy B♭ chord without a change of scale. Working like this results in an ear-grabbing chord progression, but with a smooth, logical-sounding melody over the top.

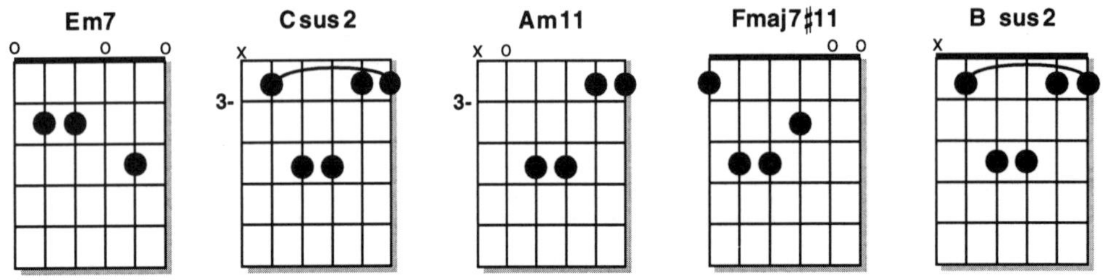

EX 3

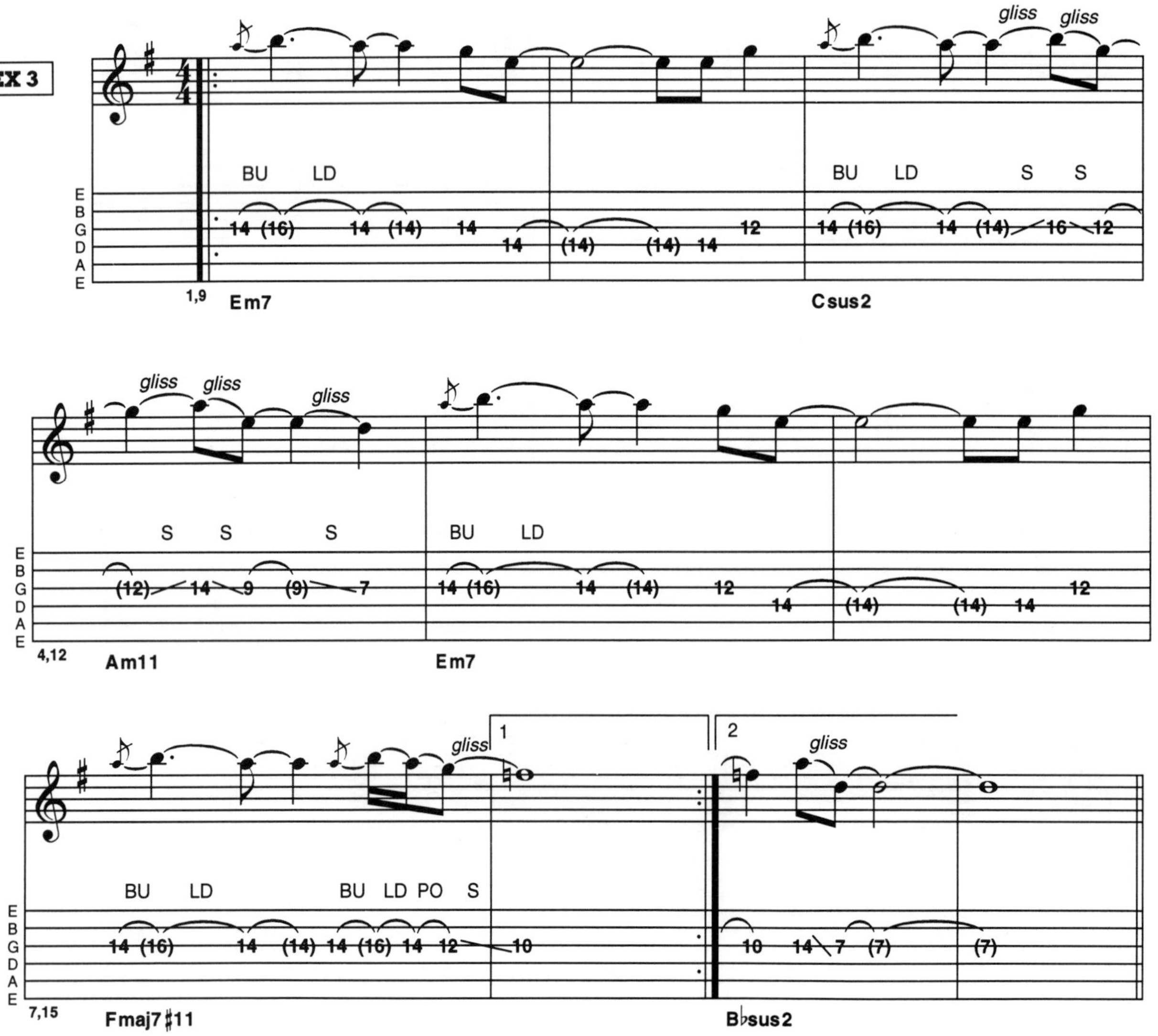

If this was a proper full-length song, you'd probably want to repeat the verse and chorus at this point, but since we've only got a limited amount of CD time, we'll jump bravely into the solo. The chord progression for the solo probably looks (and sounds!) a bit strange, but I've written it mainly as a vehicle for examining some of the scales Steve has used over the years. For the first four bars, I've alternated between two of Steve's main scales – the Lydian and Dorian modes, which make for interesting ear-grabbers, due to the raised fourth in the Lydian and the major sixth in the Dorian, notes which are not found in the standard major and minor scales respectively. After that, the C maj7 #5 allows me to demonstrate the weird and wacky Lydian Dominant mode, which is the third mode of the Melodic Minor scale – this can be heard on parts of Steve's tunes 'The Riddle' and 'Erotic Nightmares'. Finally, it's back to the Lydian for the F chord, and then the whole thing ends on E Mixolydian. Before you start the solo, this is what those scales look like.

EX 4

E LYDIAN MODE

C♯ DORIAN MODE

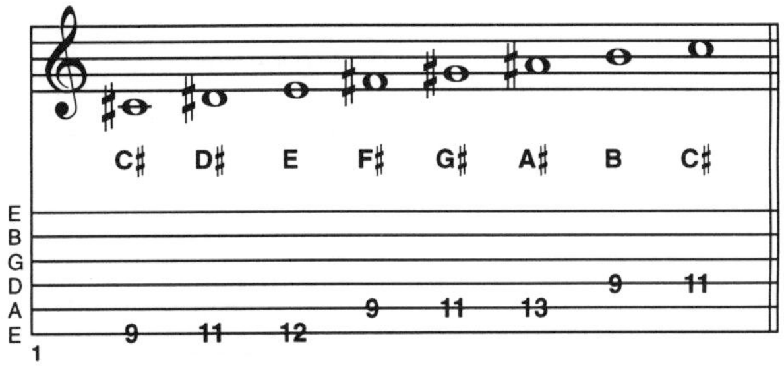

D LYDIAN MODE

B DORIAN MODE

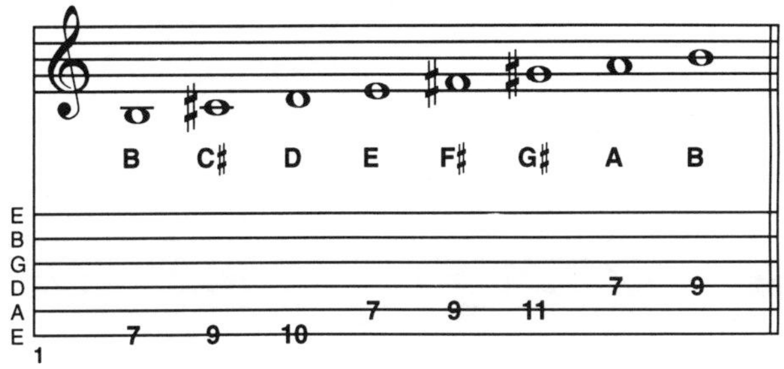

C LYDIAN DOMINANT MODE

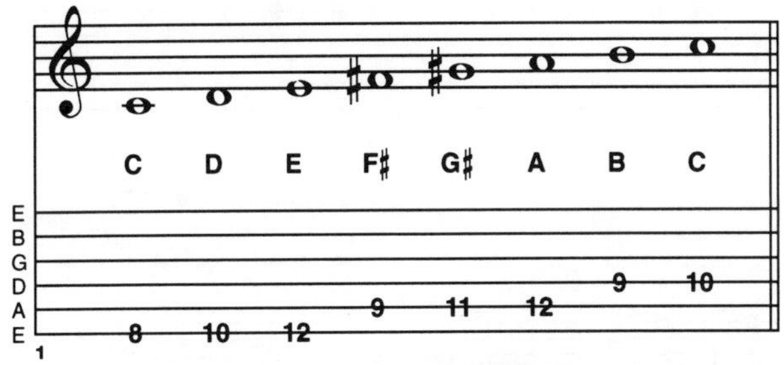

F LYDIAN MODE

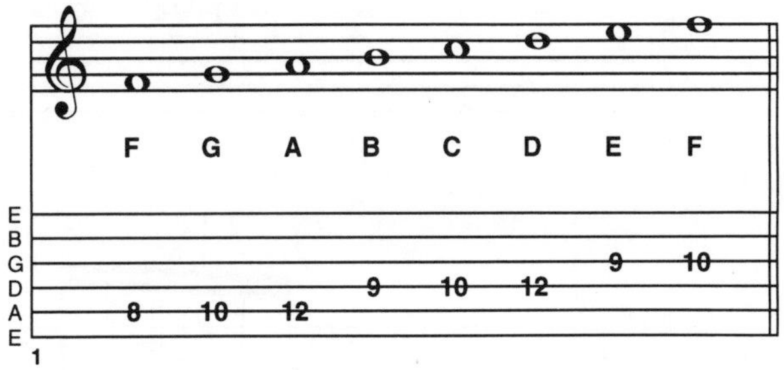

E MIXOLYDIAN MODE

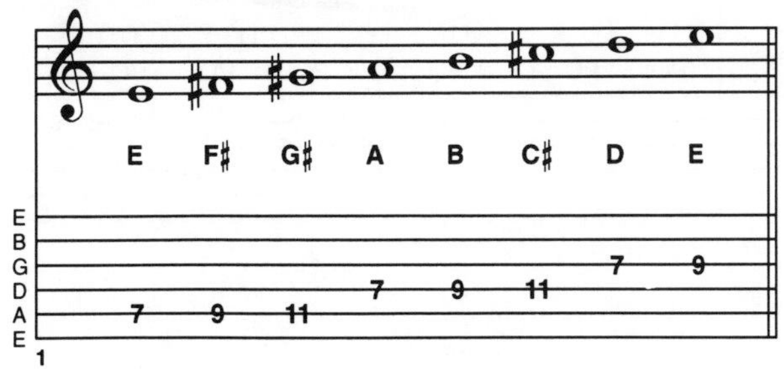

Rather than give you a complete run-down of all the techniques you're likely to come across in Steve Vai's playing (which would probably fill the rest of this book) I'll leave you to have a go at the solo itself as I've tried to fit in as many typical Vai-style lines as possible. Good luck!

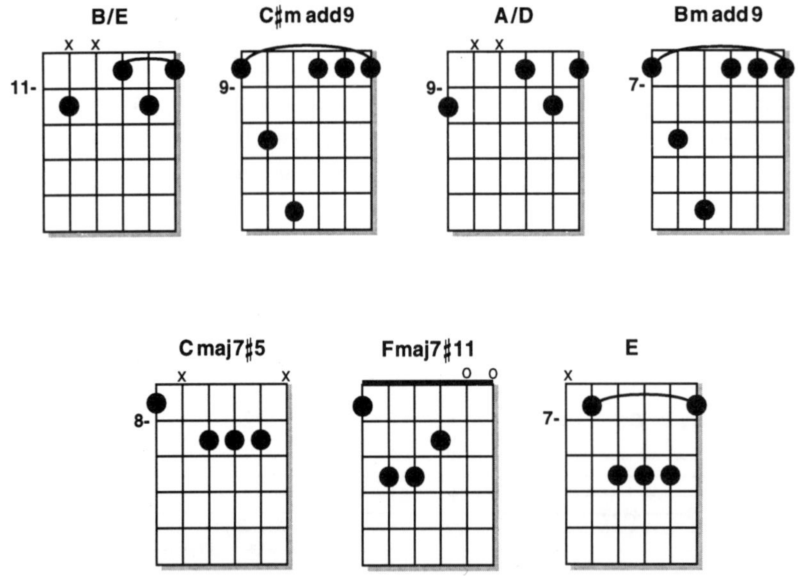

EX 5

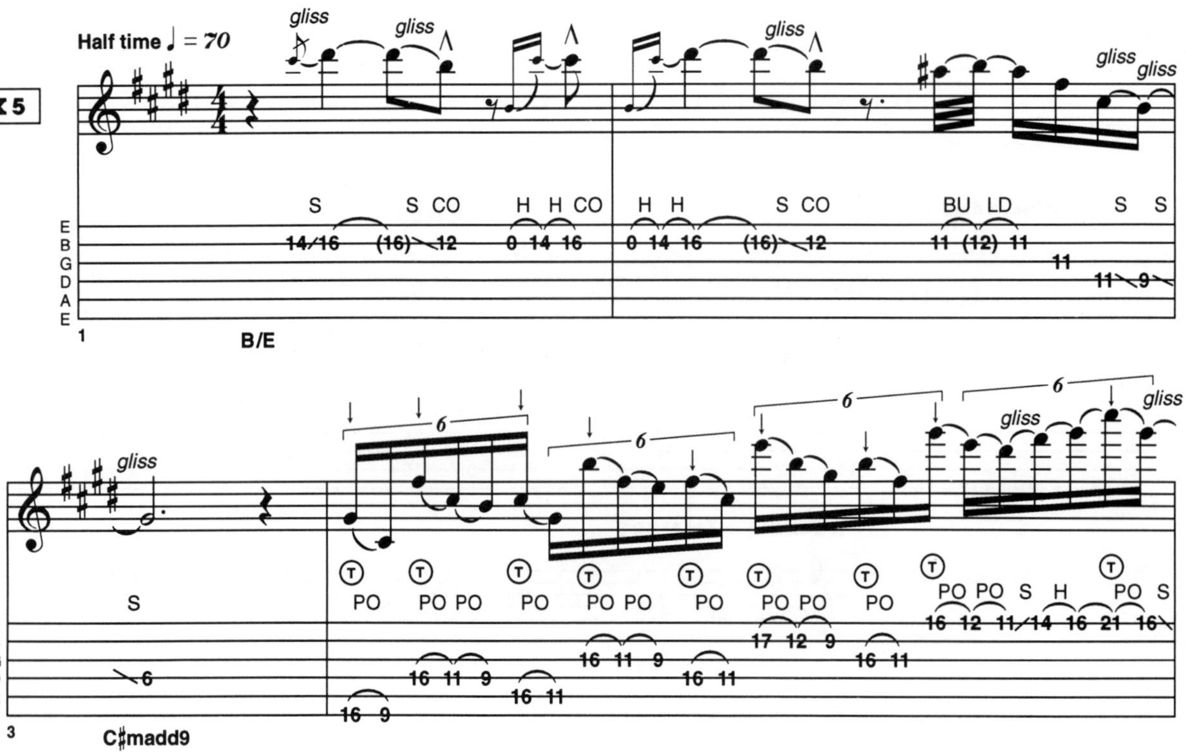

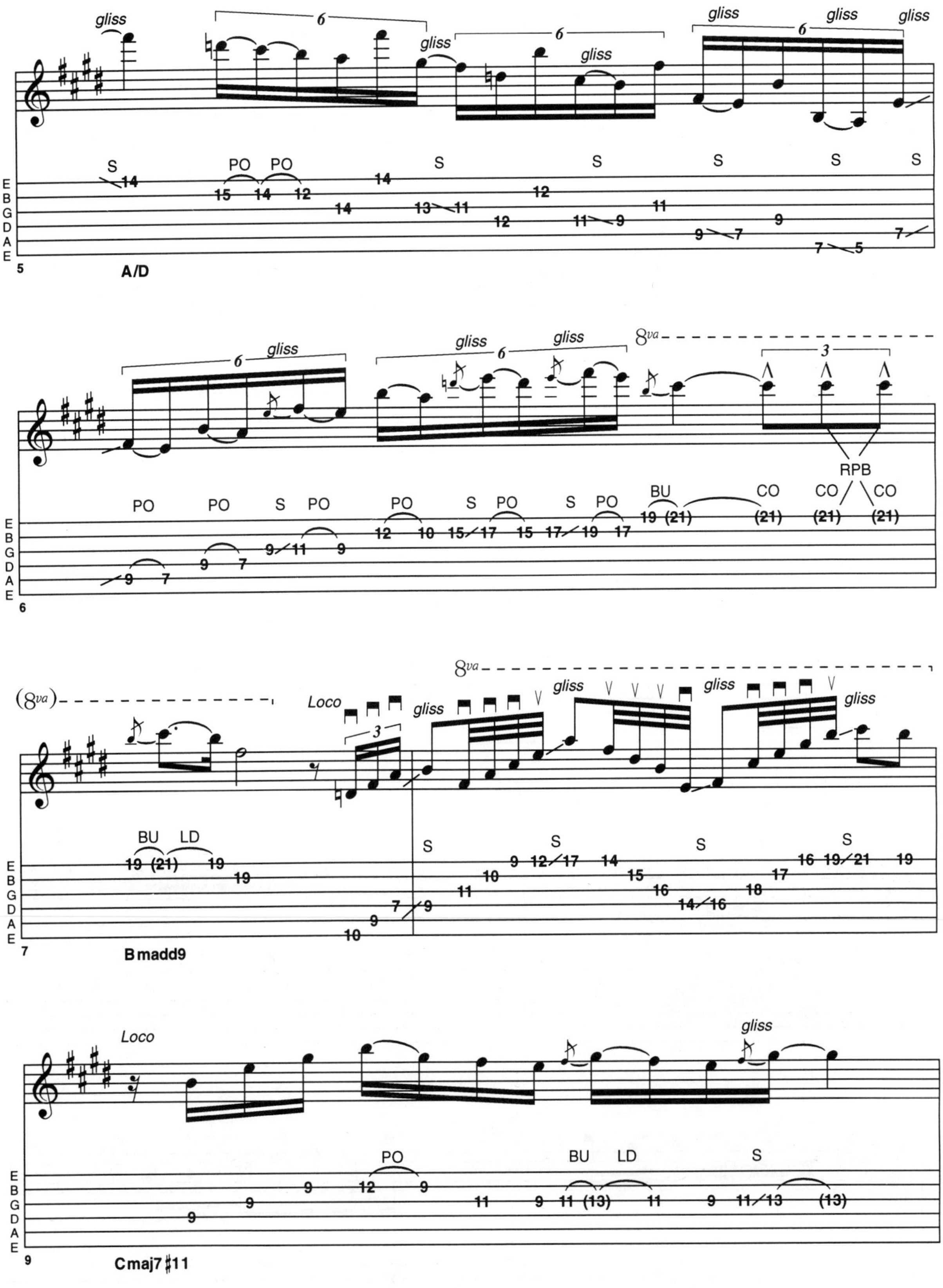
gliss
6
A/D
8va
Loco
(8va)
Bmadd9
Cmaj7♯11
PO
BU
LD
CO
RPB
S

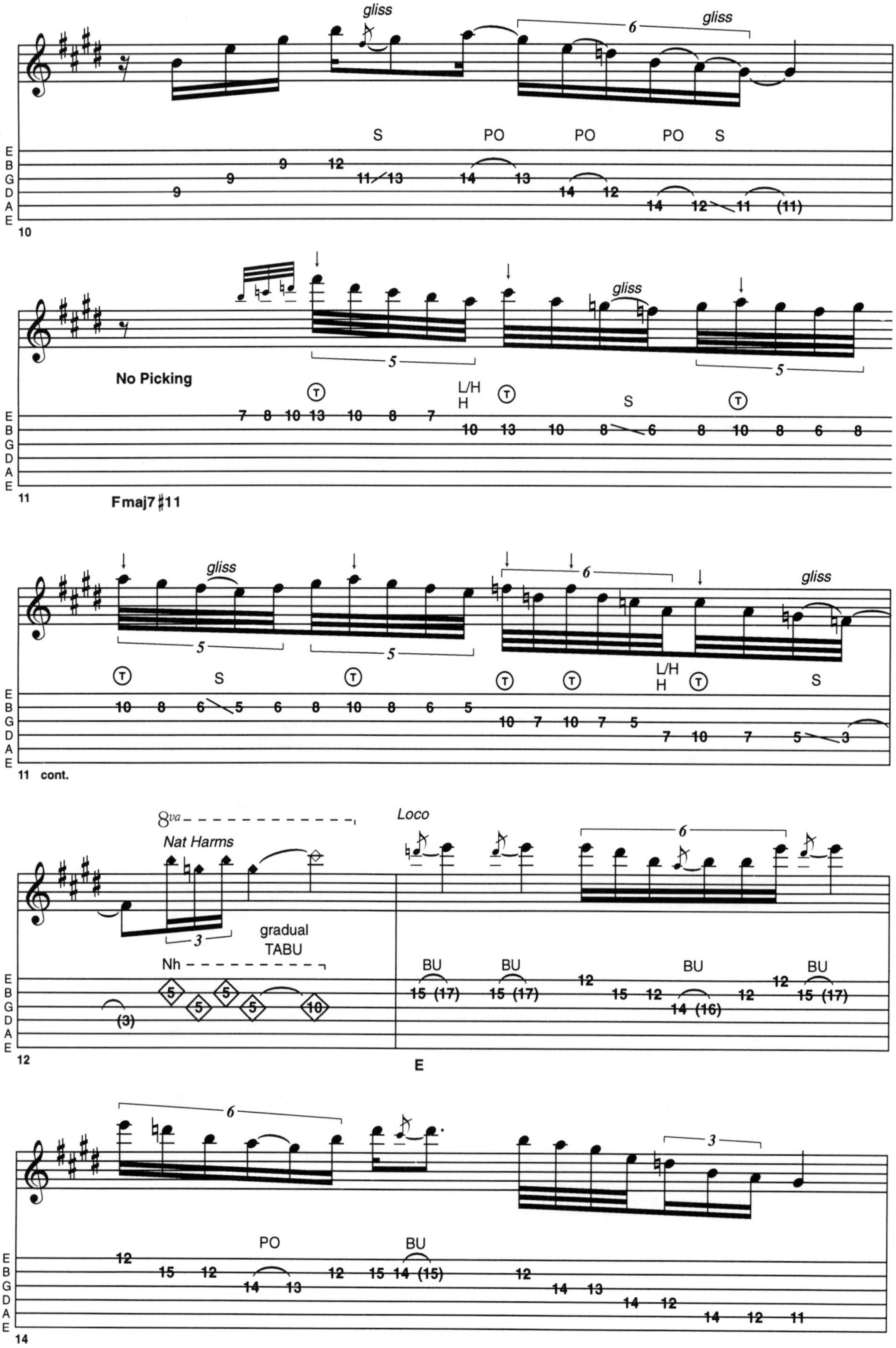
gliss
S
PO
No Picking
L/H
H
Fmaj7♯11
11 cont.
8va
Nat Harms
gradual
TABU
Nh
Loco
BU
E

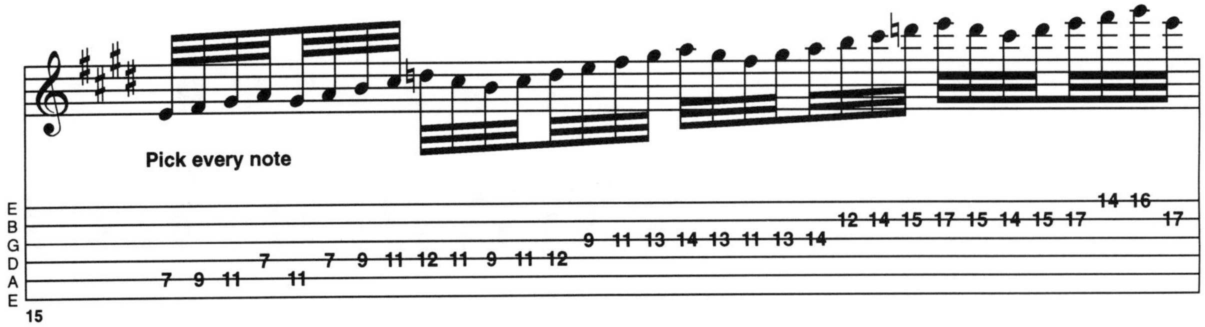

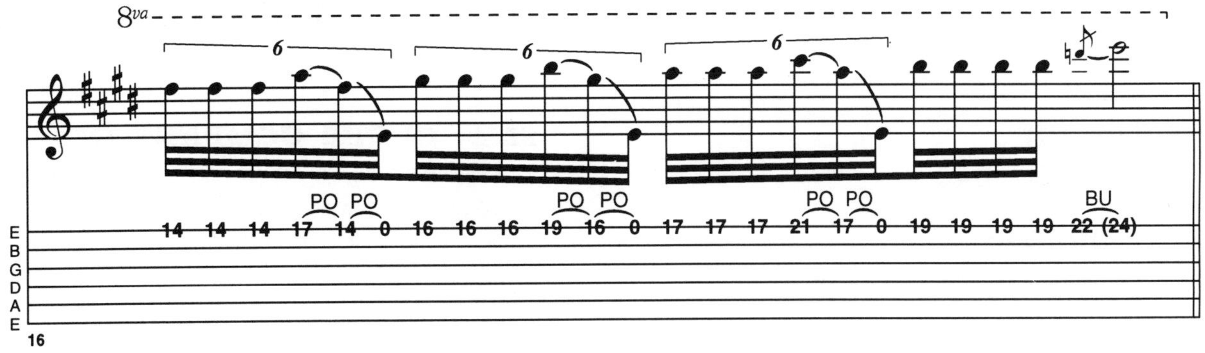

After the solo, the verse part repeats with a few different fills to keep it interesting (see if you can work them out yourself) and the whole tune ends on an F chord.

Further Exploration

Steve's earliest guitar influences were Jimi Hendrix and Jimmy Page, but it was when he decided to take lessons with a local teacher that he found one of his two major inspirations: the teacher was none other than Joe Satriani, and although their musical styles are completely different, it's clear that they share a similar attitude towards music. Steve's other mentor was of course Frank Zappa, with whom Steve gained some valuable early experience of the music business and how to survive touring. Even before he started working for FZ, Steve was a huge fan, and the influence of Zappa's penchant for odd rhythms and quirky melody can be heard in many of Steve's tunes.

Out of all the guitarists in this book, Steve Vai is possibly the most "copy-proof". His style and technical ability are incredibly advanced, and I'd wager that far more people have learnt from his attitude to composition, practising and recording.

On the web, the best point of call is http://www.vai.com but there are plenty of unofficial sites, too. As ever, some of them are swooning pubescent dross, whereas others are the work of unheralded genius.

CHAPTER 23
Edward Van Halen

biography TRACK 14

BORN:
26 January 1957.

ORIGIN:
Nijmegen, the Netherlands.

CLAIM TO FAME:
Reinvented rock guitar in the late seventies, thus becoming one of the two most important players in the history of rock guitar (the other being Jimi Hendrix, who had much the same sort of impact a decade earlier).

DISTINGUISHING FEATURES:
Ironically, these can best be heard by listening to the playing of other guitarists – two-hand tapping, extreme use of the tremolo bar, creative use of harmonics, fast tremolo picking, guitars with one pickup, a Floyd Rose tremolo and a custom paint job... for a while back in the early eighties, all the new guitarists sounded like they'd learned nothing but Van Halen solos.

FIRST SPOTTED:
Eddie and his bro' Alex formed Van Halen in 1974. Two years later, Gene Simmons (of daft make-up band Kiss) sponsored their first demo tape, but to no avail.

BIG BREAK:
Playing at LA's Starwood club in 1977, Ed and the boys were spotted by famous record producer Ted Templeman... "Kids, you're gonna be big stars. Now just sign this piece of paper and I'll do the rest." They signed. The rest is history.

SEEN IN THE COMPANY OF:
Despite his huge megastar status, Eddie's non-VH appearances have been fairly select. Apart from his legendary solo on Michael Jackson's 'Beat It', he teamed up with Brian May for the jam-tastic *Starfleet Project* in 1983, and managed to find the necessary courage to jam with – gulp – Allan Holdsworth.

THE GOOD BITS:
"Reinvented rock guitar in the late seventies..." I think I said. By 1978, the pseudo-Hendrix minor Pentatonic stuff was getting a little tired, so thank God EVH came along and provided the welcome kick up the rear.

THE BAD BITS:
Despite some routinely brilliant playing from Ed, the band have never repeated the explosive impact of the first four albums. Happens to everyone, I suppose...

NUTS AND BOLTS:
For years, Eddie was known for his "slapped together" guitars, which revolutionised the way guitars were built (looks like a Strat, sounds like Les Paul etc). More recently, he's used signature models, built first by Ernie Ball/Music Man and later by Peavey. Peavey also build Eddie's signature 5150 amplifiers.

VITAL VINYL:
The first four albums – *Van Halen* (1978), *Van Halen II* (1979), *Women And Children First* (1980) and *Fair Warning* (1981) – are essential, and despite the "old-sounding" production, the guitar playing still sounds incredible.

It was kind of inevitable I know, but somehow I just had to start this piece off with a bit of tapping (if you don't know what that means, check out the Techniques Primer where you'll find a gentle introduction). Eddie has expanded and refined his tapping technique since those heady 'Eruption'-fuelled days of the late seventies, but for this intro section, I've tried to go for the same sort of effect as he was getting on the early Van Halen albums. Here we go now...

EX 1

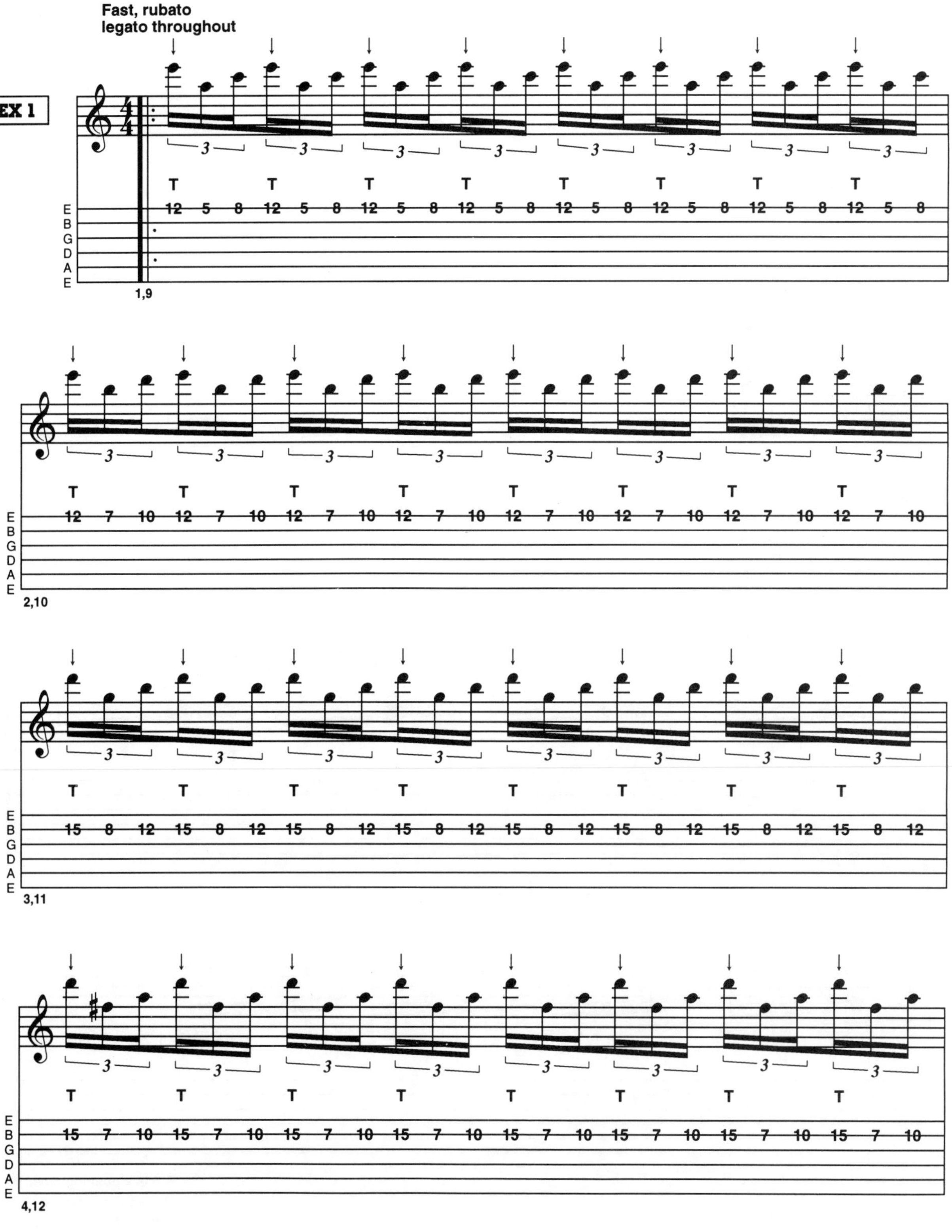

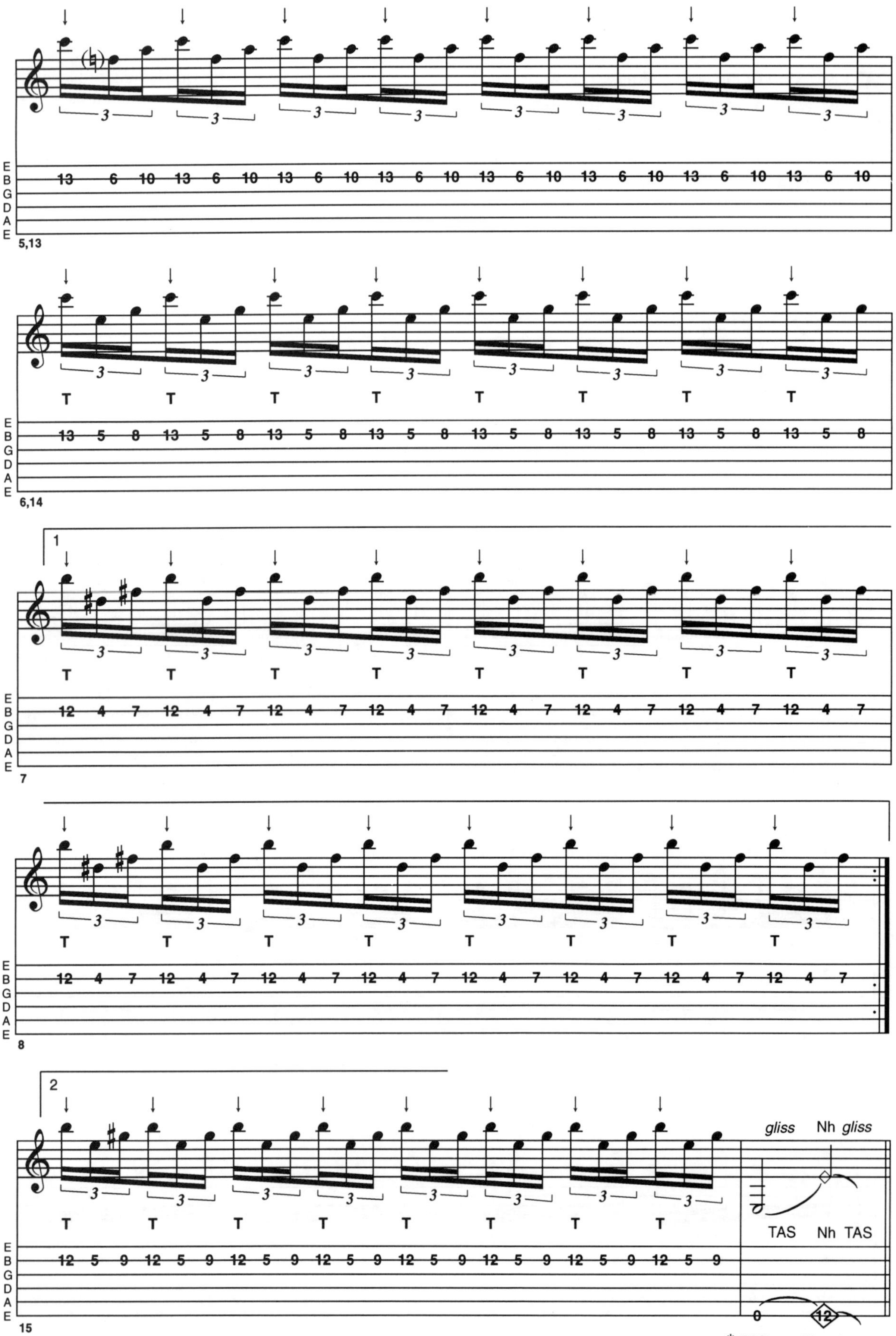

* While pushing down on tremolo bar, tap on 12th fret to produce harmonic

For the start of the song proper, I came up with this part, largely based around the A Dorian mode (A B C D E F# G A). Van Halen have done plenty of songs based on this sort of high speed boogie feel; it's not easy to play accurately at this sort of tempo, so when learning the parts, start slowly and make sure everything's sounding clean and accurate before gradually increasing speed.

EX 2

In the same sort of style, here's a verse part...

EX 3

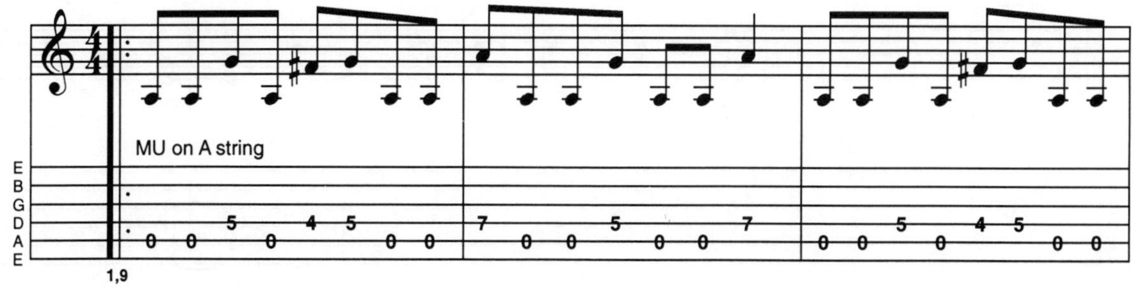

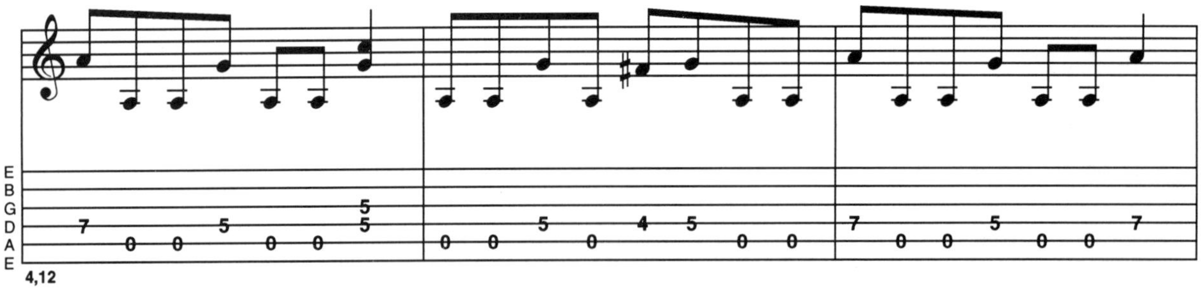

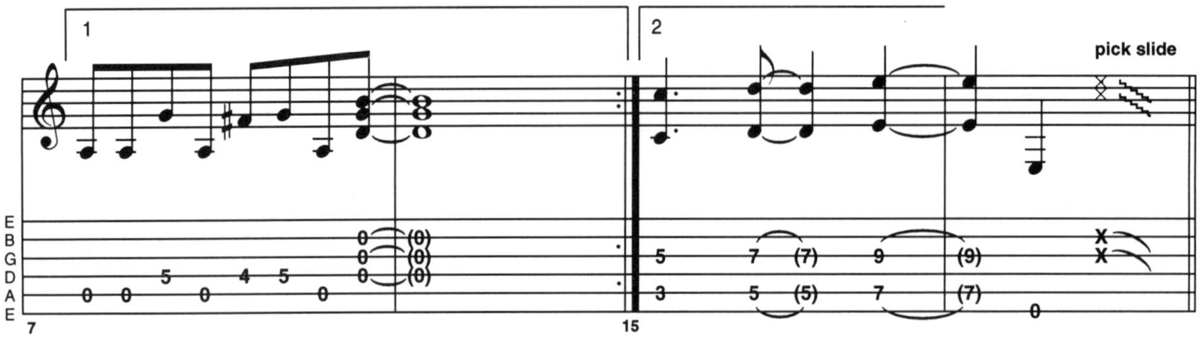

And, with that secure, soothing inevitability that comes with all classic rock songs, the chorus. (Not that this is a classic rock song, you understand, it's just a humble simulation!) Notice how I've stuck to fairly simple harmonic material: apart from fills and passing chords, I've used mainly A, D and E – the I, IV and V chords in the key of A. In standard theory, these would all be major chords, and any melody lines would use the A major scale (A B C# D E F# G# A) but in rock and blues you can be far more liberal with theoretical concerns; the result is a kind of major/minor hybrid, as discussed in other chapters, with the Dorian, Mixolydian and minor Pentatonic scales being the usual note sources. Anyway, the chorus...

EX 4

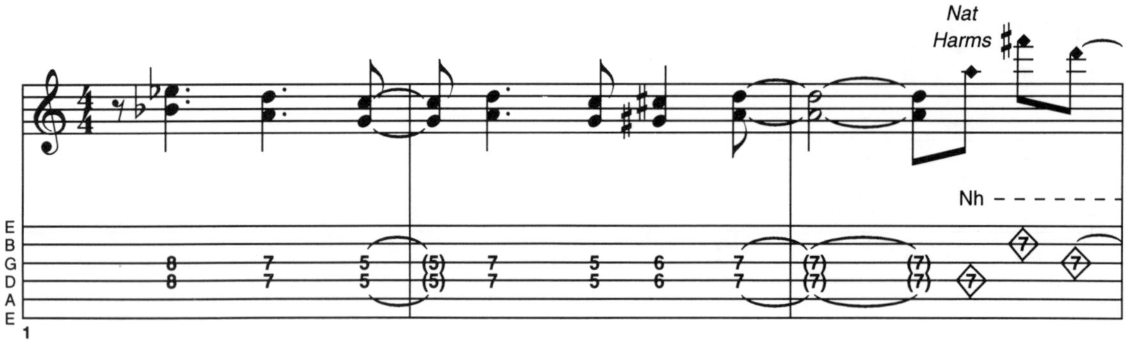

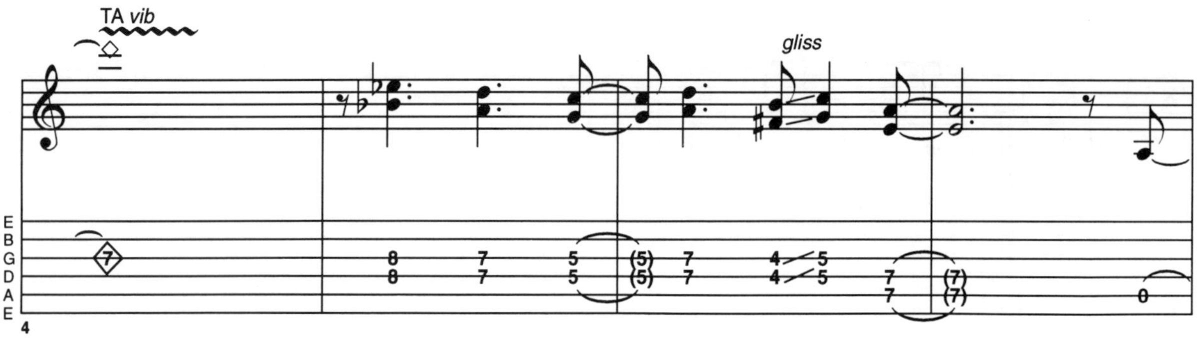

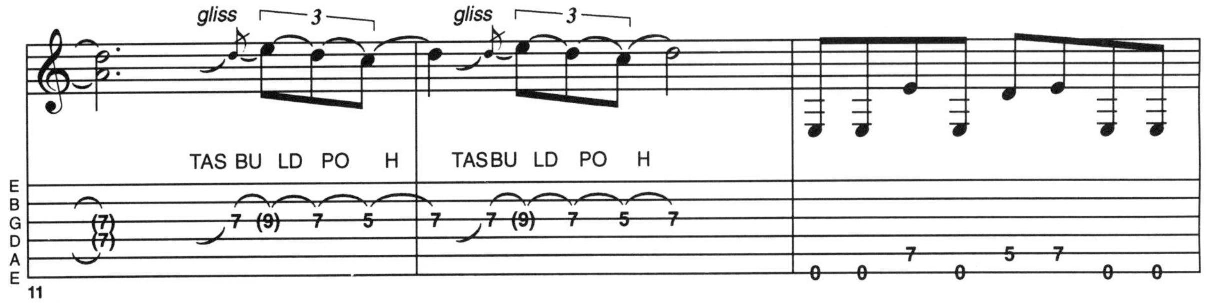

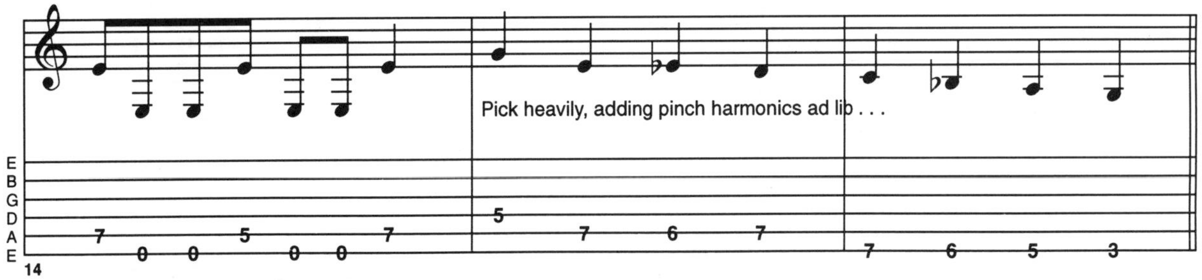

The intro returns after that, but with a slightly different ending. Play most of it as before (Ex 2) but replace the original fourth ending (the "4" box) with this:

EX 5

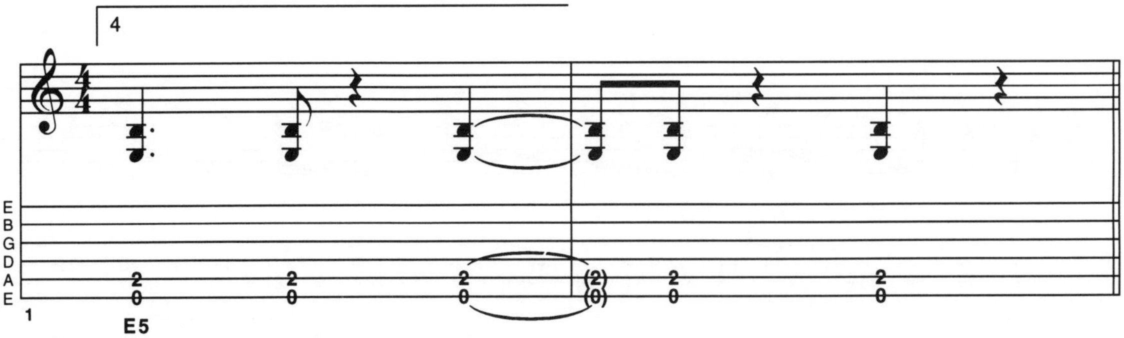

Time for a solo, and with several of Eddie's solos, you also get a key change. If you've read the chapter on Jimi Hendrix, you'll remember the tip I gave you regarding key changes: in general, move upwards. With the final E chord of the intro ringing clearly in my ears, I decided that a jump to a new key centre of F# would provide a pleasing "lift" to the tune. Halfway through the solo, I then came to the conclusion that another key change would sustain the excitement, so I moved to B. Although this might seem quite a large jump, considering what I said in the Hendrix chapter, there is a certain amount of logic to my choice: the keys of B and F# are almost identical. I used mainly the Dorian mode for both keys; take a look at their contents...

F# Dorian – F# G# A B C# D# E F# (derived from E major)
B Dorian – B C# D E F# G# A B (derived from A major)

See? There's only one note separating them. Enough of my babbling – here's the solo...

EX 6

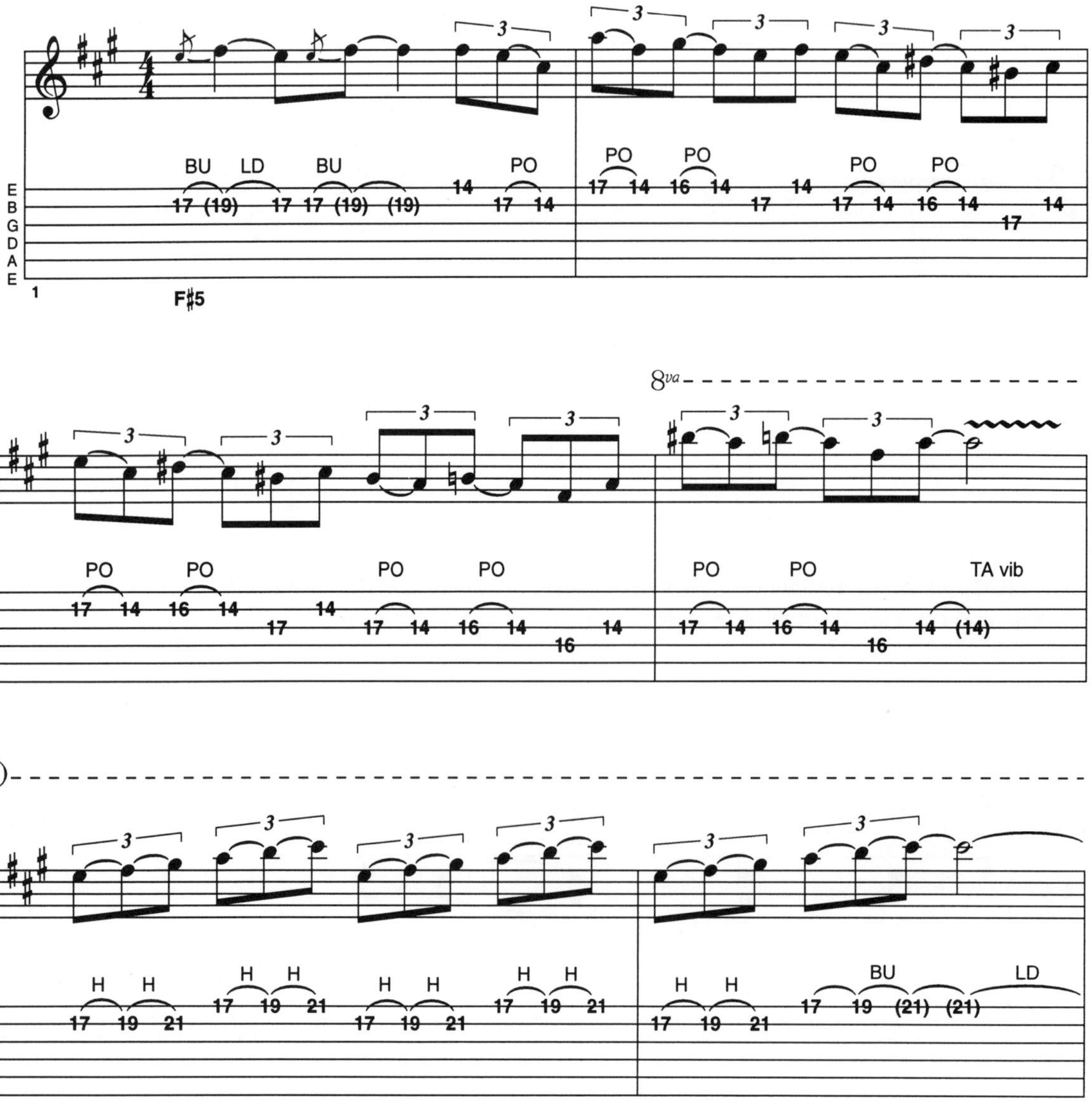

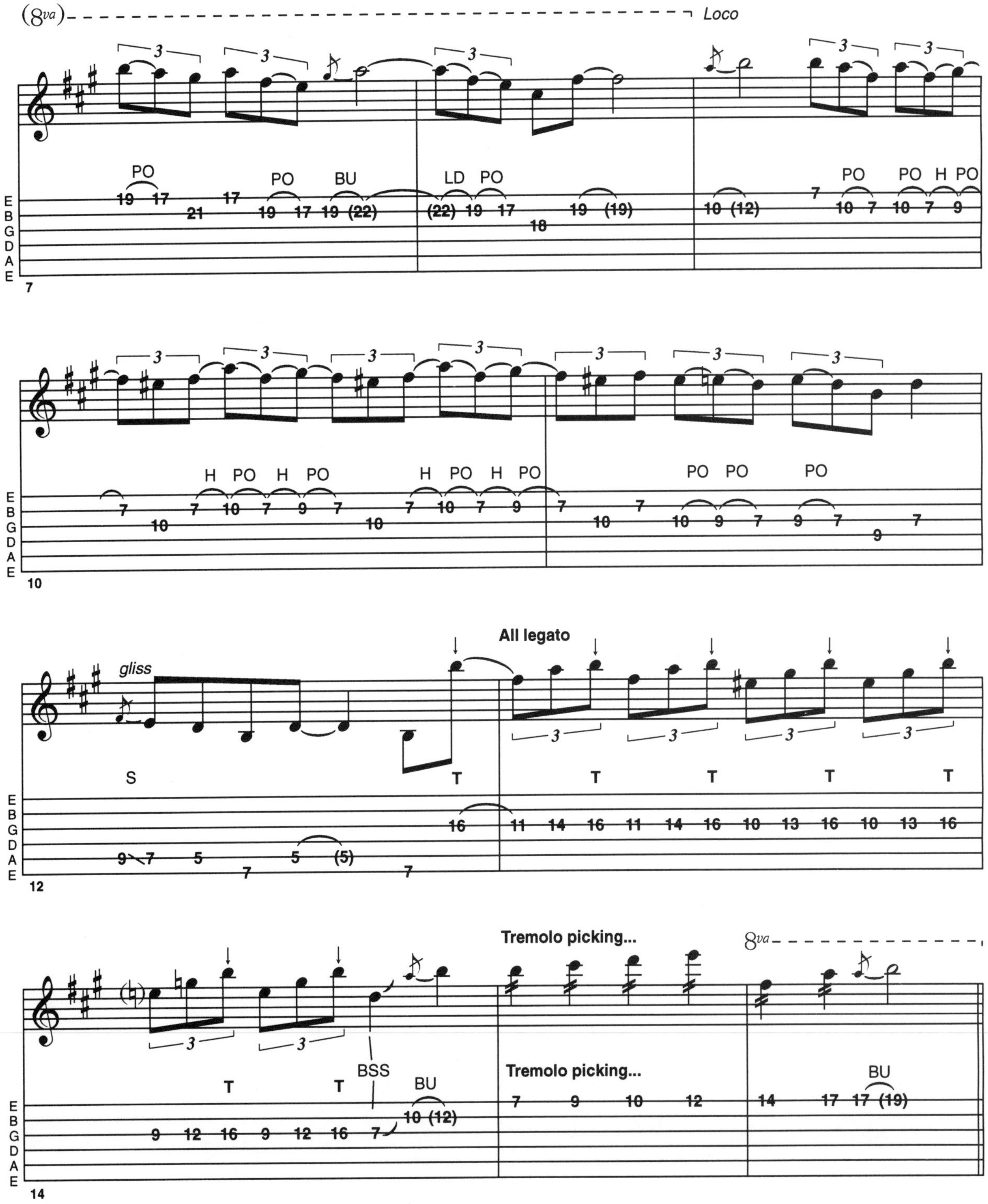

A word of warning: although Eddie is generally known as a very flash guitarist, there's an enormous amount of blues in his playing, so don't make the mistake of just concentrating on the high speed tapping workouts. Listen to his incredible phrasing – his sense of rhythm (in riffs, chord parts and solos) is totally off the wall, but it always grooves! Just to prove that all rules are made to be broken, the B minor tonality established in the second half of the solo modulates down to A with the repeat of the intro. I was tempted to change this, or add something in between, but then decided that the downward movement gives an impression of returning to the previous level; "coming home", so to speak. Anyway, all you have to do is repeat the original intro and end on an A5 chord.

Further Exploration

It's well known that Eric Clapton, especially his work with Cream, was a Eddie's biggest influence when he was learning to play guitar. While few clues to this side of these listening habits can be found in his playing, it's easy to hear how Jimi Hendrix, Jeff Beck, Ritchie Blackmore and Jimmy Page had an effect on the young EVH. Wild showmanship, sonic experimentation, a taste for classical-style precision and a genius for arrangement and composition – they're all there!

With a player like Eddie, it's not really a case of simply finding a handful of younger players who exhibit signs of the great man's influence. His influence during the late seventies and early eighties was practically universal; there's been a bit of a retro backlash in recent years, but consider the ways in which tapping, whammy bar workouts and fast legato runs have become the norms of high-energy rock playing. One particular disciple is the amazing Dweezil Zappa.

There's an awful lot of Van Halen on the Web, but go straight to the Van Halen News Desk – http://www.vhnd.com – which provides up to the minute bulletins on Ed and the boys as well as a pageful of links.

CHAPTER 24

Stevie Ray Vaughan

BORN:

3 October 1954.

DIED:

27 August 1990.

ORIGIN:

Dallas, Texas. Although Stevie's usually associated with blues city Austin, he didn't actually move there until he was eighteen.

FIRST SPOTTED:

Stevie made his first vinyl appearance in 1973, playing on 'Texas Clover' by Paul Ray And The Cobras.

BIG BREAK:

In 1982, Stevie and his band Double Trouble were invited to play at the Montreux Jazz Festival. Auspicious enough, you might think, but while there, Stevie's eyebrow-removing guitar playing attracted the interest of a certain Mr Bowie. He guested on Bowie's *Let's Dance* albumin 1983 and released his own gold-selling debut, *Texas Flood*.

SEEN IN THE COMPANY OF:

Stevie racked up quite a number of guest slots during his career, appearing on records by James Brown, Jennifer Warnes, Lonnie Mack, Bowie and many others. Arguably his most successful collaboration came in the shape of the album *Family Style*, recorded not long before his death with his elder brother Jimmie.

THE GOOD BITS:

Imagine a compendium of some of the greatest electric blues guitarists – Albert King, Lonnie Mack, Buddy Guy and Freddie King, but imbued with the fire of Jimi Hendrix. Add a little bit of funky jazz à la Grant Green or Kenny Burrell. Now turn the knob marked "Intensity" up to eleven and add a great singing voice...

THE BAD BITS:

The ultimate irony, really. Having finally straightened himself out after years of alcohol and cocaine addiction, Stevie died through circumstances beyond his control – in a helicopter crash in Wisconsin.

NUTS AND BOLTS:

The guitar you're most likely to have seen Stevie with was that battered old 1957 Strat; customised with the addition of a left-handed tremolo bridge (!) and heavy gauge Gibson frets. Most of Stevie's other guitars were Strats, including the early sixties maple-necked model he nicknamed Lenny. Amps tended most often to be Fender Vibroverbs, but he often used a Dumble head, and later in his career he started more and more to record with Marshalls.

VITAL VINYL:

Of the eight albums released (three posthumously, including the one with Jimmie Vaughan) only one is really worth avoiding: *Live Alive* (1986) comes from the period just before Stevie realised he really, desperately needed to kick his addictions. Masses of rescue work in the studio couldn't revive this lacklustre album. On the bright side, though, get hold of any of Stevie's other recordings and listen to the master at work.

One thing to bear in mind when studying the playing of Stevie Ray Vaughan is that he wasn't a Texas blues purist. No way, José – he absorbed lots of bits and pieces: from blues greats such as Albert King, Lonnie Mack and Buddy Guy, from jazz players Wes Montgomery, Grant Green and Kenny Burrell, and filtered it all through the influence of his big hero, Jimi Hendrix.

With that in mind, I've mixed together a few aspects of Stevie's style to create this little ditty. Sure, he might never have played anything quite like this, but break this piece down to its component parts and you'll find lots of things he did play.

Before we get down to the nitty gritty, let's ease into things gently by having a look at the chord sequence which provides a backdrop for the whole piece. You've heard of the twelve-bar blues, right? (If not, then consult the chapters on Chuck Berry, Scotty Moore and Charlie Christian, or look at the appropriate section in the Theory Primer). Well, this is based around a sixteen-bar blues progression. Whoo, we're flying by the seats of our pants here, folks! Oh yes, it's in the key of E and looks like this...

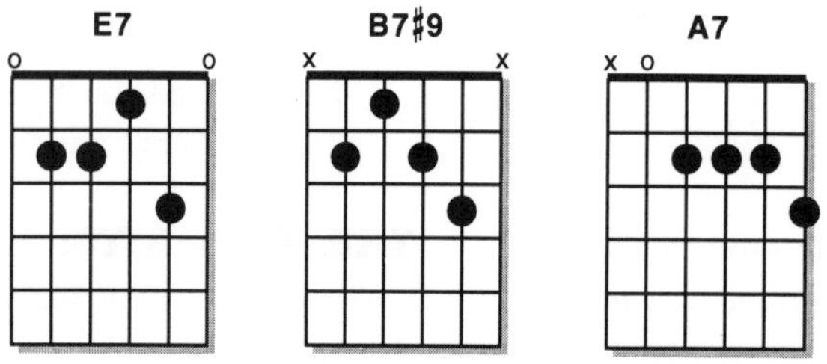

EX 1

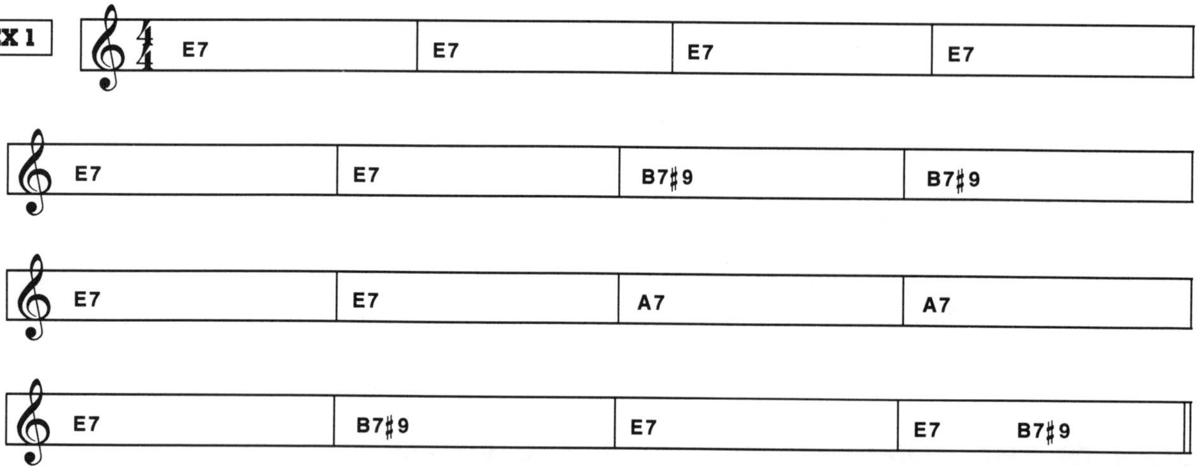

Okay? We'll now start to make something out of that humble progression. Many of Stevie's tunes (both vocal and instrumental) featured "call and response" passages. This sort of idea dates back to the sort of thing that slaves would have sung in the fields – one person sings a line, and everyone else responds. If you prefer, think of the stereotypical image of US Marines on training exercises (do they really do all that chanting stuff? Never mind...). In musical terms, the single note phrases in the following example are answered by the funky chords.

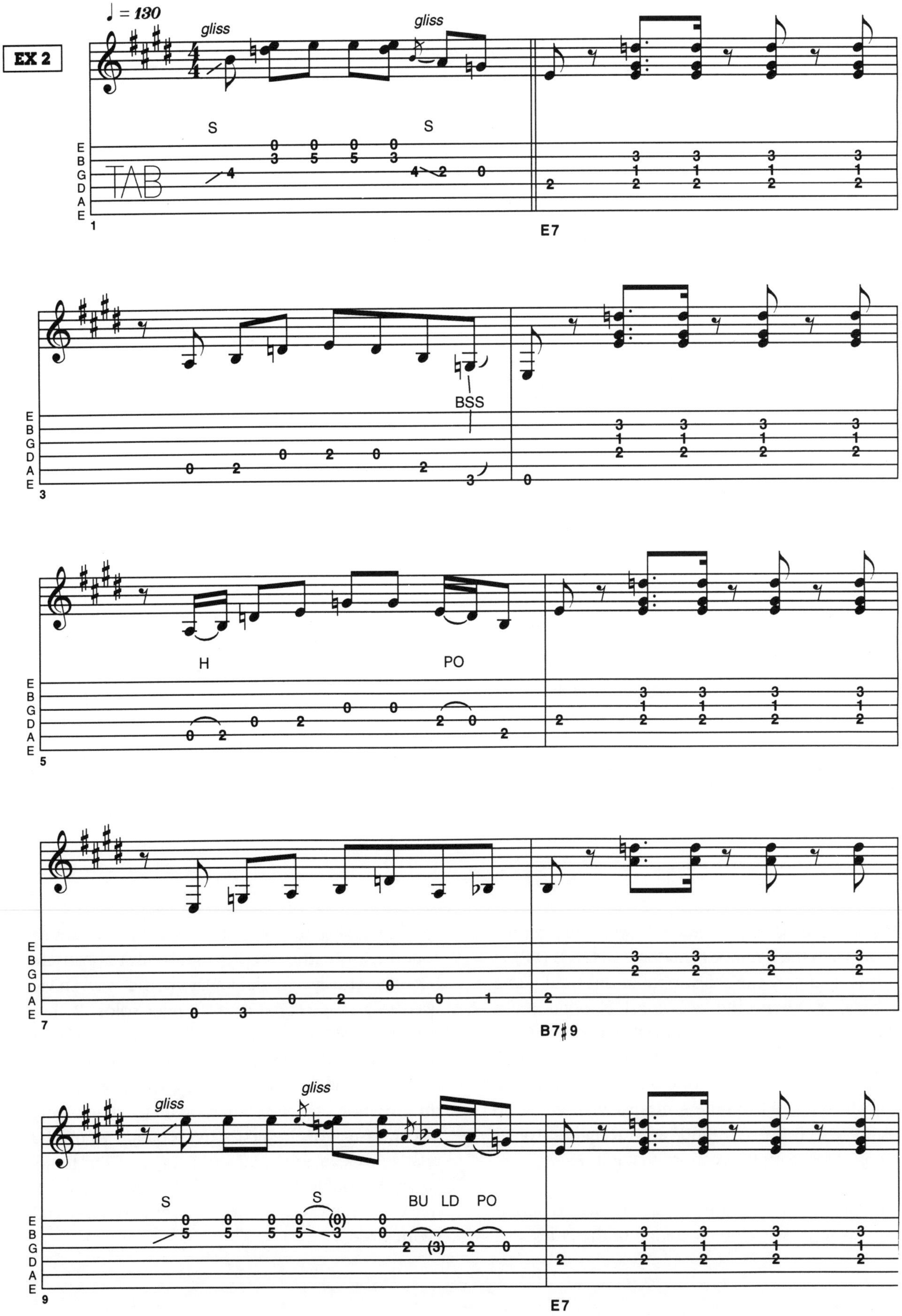
EX 2
♩ = 130
gliss
gliss
S
S
TAB
E7
BSS
H
PO
B7♯9
gliss
gliss
S
S
BU LD PO
E7

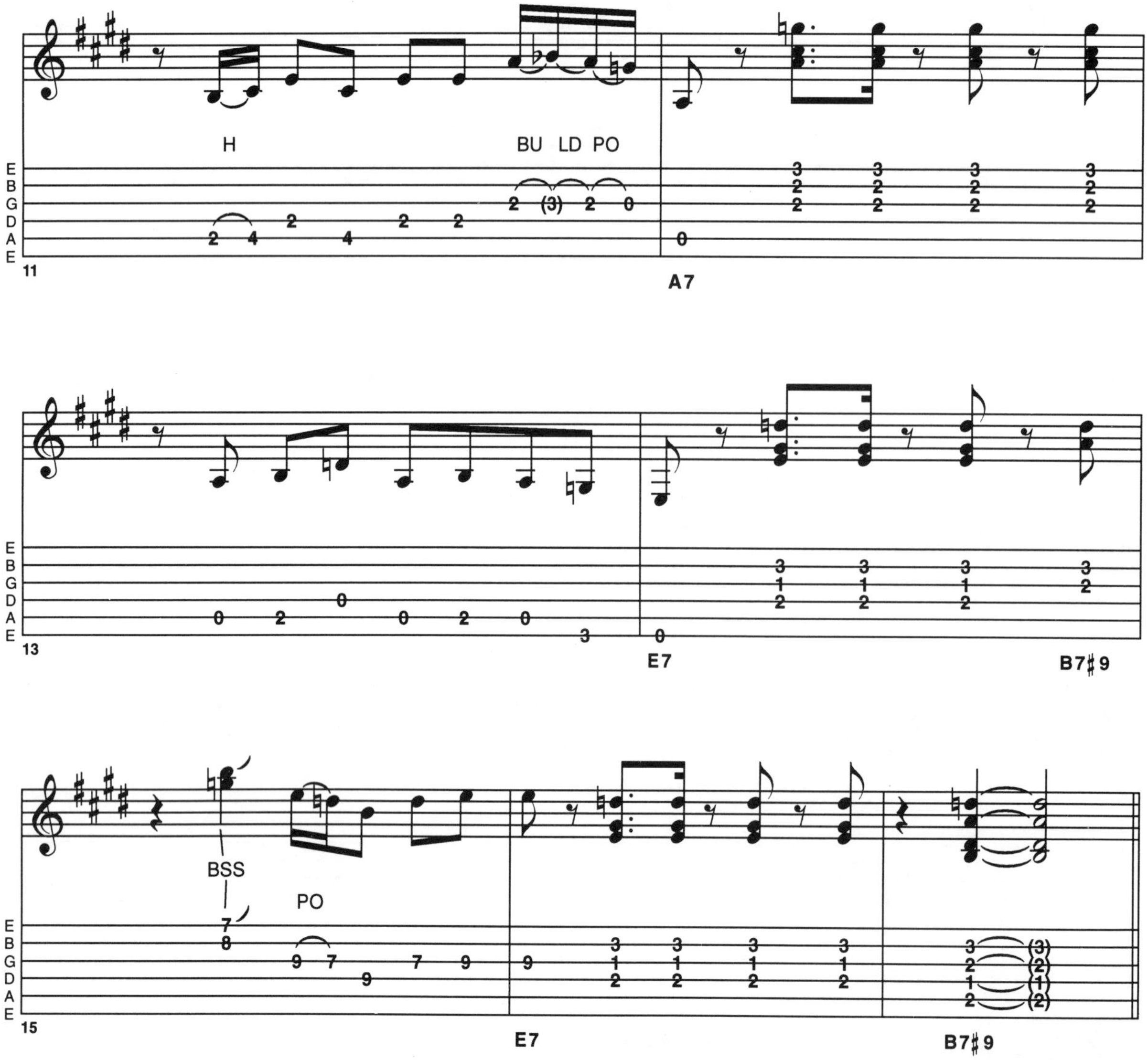

Most of the notes I used in between the chords come from the E minor Pentatonic (E G A B D E) as this is definitely the safest option, but I did add a couple of others: the occasional B♭ notes are a standard addition to the minor Pentatonic – this is the "flat 5" or "blue note" you may have heard of. There are also a couple of examples of C# in bar 10, which come from the A major Pentatonic scale (A B C# E F# A) and are designed to fit comfortably with the A chord that follows.

Time for the solo. As there were so many different aspects to Stevie's interpretation of the blues, I've split the solo into two distinct sections. This may sound like a rather sterile, methodical approach, but it's actually not dissimilar to the way Stevie used to arrange some of his longer solos. Rather than just babbling away meaninglessly with your old Pentatonic box position for four or five choruses, you'll stand more chance of capturing the attention of your listeners if you provide plenty of contrasts. For the first sixteen bars, I've used a relatively clean tone and used some of the funky jazz-style double stops and partial chords that SRV must have picked up from Kenny Burrell and Grant Green.

EX 3

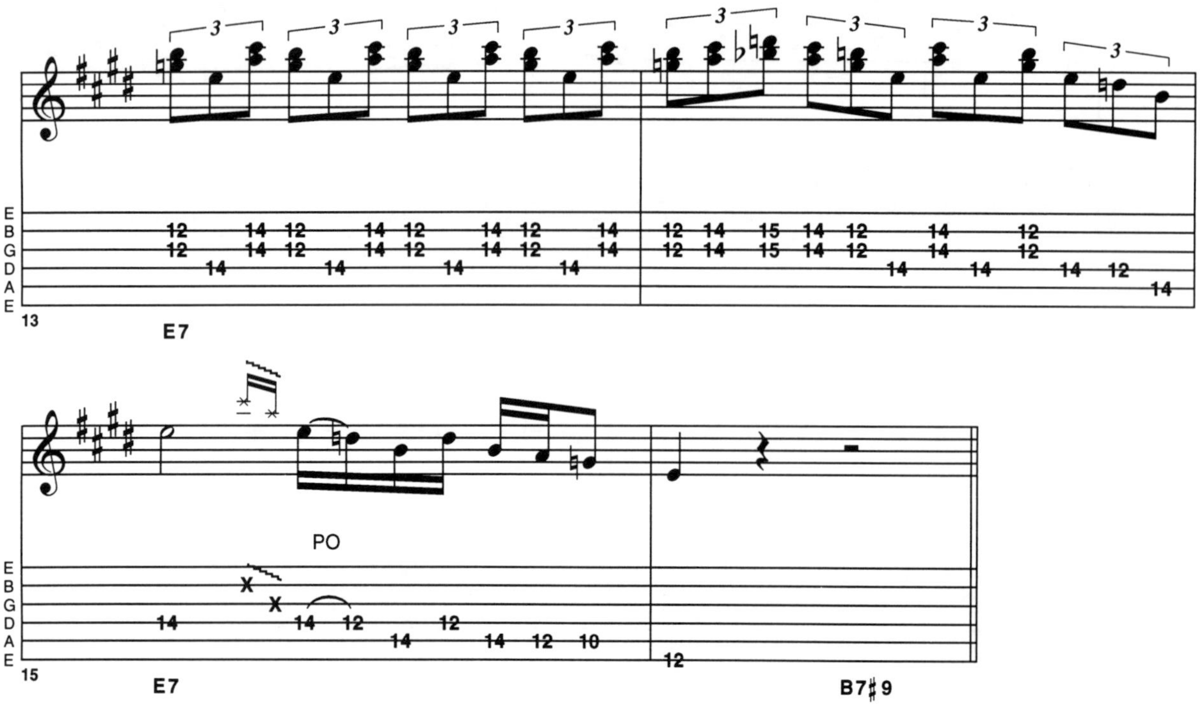

For the second chorus, I've used a more overdriven sound (by simply bringing my guitar's volume control up to its maximum position) and concentrated on single-note lines. Notice how, although I'm still basing my note choices primarily around the E minor Pentatonic, there's plenty of scope for adding extra notes to produce different effects. One of the easiest ways of doing this is to play around the chord changes, briefly ignoring the Pentatonic scale and using the chord notes as a basis for improvisation.

EX 4

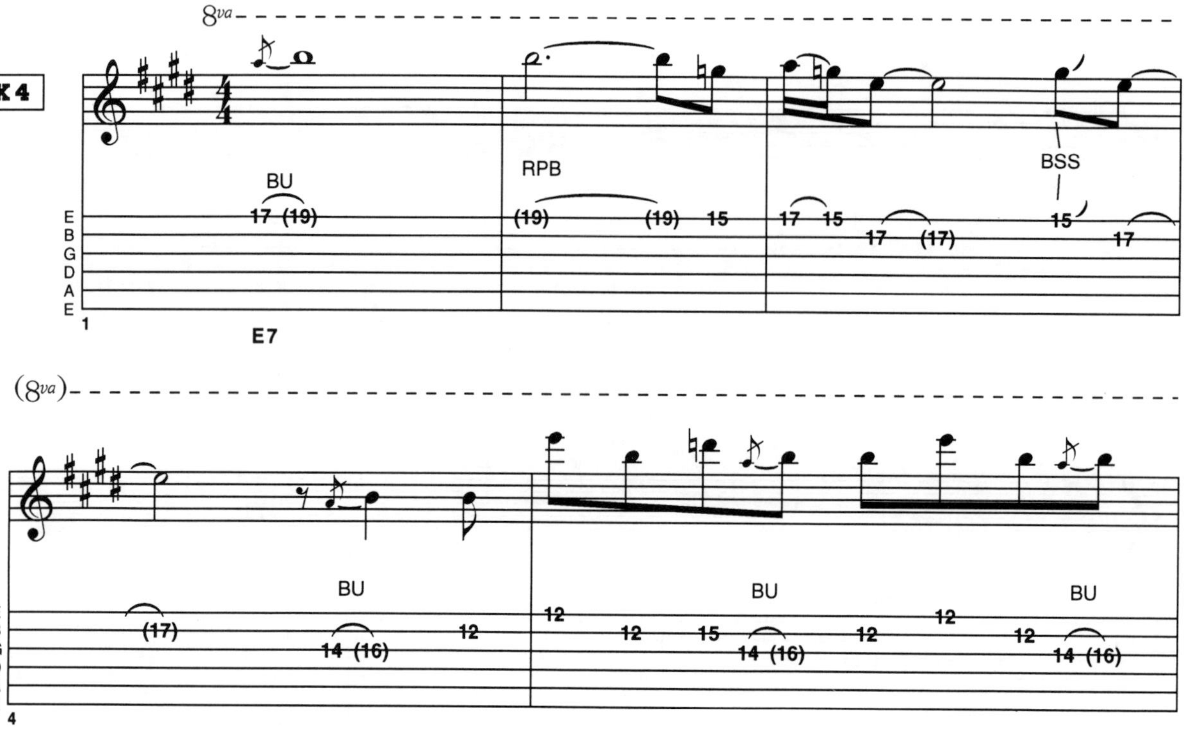

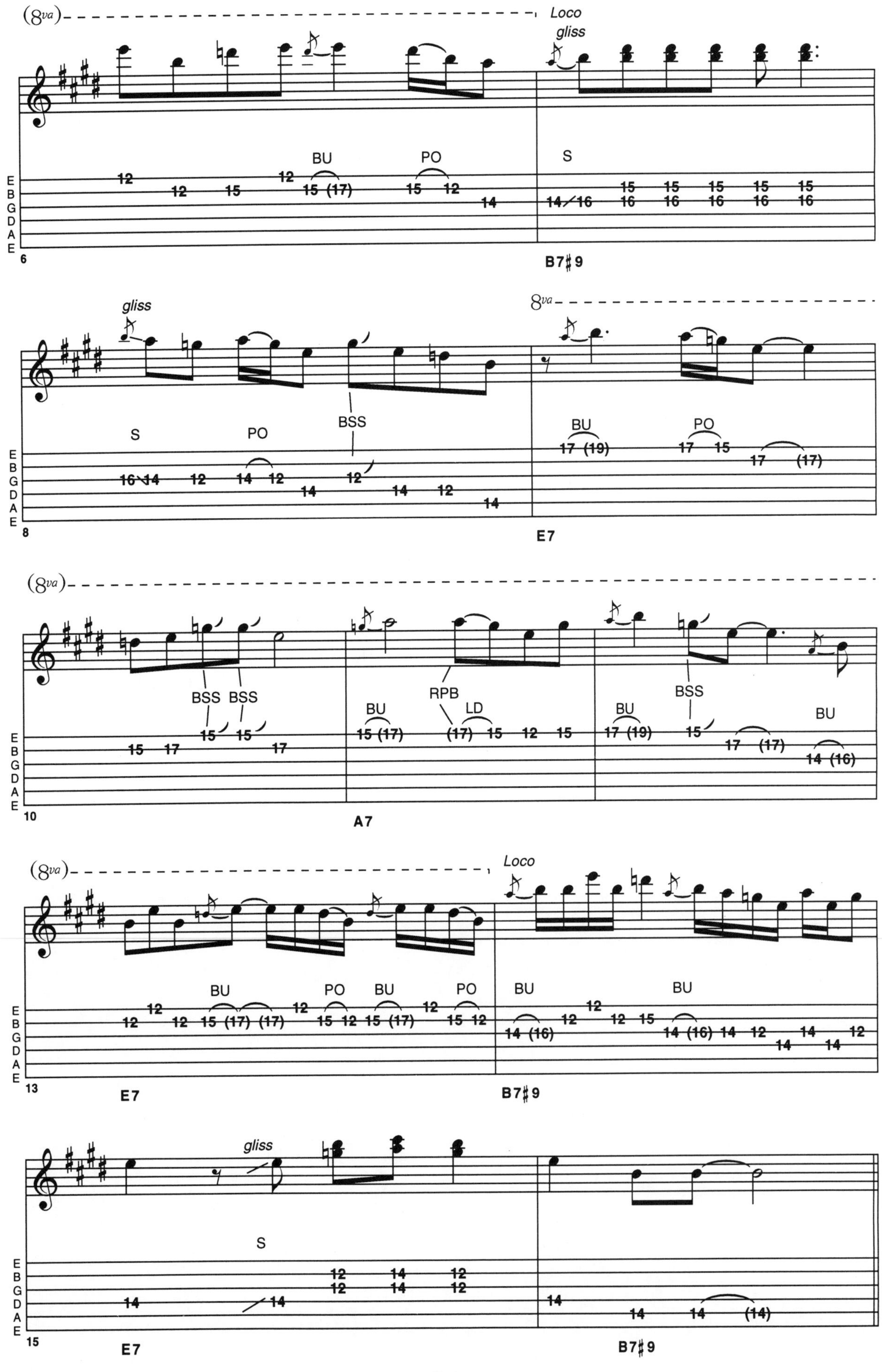
(8va)
Loco
gliss
BU
PO
S
6
B7♯9
gliss
S
PO
BSS
8va
BU
PO
8
E7
(8va)
BSS
BSS
BU
RPB
LD
BU
BSS
BU
10
A7
(8va)
Loco
BU
PO
BU
PO
BU
BU
13
E7
B7♯9
gliss
S
15
E7
B7♯9

I know this chapter isn't supposed to be about Jimi Hendrix, but it's obvious from much of Stevie's playing that Jimi had a huge influence on him. Unlike many players, though, Stevie took what he'd learnt and used it to build a style all of his own. (Hey, that's what this book is all about!) At the end, I repeated the initial "verse" part (Ex 2 with some slightly different bits). As the backing is relatively simple, why not record a few choruses of the sixteen-bar chord progression and experiment with your own call/response ideas over the top?

By the way, have you heard the "SRV fingertips" story? Not surprisingly, the frequent use of such heavy gauge strings (he sometimes went as far as a sixteen-gauge top E string!) combined with Stevie's ferocious bending and vibrato used to really take it out of his left-hand fingertips. The solution? Apparently, Stevie would apply a liberal helping of Superglue onto each finger, place his fingers on the inside of his right arm, wait until the glue had bonded and then... pull! Hey presto, a new set of fingertips!

Further Exploration

A blues fan from the beginning, Stevie's biggest influences in that genre were Albert King, Buddy Guy and Lonnie Mack. His real inspiration, though, was Jimi Hendrix, whose songs Stevie often covered: 'Voodoo Chile' and 'Little Wing', for instance.

Stevie's explosive style and his modern, post-Hendrix attitude turned plenty of young rock players on to the delights of blues guitar in the eighties, resurrecting what seemed to be a musical style in terminal decline and preparing the ground for players such as Kenny Wayne Shepherd.

If you're not too bothered about waiting a while for sites to download, the Stevie Ray Vaughan FAQ – http://www.smartlink.net/~jackklos/srvfaq1.htm – is an enormous piece of work, with details on just about every aspect of Stevie's life and music. Another site, under construction at the time of writing, is the snappily-named Stevie Ray Vaughan Was The Living Embodiment Of God which is at http://www.mcs.net/~court/stevie.html – it amused me, anyway!

TECHNIQUE PRIMER

When writing the "in-the-style-of" musical examples for this book, I tried to come up with pieces that would suit people of a variety of levels. Obviously, each piece has to reflect the technical level of the guitarist featured (if you want to learn some Steve Vai licks, you'll need a certain amount of technical ability to start with) but hopefully there's something in each chapter that even relative beginners will be able to have a stab at. Here are the most important techniques you'll need to master in order to play all the pieces effectively. (Remember: this is just a brief workout to help you hone your skills. If you've absolutely no idea of what these techniques are, you'll have to consult a more specialised book or take a few lessons with a local guitar teacher.)

ALTERNATE PICKING:

It's a good idea to get into the habit of using alternate picking as soon as possible. It's by far the most common type of picking, and for most applications it's the most effective. Think about it – every time you do a downstroke, your picking hand has to come back up to prepare for the next downstroke, so why waste that movement? Connect with the string(s) on the way up as well and – Lordy! – you've doubled your picking speed! Here are some exercises to loosen up your picking hand.

EX 1

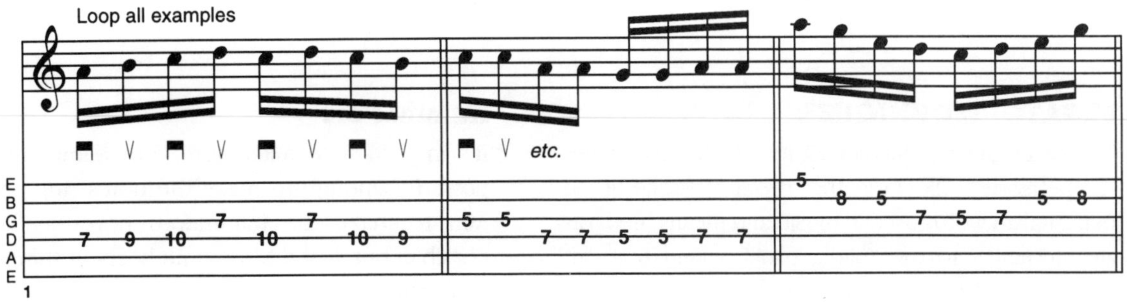

With all of the exercises here, you should start to develop another very good habit – using a metronome. Always start off at a reasonably slow speed, making sure you can play the example perfectly, and then gradually raise the metronome setting, always making sure you've ironed out every little problem before increasing speed.

SWEEP PICKING:

This is quite an advanced technique, so don't worry if you find it practically impossible – you'll be able to get through most of this book without it! Basically sweep picking is a technique whereby you use the same pick stroke to "sweep" through two or more strings, especially when playing arpeggios...

EX 2

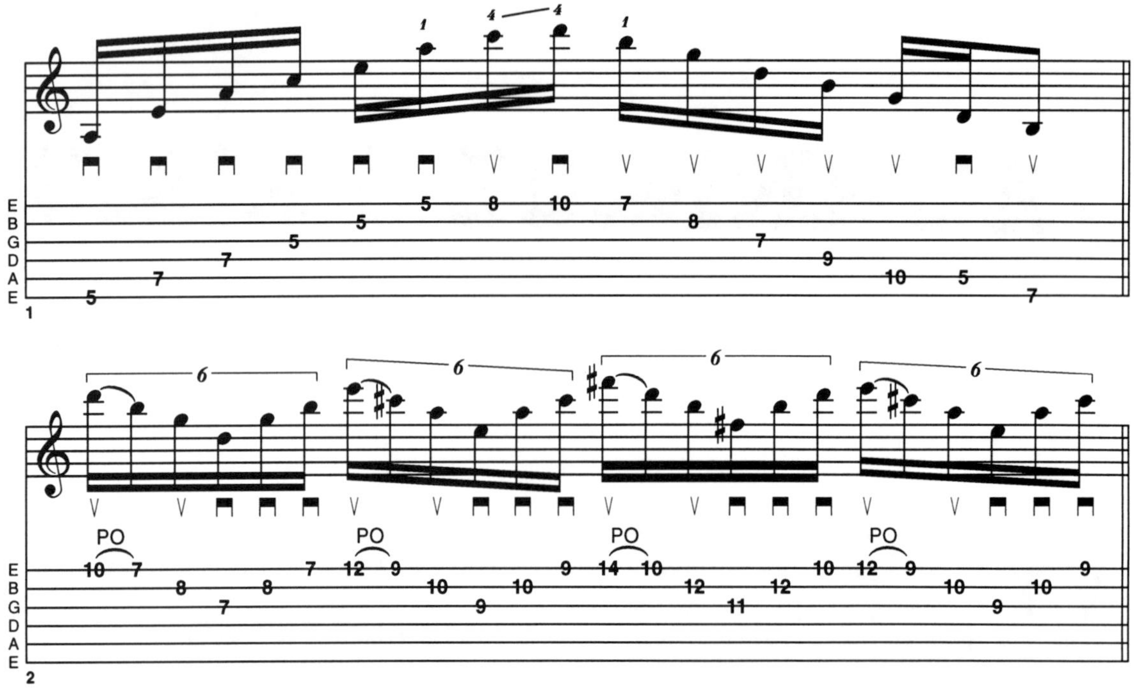

A more common use of the sweeping technique can be found in rakes. This is where you "rake" the pick through two or three muted notes in order to make the main melody note stand out.

EX 3

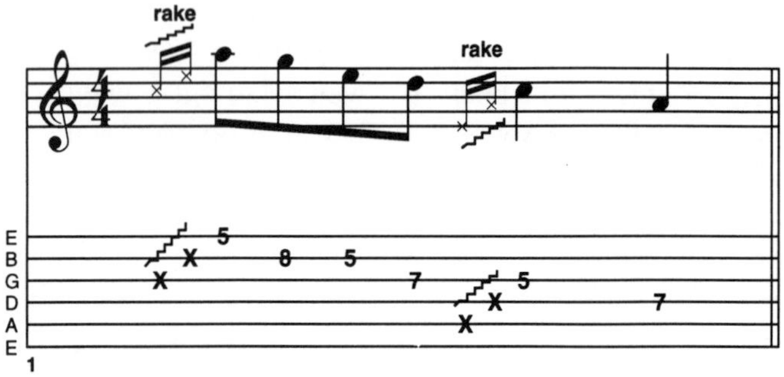

LEGATO TECHNIQUES:

The next four examples constitute ways in which notes can be made to flow together ("legato" is one of the many Italian words used in music, and means "tied") as an alternative to the "plink, plink" sound that can result from picking every note in the same way.

Hammer-on:

It's important to make sure your hammer-ons are powerful enough to make the notes ring properly. Aim to make the hammered notes as loud as possible, but at the same time keeping things clean and accurate.

EX 4

Pull-off:

Volume and accuracy are important with pull-offs, as is the angle at which you pull your finger off the string. Too much and you could bend the string out of tune; too little and the note won't ping out properly.

EX 5

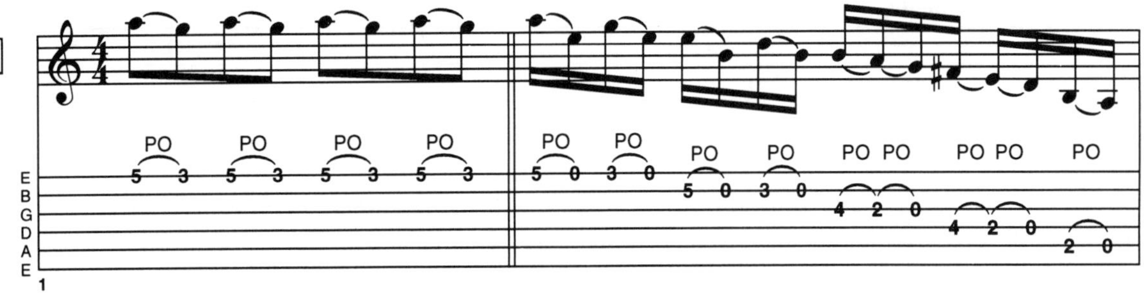

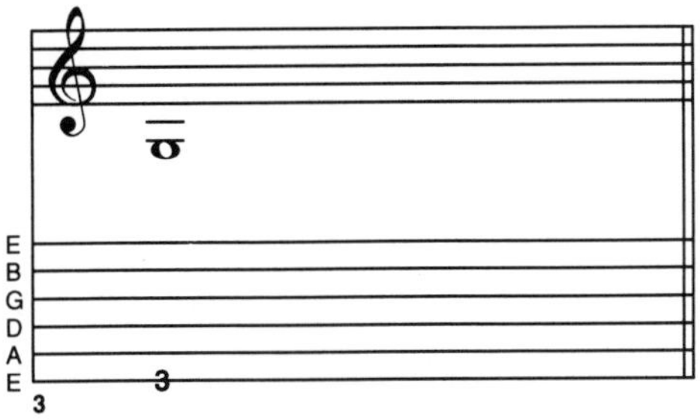

Slide ("glissando" for fans of correct nomenclature):

There's not too much to say about this one – just remember to practise slides of varying lengths, using all possible strings and fretboard positions.

EX 6

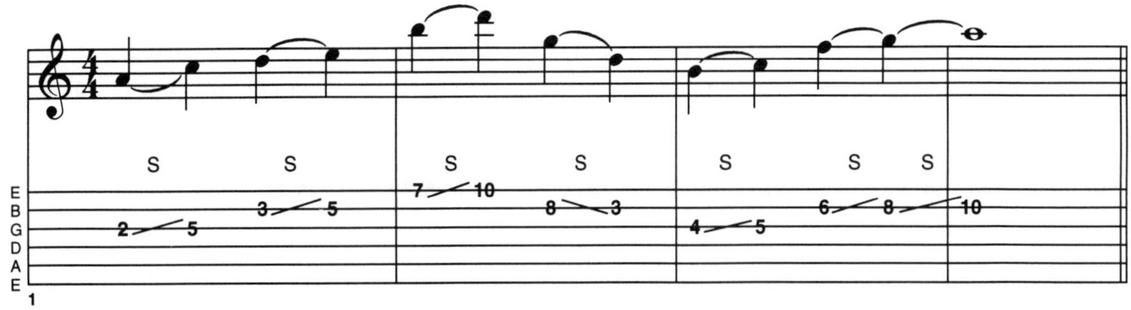

Bending:

The most difficult of all – there are so many different ways to bend a string. The best way to get a feel for the basic bending technique is to take two notes, as in Ex 7a. Play the higher one a few times until your ear becomes attuned to its pitch, then play the lower note and bend it smoothly up to the target pitch, as shown in Ex 7b. Keep referring to the normal fretted version of the target note, to gauge the accuracy of your bends. Before long, you'll know instinctively just how far you need to stretch a string in order to raise it by one, two or even three semitones. As each string reacts differently, you should practise on all of them (Example 7c).

EX 7A

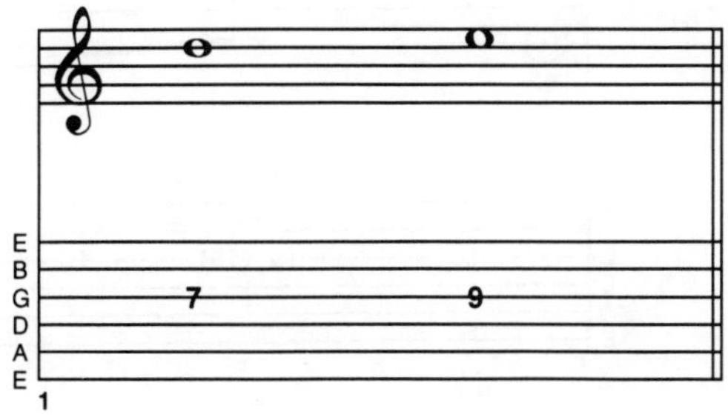

EX 7B

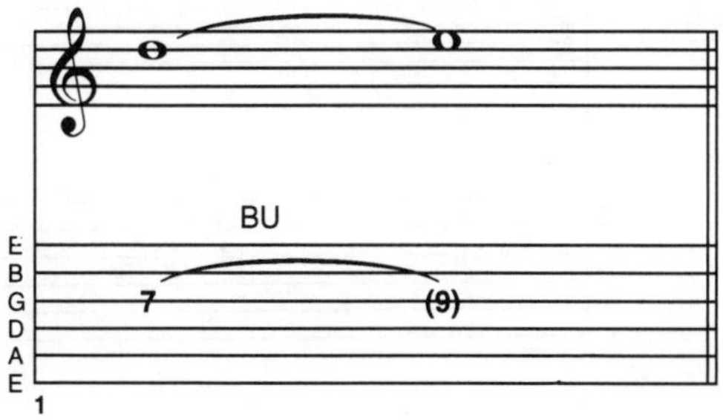

EX 7C

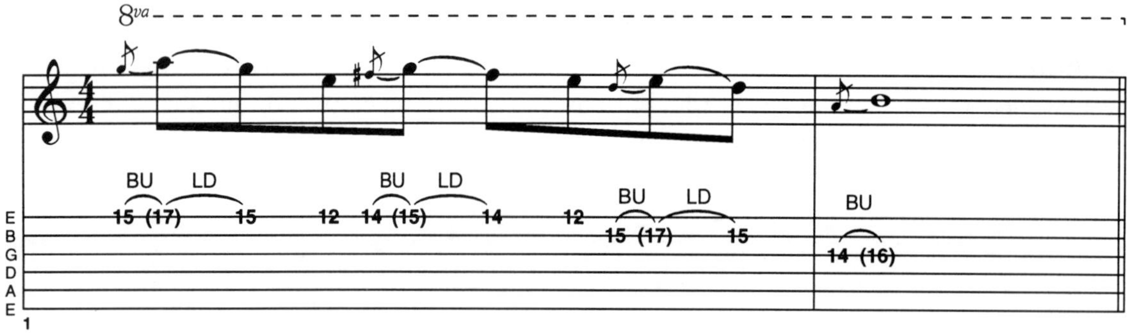

Knowing how to pitch a bend correctly is all very well, but you still need to know how to perform the actual physical motion of the bend. Here are a few tips:

a) Whenever possible, try to use your third finger for bends. This means you have two other fingers behind it for extra support.
b) Although it's frowned on among classical guitarists, placing your thumb over the edge of the neck provides yet more strength and support.
c) Take care to mute any unused strings, especially when releasing a bend – that annoying "twang" as your fingertip accidentally catches another string is guaranteed to ruin your heartfelt slow blues solo. Use every spare part of each hand to cover any potential problem strings.

In addition to all this, it's a good idea to familiarise yourself with some of the main types of bend. Ex 8 demonstrates how different bends can be built into simple, effective licks – all of these licks use the E minor scale. The simplest type involves one melody note being bent evenly up to another (Ex 8a); this can be extended by letting the string fall back to the starting note (Ex 8b). If you want to attach more importance to the target note, you could use a "grace note bend" – the original note can still be heard, but only briefly (Ex 8c and 8d). What if you want to hear the target note straight away, followed by a return to the unbent note? This is where the pre-bend (Ex 8e) comes in; it's quite a tricky technique to master, as you have to bend the note before playing it. Just go for it and trust your judgement! For your party piece, try a "grace note pre-bend" – if you've mastered the previous examples, you'll get along fine (Ex 8f). And for the real coup de grace, try this Dave Gilmour-style two-stage bend (Ex 8g). Just make sure you've got a First Aid kit handy!

EX 8A

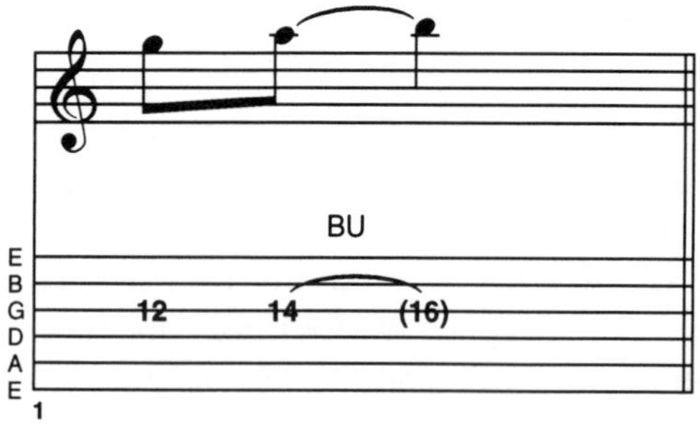

EX 8B

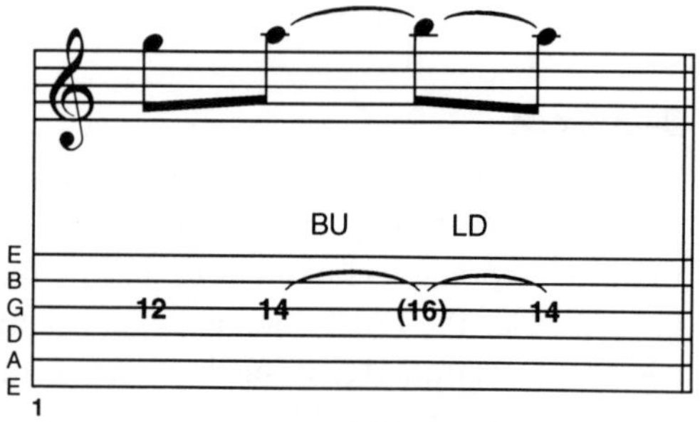

EX 8C

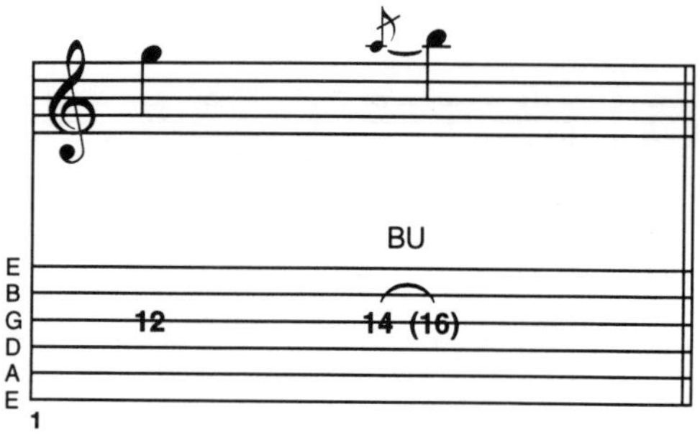

EX 8D

EX 8E

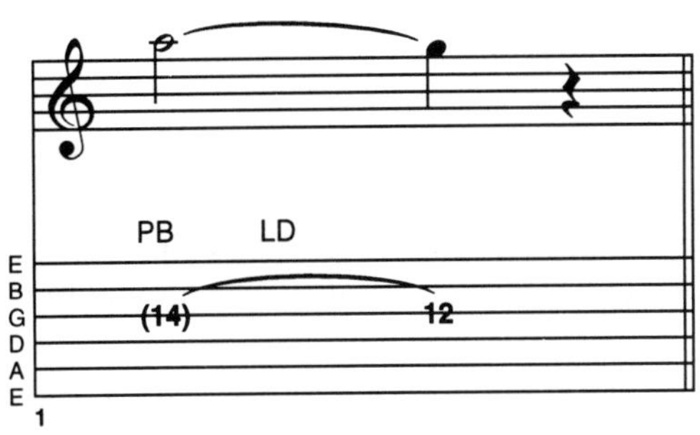

EX 8F

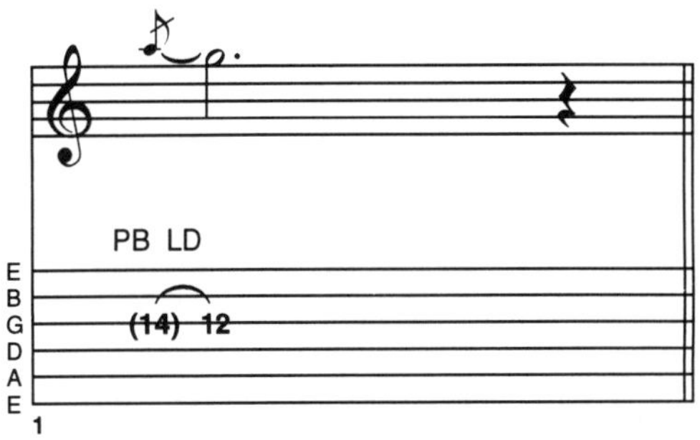

EX 8G

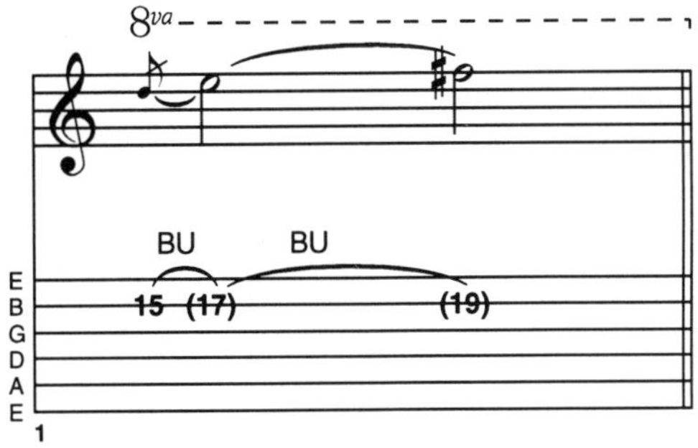

VIBRATO:

I hate to be so hard and unsympathetic, but as far as this technique is concerned, you're on your own! All I can tell you is that the basic technique is akin to lots of slight bends and releases. Keep your fretboard hand relaxed and just go for it – you'll probably find it awkward and unnatural at first, but keep at it until it becomes second nature. The main advice I can give you is that you should listen carefully to as many different players as possible; everyone has their own personal vibrato sound – fast, slow, wide, subtle or whatever.

TAPPING:

This, like sweep picking, is definitely an advanced technique, so you may wish to ignore this section if you're a beginner. However, tapping is a major component in the styles of Steve Vai, Joe Satriani and Eddie Van Halen, so your curiosity may well get the better of you. The idea behind tapping is that you use one or more of the fingers on your picking hand to fret notes; obviously you no longer have a hand free to pick notes, so you have to be able to produce the sounds using just hammer-ons and pull-offs. Try this triplet lick, picking only the very first note...

EX 9

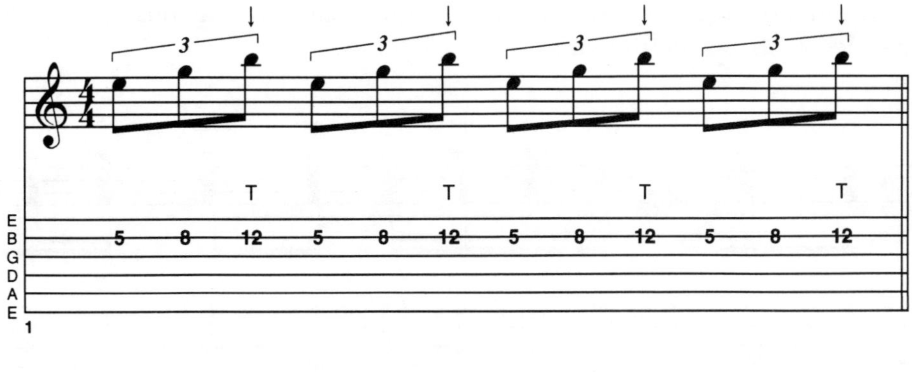

Like any guitar technique, it can take a bit of getting used to, but grit your teeth, wind up that metronome, and you'll soon have it licked. When it comes to doing pull-offs with your tapping finger, you can pull up or down; personally I tend to pull upward, but you may find it easier to do the opposite. There's also the matter of choosing which finger to tap with – I'd urge you to try using your second finger, as this means you can keep hold of your pick. Some people insist on using their index fingers, which means having to quickly stash your pick somewhere safe, until you go back to using standard technique. (Mind you, Eddie Van Halen taps with his index finger but always holds his pick between his thumb and second finger. No problemo!)

CHORD STRUMMING:

This is a large and very variable area of technique, so I'll just cover a few general points of advice...

Usually, it's a good idea to keep your strumming hand fairly relaxed. If your whole arm is tense, your music will also sound tense and awkward. Try to get most of the motion from your wrist; obviously if you're playing the sort of song that requires some big, brash acoustic strumming, you'll want to put a bit more effort into it, but in general you should aim for a compromise between accuracy and looseness.

For most musical applications, it's a good idea to get into the habit of using downstrokes for strums which land on a beat and upstrokes for strums which land on the offbeats. So, for a steady eighth note pattern of "one-and two-and three-and four-and" you'd be strumming "down-up down-up down-up down-up". Obviously you won't always be strumming on every single eighth note, but you should still keep the up-down pattern going; just make sure your pick misses the strings whenever you don't want to hear a strum. Keeping your strumming hand in this constant motion means you have a better chance of keeping time and feeling the basic pulse of the tune. As an example, try this Noel Gallagher-style strumming pattern...

EX 10

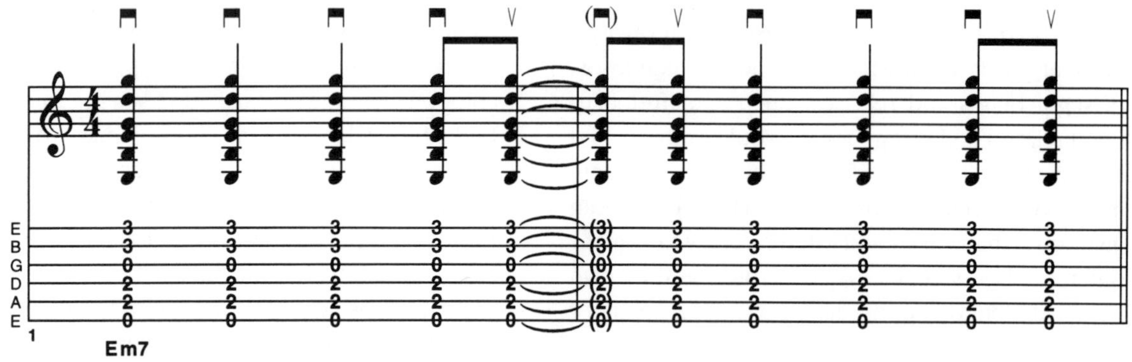

Not all music is based on an eighth-note (half-beat) pulse – many styles, such as funk, are based on a sixteenth-note (quarter-beat) feel. In this case, the method is exactly the same, but everything is doubled, so you'll have downstrokes on the beats and half-beats, and upstrokes on the quarter and three-quarter points...

EX 11

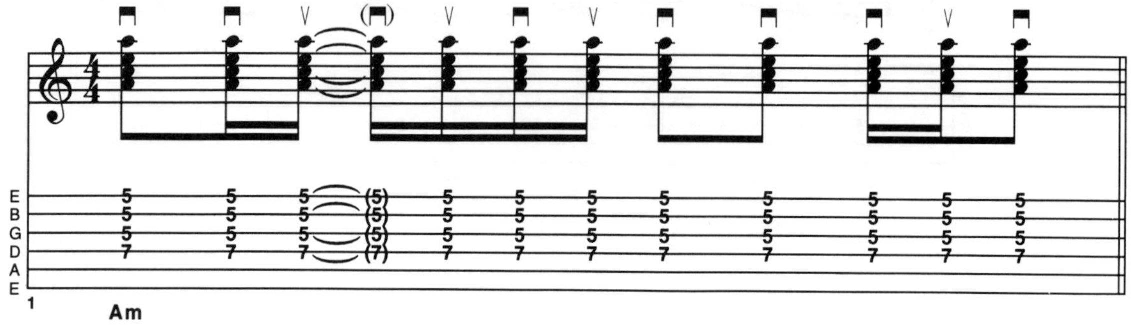

The subject of funk leads us neatly on to...

MUTED STRUMMING:

Everything I told you in the previous section still holds for this technique, but there are a couple of new features to practise. With normal strumming, if you want to vary the rhythm patterns, you just persuade your strumming hand to miss the strings on certain beats. However, there are two other things you can do. First of all, as well as missing the strings with your strumming hand, use your other hand to mute them, by lifting your fingers slightly. Don't lift them completely off the strings, just enough so the strings are no longer in contact with the frets. This provides a more obvious rhythmic effect than simply changing the strumming pattern. The other alternative is again to use your fretboard hand to mute the strings, but this time continue strumming as normal, so the sound produced is a kind of "thwack!". This sort of technique is vital in funk and reggae. The following example shows how all three possible approaches can be applied to the same phrase.

EX 12

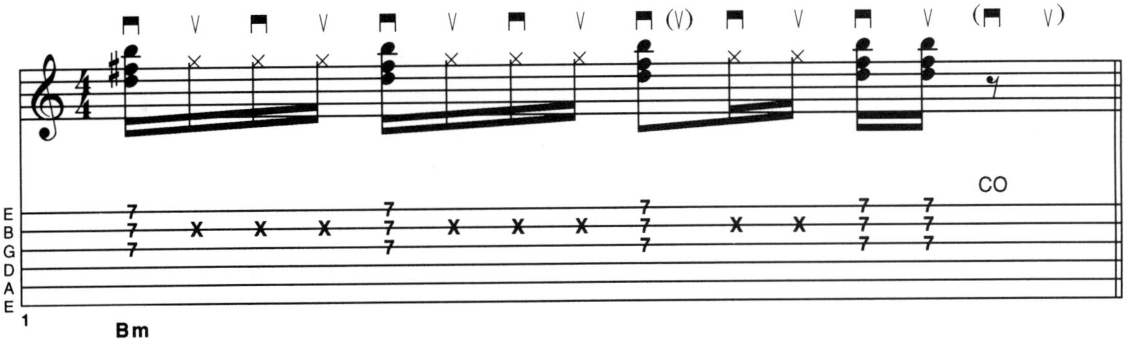

THEORY PRIMER

Now, before you dissolve in floods of tears, let me reassure you by saying that you don't actually need to understand any music theory in order to use this book. Not a jot. You can learn all the examples off by heart and play them as many times as you want. That may be fine for some people, but the whole point of *Legends* is to teach you how to use the styles of your favourite players as a jumping-off point for your own compositions. In order to use the material in that way, you'll need to understand some of the patterns and templates that lie behind the notes. That's what music theory's all about, folks.

So to help you on your way, here are a few concepts to enhance your enjoyment of this book and generally make the world a more beautiful place to live in.

KEYS:
No, not the things you lose down the back of the sofa – I'm talking about the musical variety. A key is basically just a family of notes which can be combined in various ways to create pieces of music. This family of notes can be laid end to end to form a scale, which provides the raw material for melodies, or stacked to form a series of diatonic chords (see below for a definition). Obviously there's much more to it than that, but that's the simplest basic definition. And don't forget – the "key" is not a guarantee of good music; it's simply a way of finding notes that will probably work. You can easily use notes from outside of whichever key you're supposed to be in, as long as you're prepared for a bit of unpredictability!

SCALES:
No need to be scared of scales. A scale is just a series of notes which provides a kind of recipe for a particular melodic sound. For instance, the major Pentatonic reminds me of that "southern-fried" sound, the Lydian mode is pure Steve Vai, the Phrygian Dominant is a mixture of Flamenco and the Middle East. Whenever you learn a new scale, spend some time familiarising yourself with its sound. Make up a few generalised associations, like I did above. As long as you don't restrict yourself to them too much, you'll be fine.

PENTATONIC SCALES:
You know what a pentagon is? It's a five-sided shape. By the same infallible logic, a Pentatonic scale is a scale containing five notes. For instance, the E minor Pentatonic is made up of E G A B D (after which the sequence just keeps repeating, an octave higher each time, until you run out of notes). Most people associate Pentatonic scales with blues, rock and country, but they're often used in jazz and they're positively abundant in many traditional forms of music.

DIATONIC CHORDS:
The set of chords that belongs to a particular key. There's always one chord for each note of the scale, and no notes from outside the key are included. For any major scale (and therefore major key) the series of chord types is as follows: major, minor, minor, major, major, minor, diminished. So for the key of C, you'd have the C major scale (Ex 1a) and the group of diatonic chords built from those scale notes (Ex 1b).

EX 1A

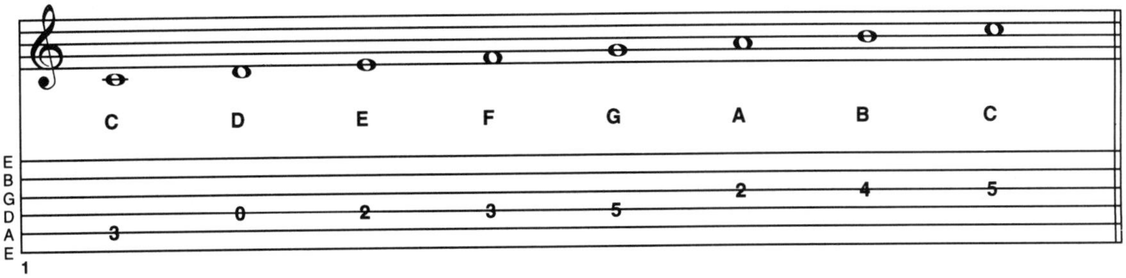

EX 1B

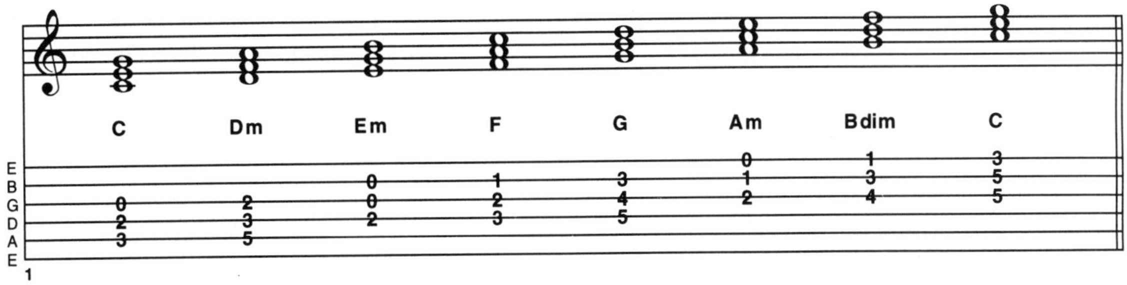

MODES:

The ones who are brave enough to read the section on scales usually lose their bottle around here. That's a shame; the concept of modes is actually quite simple, but often suffers from being over-complicated (you'll probably tell me I'm just as guilty of that as everyone else!)

Start off by playing the G major scale, as shown in Ex 2a. Finish off with a nice bold G major chord (Ex 2b) and note how the chord and scale fit very logically together. Now go back to the scale and play slowly through the notes once again, but this time stop at the F# note (the seventh note). Something's missing, isn't it? Do the same again, but after letting the F# ring for a while, resolve the scale by adding the final G. Congratulations – you've just discovered the power of the root note! The root note acts as a kind of magnetic central point, around which all the notes and chords of the key are centred.

EX 2A

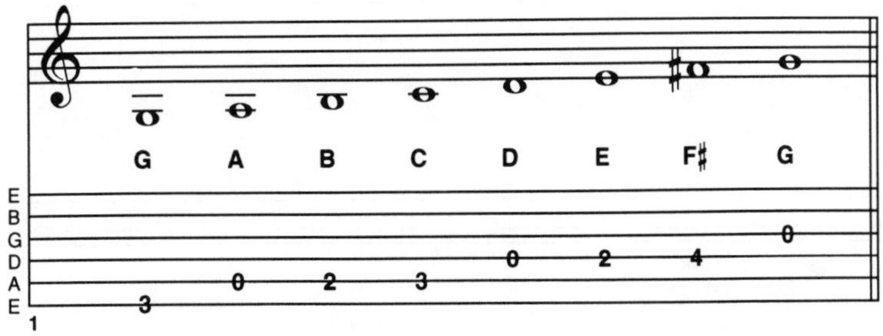

EX 2B

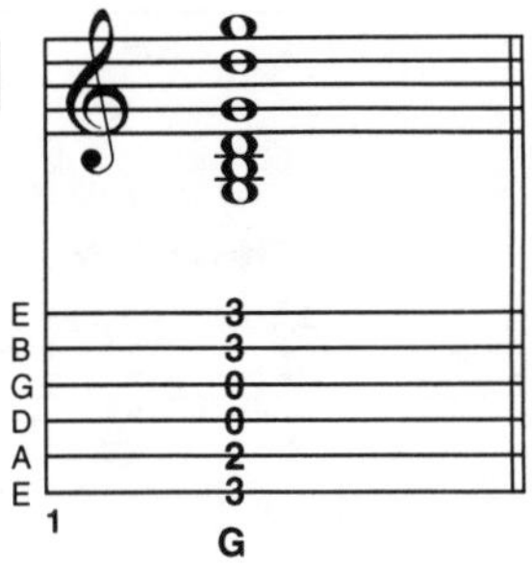

What if we take the same scale, but use a different root note? Play the G major scale again, but this time start and end on the B (Ex 3a). Once again, finish off with a big, brash chord, but this time make it a B minor chord (Ex 3b). Try playing some melodies with the notes, returning to the B minor chord every so often. Close your eyes and smile indulgently – you're using the Phrygian mode!

EX 3A

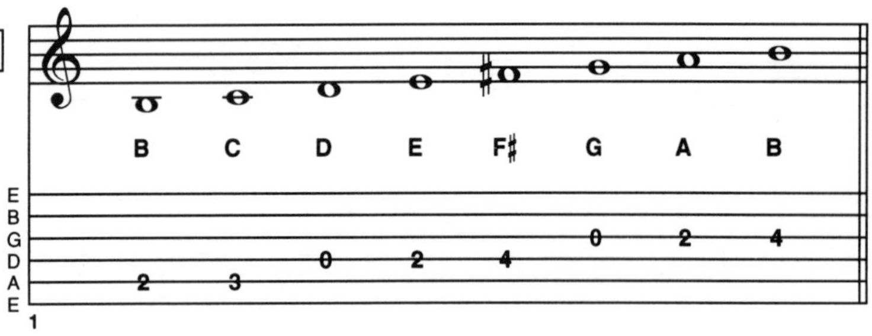

EX 3B

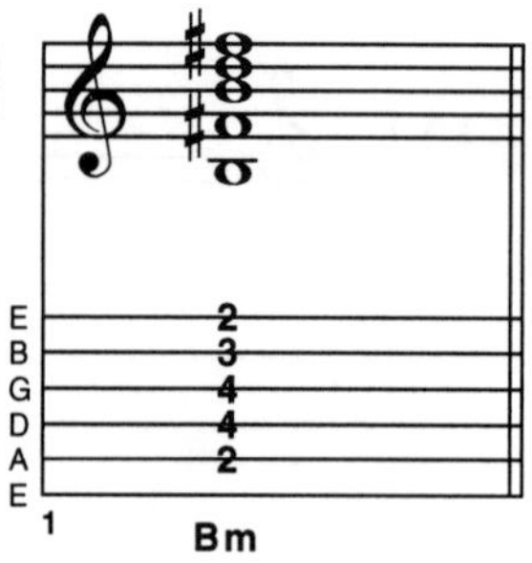

It really is as simple as that – when you use one of the modes of a particular scale/key, you're using the same scale (and the series of diatonic chords) but you're anchoring everything to a different root note; you're seeing all of the chord progressions and melodic possibilities from another point of view. Ex 4 shows the whole series of modes built from the major scale, as well as the chord built on the root of each mode. I've used the key of G again, but the pattern is the same for every key.

G IONIAN (MAJOR)

EX 4A

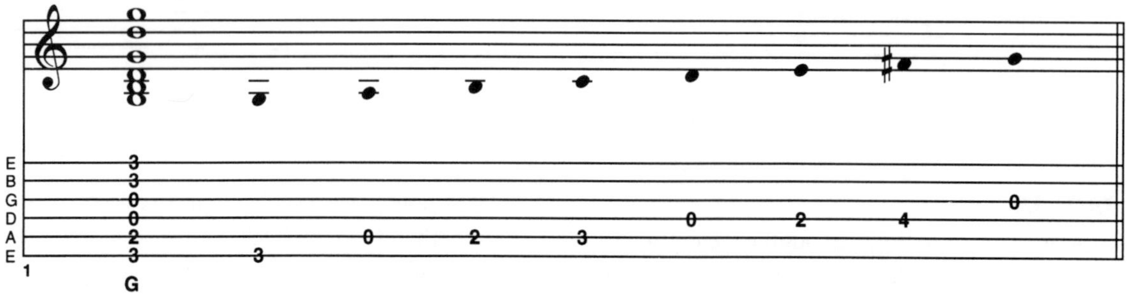

A DORIAN

EX 4B

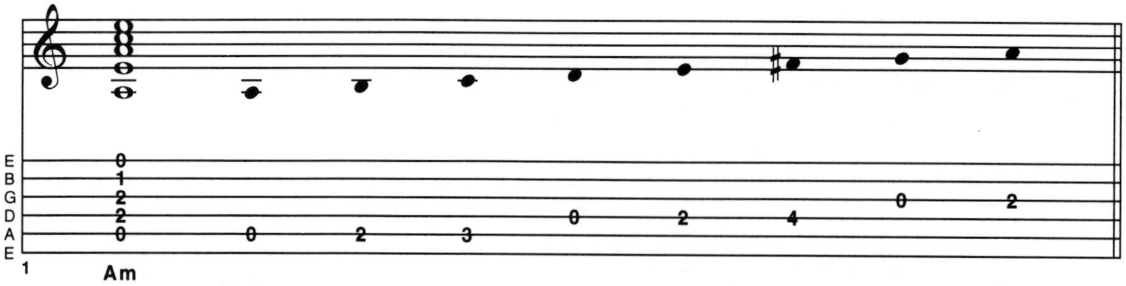

B PHRYGIAN

EX 4C

C LYDIAN

EX 4D

D MIXOLYDIAN

EX 4E

E AEOLIAN (NATURAL MINOR)

EX 4F

F♯ LOCRIAN

EX 4G

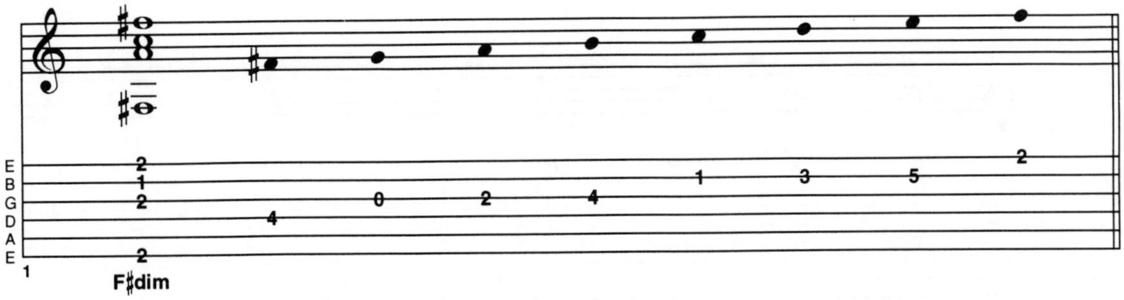

Try coming up with melodies using different modes, or if you're feeling really adventurous, why not write an entire song around a particular mode? One important point: just because you're using the B Phrygian mode, you don't have to stick entirely to a B minor chord. You can use any of the diatonic chords from the parent key (G major) as long as you remember to treat the B as the new key centre. Blimey, I'm exhausted! Let's go on to something simpler...

INTERVALS:

Quite simply, an interval is the distance between one note and the next. If you're going to do this Music Theory Thang properly, it's a good idea to learn the correct names for intervals, rather than just saying "move it up three frets" etc. Here, for your reference, is the list of interval names:

Unison – not really an interval as such, but I've included it because, er... everyone else does! A unison refers to two notes of the same pitch.

Minor Second – Also referred to as a "semitone", this is equal to a movement of one fret (on the same string, of course).

Major Second – Two frets, and you can also call it a "tone" or "whole tone".

Minor Third – Three frets.

Major Third – Four frets. The major and minor thirds are the building blocks of Western Harmony; most chords are constructed using combinations of these two intervals.

Perfect Fourth – Five frets.

Tritone – This can also be called the "augmented fourth" or the "diminished fifth" so be prepared to hear all three! Yes, you guessed... six frets, and the exact midpoint of an octave.

Perfect Fifth – Seven frets. This is the "inversion" of the perfect fourth; if you go up a perfect fourth from C, you'll end up with an F. Likewise, if you go down a perfect fifth from C, you'll also end up at F.

Minor Sixth – Eight frets, and an inverted major third.

Major Sixth – Nine frets, and an inverted minor third.

Minor Seventh – Ten frets (see if you can work out what its inversion is).

Major Seventh – Eleven frets.

Octave – Twelve frets, and the distance between one note and the next one with exactly the same name, such as E to E, G# to G#.

After that, you can go on to Tenths, Elevenths and so on, but I've always found it easier to talk about "Octave plus a major third" and so on. It may not be strictly correct in all situations, but who cares? As long as people know what you're referring to, it's the sound of the music that's important.

THE BASICS OF CHORD CONSTRUCTION (OR "WHAT ARE POWER CHORDS, DADDY?"):

If you've read this far, you won't be alarmed when I present you with this G major scale...

EX 5

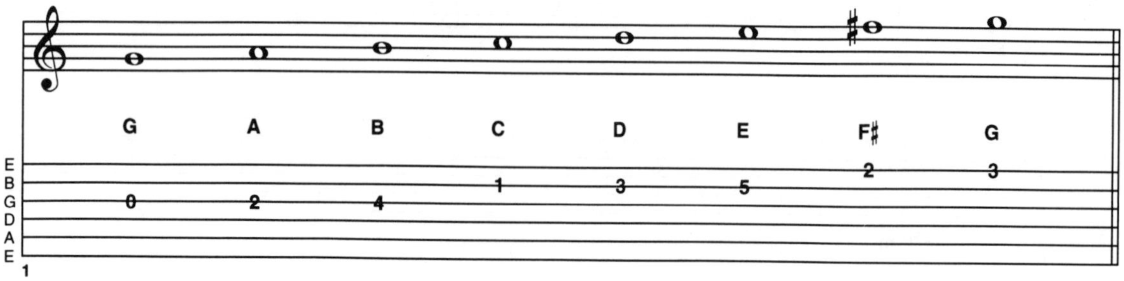

As well as being a source of countless melodic lines, that humble scale can also be used to generate chords. To form a G major chord (the chord built on the root note is known as the tonic or I chord) you take the first, third and fifth notes of the scale: G B D. To make a minor chord, do the same, but flatten the third: G B♭ D. These basic three-note groups are known as "triads".

EX 6

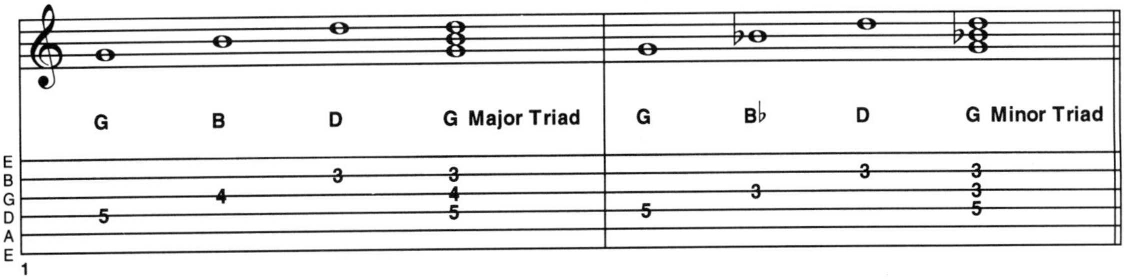

You've probably already realised that there's more to it than just that – think about any chord sequence you know, and it's pretty obvious that the chords often have more than three notes in them.

The answer, my friend, lies in "voicings". Those three notes can be doubled, trebled and arranged to create the chords we know and love. Look at these two chord shapes:

EX 7

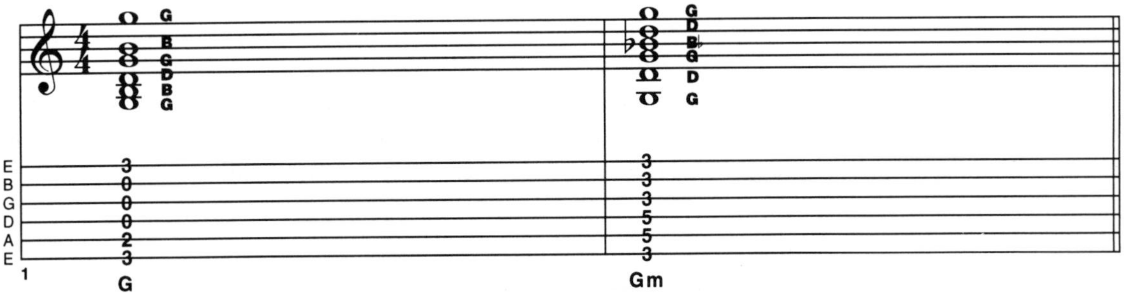

In the G major, there are three Gs, two Bs and one D; the G minor has three Gs, one B♭ and two Ds. In chord theory, the root is the safest note to duplicate, followed by the fifth and with the third as the most potentially dodgy (too many thirds can make the chord sound unbalanced). Of course, you don't necessarily have to learn how to form chords this way – most people just learn a few shapes from books or through playing songs – but it certainly opens up a new level of musical understanding. To keep you amused, here's the next level of formulas to lead on from our major and minor triads (all in the key of G for simplicity's sake).

ROOT, THIRD, ♯5 = AUGMENTED TRIAD

EX 8A

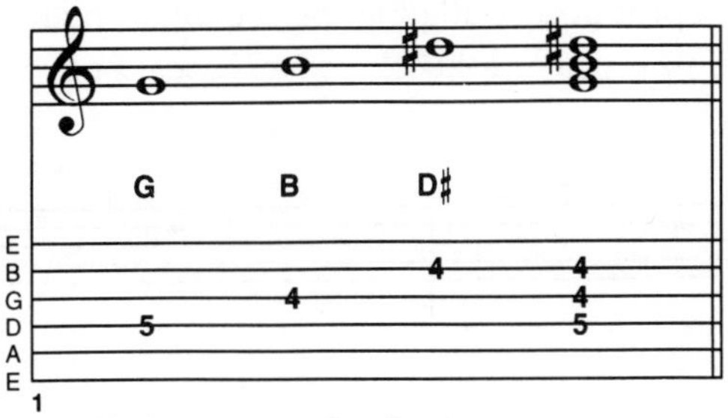

ROOT, ♭3, ♭5 = DIMINISHED TRIAD

EX 8B

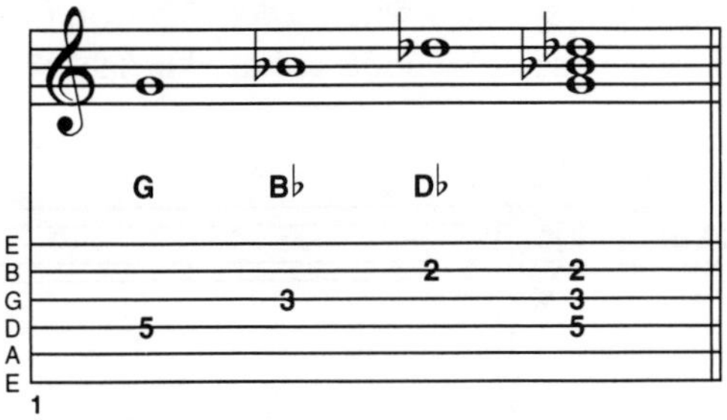

ROOT, THIRD, FIFTH, SEVENTH = MAJOR 7 CHORD

EX 8C

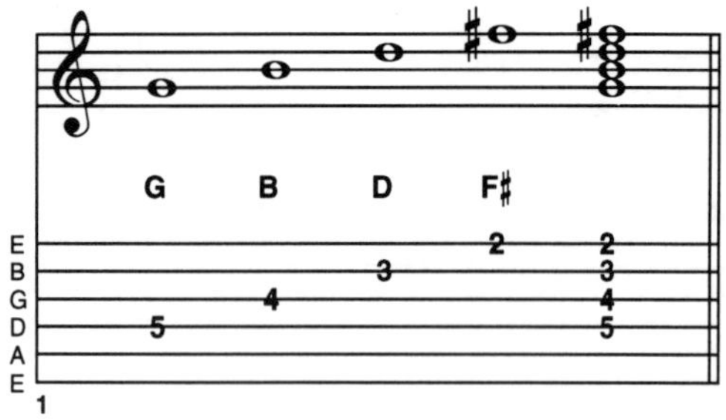

ROOT, THIRD, FIFTH, ♭7 = (DOMINANT) 7 CHORD

EX 8D

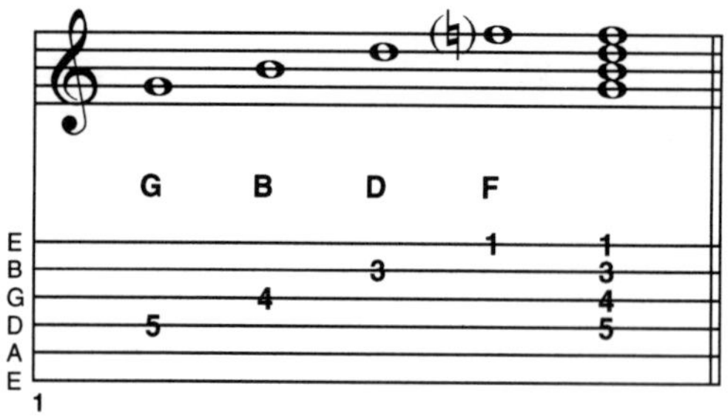

ROOT, ♭3, FIFTH, ♭7 = MINOR CHORD

EX 8E

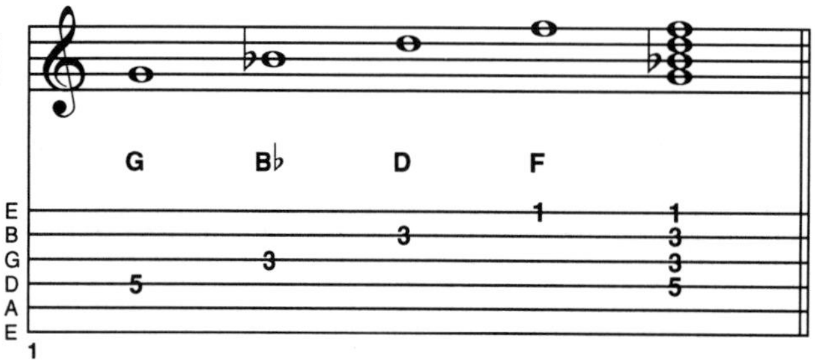

Oh yes, I almost forgot – what exactly is a power chord? Go back to the major and minor triads, and remove the third from each (remember: this refers to the third note of the parent scale, not the third note of the actual triad). You're left with the same two notes in each case (correctly known as a diad, and written G5) showing that power chords are neither major nor minor, which is why they're so versatile. Just to prove that it all works, here are some different G5 voicings.

EX 9

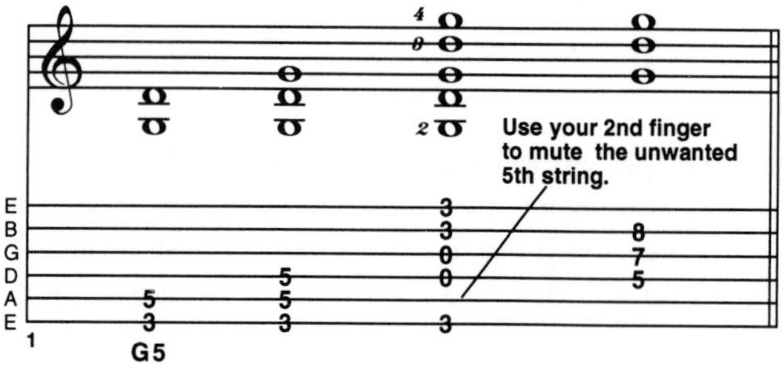

READING REPEAT SIGNS:

This isn't really part of music theory, but I've included it because it's one of those confusing notation symbols where even Tab won't help you out (the same symbols are used in Tab). There are various ways of using repeats in a piece of music...

1. When a whole section is to be repeated verbatim. In this case, you'll just find two sets of "repeat dots" outlining the section to be repeated. Unless you're told otherwise, repeat only once.

EX 10A

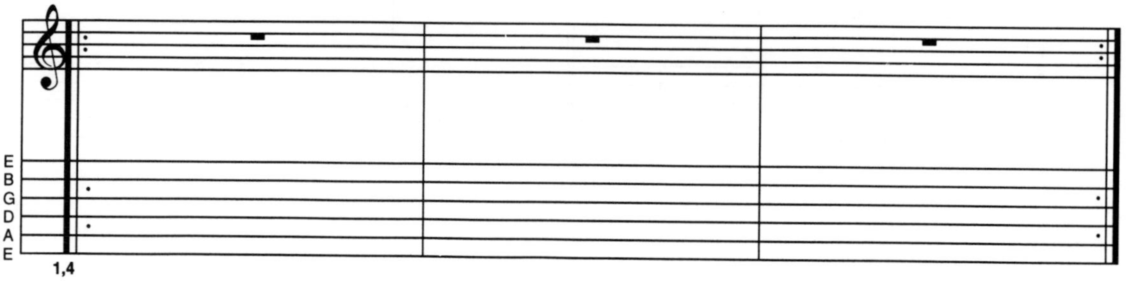

2. When a section is to be repeated, but with a different ending the second time round. The repeat dots are used as above, but you'll also see a couple of boxes marking the differing parts. In Ex 10b, start by playing right into the "1" box, as far as the second set of repeat dots. Then, as in Ex 10a, go back to the first repeat dots and start to repeat. This time, though, hop over the "1" box completely and play the "2" box instead. This method can be expanded; if you had a part that was to be played four times, with different endings each time, you'd have four different boxes.

EX 10B

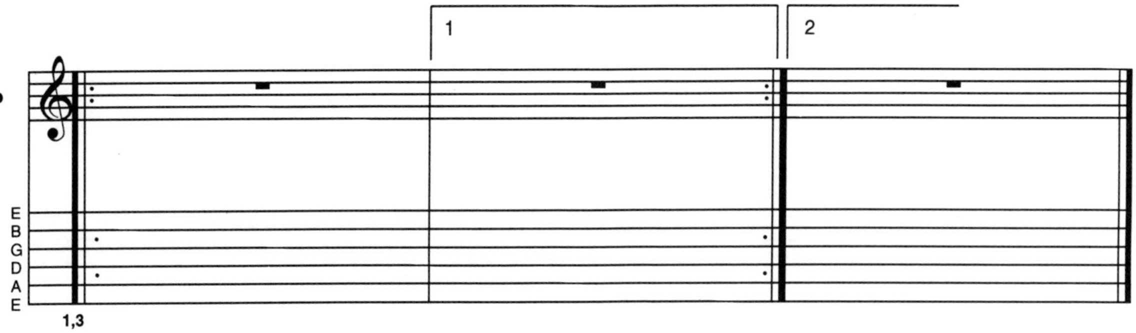

3. For more complex repeats, music writers will often use Italian terms, such as the ones I've used in the following example...

EX 10C

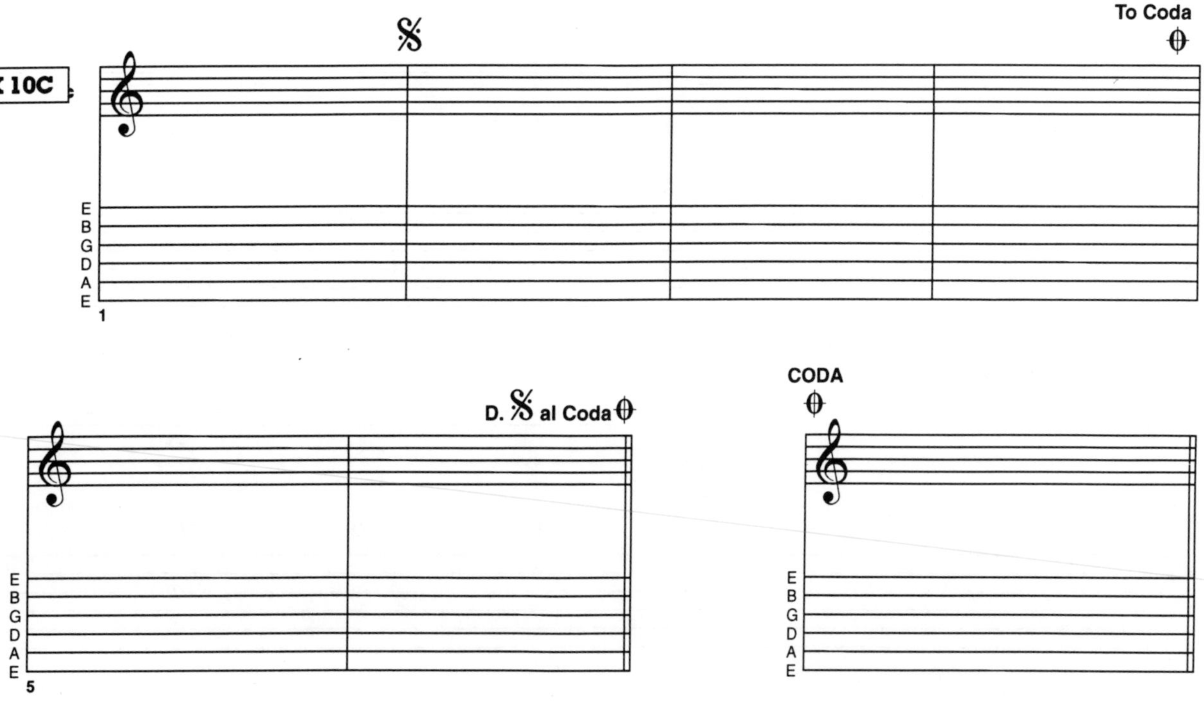

Now, the idea is that you play through the piece as normal, until you get to "DS (short for Dal Segno) al Coda", which means "go back to the sign (the strange S-like thing in bar 2) and play through until you're told to go to the Coda". So, you do that, and then at the end of bar 4, you're told to go to the Coda, or end section.

Other possibilities are "Da capo (or just DC) al Coda" (go back to the start and then play through to the Coda), "DS al Fine" (go back to the sign and then play through to the end) or "DC al Fine" (I'll leave you to figure that one out – it's every bit as logical as you'd think).

SOME USEFUL SCALES:

As a supplement to the more general guide to scales above, here are some of the most common patterns. For the sake of simplicity, they're all in the key of A.

MAJOR

EX 11

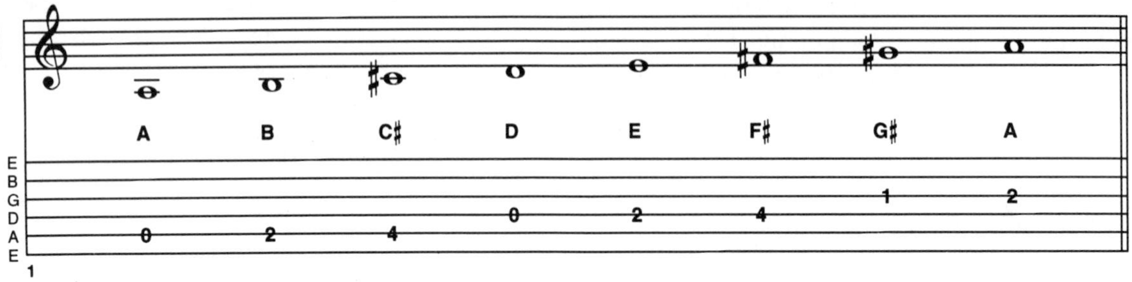

NATURAL MINOR

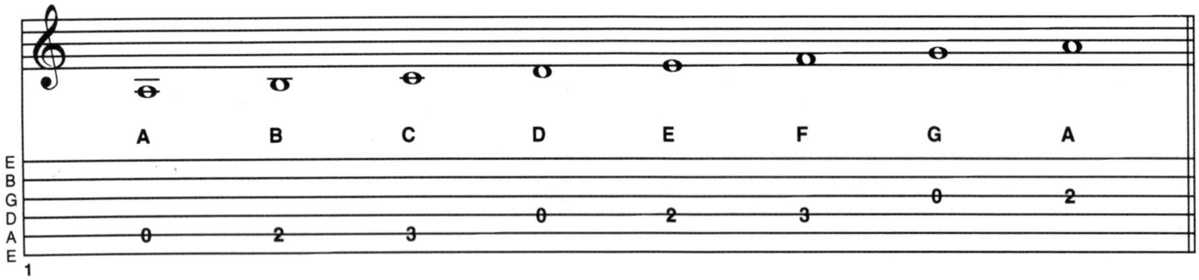

HARMONIC MINOR

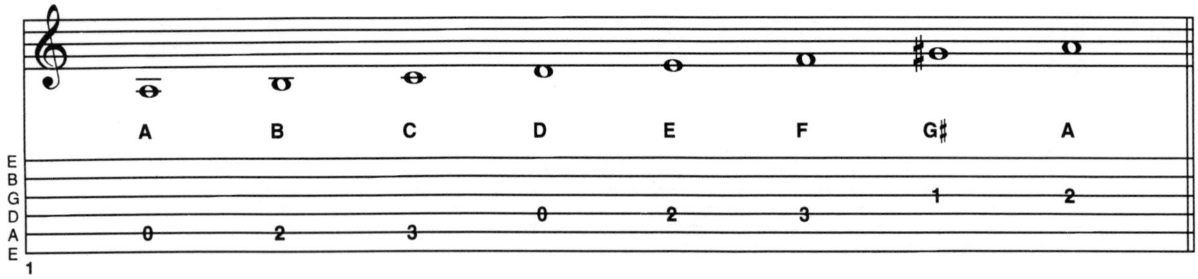

MINOR PENTATONIC

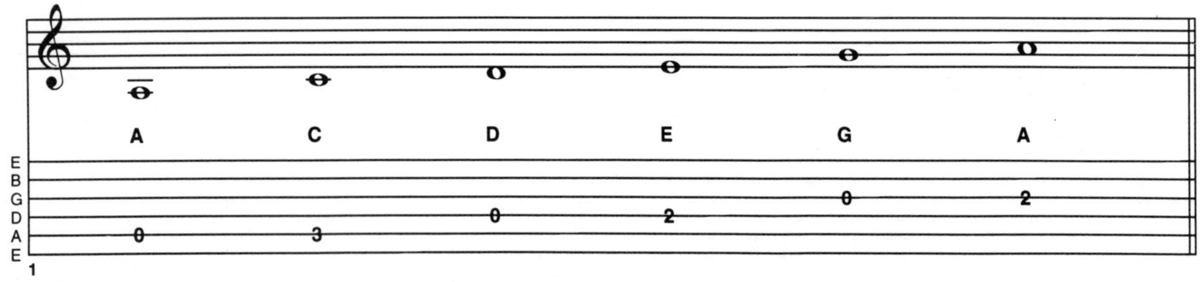

MAJOR PENTATONIC

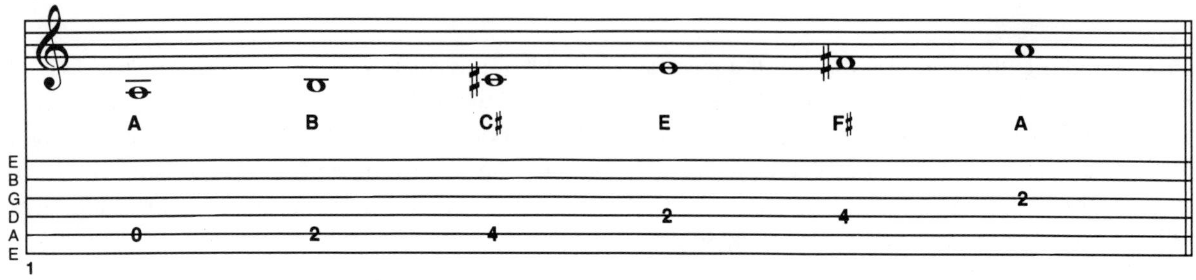